BASIC ARABIC WORKBOOK

FOR REVISION AND PRACTICE

JOHN MACE

تمارين أساسية في العربية

HIPPOCRENE BOOKS, INC

Other titles by John Mace:

Intermediate Arabic Workbook
Arabic Today—a student, business and professional course in spoken and written Arabic
Arabic Grammar, a revision and reference guide (3rd edition)
Teach Yourself Arabic Verbs
Teach Yourself Arabic Script (2nd edition)
Persian Grammar, for revision and reference

Typeset by John Mace

ISBN 0-7818-1126-0

For information, address:
HIPPOCRENE BOOKS, INC.
171 Madison Avenue
New York, NY 10016
www.hippocrenebooks.com

Cataloging-in-Publication data available from the Library of Congress

Printed in the United States of America

Contents

CONTENTS

Introduction

This is a workbook whose purpose is to help you in the early stages of learning written Arabic. It is not a course book. It can be used either for independent study or in a classroom.

It assumes that you already know the Arabic alphabet. This is the only assumption, as the text takes the grammar and vocabulary from the start to ensure that nothing important in these areas has been missed or misunderstood. You can treat as revision and consolidation any parts which are already familiar.

The Arabic used in this book is all practical. The fact that we are exercising written and not spoken Arabic does not mean that the language has to be unreal or stilted; the vocabulary and structures are up to date, and are taken from everyday living and working situations. The book bears in mind the needs not only of formal students but also of professional people needing to communicate in Arabic for their work.

The grammar is presented progressively. Each chapter centres on an important theme; in addition, certain chapters give basic vocabulary on a given subject – industry, town and country, politics, economy, information and the like. The exercises give practice in manipulating the language in the theme under study. Read aloud your answers to the exercises in order to improve your reading fluency and speed. Check your answers in the key.

Three of the chapters consist entirely of exercises revising the main areas covered: nouns, pronouns, adjectives, verbs and sentence structures.

The pronunciation shown in this book is the shortened form commonly used when reading from a text in all but the most formal or ceremonial situations. Similarly, the numbers are taught and exercised in the simplified form which is now universal.

Grammatical terms, kept to a minimum, are explained as they arise; they are chosen for maximum familiarity to western students. The more important Arabic terms (e.g. إضافة *'iḍāfa*) are introduced in parallel with the English. The book covers basic word and sentence structures, with a vocabulary of about 1,300 words.

Although the vocabulary taught and tested here is explained within the book, before long you will need a dictionary. A good dictionary for our purposes is the *Arabic Practical Dictionary* (Arabic-English and English-Arabic) by N. Awde and K. Smith, also published by Hippocrene Books.

My thanks go to Marilyn Moore and to Nick Awde for their proofreading. Any errors still found are my responsibility.

I am also very grateful to the editors of *Al-Quds al-Arabi* and *Al-Hayat* for their kind permission to reproduce in adapted form the news extracts appearing in chapters 35, 37, 38, 39 and 40.

1 Reading and writing

- Transcription
- Short and long vowels; diphthongs
- Light and dark (velarised) sounds
- Stress
- Full, pause and short pronunciation
- *hamza*
- Handwriting
- Arabic transcription

1. General

It is assumed that you already know the letters and their pronunciation in general. This chapter covers only certain special points.

2. Transcription

Arabic letters and symbols are transcribed in this book as follows:

آ	*'ā*	أ	*'a, a'*/initial *'u*	إ	*'i*	ا	initial *a, u, i*/ middle *ā*
ب	*b*	ت	*t*	ث	*th*		
ج	*j*	ح	*ḥ*	خ	*kh*	ا\ى	final *a*
د	*d*	ذ	*dh*	ر	*r*	ز	*z*
س	*s*	ش	*sh*	ص	*ṣ*	ض	*ḍ*
ط	*ṭ*	ظ	*ẓ*	ع	*'*	غ	*gh*
ف	*f*	ق	*q*	ك	*k*	ل	*l*
م	*m*	ن	*n*	ه	*h*	ة	final *a, at*
و	*w, ū*	ي	*y, ī*	ؤ	*'u, u'*	ئ	*'i, i'*
ء	*'*	اً\ىً	final *an*	ةً	final *a, atan*	ّ...	(doubled letter)

When ت *t*, د *d*, س *s*, or ك *k* is followed by ه *h* the transcription shows a hyphen (*t-h, d-h, s-h, k-h*) to avoid confusion with the letters ث *th*, ذ *dh*, ش *sh* or خ *kh*.

3. Short and long vowels; diphthongs

The distinction between these three kinds of sound is important.

- Short vowels are mostly left unwritten in everyday Arabic. There is a means of indicating them (called 'pointing'), but it is hardly ever used. It is used very little in this book. Short *a* sounds as in British-English 'man'; short *i* as in British-English 'pin'; short *u* as in British-English 'push':

  ولد *walad* boy, child　　بنت *bint* girl, daughter
  أمّ *'umm* mother

- Long *ā* is a lengthened *a* (imagine saying 'ma-a-n'); long *ī* is as in English 'machine'; long *ū* is as in English 'rule':

  باب *bāb* door　　في *fī* in
  سوق *sūq* market

  ا\ى ending a word are in theory long *-ā*, but in practice they are pronounced short as *-a*. Sometimes final و *ū* and ي *ī* are also shortened; see paragraph 8 below.

- The two diphthongs or vowel-combinations are long:
  - *ay* as in English 'day':　　بيت *bayt* house
  - *aw* like ow in English 'now':　　أو *'aw* or

4. Light and dark ('velarised') sounds

The sounds ت *t*, د *d*, س *s* and ز *z* are pronounced much as in English:

بستان *bustān* garden　　زيادة *ziyāda* increase

Each has a dark or velarised equivalent, ط *ṭ*, ض *ḍ*, ص *ṣ* and ظ *ẓ*. Pronounce *t* but with the tongue as low in the mouth as possible, forming a deep cavity. The result is velarised *t*, written ط *ṭ*. Do the same with *d*, *s* and z; this will give ض *ḍ*, ص *ṣ* and ظ *ẓ*:

طفل *ṭifl* child　　ضروري *ḍarūrī* necessary
مصر *miṣr* Egypt　　وظيفة *waẓīfa* job

The vowels *a* and *ā*, when occurring next to *ṭ*, *ḍ*, *ṣ*, *ẓ* or *q*, and often when next to *r* or *kh*, are also velarised, i.e. pronounced with a low tongue. In these examples we show velarised *a*/*ā* as *ạ*/*ạ̄*:

طاولة	*ṭạ̄wula* table	صديق	*ṣạdīq* friend
صالون	*ṣạ̄lūn* living-room	وظيفة	*wạẓīfa* job
ضروري	*ḍạrūrī* necessary	قهوة	*qạhwa* coffee
خارج	*khạ̄rij* outside	جار	*jạ̄r* neighbour

5. Stress

In words of several syllables, one syllable is stressed, i.e. sounded louder. The stress is shown here with an ..́ accent. General rules are:

- the last 'heavy' syllable is stressed. A heavy syllable is one with a long vowel or diphthong followed by a consonant, or a short vowel followed by two consonants or a doubled consonant:

صالون	*ṣālū́n* living-room	جنينة	*junáyna* garden
قهوة	*qáhwa* coffee	أمّي	*'úmmī* my mother

- if there is no heavy syllable, the first syllable is stressed:

  ولد *wálad* boy

A few words have irregular stress, marked in the text:

مجتهد *mujtáhid* hardworking

6. Full, pause and short pronunciation

For reading aloud from a text, there are three possible styles of pronunciation; full, pause and short:

- In *full pronunciation* all grammatical endings are pronounced:

  تكلّم باللغة العربية. *takallama bi-l-lughati l-'arabīyati.*
  He spoke in Arabic ('the Arabic language').

  See the Appendix for grammatical endings.

  Full pronunciation is very rare, and need not concern us here.

- In *pause pronunciation,* grammatical endings occurring before a pause, and not written with alphabetical letters, are silent:

تكلّم باللغة العربية. *takallama bi-l-lughati l-ʿarabīya.*

Pause pronunciation is used in formal reading. It is necessary to be able to understand it.

- In *short pronunciation* all grammatical endings not written with alphabetical letters are normally silent. This is an increasingly common educated style:

  تكلّم باللغة العربية. *takallam bi-l-lugha l-ʿarabīya.*

This book uses short pronunciation.

7. One-letter words

Words consisting of one letter are written as one with the next word. The transcription shows a hyphen:

شاي وقهوة *shāī wa-qahwa* tea and coffee

8. *hamza*; weak vowel; long vowel pronounced short

The consonant *hamza* is pronounced as a glottal stop or catch in the breath. We transcribe it '. It is written in Arabic as follows:

- At the beginning of a word, above or below *'alif*:

  أ *'a, 'u* أمس *'ams* yesterday, أم *'umm* mother

  إ *'i* إذا *'idha* if

  It is never written together with *madda*: آب *'āb* August

  Initial *hamza* is often left unwritten; in this book it is always written wherever sounded '.

- In the middle of a word, above *'alif, wāw* or undotted *yā'*:

  أ *'a, a'* سأل *sa'al* he asked

  ؤ *'u, u'* سؤال *su'āl* question

  ئ\ئ *'i, i'* عائلة *'ā'ila* family

- At the end of a word, as shown immediately above when next to a short vowel; or by itself after a long vowel or diphthong

  أ *'a, a'* بدأ *bada'* he began

ؤ *'u, u'* تنبّؤ *tanabbu'* forecast

ـئ\ئ *'i, i'* يبتدئ *yabtádi'* he begins

اء *ā'* جاء *jā'* he/it came

وء *ū'* مقروء *maqrū'* read

يء *ī', ay'* شيء *shay'* thing

Middle and final *hamza* are always written.

These are all the ways of writing *hamza*. The combinations shown have other sounds also, which will be shown in the text.

hamza pronounced ' is known as همزة القطع *hamzat al-qaṭ'* 'the *hamza* of severance'. In this book it is called simply *hamza*.

Some words begin with a sounded vowel with no glottal stop:

اسم *ism* name ابن *ibn* son

This unstopped initial vowel is known as همزة الوصل *hamzat al-waṣl* 'the *hamza* of connexion'. In this book we refer to it as a *weak vowel*. A weak vowel is dropped in pronunciation when preceded by another vowel in the same expression:

بنت وابن *bint wá-bn* a daughter and son (not *[wa-íbn]*)

Further, if that immediately preceding vowel is long ...و -*ū* or ...ي -*ī*, that vowel is pronounced short (*u* or *i* respectively):

في *fī* 'in' + البيت *al-bayt* 'the house'

→ في البيت *fī l-bayt* in the house (not *[fī l-]*)

9. Handwriting

Certain short cuts are common in everyday handwriting:

- two dots may be written like a hyphen (-); three dots like a circumflex accent (^):

 يبعث *yab'ath* he sends

- the indentations of سـ س *sīn* and شـ ش *shīn* may be flattened:

initial/isolated: 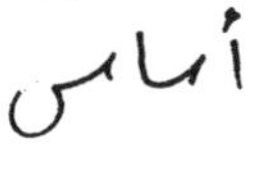 أساس *'asās* basis

middle/final: مستشفى *mustashfa* hospital

- final ه *hā'* may be simplified:

  اسمه *ismuhu* his name

- ة *tā' marbūṭa*, when pronounced -*a*, may lose its dots:

  غرفة *ghurfa* room

  but: غرفة نوم *ghurfat nawm* bedroom

- لا\ـلا *lām-'alif* is written:

  لا *lā* no

  ملابس *malābis* clothes

- ك *kāf*, كا *kāf-'alif*, كل *kāf-lām* and كلا *kāf-lām-'alif* are written:

  كتب *katab* he wrote

  شكر *shakar* he thanked

  كاتب *kātib* clerk

  مكاتب *makātib* offices

  كلّ *kull* all

  كلام *kalām* speech

- the flourish of final/isolated ك *kāf* and the dot of final/isolated ن *nūn* become a small hook:

  ترك *tarak* he left

  سكن *sakan* he lived

10. Arabic transcription

Foreign names and other words are usually transcribed as follows:

- ا for long or short a; و for long or short u or o; ي for long or short i or e; اي\ي for the sound ay; او\آو for the sound ow; آي for the sound of y as in 'my'; short vowels may also be omitted, as in Arabic words,

- for sounds foreign to Arabic: ب or the Persian letter پ for p; ج or the Persian letter چ for the sound ch;ج\غ\ق\ك for hard g; ف or the artificial letter ڤ for v,

  (In Egypt the letter ج is regularly pronounced *g* in Arabic; چ is often used in Egypt for j in foreign words.)
- the velarised letters ص and ط are often used, with or without و, for the syllables so- and to-,
- initial s + a consonant other than w becomes ..اسـ *is-*.

واشنطن	*wāshinṭon*	طوكيو	*ṭokyo*
باريس	*bārīs/pārīs*	إنترنت	*'intirnet* internet
جنيف	*jenēf* Geneva	استوكهلم	*istok-holm* Stockholm

11. Vocabulary: بيت وعائلة *bayt wa-'ā'īla*

House and family

أب	*'ab* father	سيّد	*sayyid* gentleman, Mr
سيّدة	*sayyida* lady, Mrs	شابّ	*shābb* young man/person
شبّاك	*shubbāk* window	شقّة	*shiqqa/shaqqa* apartment
طيّب	*ṭayyib* good	عنوان	*'unwān* address
كرسي	*kursī* chair	و	*wa-* and

Exercise 1. Read aloud:

e.g.: *ṣadīq* ← صديق   *bāb* ← باب

1	أمّ وأب	2	بنت أو ولد	3	شاي وقهوة
4	بيت وبستان	5	بيت أو شقّة	6	طيّب
7	كرسي وطاولة	8	اسم وعنوان	9	أمس
10	باب وشبّاك	11	عائلة	12	غرفة

Exercise 2. Which words in Exercise 1 have velarised *a* or *ā*? Why?

e.g.: *ṣadīq (ṣạdīq) a* next to *ṣ* ← صديق

Exercise 3. Write:

e.g.: *bāb wa-shubbāk* → باب وشبّاك

1	*'ab wa-'umm*	2	*qahwa 'aw shāī*	3	*bayt wa-junayna*
4	*ism 'aw 'unwān*	5	*ism wa-'unwān*	6	*ṣālūn*
7	*ṣadīq*	8	*ghurfa*	9	*ṭayyib*
10	*'ā'ila*	11	*'ams*	12	*kursī*

Exercise 4. Write *hamza* wherever it is sounded as ':

e.g.: *'ab wa-'umm* أب وأمّ ← اب وامّ

1 عا...لة
2 ابن
3 او
4 شابّ
5 سال
6 شي
7 اسم
8 سوال

Exercise 5. Transcribe, and mark the stress:

e.g.: *shubbā́k* ← شبّاك

1 غرفة
2 عنوان
3 جنينة
4 طيّب
5 صديق
6 ولد
7 كرسي
8 بستان

Exercise 6. Put these words into Arabic alphabetical order:

e.g.: عائلة، صديق، بستان، طيّب ← بستان، صديق، طيّب، عائلة

كرسي، شيء، شاي، أمّ، بيت، بنت، ولد، غرفة، أمس، اسم، قهوة، شبّاك

Exercise 7. Read these foreign names or other words:

e.g.: Ford ← فورد

1 يونسكو
2 مترو
3 برلين
4 شل
5 آي بي إم
6 رويترز
7 استالين
8 إيميل

2 Naming, qualifying and defining

- Nouns: masculine and feminine singular
- Adjectives: agreement in the singular; relative adjectives
- Indefinite and definite singular nouns and adjectives

1. Masculine and feminine nouns

A noun is the name of a person, creature, place, thing or idea: 'Ahmad', 'factory' etc. Arabic nouns are masculine (m., masc.) or feminine (f., fem.) in gender.

Feminine are:

- nouns for female persons: أمّ *'umm* mother
- nouns not denoting male persons and ending in ة... *-a*:

  سكرتيرة *sikritayra* (female) secretary

  شركة *sharika* company
- cities, continents, non-Arab countries: أمريكا *'amrīka* America
- a few others which we shall mark (f.) as they are introduced.

All other nouns are masculine. A few nouns exist in both genders:

عامل\عاملة *'āmil* (m.), *'āmila* (f.) worker, operative

زميل\زميلة *zamīl* (m.), *zamīla* (f.) colleague

2. Adjectives

An adjective qualifies (= describes or identifies) a noun. Adjectives are usually quoted in their m. form; they occur in both genders, agreeing with (= assuming the gender of) the noun which they qualify. When the m. form ends in a consonant, ة... *-a* is added for the f. form:

كبير\كبيرة *kabīr(a)* big, senior (m./f.).

The Arabic adjective follows the noun which it qualifies:

مصنع كبير *maṣna' kabīr* a big factory

شركة كبيرة *sharika kabīra* a big company

زميل كبير\زميلة كبيرة *zamīl(a) kabīr(a)* a senior colleague

3. Relative adjectives

Very many adjectives, called *relative adjectives* (in Arabic, نسبة *nisba*), can be formed from nouns by adding the ending ...ي *-ī* .

To nouns ending in a consonant, the ...ي *-ī* is added directly:

مصر *miṣr* (f.) Egypt — مصري *miṣrī* Egyptian

رئيس *ra'īs* chief — رئيسي *ra'īsī* principal

In nouns ending ...يا *-iya*, the *'alif* is dropped, leaving ...ي *-ī*:

سوريا *sūriya* (f.) Syria — سوري *sūrī* Syrian

Any ending ...ا\...ة *-a* following a *consonant* is mostly dropped before adding ...ي *-ī*:

صناعة *ṣinā'a* industry — صناعي *ṣinā'ī* industrial

أمريكا *'amrīka* America — أمريكي *'amrīkī* American

and note: سنة *sana* year — سنوي *sanawī* annual

...ي *-ī* is the m. relative ending. The f. form is ...ية\...يّة *-īya**:

صناعي\صناعية *ṣinā'ī(ya)* industrial (m./f.)

(* strictly speaking, the m. is *-iyy*, the f. therefore *-iyya*. But in practice the ending is pronounced as shown above.)

4. Full pronunciation

In full pronunciation (see Chapter 1), nouns and adjectives like those shown above have a further ending, which need not concern us here; the Appendix gives details.

5. Indefinite and definite

Common nouns in the form shown above are indefinite in meaning:

مدير *mudīr* director, a director — وظيفة *waẓīfa* job, a job

Such nouns can be made definite by adding the *definite article* ('the article'). The Arabic article is more common than its English counterpart 'the'. It is always written ...ال , joined as a prefix. Its 'standard' pronunciation is *al-* (the hyphen in the transcription does not affect the pronunciation). The stress of the word is unchanged:

المدير *al-mudī́r* the director الوظيفة *al-waẓī́fa* the job

But before a letter pronounced with the tip or near-tip of the tongue:

ت ث *t th* د ذ *d dh* ر ز *r z* س ش *s sh*
ص ض *ṣ ḍ* ط ظ *ṭ ẓ* ل *l* ن *n*

the *l* of the article assumes the sound of that letter, giving us a double letter. The double letter can be pointed with ...ّ *shadda*; the stress of the whole word remains unchanged:

التّقرير *at-taqrī́r* the report (not *[al-]*)
الرئيس *ar-ra'ī́s* the chairman, president, chief
الشركة *ash-shárika* the company

A noun used in a general sense is normally put into its definite form:

العمل *al-'amal* work الهندسة *al-handasa* engineering

Proper nouns, i.e. names seen as unique, are automatically definite. Some have the article, some not:

مصر *miṣr* Egypt العراق *al-'irāq* Iraq

An adjective qualifying a definite noun must itself be definite. The article is added to the adjective in the same way as to the noun:

المدير المصري *al-mudīr al-miṣrī* the Egyptian director

The *a-* of ...ال is weak, and therefore silent after a vowel (Chapter 1):

الشركة الكبيرة *ash-shárika͡ l-kabī́ra* the big company

(Pronounce: *[ash-shárikal-kabī́ra]*.)

The relative adjective formed from a proper noun carrying the article, like العراق, may itself be either indefinite or definite, as needed:

شركة عراقية *sharika 'irāqīya* an Iraqi company
الشركة العراقية *ash-sharika l-'irāqīya* the Iraqi company

exactly as, e.g.: (الـ)شركة (الـ)مصرية *(ash-)sharika (l-)miṣrīya*

In full pronunciation, definite nouns and adjectives also have a further ending, which need not concern us here; the Appendix gives details.

6. Adjectives as nouns

Arabic does not make our strict distinction between nouns and adjectives. Any adjective can be used as a noun where appropriate:

مصري *miṣrī* an Egyptian
المسؤول *al-mas'ūl* the responsible person

7. Vocabulary: الصناعة *aṣ-ṣinā'a* Industry

أجنبي	*'ajnabī* foreign	إنتاج	*'intāj* production
بسيط	*basīṭ* simple	تقرير	*taqrīr* report, decision
تلفون\تليفون	*tilifōn* telephone	ثقيل	*thaqīl* heavy
جديد	*jadīd* new	خفيف	*khafīf* light (weight)
دولي	*duwalī* international	سهل	*sahil* easy
صعب	*ṣa'ab* difficult	صغير	*ṣaghīr* small, junior
صنع	*ṣan', ṣun'* manufacture	طلب	*ṭalab* order, demand
طويل	*ṭawīl* long	عقد	*'aqd* contract
عملية	*'amalīya* operation, process	فنّي	*fannī* technical
قديم	*qadīm* old (things), ancient	قسم	*qism* department
قصير	*qaṣīr* short	كاتب	*kātib* clerk
كهربا	*kahraba* electricity	ماكينة	*mākīna* machine
مخزن	*makhzan* store	مشرف	*mushrif* supervisor
مشغل	*mashghal* workshop	مشغول	*mashghūl* busy
مشكلة	*mushkila* problem	معقّد	*mu'aqqad* complicated
مفيد	*mufīd* useful	مكتب	*maktab* office
منتج	*muntij* productive, *muntaj* product	مهندس	*muhandis* engineer
		موظّف	*muwaẓẓaf* employee

نوبة *nawba* shift هامّ *hāmm* important واضح *wāḍiḥ* clear

Exercise 1. Read each noun aloud and give its gender:

e.g.: *mushrif*, m. ← مشرف   *ṣinā'a*, f. ← صناعة

1 مدير   2 تلفون   3 مشكلة   4 زميل
5 تقرير   6 مكتب   7 كاتبة   8 رئيس
9 قسم   10 مشغل   11 زميلة   12 كاتب
13 مهندس   14 نوبة   15 وظيفة   16 ماكينة

Exercise 2. Make the nouns in Exercise 1 definite with the article:

e.g.: *al-mushrif* المشرف ← مشرف   *aṣ-ṣinā'a* الصناعة ← صناعة

Exercise 3. Make the adjective agree with the noun:

e.g.: *ṣun' hāmm* صنع هامّ ← صنع، هامّ
e.g.: *ṣinā'a 'ajnabīya* صناعة أجنبية ← صناعة، أجنبي

1 زميل، مصري   2 مشكلة، بسيط   3 مدير، أجنبي
4 شركة، أجنبي   5 وظيفة، صعب   6 عقد، واضح
7 قسم، منتج   8 عملية، قصير   9 كاتبة، مصري
10 شركة، دولي   11 مكتب، رئيسي   12 نوبة، طويل

Exercise 4. Make your answers to Ex. 3 definite with the article:

e.g.: *aṣ-ṣun' al-hāmm* الصنع الهامّ ← صنع هامّ
aṣ-ṣinā'a l-'ajnabīya الصناعة الأجنبية ← صناعة أجنبية

Exercise 5. Make the m. and f. relative adjective from each noun:

e.g.: *miṣrī miṣrīya* مصري مصريّة ← مصر
'amrīkī 'amrīkīya أمريكي أمريكية ← أمريكا

1 سوريا   2 رئيس   3 صناعة
4 العراق   5 هندسة   6 كهربا

Exercise 6. Rewrite, with an adjective having opposite meaning:

e.g.: *taqrīr qaṣīr* تقرير قصير ← تقرير طويل

1 مشكلة معقّدة   2 مشغل جديد   3 عملية سهلة

4 مصنع كبير 5 صناعة ثقيلة 6 عقد طويل

Exercise 7. Make your answers to Ex. 6 definite with the article:

e.g.: *at-taqrīr al-qaṣīr* التقرير القصير ← تقرير قصير

Exercise 8. Which of these expressions are always or almost always used definitely? Add the article to such expressions where appropriate:

e.g.: *al-handasa* الهندسة ← هندسة

1 إنتاج صناعي 2 عملية صناعية 3 كهربا
4 مصر 5 عامل 6 وظيفة
7 عراق 8 عمل

Which one of these is definite in meaning anyway, without an article?

Exercise 9. Select the only adjective which fits the noun both in meaning and form:

e.g.: *maṣna' muntij* مصنع منتج ← مصنع (منتجة\القديم\منتج)

1 مشرف (سوري\العراقي\أجنبية\معقّد)
2 عملية (معقّد\فنّية\المعقّدة\رئيسي)
3 الإنتاج (صناعي\فنّي\الصناعية\الصناعي\فنّية)
4 الشركة (الهامّة\الطويل\صغيرة\القصير)
5 مصر (جديدة\القديمة\قديم)

Exercise 10. Form the relative adjective from the noun shown in parentheses. Make your adjective agree with the first noun:

e.g.: *sharika 'amrīkīya* شركة امريكية ← شركة (امريكا)

ash-sharika l-'amrīkīya الشركة الأمريكية ← الشركة (امريكا)

1 مهندس (العراق) 2 المشكلة (رئيس)
3 عملية (هندسة) 4 التقرير (سنة)
5 المشغل (كهربا) 6 الإنتاج (صناعة)

3 Multiplying

- Nouns: dual, sound plural, broken plural
- Animate and inanimate
- Adjectives: dual, sound plural, broken plural, inanimate plural; agreement

1. Nouns and adjectives: dual

The *dual* form of an Arabic noun indicates 'two ...':

مُمَثِّل *mumaththil* a representative
مُمَثِّلان *mumaththil**ān*** two representatives

The number 'two' is normally not necessary, as it mostly is in English.

The dual ending is ...ان *-ấn**, added to the singular (s. or sing.) form of the noun (indefinite or definite):

- the ending is added directly after a final consonant:

  مندوب *mandūb* a delegate مندوبان *mandūbấn* two delegates

  الملفّ *al-milaff* the files الملفّان *al-milaffấn* both files

- final ة... *-a (ṭā' marbūṭa)* becomes تان... *-atān*:

  لجنة *lajna* a committee لجنتان *lajnatấn* two committees

- final ي... *-ī* becomes يّان...\يان... *-īyān*:

  أمريكي *'amrīkī* (an) American أمريكيان *'amrīkīyấn* two Americans

Adjectives are made dual in the same way. Adjectives agree not only in gender with their nouns (see Chapter 2), but also in number, in this case dual with dual:

ملفّ مكتوم *milaff maktum* a confidential file
ملفّان مكتومان *milaffān maktūmān* two confidential files
الرسالتان الخاصّتان *ar-risālatān al-khāṣṣatān* both private letters

مندوبان سوريان *mandūbān sūrīyān* two Syrian delegates

* in full pronunciation, *-āni*. See the Appendix.

2. Plural – general

It is important to remember that whereas for English, the concept 'plural' means 'more than one', for Arabic it means 'more than *two*'.

3. Animate and inanimate

Arabic makes an important distinction between nouns and other words denoting or referring to *people* ('animate' nouns or other words) and those referring to anything else ('inanimate' nouns etc.) This distinction runs right through the language, and the terms 'animate' ('an.') and 'inanimate' ('inan.') are used with these meanings in this book.

4. Nouns and adjectives: masculine sound plural

A few masculine nouns, all of them animate, i.e. denoting male persons, and some adjectives in their masc. form, make their plural (pl.) on a regular pattern (called the *sound* plural), adding the ending ...ون *-ūn* (full pronunciation *-ūna*, see Appendix). This is added to the masculine singular noun or adjective (indefinite or definite):

- it is added directly after a final consonant:

(الـ)ممثّلون *(al-)mumaththilūn* (the) representatives

مشرفون طيّبون *mushrifūn ṭayyibūn* good supervisors

مهندسون *muhandisūn* engineers

موظّفون *muwaẓẓafūn* employees

- final ...ي *-ī* becomes ...يّون\...يون *-īyūn*:

(الـ)مصريون *(al-)miṣrīyūn* (the) Eqyptians

المندوبون العراقيون *al-mandūbūn al-'irāqīyūn* the Iraqi delegates

Many masc. animate nouns, and most adjectives in the masc. form, beginning *ma-* or *mu-*, and almost all masc. relative adjectives qualifying animate nouns, make their plurals in this way. *No inanimate nouns*, and *no adjectives qualifying inanimate nouns*, take the m. sound pl. ending.

5. Nouns and adjectives: feminine sound plural

The feminine sound plural ending is ات... *-ā́t*. It forms the plural of:

- most fem. animate nouns, (i.e. nouns denoting female people), indefinite or definite; and all adjectives qualifying such nouns,
- many inanimate nouns *of either gender*, indefinite or definite.

The ending is added to the singular noun or adjective as follows:

- directly after a final consonant:

اجتماع	*ijtimā'*	اجتماعات	*ijtimā'ā́t*	meeting(s)
(الـ)ملفّ	*(al-)milaff*	(الـ)ملفّات	*(al-)milaffā́t*	(the) file(s)
كمبيوتر	*kambyūtir*	كمبيوترات	*kambyūtirāt*	computer(s)
(الـ)منتج	*(al-)muntaj*	(الـ)منتجات	*(al-)muntajāt*	(the) product(s)

- final ة... *-a (ṭā' marbūṭa)* is dropped when ات... *-āt* is added:

(الـ)رسالة	*(ar-)risāla*	(الـ)رسالات	*(ar-)risālā́t*	(the) letter(s)
سكرتيرة	*sikritayra*	سكرتيرات	*sikritayrāt*	secretary/ies
مصرية	*miṣrīya* an Egyptian lady	مصريات	*miṣrīyāt*	Egyptian ladies
زميلة سورية	*zamīla sūrīya* a Syrian colleague	زميلات سوريات	*zamīlāt sūrīyāt*	Syrian colleagues
سنة	year	سنوات	(NB) *sanawāt*	years

See the Appendix for the endings of ات... *-āt* in full pronunciation.

6. Nouns and adjectives: broken plurals

Very many nouns and adjectives do not add an ending to form their plural, but have an internal change instead (the so-called 'broken' plural). Compare the English: 'man/men', 'mouse/mice'.

Broken plurals have the same full pronunciation as the singular; see the Appendix.

There are many broken-plural patterns. The commonest ones include:

Model قسم أقسام *qism*, pl. *'aqsām*:

قسم	*qism*	أقسام	*'aqsām*	department
ولد	*walad*	أولاد	*'awlād*	boy, child
طفل	*ṭifl*	أطفال	*'aṭfāl*	child
شغل	*shughl*	أشغال	*'ashghāl*	work
عمل	*'amal*	أعمال	*'a'māl*	work
+ variants, e.g.: باب	*bāb*	أبواب	*'abwāb*	door

Model عقد عقود *'aqd 'uqūd*:

عقد	*'aqd*	عقود	*'uqūd*	contract
بيت	*bayt*	بيوت	*buyūt*	house
رأس	*ra's*	رؤوس	*ru'ūs*	head

Model تقرير تقارير *taqrīr taqārīr*:

تقرير	*taqrīr*	تقارير*	*taqārīr*	report
بستان	*bustān*	بساتين	*basātīn*	garden
شبّاك	*shubbāk*	شبابيك	*shabābīk*	window
عنوان	*'unwān*	عناوين	*'anāwīn*	address
كرسي	*kursī*	كراسي	*karāsī*	chair

* but تقريرات *taqrīrāt* (f. sound pl.) decisions

Model مكتب مكاتب *maktab makātib*:

مكتب	*maktab*	مكاتب	*makātib*	office
أجنبي	*'ajnabī*	أجانب	*'ajānib*	foreign
مخزن	*makhzan*	مخازن	*makhāzin*	store
مشغل	*mashghal*	مشاغل	*mashāghil*	workshop
مشكلة	*mushkila*	مشاكل	*mashākil*	problem
مصنع	*maṣna'*	مصانع	*maṣāni'*	factory

variants: جنينة	*junayna*	جنائن	*junā'in*	garden
وظيفة	*waẓīfa*	وظائف	*waẓā'if*	job

Model صديق أصدقاء *ṣadīq 'aṣdiqā'*:

صديق	*ṣadīq*	أصدقاء	*'aṣdiqā'*	friend
variants: أب	*'ab*	آباء	*'ābā'*	father
ابن	*ibn*	أبناء	*'abnā'*	son
اسم	*ism*	أسماء	*'asmā'*	name

Model مدير مدراء *mudīr mudarā'*:

مدير	*mudīr*	مدراء	*mudarā'*	director
بسيط	*basīṭ*	بسطاء	*busaṭā'*	simple
ثقيل	*thaqīl*	ثقلاء	*thuqalā'*	heavy
رئيس	*ra'īs*	رؤساء	*ru'asā'*	president
زميل	*zamīl*	زملاء	*zumalā'*	colleague

Model كبير كبار *kabīr kibār*:

كبير	*kabīr*	كبار	*kibār*	big
صعب	*ṣa'b*	صعاب	*ṣi'āb*	difficult
صغير	*ṣaghīr*	صغار	*ṣighār*	small
طويل	*ṭawīl*	طوال	*ṭiwāl*	long
قصير	*qaṣīr*	قصار	*qiṣār*	short

Other examples (from the many remaining patterns):

كاتب	*kātib*	كتّاب	*kuttāb*	clerk
عامل	*'āmil*	عمّال	*'ummāl*	worker
غرفة	*ghurfa*	غرف	*ghuraf*	room
نوبة	*nawba*	نوب	*nuwab*	shift
شابّ	*shābb*	شباب	*shabāb*	young man/person
جديد	*jadīd*	جدد	*judud*	new
سيّد	*sayyid*	سادة	*sāda*	gentleman, Mr
بنت	*bint*	بنات	*banāt*	girl, daughter

It is wise to learn new words with broken plurals thus: قسم أقسام *qism 'aqsām*. The broken plural is given in this manner in the vocabulary. Where no plural is shown, it is sound, *-ūn/-āt*.

7. Agreement of adjectives: animate and inanimate plural

See Chapter 2. An adjective agrees also in number with the noun it qualifies or replaces:

- a singular or dual noun has a singular or dual adjective respectively, agreeing in gender (m./f.); see examples above,
- a m. or f. animate plural noun has a m. or f. plural adjective respectively; see examples above. Mixed company is treated as masculine:

  زملاء جدد *zumalā' judud* new colleagues (male or mixed)
- (most important:) an *inanimate* plural noun has its adjective in the *inanimate plural* form, which is identical to the *feminine singular*:

  عقد جديد *'aqd jadīd* a new contract

  عقود جديدة *'uqūd jadīda* new contracts

8. Vocabulary: الإدارة *al-'idāra* **Administration**

اجتماع *ijtimā'* meeting
أسلوب أساليب *'uslūb 'asālīb* method
أمر أمور *'amr 'umūr* matter, affair
أمر أوامر *'amr 'awāmir* command
بحث بحوث *baḥth buḥūth* discussion
تاريخ تواريخ *tārīkh tawārīkh* date, history
حديث حداث *ḥadīth ḥidāth* modern
جواب أجوبة *jawāb 'ajwiba* answer
خاص *khāṣṣ* special, private
رقم أرقام *raqm 'arqām* figure
ضعيف ضعفاء *ḍa'īf ḍu'afā'* weak
قليل أقلاء *qalīl 'aqillā'* little, slight
كثير كثار *kathīr kithār* much, many

لجنة لجان *lajna lijān* committee, commission
مبلغ مبالغ *mablagh mabāligh* amount
مشهور *mashhūr* famous
منظّمة *munaẓẓama* organisation
نمرة نمر *numra numar* number (in a series)
وثيقة وثائق *wathīqa wathā'iq* document
وفد وفود *wafd wufūd* delegation
وقت أوقات *waqt 'awqāt* time
وكيل وكلاء *wakīl wukalā'* agent
يوم أيام *yawm 'ayyām* day
اليوم *al-yawm* today

Exercise 1. Give (a) the dual and (b) the plural of each noun:

e.g.: *risālatān, risālāt* رسالتان، رسالات ← رسالة

al-mablaghān, al-mabāligh المبلغان، المبالغ ← المبلغ

1 وفد	2 مندوب	3 الكمبيوتر
4 زميل	5 لجنة	6 ممثّل
7 مكتب	8 منظّمة	9 الوثيقة
10 الملفّ	11 رئيس	12 الكاتب
13 مهندس	14 النوبة	15 وظيفة
16 جواب	17 بحث	18 الصديق
19 مصري	20 مدير	21 رأس

Exercise 2. Put each expression into the plural:

e.g.: *risālāt maktūma* رسالات مكتومة ← رسالة مكتومة

al-mandūbūn al-'ajānib المندوبون الأجانب ← المندوب الأجنبي

1 صديق جديد	2 يوم طويل	3 المدير الفنّي
4 مدير سوري	5 وقت صعب	6 زميلة أجنبية
7 المشكلة المعقّدة	8 ممثّل طيّب	9 المخزن القديم
10 الزميل الرئيسي	11 الرئيس الجديد	12 شركة دولية

13 اجتماع قصير
14 سكرتيرة طيّبة
15 مهندس عراقي
16 رقم واضح
17 المشرف المسؤول
18 طفل صغير
19 البستان الصغير
20 وظيفة هامّة

Exercise 3. Put each expression into the singular:

e.g.: *ṣadīq ṭayyib* صديق طيّب ← أصدقاء طيّبون

1 مديران جديدان
2 بيوت كبيرة
3 وثائق معقّدة
4 مدراء جدد
5 مصانع منتجة
6 تقارير هامّة
7 التقريرات الهامّة
8 عقود قديمة
9 أساليب مفيدة
10 النوب اليومية
11 اجتماعان طويلان
12 وفود كبيرة
13 اللجان الرئيسية
14 بنات صغيرات
15 الموظّفان المسؤولان
16 أرقام بسيطة
17 العمّال المنتجون
18 موظّفون سوريون
19 الوثائق الخاصّة
20 أجوبة طويلة

Exercise 4. Select the only adjective which fits the noun both in meaning and form:

e.g.: ملفّات مكتومة ← ملفّات (جدد\المكتومة\مكتومة)
milaffāt maktūma

1 الوثيقة (البسيطة\الطويل\طويلة\البسطاء)
2 وثائق (بسطاء\معقّد\بسيطة\البسيطة)
3 مبالغ (كبير\كبار\الصغيرة\كبيرة)
4 العمّال (السوريون\مصري\مفيدة\المنتجة)
5 مدراء (مسؤولون\مسؤولان\مسؤولة\الأجانب)

Now add to each noun a different adjective of your own choice.

4 Indicating

- Demonstratives

1. Demonstrative adjectives

The demonstrative adjectives ('this, these, that, those') are in Arabic:

	Singular	Dual	Plural
m.	هذا *hādha* this	هذان *hādhāni* these two	هؤلاء *hā'ulā'i* these
f.	هذه *hādhihi* this	هاتان *hātāni* these two	
m.	ذلك *dhālika* that	ذانك *dhānika* those two	أولئك *'ūlā'ika* those
f.	تلك *tilka* that	تانك *tānika* those two	

Note:

- In over half of these forms a middle *'alif* is missing from the spelling. The pronunciation is as shown; note also the *-i*, usually dropped in short pronunciation, in the 'these two' forms.
- The feminine singular forms are of course also used for the inanimate plural 'these/those' (see Chapter 3). The plural forms shown are masculine and feminine plurals, animate.
- Used as adjectives, the demonstratives agree with and *precede* their noun, which is definite and always has the article:

هذه الرسالة *hādhihi r-risāla* this letter
هذا البلاد *hādha l-bilād* this country
هذه الرسالات الخاصّة *hādhihi r-risālāt al-khāṣṣa* these private letters
تلك محلاّت *tilka l-maḥallāt* those places
هؤلاء الناس *hā'ulā'i n-nās* these people
أولئك الأشخاص الحاضرون *'ūlā'ika l-'ashkhāṣ al-ḥāḍirūn* those persons present

هذان المأموران السابقان *hādhān al-ma'mūrān as-sābiqān*
these two former officials

2. Demonstrative pronouns

The demonstrative can also act as a *pronoun*, i.e. standing for an implied but unstated noun:

هذا وذلك *hādha wa-dhālika* this (one) and that

هذه الصغيرة *hādhihi ṣ-ṣaghīra* this small one/these small ones

When the gender of the implied noun is not known, the masc. is used. The demonstrative pronoun is studied further in Chapters 5, 7 and 12.

3. Vocabulary: الناس والبلدان والمهن *an-nās wa-l-buldān wa-l-mihan* People, countries, professions

أفريقيا *'afrīqiya* Africa

ألمانيا *'almāniya* Germany

إنجلترا\إنكلترا *'ingiltira* England, Great Britain

إنجليزي إنجليز\إنكليزي إنكليز *'ingilīzī 'ingilīz* English, British

إيطاليا *'īṭāliya* Italy

بريطانيا *barīṭāniya* Britain

بلاد بلدان *bilād buldān* country

بوّاب *bawwāb* doorman

تاجر تجّار *tājir tujjār* merchant, trader

حاضر *ḥāḍir* present (adjective)

حمّال *ḥammāl* porter, carrier

روسيا *rūsiya* Russia

سابق *sābiq* former

سائق\سوّاق *sā'iq/sawwāq* driver

السعودية *as-sa'ūdīya* Saudi Arabia

شخص أشخاص *shakhṣ 'ashkhāṣ* person

شرطة *shurṭa* police

شرطي *shurṭī* policeman
الصين *aṣ-ṣīn* China
عامّ *'āmm '* general, public
عربي عرب *'arabī 'arab* Arab(-ic/-ian)
غائب *ghā'ib* absent
فرنسا\فرنسة *faransa* France
فرنسي\فرنساوي *faransī/faransāwī* French
الكويت *al-kuwayt* (f.) Kuwait
مأمور *ma'mūr* official (noun)
مجتهد *mujtáhid* hardworking
محاسب *muḥāsib* accountant
محلّ *maḥall* place
مهنة مهن *mihna mihan* profession
ناس (an. pl.) *nās* people
هنا *huna* here
هناك *hunāka* there
الهند *al-hind* India
هندي هنود *hindī hunūd* Indian
الولايات المتّحدة *al-wilāyāt al-muttáḥida* United States
اليابان *al-yābān* Japan

Exercise 1. Put the demonstrative with each noun:

e.g.: *hādha l-bilād, dhālika l-bilād* بلاد ← هذا البلاد، ذلك البلاد

1 محاسب سعودي 2 محاسبون طيّبون 3 رسالة
4 ناس 5 مهنة هامّة 6 وفود غائبة
7 منظّمة يابانية 8 مأموران صينيان 9 وقت
10 مبلغ كبير 11 مبالغ كبيرة 12 شرطيون
13 مشاكل شخصية 14 سائق مجتهد 15 شخص
16 تجّار فرنساويون 17 محلاّت قديمة 18 أشخاص
19 بنت صغيرة 20 زميل سابق

Exercise 2. Put each expression into the plural:

e.g.: هذا المأمور الياباني ← هؤلاء المأمورون اليابانيون

hā'ulā'i l-ma'mūrūn al-yābānīyūn

1 ذلك السيّد الإنجليزي
2 هذه السيّدة الألمانية
3 هذا الكمبيوتر الياباني
4 تلك المشكلة العامّة
5 هذة الصديقة العربية
6 هذا الصديق العربي
7 ذلك الزميل الغائب
8 هذه السكرتيرة الهندية
9 هذا المهندس الهندي
10 هاتان البنتان الصغيرتان

Exercise 3. Replace 'this/these' with 'that/those', and vice versa:

e.g.: هؤلاء المحاسبون ← أولئك المحاسبون *'ūlā'ika l-muḥāsibūn*

1 تلك المشاكل
2 هذا الشخص
3 أولئك الناس
4 ذلك الشرطي
5 هؤلاء الأشخاص
6 هذا البوّاب
7 تلك الأجوبة
8 هذه السيّدة

Exercise 4. Make expressions with relative adjectives, s. and pl.:

e.g.: تاجر، اليابان ← تاجر ياباني، تجّار يابانيون

tājir yābānī, tujjār yābānīyūn

1 المأمور، إيطاليا
2 محاسب، الكويت
3 شرطي، السعودية
4 شخص، الهند
5 المدير، فرنسا
6 المهندس، ألمانيا
7 وكيل، الصين
8 مندوب، روسيا

Exercise 5. Make an expression with the opposite meaning:

e.g.: هذا البلاد الكبير ← ذلك البلاد الصغير

dhālik al-bilād aṣ-ṣaghīr

1 تلك المشكلة المعقّدة
2 هذه الرسالات الطويلة
3 هؤلاء المأمورمن الغائبون
4 هذه المشكلة العامّة
5 هذا المكتب الحديث

5 Identifying

- Subject pronouns
- Equations (verbless sentences)

1. Subject pronouns

The pronouns used as subject of a sentence ('I', 'he', 'they' etc.) are in Arabic:

Person	Singular	Plural
1 m./f.	أنا *'ana* I	نحن *naḥnu* we
2 m. 2 f.	أنتَ *'anta* you (m.) أنتِ *'anti* you (f.)	أنتم *'antum* you
3 m 3 f.	هو *huwa* he, it هي *hiya* she, it, they (inan.)	هم *hum* they

Note:

- 2nd person: the singular varies for gender. The plural shown here is masculine; it refers also to a group of mixed gender.
- 3rd person: the singular varies for gender. The masculine refers to any masculine singular noun; the feminine refers to any feminine singular noun, or any inanimate pl. noun; see Chapter 3 and examples given below. The plural form shown here is animate masculine, i.e. denotes male people or a group of mixed gender.
- There are other 2nd and 3rd persons, i.e. the dual and the feminine plural, too rare to concern us here. The Appendix gives full details.

The pronoun can be used to emphasise the subject of the verb:

أنا كتبت الإنشاء. *'ana katabt al-'inshā'*. *I* wrote the essay.

but it is mostly omitted when the verb makes its own subject clear. The main use of the subject pronouns is in sentences with no verb; see immediately below.

2. Equations (verbless sentences)

Examine the sentences

هذا الطالب مصري. *hādha ṭ-ṭālib miṣrī.*
This student is Egyptian.

الدورات الفنّية مختلفة. *ad-dawrāt al-fannīya mukhtálifa.*
The technical courses are varied.

هي مختلفة. *hiya mukhtálifa.* They are varied.

أنا سوري\سورية. *'ana sūrī(ya).* I am Syrian.

الأستاذ طبيب مشهور. *al-'ustādh ṭabīb mashhūr.*
The professor is a famous doctor.

In such sentences the Arabic shows no equivalent for our verb 'to be' in present time ('am/is/are'). The *subject*, which is definite, is followed directly by a *predicate* qualifying the subject. The predicate (most often an adjective or noun) is usually indefinite.

We can call such a verbless sentence an *equation.*

The English equivalent of an equation may have an indefinite subject; the Arabic subject will be definite:

الكتب الطبّية معقّدة. *al-kutub aṭ-ṭibbīya mu'aqqada.*
Medical books (i.e. in general) are complicated.

The predicate can also be a different type of expression, not describing or identifying the subject but (for example) locating it:

المكتبة هناك. *al-maktaba hunāka.* The library is there.

Distinguish between, e.g.:

الطالب مصري. *aṭ-ṭālib miṣrī.* The student is Egyptian.

and الطالب المصري *aṭ-ṭālib al-miṣrī* the Egyptian student

the first of which is an equation; the second is not any kind of sentence but only a definite noun plus adjective, as shown in Chapter 2. It would need expanding to turn it into a sentence, e.g.:

الطالب المصري ذكي. *aṭ-ṭālib al-miṣrī dhakī.*
The Egyptian student is intelligent

A demonstrative pronoun (Chapter 4) may stand as the subject of an equation:

هذا تلميذ جديد. *hādha tilmīdh jadīd.* This is a new pupil.

An equation can only have the implied meaning 'to be', it must be *present* in timing, and affirmative. When the statement is past or future, or negative, then a verb is needed; see Chapters 18, 19 and 23.

Equations in the form of a question are studied in Chapter 13.

(The Appendix gives the noun and adjective endings used in full pronunciation.)

3 . Equations with a definite predicate

Some equations, less common, have a definite predicate:

هو الخبير. *huwa l-khabīr.* He is the expert.

But for 'This is the.../These are the...', where we use the demonstrative **هذا** *hādha* etc. as a pronoun with a predicate having the article **..الـ**, then we restate the subject with the appropriate subject pronoun:

هذه هي التمارين الفنّية. *hādhihi hiya t-tamārīn al-fannīya.*
These ('they') are the technical exercises.

since **هذه التمارين الفنّية** *hādhihi t-tamārīn al-fannīya* means only 'these technical exercises', and is not a sentence.

Similarly, the subject pronoun (**هو\هي** etc.) is usually added when both subject and predicate have the article:

الأستاذ هو الخبير. *al-'ustādh huwa l-khabīr.*
The professor ('he') is the expert.

4. There is, there are

Arabic expresses 'there is/are ...' with an equation in which the order of subject and predicate is reversed. The subject is indefinite, and the predicate usually expresses a place or time:

في الجامعة مكتبة كبيرة. *fī l-jāmiʿa maktaba kabīra.*

('In the university a big library') There is a big library in the university.

هناك كتب جديدة. *hunāka kutub jadīda.*

There are new books there.

هذه السنة أستاذ سعودي. *hādha s-sana 'ustādh saʿūdī.* There is a Saudi professor this year./This year there is a Saudi professor.

Another formula for 'there is/are' is studied in Chapter 11.

5. Vocabulary: التربية والتدريب ***at-tárbiya wa-t-tadrīb***

Education and training

ابتدائي *ibtidā'ī* primary, elementary

اختبار *ikhtibār* experiment

أساسي *'asāsī* basic

أستاذ أساتذة *'ustādh 'asātidha* professor

امتحان *imtiḥān* examination

تجربة تجارب *tajriba tajārib* test, experiment

تدريس *tadrīs* instruction

ترجمة تراجم *tarjama tarājim* translation

تعليم *taʿlīm* tuition, education

تلميذ تلاميذ *tilmīdh talāmīdh* pupil

تمرين تمارين *tamrīn tamārīn* exercise

ثانوي *thānawī* secondary

ثقافة *thaqāfa* culture

جامعة *jāmiʿa* university

خبير خبراء *khabīr khubarā'* expert

دبلوم *diblōm* diploma

دراسة *dirāsa* study

درس دروس *dars durūs* lesson

دكتور *duktūr* Dr, Doctor (title)
دورة *dawra* course
ذكي أذكياء *dhakī 'adhkiyā'* intelligent
شهادة *shahāda* certificate
صفّ صفوف *ṣaff ṣufūf* class(room)
طالب طلاّب *ṭālib ṭullāb* student
طبّ *ṭibb* medicine
طبيب أطبّة *ṭabīb 'aṭibba* doctor
علم علوم *'ilm 'ulūm* science, knowledge
عملي *'amalī* practical
كتاب كتب *kitāb kutub* book
كلّية *kullīya* college, faculty
مادّة موادّ *mādda mawādd* material, (school) subject
متخرّج *mutakharrij* graduate
متوسط *mutawassiṭ* middle (adj.)
مثقّف *muthaqqaf* cultured, educated
محاضرة *muḥāḍara* lecture
مختبر *mukhtábar* laboratory
مدرّس *mudarris* instructor
مدرسة مدارس *madrasa madāris* school
معلّم *mu'allim* teacher
مرشّح *murashshaḥ* candidate
مكتبة مكاتب *maktaba makātib* library
ممتاز *mumtāz* excellent, distinguished
موضوع مواضيع *mawḍū' mawāḍī'* subject, theme
نظري *naẓarī* theoretical

Exercise 1. Replace each subject noun or noun expression with the right pronoun:

e.g.: *hiya kabīra*. هي كبيرة. ← الجامعة كبيرة.

1 التمرين قصير.

2 هؤلاء الطلاّب مصريون.

3 هذه المشاكل معقّدة.

4 الإنشاءات طويلة.

5 التجربة نظرية.

6 التجارب نظرية.

7 الدرس عملي.

8 الدروس عملية.

9 الأستاذ خبير مشهور.

10 هذه الترجمة ممتازة.

11 المرشّح مصري.

12 المرشّحة مصرية.

Exercise 2. Make a standard equation (definite subject, indefinite predicate) from each pair of expressions:

e.g.: *hum muhandisūn.* هم، مهندس ← هم مهندسون.

al-mudarris miṣrī. مدرّس، مصري ← المدرّس مصري.

1 طالبة، سوري

2 دروس، طويل

3 تدريب، عملي ونظري

4 هي، مثقّف

5 مدرّس، في الصفّ

6 مختبر، هناك

7 مختبر، مشهور

8 إنشاء، سهل

9 أستاذ، خبير في الكهربا

10 تلاميذ، في المكتبة

11 أفريقيا، كبير

12 وثيقة، طويل

13 نحن، مصري

14 رسالات، مكتوم

15 سوّاق، حاضر

16 أستاذ سابق، مشهور

Exercise 3. Put the expressions into two columns, as shown:

e.g.:

equation	not an equation
المشكلة بسيطة	المشكلة البسيطة
al-mushkila basīṭa	*al-mushkila l-basīṭa*

1 شخص مثقّف

2 هذا الطالب

3 هذا طالب

4 هذا هو الطالب الجديد

5 هذا الطالب جديد

6 في المختبر تجارب عملية

7 التمارين الفنّية الصعبة

8 التمارين الفنّية صعبة

9 الزميل مهندس

10 هو المسؤول الرئيسي

11 الكتب الدراسية

12 كتب دراسية

13 الدورة العملية طويلة
14 المدرسة الفنّية هنا
15 التدريب الفنّي
16 التدريب فنّي

Exercise 4. Make an equation with a definite predicate from each pair of expressions:

e.g.: هذه، مشكلة رئيسية ← هذه هي المشكلة الرئيسية.
hādhihi hiya l-mushkila r-ra'īsīya.

1 هذا الزميل، خبير طبّي
2 هم، معلّمون أجانب
3 المدرّس، خبير في الكمبيوتر
4 التربية، مشكلة كبيرة
5 الموادّ الرئيسية، دراسات طبّية وعلوم عامّة

Exercise 5. Make the singular equations plural and the plural equations singular:

e.g.: التجربة مفيدة ← التجارب مفيدة. *at-tajārib mufīda.*

1 هذا الطالب ذكي.
2 الدراسات نظرية
3 المشرفون مسؤولون.
4 هذا الزميل خبير.
5 الأستاذ زميل.
6 في الصفّ مرشّح أجنبي.
7 المشكلة الرئيسية هي الترجمة.
8 المشرف حاضر.
9 الامتحانات العملية صعبة.
10 التلميذ هناك في الصفّ.
11 هو شخص مثقّف.
12 الطلاّب غائبون.

Exercise 6. Make an equation by selecting the only predicate which fits the subject both in meaning and form:

e.g.: الدورة (طويل\المعقّدة\قصيرة) ← الدورة قصيرة.
ad-dawra qaṣīra.

1 الترجمة (البسيطة\ذكية\معقّدة\بسيط)
2 هذه العملية (معقّد\طويلة\المعقّدة\الممتازة)
3 هذه الطالبة (الذكية\إيطالية\الإيطالية\نظرية)
4 هذه هي الطالبة (إيطالية\الإيطالية\النظرية)
5 مصر بلاد (عملية\الحديث\قديم)

Now add to each subject a different predicate of your own choice.

Exercise 7. Make an equation by providing a suitable noun subject:

e.g.: ... شخص مثقّف. ← المدرّس شخص مثقّف.

al-mudarris shakhṣ muthaqqaf.

في المصنع .... ← في المصنع مشغل كبير.

fī l-maṣna' mashghal kabīr.

1 ... معلّم في العلوم الأساسية. 2 ... المرشّحة الجديدة.
3 ... في الصفّ الرئيسي. 4 في الصفّ الرئيسي ...
5 ... المدرسة الابتدائية. 6 ... علم معقّد.

Exercise 8. Read this passage aloud:

هذه الجامعة كبيرة. نحن تلاميذ جدد هنا. أنا طالب\طالبة في الدراسات الطبّية. في الجامعة طلاّب وطالبات كثار. في هذة الجامعة كلّيات مختلفة وفي الكلّيات تعليم نظري وعملي. المعلّم الرئيسي أو المعلّمة الرئيسية في الكلّية هو أو هي الأستاذ أو الأستاذة. هذا الأستاذ خبير مشهور في العلم الطبّي والمدرّسون ناس مثقّفون. الكتب في المكتبة الطبّية حديثة ومفيدة، والمختبرات ممتازة.

Now complete these sentences, using the text as key:

1 هذا الأستاذ ... 2 نحن ... .
3 أنا طالب\طالبة في ... . 4 ... خبير مشهور في العلم الطبّي.
5 في الكلّيات .... 6 هذه الجامعة ... .
7 ... حديثة ومفيدة. 8 المختبرات ....

6 Associating – 1

- Prepositions

1. Prepositions

Prepositions ('in', 'for' etc.) show the association between a noun or pronoun and the rest of the sentence. Common prepositions are:

في	*fī* in	على	*'ala* on, against
مع	*ma'a* with	ل	*li-* for, of
دون\بدون	*dūna, bi-dūni* without	ب	*bi-* in, with, by means of
فوق	*fawqa* above, over	تحت	*taḥta* below, under
إلى	*'ila* to	من	*min* from
عن	*'an* from, about	عند	*'inda* at, among, with
قبل	*qabla* before, ago	بعد	*ba'da* after
خلال	*khilāla* during	بين	*bayna* between, among
ضدّ	*ḍidda* against	من أجل	*min ajli* for (the sake of)
مثل	*mithla* like	ك	*ka-* as, like
حتّى	*ḥatta* up to, until	منذ	*mundhu* since
امام	*'amāma* in front of	وراء	*warā'a* behind
داخل	*dākhila* inside	خارج	*khārija* outside
جنب	*jamba* (NB) beside	بخصوص	*bi-khuṣūṣi* concerning
بسبب	*bi-sababi* because of	حول\حوالى	*ḥawla, hawāla* about
بالرغم من\على رغم	*bi-r-raghm min, 'ala raghmi* despite		

When used before a noun, the preposition usually drops its full-pronunciaton ending (small type). The noun (+ its adjective if any) stands in the *genitive case* (الجرّ *al-jarr*); but the only genitive endings shown in writing and heard in short pronunciation are the *m. sound pl.* *-īn* and the *dual -ayn*, both spelt ين...:

خلال يومين *khilāl yawmayn* for ('during') two days

بين الشركتين الأجنبيتين *bayn ash-sharikatayn al-'ajnabīyatayn* between both foreign companies

مع (الـ)مندوبين (الـ)ألمانيين *ma' (al-)mandūbīn (al-)'almānīyīn*
with (the) German delegates

The dual demonstratives (Chapter 4) have the genitive forms هذين *hādhayn* (m.), هاتين *hātayn* (f.) 'these', and ذينك *dhaynika* (m.), تينك *taynika* (f.) 'those':

مع هذين\ذينك الزميلين *ma' hādhayn az-zamīlayn/ dhaynika z-zamīlayn* with these/those two colleagues

With other noun and adjective forms, the genitive looks and sounds (in short pronunciation) the same as the subject form:

مع الخبير\الخبراء *ma' al-khabīr/al-khubarā'*
with the expert(s)

في مصنع جديد *fī maṣna' jadīd* in a new factory

قبل سنة *qabl sana* a year ago

while the sing. and pl. demonstratives do not change for case anyway:

من أجل هذه اللجنة *min 'ajl hādhihi l-lajna* for this committee

After لـ *li-* 'for, of', the article drops its *'alif* in writing:

للعامل ، للعمّال *li-l-'āmil, li-l-'ummāl* for the worker(s)

للّجنة الفنّية *li-l-lajna l-fannīya*
for the technical committee

Remember (Chapter 1) that a final long vowel is pronounced short before a dropped weak vowel, e.g. the *a-* of the article:

في مصر *fī miṣr* in Egypt

but: في الولايات المتّحدة *fi l-wilāyāt al-muttáḥida*
in the United States

The Appendix shows the full-pronunciation case-endings for nouns and adjectives.

2. like this etc.

Note the structure مثل هذا الكتاب *mithl hādha l-kitāb* 'a book like this', 'such a book'.

3. Prepositions with pronouns

A pronoun following a preposition is attached to it as a suffix:

Person	Singular	Plural
1 m/f.	...ي *-ī* me	...نا *-na* us
2 m. 2 f.	...ك *-ka* you ...ك *-ki* you	...كم *-kum* you
3 m 3 f.	...ه *-hu (-hi)* him, it ...ها *-ha* her, it, them (inan.)	...هم *-hum (-him)* them

The three indents of Chapter 5, paragraph 1, apply also here.

When the suffix ...ي 'me' is added to a preposition:

- any full-pronunciation ending of the preposition is first dropped:

  معي *ma'ī* with me ورائي *warā'ī* behind me
- ل *li-* 'for, of' loses its vowel: لي *lī* for/to me
- final ...ى *-a* + ...ي becomes ...يّ *-ayya*; final ...ي *-ī* + ...ي becomes ...يّ *-īyya*:

  إليّ *'ilayya* to me فيّ *fīyya* in me
- من *min* 'from' and عن *'an* 'from, about' double their *n*:

  منّي *minnī* from me عنّي *'annī* from/about me

When the other suffixes are added:

- any full-pronunciation ending of the preposition is first restored:

  معهم *ma'ahu* with them ضدّكم *ḍiddaka* against you
- ل 'for, to' is pronounced *la-*: لها *laha* for her/it/them
- final ...ي\...ى becomes ...يْ *-ay*: إلينا *'ilayna* to us
- after the endings *-i*, ...ي *-ī* or *-ay-* (see above), the suffixes ...ه and ...هم are pronounced *-hi* and *-him*:

  به *bihi* in/with him/it فيهم *fīhim* in them

إليهم *'ilayhim* to them   عليه *'alayhi* on him/it

The ending *-i* may be a restored full-pronunciation ending *-i*:

من أجله *min 'ajlihi* for his sake

بين *bayn* governs two concepts; when one is a pronoun (or both are), بين is repeated:

بين الكويت والصين *bayn al-kuwayt wa-ṣ-ṣīn*
between Kuwait and China

but: بيننا وبين الصين *baynana wa-bayn aṣ-ṣīn*
between China and us ('us and China')

بيني وبينك *baynī wa-baynaka* between you and me

The prepositions حتى *ḥatta* and ك *ka-* are not used with a suffix.

Exercise 1. Add the noun to the preposition:

e.g.: *li-l-muhandisīn* للمهندسين ← ل، المهندسون

1 تحت، التجربة	2 في، اليابان	3 في، المشغل
4 في، هذا الوقت	5 بعد، الاجتماعان	6 ك، تلميذ
7 داخل، المكاتب	8 منذ، سنتان	9 خلال، الدورة
10 خلال، الدورات	11 ضدّ، الموظّفون	12 ل، الرئيس

Exercise 2. Add the pronoun to the preposition:

e.g.: *ḥawlahu* حوله ← حول، هو

1 على، أنا	2 في، أنتم	3 في، هي
4 في، هم	5 جنب، أنا	6 عن، أنت
7 داخل، هي	8 خارج، هو	9 جنب، هو
10 بخصوص، أنا	11 عن، أنا	12 ل، هم

Exercise 3. Replace the noun or noun expression with the appropriate pronoun:

e.g.: *min 'ajliha* من أجلها ← من أجل التربية العربية

1 خلال البحث	2 للمشاكل	3 إلى المندوبين

4 في البحث　5 خلال البحوث　6 في البحوث
7 من أجل الإنتاج　8 للرئيس　9 ضدّ العقد
10 بخصوص الزملاء　11 على الرأس　12 عند الوكلاء

Exercise 4. Replace the preposition with one having opposite meaning:

e.g.: *khārijahu* خارجه ← داخلوه

1 قبل سنتين　2 من أجل الشركة　3 فوقها
4 عنه　5 معه　6 إلى الكويت
7 حتّى اليوم　8 أمامهم　9 منّي
10 بسبب التجارب المختلفة

Exercise 5. Replace the pronoun with an appropriate noun:

e.g.: من أجلها ← من أجل الشركة\الشركات

min 'ajl ash-sharika/ash-sharikāt

1 بعدها　2 ضدّهم　3 وراءه
4 فيه　5 بخصوصها　6 خلاله
7 خلالها　8 لها　9 عليها
10 إليه　11 عندهم　12 بها

Exercise 6. Make the noun or noun expression (a) dual, (b) plural:

e.g.: إلى المرشّح ← إلى المرشّحين\المرشّحين

'ila l-murashshaḥayn/al-murashshaḥīn

1 مع هذا الوكيل　2 في المدرسة
3 بيني وبين المدير　4 في المشكلة الحاضرة
5 بعد اجتماع طويل　6 عن التاجر العربي
7 للممثّل السابق　8 عند الشرطي
9 خلال بحث خاصّ　10 بخصوص النوبة اليومية

Exercise 7. Add (a) في , (b) لـ and (c) بـ to each noun:

e.g.: القسم ← في القسمه، للقسم، بالقسم

fī l-qism, li-l-qism, bi-l-qism

1 العقد	2 الشركات	3 التقرير
4 البيت	5 الوظيفة	6 المختبرات
7 الصناعة	8 المدير	9 الزملاء
10 الرسالة	11 المدراء	12 المكتب

Now do the same exercise again, first making the noun indefinite.

7 Associating – 2

- Construct
- Preposition ل *li*

1. Construct

Examine the noun expressions

استقرار البلاد *istiqrār al-bilād* the stability of the country
برنامج الحكومة *barnāmaj al-ḥukūma* the government('s) programme ('the programme of the government')
لحلّ هذه المشاكل *li-ḥall hādhihi l-mashākil* for the solution to/of these problems
في قسم سوريا *fī qism sūriya* in Syria Department
مشكلة الانتخابات *mushkil**at** al-intikhābāt* the problem of the elections
حكومة مصر *ḥukūm**at** miṣr* the government of Egypt
مأمورو الوزارة *ma'mūr**ú** l-wizāra* the ministry officials
مأمورا الوزارة *ma'mūr**á** l-wizāra* both ministry officials

This type of expression is a *construct* (in Arabic: إضافة *'iḍāfa*); the two nouns are *in construct state*. They are associated by simply being put together, with no preposition. We can call the first noun the *theme* (المضاف *al-muḍāf*), and the second noun the *attribute* (المضاف إليه *al-muḍāf 'ilayhi*) Note:

- the *theme* is limited or qualified by the *attribute*.
- the association between the nouns may often be that of possession, but is not always so.
- in these examples the whole expression is definite, but (most important) the theme *never has the definite article* (Chapter 2); it is deemed to be defined by the attribute, which *is* 'explicitly' definite; here it has the article, or it is a (definite) proper name

(سوريا , مصر).

- a final ة... on the theme (حكومة , مشكلة) is pronounced *-at*.
- when the theme is in the sound m. pl. or the dual (Chapter 3), the final ن... *-n* of the plural or dual ending is dropped (مأمورو, مأمورا) but the final vowel keeps its original stress, e.g. *ma'mūrú* (pl.), *ma'mūrá* (dual).

The attribute is always in the *genitive* case; but this is normally evident only with the endings ين... *-īn/-ayn* (see Chapter 6):

مسؤولية المأمورين *mas'ūlīyat al-ma'mūrīn/al-ma'mūrayn*
the responsibility of the (two) officials

سياسة الوزارتين *siyāsat al-wizāratayn*
the policy of both ministries

Most compound prepositions are in fact the theme of a construct:

بسبب المشاكل *bi-sabab al-mashākil* (المشاكل is the attribute)
because of ('by reason of') the problems

2. Indefinite construct

Indefinite constructs are less common; they follow all the rules of the definite construct, except that their attribute is indefinite:

مأمورو وزارة *ma'mūrū wizāra* ministry officials
وظيفة سفير *waẓīfat safīr* an ambassador's job
قوانين بلاد *qawānīn bilād* a country's laws

(قوانين is a broken, not a sound plural; the final ن is part of the root.)

Only the attribute shows whether the whole construct is definite or indefinite in meaning.

3. Longer constructs

Constructs with more than two nouns also exist. There are two types:

- 'multiple' constructs, with two* themes or two* attributes, the pair being connected with و *wa/u* 'and' or او *'aw* 'or':

تاريخ و برنامج المؤتمر *tārīkh wa-barnāmaj al-mu'tamar*
the date and programme of the conference

وظيفة وزير أو سفير *waẓīfat wazīr 'aw safīr*
a minister's or ambassador's job

(* More than two is possible, but unwieldy; see para. 5 below.)

- 'string' constructs, with each noun limited/qualified by the next:

انتخاب رئيس المجلس *intikhāb ra'īs al-majlis*
the (s)election of the president of the assembly

4. Adjective or demonstrative with a construct

An adjective other than a demonstrative may not interrupt a construct. It follows the whole expression, regardless of which noun it qualifies. It carries the article when the noun which it qualifies is definite:

برنامج الحكومة الجديدة *barnāmaj al-ḥukūma l-jadīda*
the new government's programme

برنامج الحكومة الجديد *barnāmaj al-ḥukūma l-jadīd*
the government's new programme

See paragraph 5 below for a way to avoid ambiguity.

(In modern business or newspaper Arabic you may find e.g.:

مدير عامّ الشركة *mudīr 'āmm ash-sharika*
the company('s) general manager

where عامّ is indeed an intrusive adjective, but مدير عامّ is seen in this context as an indivisible compound, and [مدير الشركة العامّ] would not do, as it would break up the G.M.'s job title. Use such examples sparingly. Paragraph 5 below offers a safe way out of the dilemma.)

A demonstrative qualifying the attribute precedes it as usual. A demonstrative qualifying a theme follows the whole construct:

أحزاب هذه الحكومة *'aḥzāb hādhihi l-ḥukūma*
the parties in ('of') this government

أحزاب الحكومة هذه *'aḥzāb al-ḥukūma hādhihi*

these government parties

5. Preposition ل *li*

See paragraphs 3 and 4 above. Some complicated constructs may be re-expressed more simply and clearly by using ل *li* 'of' instead of part of the construct, thereby avoiding some of the latter's constraints:

بحث البرنامج المالي الجديد للحزب *baḥth al-barnāmaj al-māli l-jadīd li-l-ḥizb* discussion of the party's new financial programme

which is looser and more transparent than the following would be:

[بحث برنامج الحزب المالي الجديد *baḥth barnāmaj al-ḥizb al-māli l-jadīd*]

and makes clear which noun is qualified by مالي and which by جديد .

The reference to the general manager (paragraph 4 above) can become:

المدير العامّ للشركة *al-mudīr al-ʿāmm li-sh-sharika*

6. Vocabulary: السياسة *as-siyāsa* Politics

إجراء *'ijrā'* (administrative) measure
استقرار *istiqrār* stability
اشتراكي *ishtirākī* socialist
إقليم أقاليم *'iqlīm 'aqālīm* region
برلمان *barlamān* parliament
برنامج برامج *barnāmaj barāmij* programme
جزء أجزاء (من) *juz 'ajzā' (min)* part (of)
جمهورية *jumhūrīya* republic
حرّ أحرار *ḥurr 'aḥrār* free, liberal
حزب أحزاب *ḥizb 'aḥzāb* party
حلّ حلول *ḥall hulūl* solution
خارجية *khārijīya* Foreign Affairs
خطاب أخطبة *khiṭāb 'akhṭiba* speech, address
داخلية *dākhilīya* Home/Internal Affairs

دفاع *difā'* defence
رسمي *rasmī* official
رئيس وزراء *ra'īs wuzarā'* Prime Minister
رئاسة\رياسة *ri'āsa, riyāsa* chairmanship, presidency
سلام\سلم *salām, silm* peace
سلطة *sulṭa* authority
سياسة *siyāsa* policy, politics
سياسي *siyāsī* political, politician
شعب شعوب *sha'ab shu'ūb* people
صحّة *ṣiḥḥa* health
ضروري *ḍarūrī* necessary
عضو أعضاء *'uḍw 'a'ḍā'* member
قانون قوانين *qānūn qawānīn* law
مالية *mālīya* finance
مجلس مجالس *majlis majālis* assembly
مجلس وزراء *majlis wuzarā'* cabinet
محافظ *muḥāfiẓ* conservative
منطقة مناطق *minṭaqa manāṭiq* area, region
معارضة *mu'āraḍa* opposition
مؤتمر *mu'tamar* conference
نائب نوّاب *nā'ib nuwwāb* deputy, member of parliament
بواسطة *bi-wāsiṭat* by means of
وزارة *wizāra* ministry
وزير وزراء *wazīr wuzarā'* minister
وطن أوطان *waṭan 'awṭān* homeland
وطني *waṭanī* national

Exercise 1. Make a definite construct:

e.g.: *'uḍw al-ḥizb* عضو الحزب ← العضو، الحزب

1 الاستقرار، البلاد 2 الأسماء، الأعضاء

3 الحكومة، مصر
4 البرامج، الحكومة
5 هم المندوبون، البرلمان
6 على الرأس، الوفد
7 مع المندوبين، البرلمان
8 تحت الرياسة، الوزير
9 للحزبين، الحكومة
10 السياسة أو البرامج، الحزب الممثّل، العراق

Exercise 2. Make the adjective and/or demonstrative qualify the underlined word:

e.g.: برنامج الحزب، رسمي ← برنامج الحزب الرسمي
barnāmaj al-ḥizb ar-rasmī

1 سياسة الحزب، رئيسي
2 سياسة الحزب، رئيسي
3 مأمور الوزارة، هذا
4 مأمور الوزارة، هذا
5 مسؤوليات الوزارة، هذا، هامّ
6 قانون العمل، جديد

Exercise 3. Make a meaningful expression using ل:

e.g.: برنامج، عمل، جديد، وزارة
← برنامج عمل الجديد للوزارة\برنامج الوزارة الجديد للعمل
barnāmaj 'amal al-jadīd li-l-wizāra/
barnāmaj al-wizāra l-jadīd li-l-'amal

1 رئيس، سابق، لجنة، مالي
2 إجراءات، دفاع، بلاد
3 صناعة، خفيف، هذا، بلاد
4 رئيس، حزب، سابق
5 سياسة، الحزب، تدريب، شباب
6 انتخابات، برلماني، حكومة، جديد

Exercise 4. Identify definite and indefinite constructs:

e.g.: *ra'īs wuzarā'*, indefinite ← رئيس وزراء
ra'īs al-wuzarā', definite ← رئيس الوزراء

1 برلمان مصر
2 هذه هي وزارة الدفاع
3 مشاكل وفد العراق معقّدة
4 انتخاب مرشّحين جدد
5 حلّ مشاكل الحزب
6 من أجل استقرار الوطن

7 وزير المالية السابق 8 حلّ هذه المشاكل

Exercise 5. Make the theme of the construct plural:

e.g.: عضو مجلس الوزراء ← أعضاء مجلس الوزراء
'a'ḍā' majlis al-wuzarā'
لمندوب الحكومة ← لمندوبي الحكومة *li-mandūbí l-ḥukūma*

1 سياسة هذه الحكومة 2 من أجل ممثّل الحزب
3 قانون العمل المعقّد 4 بلاد أفريقيا
5 عن مهندس هذا القسم 6 انتخاب النوّاب السنوي
7 رئيس وممثّل حكومة مصر 8 هو مندوب الحزب

Exercise 6. Put the preposition عن before the expression:

e.g.: *'an ma'mūri l-wizāra* مأمورو الوزارة ← عن مأموري الوزارة

1 سكرتيرات هذا المكتب 2 مندوبو الوزارة
3 أعضاء الحزبين 4 نائبا هذا الحزب
5 الاشتراكيون والأحرار والمحفظون في البرلمان

Which of these expressions are not constructs?

Exercise 7. Put together an expression from each column to make a meaningful construct:

e.g.:

Theme	Attribute
الوزارة	الدفاع

← وزارة الدفاع *wizārat ad-difā'*

Theme	Attribute
1 الاستقرار	7 الجامعة
2 الوزارات	8 الوزير
3 المكتبة الرئيسية	9 البلدان العربية
4 تحت الرئاسة	10 الوزراء
5 المجلس	11 الولايات المتّحدة
6 الحكومة	12 الإقليم

Now substitute an attribute of your own choice for each answer.

Exercise 8. Make a string construct by adding a suitable noun in the space:

e.g.: ... وزارة الخارجية ← مسؤوليات وزارة الخارجية

mas'ūlīyāt wizārat al-khārijīya

مسؤوليات الوزارة ... ← مسؤوليات وزارة الخارجية

mas'ūlīyāt wizārat al-khārijīya

1 ... برلمان مصر
2 صحّة رئيس ...
3 اسم صديق ...
4 ... رئيس الوزراء
5 تقرير مدير ...
6 طلبات عمّال ... الوطنيين
7 ... صناعة هذا البلاد
8 ... حكومة الكويت
9 تدريب معلّمي ... ابتدائية
10 برنامج تدريب ... جدد

Exercise 9. Add an attribute of your own choice to make a construct, making any necessary changes:

e.g.: مجلس ... ← مجلس وزراء *majlis wuzarā'*

المجلس ... ← مجلس الوزراء *majlis al-wuzarā'*

1 رئيس ...
2 الانتخاب ...
3 القانون ...
4 مؤتمر ...
5 المشاكل ...
6 للممثّلين ...
7 الأساليب ...
8 سلطة ...
9 التاريخ والمحل ...
10 الوزارة ... أو...

Exercise 10. 1. List as many likely ministers and ministries as you can, in the form of a construct:

e.g.: وزير\وزارة الخارجية ... *wazīr/wizārat al-khārijīya* ...

2. Now list likely directors and departments:

e.g.: مدير\قسم الهندسة ... *mudīr/qism al-handasa* ...

3. And now professors and faculties:

e.g.: أستاذ\كلّية الطبّ ... *'ustādh/kullīyat aṭ-ṭibb* ...

8 Distinguishing – 1

- Comparative and superlative of simple adjectives

1. Comparative of adjectives

The comparative form ('bigger', 'better') of adjectives is formed on the model

كبير *kabīr* big → أكبر *'akbar* bigger

so also, from adjectives already studied:

أصغر *'aṣghar* smaller (صغير *ṣaghīr*)
أبسط *'absaṭ* simpler (بسيط *basīṭ*)
أسهل *'as-hal* easier (سهل *sahil*)
أصعب *'aṣ'ab* more difficult (صعب *ṣa'b*)

أحدث	*'aḥdath* more modern	أثقل	*'athqal* heavier
أطول	*'aṭwal* longer	أقصر	*'aqṣar* shorter
أكثر	*'akthar* more	أضعف	*'aḍ'af* weaker
أقدم	*'aqdam* older	أوضاح	*'awḍaḥ* clearer

and others:

خطر	*khaṭir* dangerous	→	أخطر	*'akhṭar* more dangerous
واطئ	*wāṭi'* low		أوطأ	*'awṭa'* lower
لطيف لطفاء	*laṭīf luṭafā'* kind		ألطف	*'alṭaf* kinder
واسع	*wāsi'* wide		أوسع	*'awsa'* wider
عميق	*'amīq* deep		أعمق	*'a'maq* deeper
قريب (من)	*qarīb (min)* near (to)		أقرب (من)	*'aqrab (min)* nearer (to)
بعيد (عن)	*ba'īd ('an)* far (from)		أبعد (عن)	*'ab'ad ('an)* farther (from)
سريع سراع	*sarī' sirā'* fast		أسرع	*'asra'* faster
جميل	*jamīl* beautiful		أجمل	*'ajmal* more beautiful

'akbar is the model for adjectives with three different root consonants, e.g. *k-b-r* (و\ي when pronounced *w/y* are consonants). For adjectives whose last two root consonants are identical, the model is أجدّ *'ajadd*

'newer' (جديد *jadīd* 'new'):

أجدّ	*'ajadd* newer	أخفّ	*'akhaff* lighter
أقلّ	*'aqall* less	أحرّ	*'aḥarr* freer
أهمّ	*'ahamm* more important	أخصّ	*'akhaṣṣ* more special

أطيب *'aṭyab* (from طيّب *ṭayyib*) means 'kinder, pleasanter'; for 'better' use one of the comparatives أحسن *'aḥsan* or أفضل *'afḍal*, derived from other roots.

Final ي... *-ī* as a *root letter* (i.e. not as the ending of a relative adjective) becomes ى... *-a* in the comparative:

ذكي	*dhakī* intelligent	→	أذكى	*'adhka* more intelligent
قوي أقوياء	*qawī 'aqwiyā'* strong		أقوى	*'aqwa* stronger
غني أغنياء	*ghanī 'aghniyā'* rich		أغنى	*'aghna* richer

The preposition 'than' used with a comparative is من *min*:

هذا السؤال أصعب من ذلك. *hādha s-su'āl 'aṣ'ab min dhālika.*
This question is harder than that.

المبدأ أهمّ من التفاصيل. *al-mabda' 'ahamm min at-tafāṣīl.*
The principle is more important than the details.

Comparative adjectives are invariable for gender and number, and *indefinite* in meaning. They follow the noun which they qualify:

فكرة\أفكار أوضح	*fikra/'afkār 'awḍaḥ* (a) clearer idea(s)
تفصيل\تفاصيل أصغر	*tafṣīl/tafāṣīl 'aṣghar* (a) smaller detail(s)
فرق أكبر	*farq 'akbar* a greater difference
فرص أفضل	*furaṣ 'afḍal* better opportunities

2. Superlative

The superlative form ('biggest', 'best') is expressed by making the comparative definite, in one of two ways. The first and commonest is to put it before the indefinite noun standing in the genitive case, similarly to an indefinite construct (Chapter 7):

أكبر فرق *'akbar farq* the greatest difference

أحسن مهندسين *'aḥsan muhandisīn* the best engineers
أهمّ فكرة *'ahamm fikra* the most important idea

Note that these expressions are *definite* in meaning.

The second structure, less common, uses the comparative as a definite adjective in its usual position, after the definite noun:

العبارة الأوضح *al-'ibāra l-'awḍaḥ* the clearest expression
السؤال الأسهل *as-su'āl al-'as-hal* the easiest question

Most superlatives have the invariable comparative form. But a few have also a fem./inan. pl. form, ending in ى... *-a*. Not all of these words have a clearly superlative meaning in English. Some common examples:

masc.		fem./inan. pl.		
الأكبر	*al-'akbar*	الكبرى	*al-kubra*	the greatest
الأصغر	*al-'aṣghar*	الصغرى	*aṣ-ṣughra*	the smallest
الأوّل	*al-'awwal*	الأولى	*al-'ūla*	the first
الأحسن	*al-'aḥsan*	الحسنى	*al-ḥusna*	the best

and one non-superlative used either definitely or indefinitely:

(الـ)آخر *(al-)'ākhar* (الـ)أخرى *(al-)'ukhra* (the) other

The special fem. form must be used following a fem. or inan. pl. noun, e.g. in the second of the two superlative structures explained above. Examine:

أوّل فكرة *'awwal fikra* the first idea
آخر عبارات *'ākhar 'ibārāt* the other expressions
but: الفكرة الأولى *al-fikra l-'ūla*
(الـ)عبارات (الـ)أخرى *(al-)'ibārāt (al-)'ukhra*
(the) other expressions

Like all adjectives, the superlative can be used as a noun where the meaning permits. Here again the special fem. form must be used when appropriate:

هو أحسن المعلّمين. *huwa 'aḥsan al-mu'allimīn.*
He is the best (one) of the teachers

هي حسنى المعلّمات. *hiya ḥusna l-mu'allimāt.*
She is the best of the teachers.

أهمّ النقط هي ... *'ahamm an-nuqaṭ, hiya ...*
The most important of the points is ...

3. Derived adjectives

All the adjectives described above are simple, i.e. not derived from other parts of speech. Derived adjectives such as *relative* adjectives (Chapter 2), e.g. عملي *'amalī*, نظري *naẓarī*; and adjectives beginning *mu-*, e.g. مفيد *mufīd*, مختلف *mukhtálif*, form their comparatives differently. They are examined in Chapter 28.

4. Construct expressions

We have seen one use of superlatives as nouns. Note also these examples, some with broken plurals, in definite constructs:

أوّل السنة\الشهر ... *'awwal as-sana/ash-shahr* (etc.)
the beginning of the year/month (etc.)

أوائل السنة ... *'awā'il as-sana* the early part of the year (etc.)

آخر السنة ... *'ākhir as-sana* the end of the year (etc.)

أواخر السنة ... *'awākhir as-sana* the later part of the year (etc.)

Do not confuse آخر أواخر *'ākhir 'awākhir* 'last' with آخر أخرون *'ākhar 'ākharūn* 'other'.

5. Broken plurals

Apart from أوائل *'awā'il* and أواخر *'awākhir* shown above, a few other comparative forms also have a broken noun plural, used with special meaning. Note these two:

(الـ)أكابر *(al-)'akābir* adults, older/prominent people (from أكبر)

(الـ)أقارب *(al-)'aqārib* relatives (from أقرب)

6. Vocabulary: الأفكار *al-'afkār* **Ideas**

احترام *iḥtirām* respect
أخير *'akhīr* recent
إرادة *'irāda* will, wish
أساس أسس *'asās 'usus* basis
إمكانية *'imkānīya* possibility
أهمّية *'ahammīya* importance
إيجابي *'ījābī* positive
تسوية *táswiya* settlement (dispute etc.)
تفصيل تفاصيل *tafṣīl tafāṣīl* detail
تنظيم *tanẓīm* (act of) organisation
حقل حقول *ḥaql ḥuqūl* field, domain
حقيقة *ḥaqīqa* truth
خطوة *khuṭwa* step
خلاف *khilāf* dispute, disagreement
رأي آراء *ra'y 'ārā'* opinion
سبب أسباب *sabab 'asbāb* cause, reason
سؤال أسئلة *su'āl 'as'ila* question
شديد أشدّاء *shadīd 'ashiddā'* severe
شهر أشهر *shahr 'ashhur* month
شيء أشياء *shay' 'ashyā'* thing
طريقة طرائق *ṭarīqa ṭarā'iq* way
عادة عوائد *'āda 'awā'id* habit
عبارة *'ibāra* expression
غرض أغراض *gharaḍ 'aghrāḍ* purpose
فرصة فرص *furṣa furaṣ* opportunity
فرق فروق *farq furūq* difference
فكرة أفكار *fikra 'afkār* idea
كامل كملة *kāmil kamala* complete, perfect
لغة *lugha* language

مبدأ مبادئ *mabda' mabādi'* principle
مساعدة *musā'ada* aid, help
ممكن *mumkin* possible
موافقة *muwāfaqa* agreement, consent
نتيجة نتائج *natīja natā'ij* result
نقطة نقط *nuqṭa nuqaṭ* point
وسيلة وسائل *wasīla wasā'il* means
وضع أوضاع *waḍ' 'awḍā'* situation

Exercise 1. Form the comparative of the adjective:
e.g.: *'aṣghar* أصغر ← صغير

1 شديد	2 طويل	3 واضح
4 قصير	5 هامّ	6 ضعيف
7 قوي	8 صعب	9 ذكي
10 جديد	11 خفيف	12 سهل

Exercise 2. Make the expression (a) comparative, (b) superlative (without the article):
e.g.: *farq 'akbar, 'akbar farq* فرق كبير ← فرق أكبر، أكبر فرق

1 شيء هامّ	2 فكرة واضحة	3 وضع خطر
4 الفكرة الواضحة	5 طريقة طيّبة	6 ناس لطفاء
7 خلاف عميق	8 خطوة شديدة	

Exercise 3. Complete the sentence with an appropriate comparison:
e.g.: هذه النقطة ... التفاصيل الأخرى.
← هذه النقطة أهمّ من التفاصيل الأخرى.
hādhihi n-nuqṭa 'ahamm min at-tafāṣīl al-'ukhra.

1 رأي الرئيس ... ذلك.	2 روسيا ... المانيا.
3 تنظيم المؤتمر ... هذه المشاكل الصغيرة	4 السنة ... الشهر
5 الموافقة ... الخلاف.	6 التقرير ... رسالة الوكيل

Exercise 4. Express the superlative differently:

e.g.: *an-nuqṭa l-'ūla* النقطة الأولى ← أوّل نقطة

'ahamm shay' أهمّ شيء ← الشيء الأهمّ

1 أجمل عبارة 2 الخلاف الأخطر 3 أوضح آراء

4 أصعب وضع 5 الجواب الأقصر 6 أهمّ خطوة

7 النتائج الحسنى 8 آخر نقطة

Exercise 5. Give the opposite of each expression:

e.g.: *lugha 'aṣ'ab* لغة اصعب ← لغة أسهل

1 عبارة أطول 2 أول فرصة 3 بيت أقدم

4 أواخر السنة 5 أقرب من المكتب 6 الخلاف الأكبر

7 الصناعات الأثقل 8 احترام أكثر

Exercise 6. Use the expressions shown in parentheses to make a comparative sentence:

e.g.: الممثّل (ذكي) المدير

← الممثّل أذكى من المدير. *al-mumaththil 'adhka min al-mudīr.*

1 هو (قوي) (أنا) 2 الجواب (طويل) السؤال

3 الحقيقة (هامّ) رأي الناس

4 الفكرة الأساسية (بسيط وسهل) ذلك

Exercise 7. Complete the sentence with your own words:

e.g.: أهمّ شيء ... ← اهمّ شيء هو نتيجة الانتخاب.

'ahamm shay' huwa natījat al-intikhāb.

1 أوّل خطوة ... 2 ... هي تسوية الخلاف.

3 أحسن جواب لهذه السؤال ... 4 ... أغنى من الآخرين

5 ... أكبر وأقوى من الحزب الاشتراكي. 6 المكتب أبعد ...

Exercise 8. Give the *positive* (i.e. non-comparative, non-superlative) form of each adjective:

e.g.: *kabīr* أكبر ← كبير

1 الأطول	2 أقصر	3 الكبرى
4 أذكى	5 أهمّ	6 أقلّ
7 أكثر	8 أقدم	9 أشدّ
10 أثقل	11 أغنى	12 أوطأ

Exercise 9. Put a suitable noun with each adjective:

e.g.: مشكلة ← مشكلة أسهل\أسهل مشكلة

mushkila 'as-hal/'as-hal mushkila

1 أوّل	2 الأوّل	3 أخرى
4 الأقرب	5 الأفضل	6 الأولى
7 الكبرى	8 أقوى	9 أغنى
10 أشدّ		

9 Distributing

- Expressing all or part

1. All, some

كلّ ***kull.*** This noun means 'whole'; but it is has other, commoner English equivalents. It is used:

- with the article, mostly translated as 'everybody, everything, all':

هذا هو الكل. *hādha huwa l-kull.* That is everything.

عند الكلّ *'ind al-kull* with everybody/all

- in an indefinite singular construct (Chapter 7), 'each/every':

كلّ مشروع *kull mashrū'* each/every project

- in a definite construct (singular or plural), 'the whole/all (of)':

في كلّ الاقتصاد *fī kull al-iqtiṣād* in the whole economy

كلّ المستوردات *kull al-mustawradāt* all (of) the imports

جميع ***jamī'.*** Also meaning 'whole', this noun is used as in the first and third indents for **كلّ** shown above, with the same meanings:

للجميع *li-l-jamī'* for everybody/all

جميع الحسابات *jamī' al-ḥisābāt* all the accounts

بعض ***ba'ḍ*** 'part' is used in a definite construct, (s. or pl.) 'some (of)':

بعض الوقت *ba'ḍ al-waqt* some of the time

في بعض القطاعات *fī ba'ḍ al-qiṭā'āt* in some (of the) sectors

Although each of these distributive nouns is singular, it is the noun following it which determines whether the expression as a whole is singular or plural:

كلّ تلميذ حاضر. *kull tilmīdh ḥāḍir.* Every pupil is present.

كلّ\جميع التلاميذ حاضرون. *kull/jamī' at-talāmīdh ḥāḍirūn.*

(not [حاضر]) All the pupils are present.

بعض البنوك محلّية. *ba'ḍ al-bunūk maḥallīya.*

(not [محلّي *maḥallī*]) Some of the banks are local.

(بعض *ba'ḍ* is also used, with or without the article and with no following noun, for 'each other':

عن (الـ)بعض *'an (al-)ba'ḍ* from/about each other)

2. Any

'Any' is expressed with the pronoun أيّ *'ayy* (m.) or أيّة *'ayya* (f.) in indefinite construct. The singular form is used also for the animate plural:

مع أيّ معلّم\معلّمين *ma' 'ayy mu'allim(īn)* with any teacher(s)
في أيّة مدرسة *fī 'ayya madrasa* in any school

'any of the' is expressed with a definite plural construct, or with أيّ من *'ayy min* or أيّة من *'ayya min* plus plural noun:

إلى أيّ (من) الحسابات *'ila 'ayy (min) al-ḥisābāt*
to any of the accounts

3. The same

The singular form of the noun نفس أنفس *nafs 'anfus* (f.) 'self', 'soul' is commonly used in definite (singular or plural) construct, to give the meaning of the English adjective 'the same':

نفس الشيء\الأشياء *nafs ash-shay'/al-'ashyā'*
the same thing(s)
لنفس الراتب *li-nafs ar-rātib* for the same salary

4. A number of, several

We can express an indeterminate quantity with various nouns.

- عدّة *'idda* 'number' gives 'a number of, several'; it is used in an indefinite plural construct:

  عدّة بنوك *'iddat bunūk* a number of/several banks
  مع عدّة أشخاص *ma' 'iddat 'ashkhāṣ* with several people

- أكثرية *'aktharīya* 'majority' expresses 'most (of)'; it is used in a definite plural construct:

في أكثرية المشاريع الحكومية *fī 'aktharīyat al-mashārī' al-ḥukūmīya* in most (of the) government projects

The following two expressions are followed by a definite plural noun or construct, or a plural pronoun suffix:

- from عدد أعداد *'adad 'a'dād* 'number'; عدد من *'adad min* 'a number of, several':

  عدد من تجّار البلاد *'adad min tujjār al-bilād* a number of/several of the merchants in ('of') the country

  مع عدد منهم *ma' 'adad minhum* with several of them
- كثير من *kathīr min* 'many of' and قليل من *qalīl min* 'few of':

  كثير من\قليل من أسواق اليوم *kathīr min/qalīl min 'aswāq al-yawm* many of/few of today's markets

The comment found at the end of paragraph 1 above applies also here:

أكثرية النوّاب غائبون. *'aktharīyat an-nuwwāb ghā'ibūn.*
(not [غائبة]) Most of the MPs are absent.

Distinguish between عدّة and عدد, which have the same root but different uses. عدّة is used as the theme of an indefinite construct; عدد is followed by a definite noun expression (which may be a construct), connected and governed by the preposition من:

عدة تجّار أجانب *'iddat tujjār 'ajānib* several foreign traders

عدد من التجّار الأجانب *'adad min at-tujjār al-'ajānib* several of the foreign traders

5. One of

The pronoun أحد *'aḥad* (m.), إحدى *'iḥda* (f.) 'one (of)' is used in a definite plural construct:

مدير أحد البنوك الوطنية *mudīr 'aḥad al-bunūk al-waṭanīya* the director of one of the national banks

في إحدى الوزارات *fī 'iḥda l-wizārāt* in one of the ministries

6. Possessive expressions

Most of the distributive expressions given above can be used also in possessive expressions; these are studied in Chapter 15.

7. Vocabulary: الاقتصاد والمالية *al-iqtiṣād wa-l-mālīya*

Economy and finance

استثمار *istithmār* investment
بضاعة بضائع *biḍā'a baḍā'i'* merchandise
بنك بنوك *bank bunūk* bank
تجارة *tijāra* trade
تطوّر *taṭawwur* development
تعويض *ta'wīḍ* compensation
تكليف تكاليف *taklīf takālīf* cost, expense
تنمية *tánmiya* development
ثمن أثمان *thaman 'athmān* cost, value
حساب *ḥisāb* account, bill
دفع مدفوعات *daf' madfū'āt* payment
دكّان دكاكين *dukkān dakākīn* shop
دين ديون *dayn duyūn* debt
راتب رواتب *rātib rawātib* salary
رأسمال *ra'smāl* capital
رخيص *rakhīṣ* cheap
سعر أسعار *si'r 'as'ār* price, rate
سوق أسواق *sūq 'aswāq* (f.) market
صادرات *ṣādirāt* exports
عالم أعوالم *'ālam 'a'wālim* world
غرفة تجارة *ghurfat tijāra* Chamber of Commerce
فلوس *fulūs* (inan. pl.) money

قرض قروض *qarḍ qurūḍ* loan
قطاع *qiṭā'* sector
مال أموال *māl 'amwāl* property
مستوردات *mustawradāt* imports
مشروع مشاريع *mashrū' mashārī'* project
مصرف مصارف *maṣrif maṣārif* bank
ميزانية *mīzānīya* budget
نقود *nuqūd* (inan. pl.) money
الوحيد *al-waḥīd* the only
وكالة *wikāla* agency

Exercise 1. Put (a) عدّة and (b) عدد من before each expression, making any necessary changes:

e.g.: استثمار ← عدّة استثمارات\عدد من الاستثمارات

'iddat istithmārāt, 'adad min al-istithmārāt

1 مصرف محلّي
2 راتب
3 حساب
4 أستاذ
5 وكالة
6 مشروع دولي
7 رأي
8 مكاتب حكومية
9 تكليف
10 صادرات
11 عضو
12 هذه البضائع

Exercise 2. Make an equation with the attribute which is shown in parentheses:

e.g.: بعض الأعضاء (جديد) ← بعض الأعضاء جدد.

ba'ḍ al-'a'ḍā' judud.

1 عدد من الديون (صغير)
2 كلّ الاستثمارات (خاصّ)
3 أحد بنوك التنمية (محلّي)
4 جميع المدفوعات (معقّد)
5 هذه (المشكلة الوحيدة)
6 كثير من العمليات (رخيص)
7 عدّة أصدقاء (حاضر)
8 بعض الطلاّب (غائب)

Exercise 3. Select the only correct distributive noun or pronoun for the expression:

e.g.: (كلّ\عدّة\بعض) حسابات في البنك

← عدّة حسابات في البنك *'iddat ḥisābāt fi l-bank*

1 (أيّ\نفس\عدد من) حلّ كامل للمشكلة
2 (عدّة\كثير من\جميع\كلّ) ميزانية سنوية
3 (عدد من\أيّة\أيّ) الصادرات الصناعية للبلاد
4 (أيّ\نفس\عدد من) الحلّ للمشكلة
5 في (بعض\أكثرية\قليل من\أيّة) سوق العالم
6 من أجل دفع (كثير من\عدّة\أيّة) القروض الأجنبية

Exercise 4. Select the only correct expression to follow the distributive noun or pronoun:

e.g.: بعض (حساب\التاجر\الحسابات) ← بعض الحسابات

ba'ḍ al- ḥisābāt

1 نفس (العملية\عمليات\عمليات تجارية)
2 كلّ (ميزاتيات\ميزانية\قروض)
3 كلّ (القروض\ديون\ميزانيات)
4 كلّ (صادرات\مستوردات\صادرات الشركة)
5 أيّ (حساب\حسابات\الحساب)
6 لأحد (حسابات\حساب\هذه القطاعات)

Exercise 5. Collect together words having the same root:

e.g.: *kabīr 'akbar kubra* كبير أكبر كبرى

أكثرية مال أهمّية كثير خلاف عدّة كلّية أهمّ جميع كلّ أكثر أموال مختلف مالية عدد هامّ جامعة

10 Deriving

- Collective and abstract nouns
- Adjectives of colour and defect
- Weak nouns and adjectives

1. Collective nouns

A collective noun denotes a group, e.g. 'cattle' in English. Arabic collectives are m. sing., mostly with no pl. They denote living things and simple products. e.g.:

بقر	*baqar* cattle	إبل	*'ibil* camels	سمك	*samak* fish
دجاج	*dajāj* chickens	خيل	*khayl* horses	تفّاح	*tuffāḥ* apples
تمر	*tamr* dates	عنب	*'inab* grapes	تين	*tīn* figs
زهر	*zahr* flowers	بيض	*bayḍ* eggs	شجر	*shajar* trees
حبّ	*ḥabb* grains, seeds	طوب	*ṭūb* bricks	ورق	*waraq* foliage, paper

The unit noun is derived by adding ...ة *-a*: بقرة *baqara* 'cow'. Some unit nouns have sound plurals. Among those with broken plurals are:

سمكة أسماك	*samaka 'asmāk* fish
حبّة حبوب	*ḥabba ḥubūb* grain, seed
شجرة أشجار	*shajara 'ashjār* tree
زهرة زهور	*zahra zuhūr* flower
عنبة أعناب	*'inaba 'a'nāb* grape
ورقة أوراق	*waraqa 'awrāq* leaf, sheet of paper
تمرة تمور	*tamra tumūr* date

In some cases a different unit noun is used:

جمل أجمال	*jamal 'ajmāl* camel
حصان حصن	*ḥiṣān ḥuṣun* horse

and some living things have no collective nouns:

طير طيور	*ṭayr ṭuyūr* bird	حيوان	*ḥayawān* animal

حشرة *ḥashara* insect

2. Abstract nouns

Many abstract nouns denoting activities or ideas have a form identical to that of the feminine relative adjective (Chapter 2), with the ending ...ية *-īya*:

حرّية	*ḥurrīya* freedom	اشتراكية	*ishtirākīya* socialism
ديموقراطية	*dimoqrāṭīya* democracy	نظرية	*naẓarīya* theory
عملية	*'amalīya* operation	رأسمالية	*ra'smālīya* capitalism
بلدية	*baladīya* municipality	هوية	*huwīya* identity

3. Adjectives of colour and defect

An important group of adjectives denoting colours and physical afflictions has a m. form similar to that of the comparative adjectives (Chapter 8). Common examples:

m. sing.		f. sing./inan. pl.		m. + f. an. pl.		
أحمر	*'aḥmar*	حمراء	*ḥamrā'*	حمر	*ḥumr*	red
أبيض	*'abyaḍ*	بيضاء	*bayḍā'*	بيض	*bīḍ*	white
أسود	*'aswad*	سوداء	*sawdā'*	سود	*sūd*	black
أزرق	*'azraq*	زرقاء	*zarqā'*	زرق	*zurq*	blue
أصفر	*'aṣfar*	صفراء	*ṣafrā'*	صفر	*ṣufr*	yellow
أخضر	*'akhḍar*	خضراء	*khaḍrā'*	خضر	*khuḍr*	green
أعمى	*'a'ma*	عمياء	*'amyā'*	عمي	*'umy*	blind
أطرش	*'aṭrash*	طرشاء	*ṭarshā'*	طرش	*ṭursh*	deaf

For the dual: m. أحمران\أحمرين *'aḥmarān, 'aḥmarayn*
أعميان\أعميين *'a'mayān, 'a'mayayn* (etc.)
f. حمراوان\حمراوين *ḥamrāwān, ḥamrāwayn*
عمياوان\عمياوين *'amyāwān, 'amyāwayn* (etc.)

4. Weak nouns and adjectives

Some important nouns and adjectives, called weak (ناقصة *nāqiṣa*), have different indefinite and definite forms:

Indefinite singular *-in*, definite singular ي... *-ī*, masculine:

Indefinite sing.		Definite sing.		Plural		
قاضٍ*	*qāḍin*	القاضي	*al-qāḍī*	(الـ)قضاة	*(al-)quḍā*	judge
فاضٍ	*fāḍin*	الفاضي	*al-fāḍī*	(الـ)فاضون\ين	*(al-)fāḍūn/īn*	vacant, free
ماض	*māḍin*	الماضي	*al-māḍī*	(الـ)ماضون\ين	*(al-)māḍūn/īn*	past
جار	*jārin*	الجاري	*al-jārī*	(الـ)جارون\ين	*(al-)jārūn/īn*	current
خال	*khālin*	الخالي	*al-khālī*	(الـ)خالون\ين	*(al-)khālūn/īn*	empty
غال	*ghālin*	الغالي	*al-ghālī*	(الـ)غالون\ين	*(al-)ghālūn/īn*	expensive
عال	*ʿālin*	العالي	*al-ʿālī*	(الـ)عالون\ين	*(al-)ʿālūn/īn*	high
محام	*muḥāmin*	المحامي	*al-muḥāmī*	(الـ)محامون\ين	*(al-)muḥāmūn/īn*	lawyer

(* The ... *kasra tanwīn* is hardly ever seen outside grammar books.)

Indefinite singular ىً... *-an*, definite singular ى... *-a*, masc.:

مستشفىً	*mustashfan*	المستشفى	*al-mustashfa*	(الـ)مستشفيات	*(al-)mustashfayāt*	hospital
مستوىً	*mustawan*	المستوى	*al-mustawa*	(الـ)مستويات	*(al-)mustawayāt*	level

Indefinite plural *-in*, definite plural ي... *-ī*, masc. and fem.:

Singular		Indefinite plural		Definite plural		
(الـ)أهل	*(al-)'ahl* (m.)	أهال	*'ahālin*	الأهالي	*al-'ahālī*	relative

(الـ)أرض *(al-)'arḍ* (f.) أراض *'arāḍin* الأراضي *al-'arāḍī* land
(الـ)يد *(al-)yad* (f.) أياد *'ayādin* الأيادي *al-'ayādī* hand

Indefinite plural ىً... ***-an*****, definite plural** ى... ***-a*****, feminine:**

(الـ)قرية *(al-)qáriya* قرىً *quran* القرى *al-qura* village

The adjectives have a regular feminine/inanimate plural and, where meaningful, a regular comparative (see Chapter 8):

(الـ)فاضية\خالية\ماضية\جارية *(al-)fáḍiya, kháliya, máḍiya, járiya*
(الـ)غالية *(al-)gháliya* أغلى *'aghla*
(الـ)عالية *(al-)'áliya* أعلى *'a'la*
(f. superlative العليا *al-'ulya*)

Remember that the theme of a construct always has a definite ending:

قاضي المحكمة العليا *qāḍi l-maḥkama l-'ulya* the high court judge

It is common today to pronounce the definite form for the indefinite of the weak nouns and adjectives. The spelling, however, is respected:

هو محام. *huwa muḥāmin/muhāmī.* He is a lawyer.

Conversely, the word سنة *sana* 'year' often gets full pronunciation in expressions such as:

في السنة الماضية *fi s-sanati l-máḍiya* (in the) past/last year
في السنة الجارية *fi s-sanati l-járiya* in the current year

This is the full *genitive case* ending, explained in Chapter 15.
We shall mark weak nouns and adjectives '(weak)' in the vocabulary.

5. Vocabulary: البلاد والريف *al-bilād wa-r-rīf*

Town and country

أهل القرى *'ahl al-qura* country people
أهل المدن *'ahl al-mudun* townspeople
بلد بلاد *balad bilād* (m./f.) town
بناية *bināya* building
بيروت *bayrūt* Beirut
جبل جبال *jabal jibāl* mountain

خريف *kharīf* autumn
دمشق *dimashq* Damascus
ربيع *rabī'* spring (season)
ريف أرياف *rīf 'aryāf* country(side)
زراعة *zirā'a* agriculture
ساحل سواحل *sāḥil sawāḥil* coast
شتاء أشتية *shitā' 'áshtiya* winter
شريع شواريع *shārī' shawārī'* street
صحراء صحارى *ṣaḥrā' ṣaḥāra* (f.) desert
صيف أصياف *ṣayf 'aṣyāf* summer
طريق طرق *ṭarīq ṭuruq* (m./f.) road
فلاّح *fallāḥ* farmer, peasant
القاهرة *al-qāhira* Cairo
كنيسة كنائس *kanīsa kanā'is* church
مدينة مدن *madīna mudun* city
مسجد مساجد *masjid masājid* mosque
مكان أماكن *makān 'amākin* place
ميدان ميادين *maydān mayādīn* square
نهر أنهر *nahr 'anhur* river
النيل *an-nīl* the Nile

Exercise 1. Make the adjective agree with the noun:

e.g.: *zahra zurqa* زهرة زرقة ← زهرة، أزرق

1 زهر، أزرق
2 زهور، أزرق
3 الورقة، أبيض
4 ناس، أعمى
5 الأشجار، أخضر
6 طوبة، أحمر
7 الحصان، أسود
8 زوّار، أجنبي

Exercise 2. Make each expression definite with the article:

e.g.: *al-'arāḍi r-rīfiya* الأراضي الريفية ← أراض ريفية

1 قاض سابق	2 محلاّت فاضية
3 على مستوىً عال	4 إلى مستشفىً عامّ
5 لمحام غال	6 بنايات قرىً

Exercise 3. Make definite constructs:

e.g.: أراض، هذه القرية ← أراضي هذه القرية

'arāḍī hādhihi l-qáriya

1 قرىً، منطقة	2 في أياد، سلطات محلّية
3 محام، هذه الشركة	4 محامون، هذه الشركة
5 أراض، منطقة، النيل الأبيض	6 طريق، دمشق

Exercise 4. Take your answers to Exercise 3. Add to each theme respectively the adjective listed below and recast your construct as a prepositional expression with ل:

e.g.: واسع ← الأراضي الواسعة لهذه القرية

al-'arāḍi l-wāsi'a li-hādhihi l-qáriya

1 مختلف	2 خبير	3 غال
4 سابق	5 زراعي	6 طويل

Do the same again, using another adjective of your own choice.

Exercise 5. Put the words from the list into the blanks in the passage:

القاهرة هي أكبر ... أفريقيا و ... أقدم مدن العالم. مصر بلاد هامّ من أجل ثقافة وسياسة الـ... العربي الشرقي والـ... . كتب الكتّاب* المصريين ... عند جميع العرب المثقّفين. وفي نفس الوقت مصر ... في ... الدولية. القاهرة على نهر ... . هذا ... هو ... نهر العالم، وهو هامّ لـ ... كلّ الإقليم.

(زراعة، عالم، مدينة، منظّمات، أطول، غربي، مشهور، نهر، إحدى، النيل، هامّ)

* كاتب كتّاب here: author, writer

11 Recounting – 1

- Past tense, Form I: sound, hamzated and initial-*wāw* verbs
- Verbal sentences; قد *qad*, لقد *laqad*
- there is, there are

1. Past tense of verbs

A verb expresses an action or state: 'write', 'seem'. Arabic verbs have two main tenses (= time connotations), *past* and *present.*

The Arabic past tense (الماضي *al-māḍī*) is used for actions and situations already completed. To derive this tense we take the *first principal part* (the verb form found in most dictionaries). The principal part itself is the 3rd. person m. sing. ('he', 'it') of the past tense. For the other persons, drop the final *-a* of this part and then add the past personal endings shown in the table. Thus, for كتب *kataba* 'to write', with the three root letters *k t b,* we have:

Person	Singular	Plural
1 m/f.	كتبت *katabtu* I wrote	كتبنا *katabna* we wrote
2 m. 2 f.	كتبت *katabta* you (m.) wrote كتبت *katabti* you (f.) wrote	كتبتم *katabtum* you wrote
3 m 3 f.	كتب *kataba* he wrote كتبت *katabat* she wrote	كتبوا *katabū* they wrote

(or: I have written etc.)

Note:

- The three persons correspond in use to those shown in Chapter 5 for the subject pronouns. Remember that the subject pronoun is used with the verb sparingly, e.g. for emphasis, since it is mostly implicit in the form of the verb itself.
- Where the vowel of the ending is transcribed in small type, it is

mostly dropped in short pronunciation; see Chapters 1 and 12. You will note that this happens to the final *-a* of the هو form itself.

- There is no infinitive form ('to do', 'to write' etc.) in Arabic. The first principal part, e.g. كتب *kataba* (which is read in this context with full pronunciation), is listed in English dictionaries and vocabularies as 'to write'. Used in a sentence كتب must however mean 'he wrote/has written'.
- In the ending ...وا *-ū* the *'alif* is silent.
- As with the pronouns, there are other 2nd and 3rd persons, i.e. the dual and the f. plural; these rarer persons need not concern us here. The Appendix has details.

Similarly, for عمل *'amila* 'to do', 'to work', 'to make':

عملت *'amiltu,* عملت *'amilta,* عملت *'amilti,* عمل *'amila,*
عملت *'amilat;* عملنا *'amilna,* عملتم *'amiltum,* عملوا *'amilū*

I, you, he (etc.) did/have done/has done, (have/has) worked/made

This pattern is valid for verbs with three consonants ('sound' verbs), or ء and two other consonants ('hamzated' verbs), as root letters, or with و *wāw* as *first* root letter, and two consonants as the other root letters ('initial-*wāw*' verbs).

قرأ *qara'a* to read:

قرأت *qara'tu,* قرأت *qara'ta,* قرأت *qara'ti,* قرأ *qara'a,*
قرأت *qara'at;* قرأنا *qara'na,* قرأتم *qara'tum,* قرأوا *qara'ū*

I, you, he (etc.) (have/has) read

قرأوا is the easiest spelling for *qara'u*; you will also encounter قرؤوا .

وصل *waṣala* to arrive:

وصلت *waṣaltu,* وصلت *waṣalta,* وصلت *waṣalti,* وصل *waṣala,*
وصلت *waṣalat;* وصلنا *waṣalna,* وصلتم *waṣaltum,* وصلوا *waṣalū*

I, you, he (etc.) (have/has) arrived

2. Masculine and feminine; animate and inanimate

Look back to Chapters 2 and 3. The 3rd person singular forms are made to agree with the (m. or f.) subject noun to which they refer:

التقرير طويل. وصل أمس. *at-taqrīr ṭawīl. waṣal 'ams.*
The report is long. It arrived yesterday.

الرسالة طويلة. وصلت أمس. *ar-risāla ṭawīla. waṣalat 'ams.*
The letter is long. It arrived yesterday.

المندوبون حاضرون. وصلوا أمس. *al-mandūbūn ḥāḍirūn. waṣalū 'ams.* The delegates are present. They arrived yesterday.

A verb with an *inanimate* (= non-people) plural as subject stands in the inanimate plural form, which is identical to the feminine singular:

التقارير طويلة. وصلت أمس. *at-taqārīr ṭawīla. waṣalat 'ams.*
The reports are long. They arrived yesterday.

A noun denoting a group of people is itself inanimate:

الوفود حاضرة. وصلت أمس. *al-wufūd ḥāḍira. waṣalat 'ams.*
The delegations are present. They arrived yesterday.

3. Verb Forms

The verbs quoted in this chapter are in Form I, which is the simplest form using the three root letters of the verb. In later chapters we shall study eight *increased* forms (II to VIII, and X), which are variants of Form I in pattern and meaning.

4. Verbal sentences

In an Arabic sentence the verb most often stands first. This structure is called a *verbal sentence* (جملة فعلية *jumla fi'līya*).

In a verbal sentence having a *noun* as subject, the verb preceding it always stands in the singular; for our purposes this rule affects only the هم form, which in the past tense loses its ending ...وا *-ū*:

قرأ الخبراء التقرير. *qara' al-khubarā' at-taqrīr.*
(not [قرأوا]) The experts read the report.

An inanimate plural form counts as singular, so that form is retained:

وصلت الرسالات أمس. *waṣalat ar-risālāt 'ams.*
The letters arrived yesterday.

The noun subject follows the initial verb. Any further verb with the same subject follows that subject and agrees fully with it:

دخل الخبراء وجلسوا. *dakhal al-khubarā' wa-jalasū.*
The experts entered and sat down.

All other persons we have studied, and all verbs having a subject other than a noun, agree fully with their subject, when they begin the sentence:

قرأنا التقرير. *qara'na t-taqrīr.* We read the report.
قرأوا التقرير. *qara'u t-taqrīr.* They read the report.

5. Adverbial expressions

Adverbs are explained in Chapter 32. But note here that adverbial expressions such as those indicating time and place can precede the verb. The sentence remains a verbal sentence as long as the verb is situated earlier than its subject. Compare:

بعد بحث هذه النقطة ترك الوزراء المؤتمر.
ba'd baḥth hādhihi n-nuqṭa tarak al-wuzarā' al-mu'tamar.
After discussion of this point the ministers left the conference.

ترك الوزراء المؤتمر بعد بحث هذه النقطة.
tarak al-wuzarā' al-mu'tamar ba'd baḥth hādhihi n-nuqṭa.
The ministers left the conference after discussion of this point.

6. قد *qad*

The particle قد *qad*, or لقد *laqad*, can be put before a past-tense verb. It is optional, and emphasises that the action is completed:

قد حضر المثّلون الاجتماع. *qad ḥaḍar al-mumaththilūn al-ijtimā'.*
The representatives attended the meeting (= which is now over).
لقد كتب التقرير. *laqad katab at-taqrīr.*
He has written (= finished writing) the report.

7. There is, there are

In Chapter 5 we studied 'there is, there are' expressed with a reversed equation.

'There is/are' can also be expressed with a verbal sentence. The verb used is **يوجد** *yūjad* (m. s.) or **توجد** *tūjad* (f.s./inan. pl.), ('it is found'). Examine:

يوجد مؤتمر في غرفة التجارة. *yūjad mu'tamar fi ghurfat at-tijāra.*
There is a conference in the Chamber of Commerce.
توجد لجان مختلفة. *tūjad lijān mukhtálifa.*
There are various committees.

8. Vocabulary: sound, hamzated and initial-*wāw* verbs, Form I

أخذ *'akhadha* to take	أكل *'akala* to eat
بدأ *bada'a* to begin	حمل *ḥamala* to carry
خرج (من) *kharaja (min)* to go/come out (of)	درس *darasa* to study
ذكر *dhakara* to mention, recall	ذهب *dhahaba* to go
رجع *raja'a* to go/come back	رفض *rafaḍa* to reject, refuse
ركب *rakiba* get on/into	سأل *sa'ala* to ask (enquire)
سكن *sakana* to live	سمع *sami'a* to hear
شرب *shariba* to drink	شرح *sharaḥa* to explain
شكر *shakara* to thank	ضرب *ḍaraba* to hit
طلب *ṭalaba* to ask for	عرف *'arafa* to know, recognise
فتح *fataḥa* to open	فشل *fashila* to fail
فهم *fahima* to understand	لبس *labisa* to wear

لعب	*la'iba* to play	نجح	*najaḥa* to succeed
نزل	*nazala* to go/come/get down	نشر	*nashara* to publish
وجد	*wajada* to find (a thing)	وضع	*waḍa'a* to put, place

Exercise 1. Put the verb into the correct form of the past tense:

e.g.: *katabt* كتبت ← (كتب، أنا)

waṣalat ar-risāla. وصلت الرسالة. ← (وصل) الرسالة

1 (دخل) الطالب
2 (دخل) الطلاّب
3 (شرح، هم)
4 (ذهب، نحن)
5 (رجع، أنتم)
6 (فهم، هي)
7 (وصل، هم)
8 (خرج) الأطفال
9 (نجح) مشاريع الشركة
10 (شرب) الحيوانات

Exercise 2. Put singular verbs into the plural and plural verbs into the singular:

e.g.: *dakhalū wa-jalasū* دخلوا وجلسوا ← دخل وجلس

'araft wa-sharaḥt عرفت وشرحت ← عرفتم وشرحتم

1 سمعت وفهمت (أنا)
2 أكلنا وشربنا
3 بدأوا ونجحوا
4 أخذ الملفّ وترك المكتب.
5 كتبت ونشرت (أنت)
6 قرأنا التقرير.
7 وجدت (أنا) الرسالة هنا.
8 سكن في بيروت.
9 فتحوا باب البيت.
10 طلب الفلوس.

Exercise 3. Put the verb into the correct form of the past tense:

e.g.: *qara't at-taqrīr.* قرأت التقرير. ← (قرأ، أنا) التقرير

دخل الطلاّب وجلسوا. ← (دخل) الطلاّب و(جلس).

dakhal aṭ-ṭullāb wa-jalasū.

1 (كتب) الزميل التقرير أمس.
2 (دخل، أنا) المصنع.
3 (خرج، هم) من المكتب.
4 قد (نشر) اللجنة التقرير.

5 (رجع، أنتم) إلى المكتب. 6 (كتب، نحن) التقرير.
7 (شرب) الأصدقاء القهوة و(ترك) البيت.
8 (ذهب) المدير والزملاء إلى البنك.
9 لقد (ترك) الوفود بيروت. 10 (فهم، هو) السؤال.

Exercise 4. Select the only correct verb form for the subject:

e.g.: (كتبنا\قرأتم\فهمت\شرحوا، نحن) الرسالة الرسمية.

← كتبنا الرسالة الرسمية. *katabna r-risāla r-rasmīya.*

1 (سمع\سألنا\عرفت\فهموا، نحن) ممثّل الشركة.
2 (ذهب\خرجنا\رجعوا\دخلت) الموظّفون إلى بيروت و(ذهب\خرجنا\رجعوا\دخلت) إلى المكتب.
3 (وضعوا\وجدتم\نشرت\كتب) الوكالة الأرقام في التقرير.
4 (ذكرتم\كتب\سألوا\عرفت، أنا) تفاصيل المشروع و(ذكروا\كتبت\سأل\عرفتم) الاسم والنمرة الكاملة في الملف.
5 قد (وصلت\رجعتم\حضر\ذهبوا) الوفود أمس.

Exercise 5. Select the only correct subject for the verb:

e.g.: شرح (أنا\الوكالة\الوكيل\السكرتيرة) أهمّية الأرقام.

← شرح الوكيل أهمّية الأرقام.

sharaḥ al-wakīl 'ahammīyat al-'arqām.

1 قد بدأ (المهندسون\هم\الشركة\نحن) المشروع الجديد أمس.
2 بدأت (المهندسون\هم\الشركة\نحن) المشروع الجديد أمس.
3 أخذت (هم\نحن\الممثل\السكرتيرة) الملفّ من المكتب.
4 أخذ (هي\نحن\الممثّل\السكرتيرة) الملفّ من المكتب.
5 لقد وصلت (الوفد\المندوب\الوفود\المندوبون) أمس.

Exercise 6. Add a suitable noun subject to the sentence, making any changes needed:

e.g.: دخلوا الصفّ. ← دخل الطلاب الصفّ.

dakhal aṭ-ṭullāb aṣ-ṣaff.

1 فشلت بعد سنة. 2 رفضوا الميزانية الفنية.
3 قد بدأوا دراسة المشروع. 4 قد بدأ بحث المشاريع.
5 شرح لنا تفاصيل التقرير. 6 ذهبوا إلى البلد ورجعوا أمس.

Exercise 7. Replace each verb with another suitable one, making any changes needed:

e.g.: قرأنا التقرير الفنّي. ← شرحنا التقرير الفنّي.
sharaḥna t-taqrīr al-fannī.

1 خرج الاشتراكيون من البرلمان. 2 ترك الزملاء الاجتماع.
3 نشرت الوزارة القانون المالي. 4 درس التلاميذ اللغة العربية.
5 نجحت مشاريع الحكومة. 6 رفضوا سياسة الحزب.

Exercise 8. Recast the equation as a verbal sentence with يوجد\توجد:

e.g.: هناك أقسام مختلفة.← هناك توجد أقسام مختلفة.
hunāka tūjad 'aqsām mukhtálifa.

1 في البستان زهور جميلة. 2 هناك سؤال اقتصادي معقّد.
3 وراء البيت جنينة كبيرة. 4 في التقرير عدّة أسئلة صعبة.
5 في الكلّية مختبر حديث.

Exercise 9. Read this passage aloud, then make complete sentences based on the text:

كتب الخبراء الاقتصاديون التقرير السنوي على طلب الوزراء. درس الوزراء الوثيقة خلال اجتماع اللجنة المالية مع ممثلي الأقسام. بعد بحث طويل رفضوا عدّة تفاصيل. سأل أعضاء اللجنة أسئلةً فنّيةً مختلفةً وسمعوا جواب الخبراء. ذكرت اللجنة عدد من المشاكل المالية المعقدة وطلبت دراسة هدّة نقط.

1 ... على طلب ... 2 رفضوا ...
3 ... وطلبت دراسة عدّة نقط. 4 سأل أعضاء اللجنة ...
5 ذكرت اللجنة عدد ... 6 درس الوزراء الوثيقة ...

12 Entailing

- Direct and prepositional objects of the verb

1. Direct object of the verb: regular nouns and adjectives

The direct object of a verb is that which is directly affected by the verb's action. The Arabic direct object noun and/or adjective stands in the *accusative* case (النصب *an-naṣb*), the endings of which depend on the type of noun or adjective.

Singular and broken plural. In the singular and the broken plural, the accusative is normally written and pronounced only when the noun or adjective is indefinite. Its regular ending is *-an*:

- After a final consonant other than *hamza*, it is spelt ...اً (*'alif tanwīn*) pronounced *-an*. It is added directly after the consonant:

  حجزوا أوتيلاً. *ḥajazū 'utaylan.* They booked a hotel.

  عرفوا ضيوفاً جدداً هناك. *'arafū ḍuyūfan judūdan hunāka.* They recognised new guests there.

- The relative ending ...ي *-ī* becomes ...يّاً *-íyan*; the final *-ī* of weak words like *qāḍī* (Chapter 10) becomes ...ياً *-iyan* (NB different pronunciation and stress):

  حجزوا أوتيلاً ساحلياً غالياً. *ḥajazū 'utaylan sāḥilíyan ghắliyan.* They booked an expensive seaside ('coastal') hotel.

- ...ة becomes ...ةً, still sounded *-a* in short pronunciation (for the record, *-atan* in full pronunciation):

  عمل رحلةً بحريةً. *'amil riḥla baḥrīya.* He made a sea trip.

- After final ...اء *-ā'* in masc. sing. nouns and adjectives, it is written ...ً pronounced *-an*:

  دخلت الباخرة ميناءً أجنبياً. *dakhalat al-bākhira mīnā'an 'ajnabīyan.* The ship entered a foreign port.

The symbol ...ً *fatḥa tanwīn* is omitted in many texts.

(Some nouns and adjectives [see below] have none of these endings in the accusative.)

Dual and sound m. plural. In the dual and in the sound m. pl., both indefinite and definite, the accusative is identical to the *genitive* الجرّ *al-jarr*, see Chapter 6):

أخذنا (الـ)جدولين (الـ)جوّيين. *'akhadhna (l-)jadwalayn (al-)jawwīyayn* We took (the) two air timetables.

شكرنا المأمورين الحكوميين. *shakarna l-ma'mūrīn al-ḥukūmīyīn.* We thanked the government officials.

ذكروا هذين الأوتيلين. *dhakarū hādhayn al-'utaylayn.* They mentioned these two hotels.

These are the only accusative endings sounded in short pronunciation when no suffix follows. Chapter 15, and the Appendix, show the endings pronounced before a suffix.

Sound f. plural. The sound f. pl. ending ...ات *-āt* is unchanged in short pronunciation for the accusative, whether indefinite or definite:

حجزوا أوتيلات غاليةً. *ḥajazū 'utaylāt ghāliya.* They booked expensive hotels.

2. Direct object of the verb: irregular nouns and adjectives

The following nouns and adjectives do not take the ending *-an* (however spelt):

- those like أبيض *'abyaḍ,* أكبر *'akbar,* أخرى *'ukhra* (colours and comparatives, Chapters 8 and 10),
- broken plurals with vowel patterns

  -a-ā-ī-, e.g. تقارير *taqārīr* reports

  -a-ā-i-, e.g. تذاكر *tadhākir* tickets
- all fem. and almost all (see * below) pl. forms ending ...اء *-ā'*.

أخذنا تذاكر أرخص. *'akhadhna tadhākir 'arkhaṣ.* We took cheaper tickets.

ذكروا تفاصيل أخرى. *dhakarū tafāṣīl 'ukhra.*
They mentioned other details.

عرفنا زملاء كثاراً. *'arafna zumalā' kithāran.*
We recognised many colleagues.

Nouns and adjectives of this type are called *diptote* (غير منصرف *ghayr munṣarif*). The Appendix gives details, including full-form endings.

Weak nouns ending in ى... *-a* (e.g. مستشفىً *mustashfan*, Chapter 10) do not change for case in the singular; they have, as you will recall, ىً... *-an* (indefinite) and ى... *-a* (definite).

(* The rare exceptions occur when either ا or ء is, or represents, a *root letter*, e.g. أجزاء *'ajzā'* 'parts', indef. accusative أجزاءً *'ajzā'an.*)

3. Accusative in constructs

The theme of a construct (Chapter 7) always has definite form; so it cannot take the indefinite ending *-an* (however spelt), even when it is a direct object:

سألت سائق تاكسي. *sa'alt sā'iq taksī.*
(not [سائقاً *sā'iqan*]) I asked a taxi driver.

قد نشروا دراسة مشروع جديد. *qad nasharū dirāsat mashrū' jadīd.*
They have published a study of a new project.

Remember to drop final ن... *-n* in the dual and the sound m. pl.:

سألنا مأموري وكالة. *sa'alna ma'mūray/ma'mūri wikāla.*
(not [ين... *-ayn/-īn*]) We asked (two) agency officials.

4. Pronoun direct objects

The direct-object pronouns ('me', 'him' etc.) are suffixed to their verb; the suffixes are identical to those used after prepositions (Chapter 6), with the exception of 'me', which is ني... *-nī.*

Before adding the object suffix, we restore any 'suppressed' final vowel of the singular verb (Chapter 11):

دفعت الأجرة. *dafa't al-'ujra*. I paid the fare.

but: دفعتها. *dafa'tuha*. I paid it.

so also: شكرني. *shakaranī*. He thanked me.

The plural persons of the verb change before the suffix is added:

- نا... *-na* is pronounced *-nā́-*; the spelling is unchanged
- تم... *-tum* becomes ...تمو... *-tumū́-*
- وا... *-ū* is written ...و... *-ū́-*

(NB stress:) ذكرناهم. *dhakarnā́hum*. We mentioned them.

أخذتموها. *'akhadhtumū́ha*. You took it/them.

سمعوك. *sami'ū́ka/sami'ū́ki*. They heard you.

5. Prepositional objects

Many verbs have a *prepositional* object (i.e. an object governed by a preposition):

دفع الأجرة إلى السائق. *dafa' al-'ujra 'ila s-sā'iq*.

He paid the fare to the driver.

In English the prepositions 'to' and 'for' may be omitted; the equivalents cannot be omitted in Arabic. 'He paid the driver the fare' is still دفع الأجرة إلى السائق.

Arabic and equivalent English verbs may differ in their objects:

طلبوا منّي الأجرة. *ṭalabū minni l-'ujra*.

They asked me for the fare. ('They asked from me the fare.')

A few verbs offer a choice of direct or prepositional object:

بعث (بـ)رسالة. *ba'ath (bi-)risāla*. He sent a letter.

6. Accusative of time

A noun which has no preposition and which indicates when the action of a verb happens, also stands in the accusative:

سكنوا شهراً كاملاً في مصر. *sakanū shahran kāmilan fī miṣr*.

They lived (for) a full month in Egypt.

عملت هنا سنتين. *'amilat huna sanatayn.*
She worked here (for) two years.

7. Vocabulary: النقل والسفرات *an-naql wa-s-safarāt* Transport and travel

أوتوبيس\باص *'otobīs, bāṣ* bus
باخرة بواخر *bākhira bawākhir* ship
بحر أبحار *baḥr 'abḥār* sea
تأخير *ta'khīr* delay
تأمين *ta'mīn* insurance
تذكرة تذاكر *tadhkara tadhākir* ticket
جدول جداول *jadwal jadāwil* schedule, timetable
جمرك جمارك *jumruk jamārik* customs
جولة *jawla* trip, tour
إلى\في الخارج *'ila/fī l-khārij* abroad
خطّ خطوط *khaṭṭ khuṭūṭ* line
راكب ركّاب *rākib rukkāb* passenger, rider
رجوع *rujū'* return
زائر زوّار *zā'ir zuwwār* visitor
سائح سيّاح *sā'iḥ suyyāḥ* tourist
سفر *safar* journey, travel
سفينة سفن *safīna sufun* ship
سكّة (سكك) حديدية *sikka* (pl. *sikak*) *ḥadīdīya* railway
سياحة *siyāḥa* tourism
سيّارة *sayyāra* car
شحن *shaḥn* load
شنطة شنط *shanṭa shunaṭ* suitcase
ضيف ضيوف *ḍayf ḍuyūf* guest
طائرة *ṭā'ira* aeroplane
قطار قطر *qiṭār quṭur* train

متأخّر *muta'akhkhir* delayed
محطّة *mahaṭṭa* station
مسافر *musāfir* traveller
مطار *maṭār* airport
مغادرة *mughādara* departure
ميناء موان\الموانى *mīnā' mawānin/al-mawānī* (weak) port
مهاجرة *muhājara* immigration
نقل *naql* transport
هواء *hawā'* air
وصول *wuṣūl* arrival

Exercise 1. Add the expression shown in parentheses to the verb, as object (direct or prepositional):

e.g.: حملت السفينة (شحن كبير). ← حملت السفينة شحنًا كبيراً.
ḥamalat as-safīna shaḥnan kabīran.
دفعوا (الحمّال، الأجرة). ← دفعوا الأجرة للحمّال.
dafa'u l-'ujra li-l-ḥammāl.

1 أخذنا (قطار خاصّ).
2 حجزنا (غرفتان).
3 حجزنا (الغرفتان).
4 أخذنا (قطر خاصّة).
5 حجزنا (تذكرتان للقطار).
6 ركب (التاكسي).
7 طلبنا (المأمور، تذاكر أرخص).
8 أخذ (أوتوبيس).
9 سألوا (موظّفو وكالة).
10 نشروا (جداول جديدة).
11 أخذ الزوّار (جدول جديد) معهم.
12 ركب (تاكسي).

Exercise 2. Make plural everything possible:

e.g.: أخذ المسافر قطاراً خاصّاً. ← أخذ المسافرون قطراً خاصّةً.
'akhadh al-musāfirūn quṭuran khāṣṣa.

1 طلب المأمور من الراكب أجرة أخرى.
2 عرف موظّف الجمرك سائحًا أجنبيًا فى الطائرة.
3 طلب الراكب من الوكيل تذكرةً للرجوع.

4 نشرت شركة السياحة جدولاً جديداً.
5 حملت (أنا) شنطةً كبيرةً معي.
6 سمعت (أنا) باخرةً في الميناء.
7 شكرت (أنا) الموظّف المصري.
8 شرح لي الوكيل تفصيل الجدول.
9 شكرت (أنا) موظّف شركة السياحة.
10 فهم المأمور مشكلة التذكرة.

Exercise 3. Replace the noun objects (direct and prepositional) with pronouns:

e.g.: *fahimaha.* فهمها. ← فهم المشكلة.

sharaḥaha lī. شرحها لي. ← شرح لي المشكلة.

1 شرحت (أنا) البرنامج للضيوف. 2 قرأوا الجداول.
3 قرأوا الجدول. 4 دفع الأجرة إلي السائق.
5 دفع الأجرة إلي السائقين. 6 ركب التاكسي.
7 طلبنا الجدول من الوكيل. 8 أخذ المسافر التاكسي.
9 دفعنا حساب الأوتيل. 10 تركنا الأوتيل.

Exercise 4. Replace the pronoun objects (direct and prepositional) with nouns taken from this chapter:

e.g.: *sami'u l-bākhira.* سمعوا الباخرة. ← سمعوها.

طلبها منه. ← طلب الأجرة من الراكب.

ṭalab al-'ujra min ar-rākib.

1 خرجنا منه. 2 شرحوه لهم. 3 أخذها.
4 دفعها. 5 بدأها أمس. 6 ركبناه
7 ركبناها. 8 سمعوهم. 9 حملها.
10 تركوه. 11 فهموه. 12 شكرناهم.

Exercise 5. Make the direct object indefinite:

e.g.: شرح البرنامج للسيّاح. ← شرح برنامجًا للسيّاح.

sharaḥ barnāmajan li-s-suyyāḥ.

1 ركبوا القطار الخاصّ. 2 حجزنا التذاكر.
3 أخذ التأمين الرخيص. 4 كتب الرسالتين.
5 دخل الأوتيل الأرخص. 6 بدأ السفر الطويل.
7 قرأوا الجدول. 8 شرحنا النقط الهامّة.
9 فتحوا الأوتيل الجديد. 10 قرأ الكتاب المعقّد .
11 وجدوا الجدول الجوّي. 12 عملنا الرحلة الأرخص.

Exercise 6. Add a suitable adjective to the direct-object noun:

e.g.: حجز المسافرون تذاكر. ← حجز المسافرون تذاكر خاصّة.

ḥajaz al-musāfirūn tadhākir khāṣṣa.

1 حمل الحمّالون الشنط. 2 حجزنا التذاكر.
3 طلبوا غرفًا. 4 أخذنا طائرةً.
5 دخلَت السفينا ميناءً. 6 بدأ الجولة.
7 تركوا المطار. 8 قرأت جدولاً.
9 شكر الضيوف الوكيلين. 10 نشروا جداول.
11 سألنا ممثّلين. 12 سألنا أصدقاء.

Exercise 7. Read this passage aloud, then make the sentences complete, drawing on the text:

خلال الربيع عملنا رحلةً بحريةً من بيروت. قد حجزنا عند وكالة سفر تذاكر لباخرة سيّاحية كبيرة. ركبنا اتوبيسًا خاصًا في البلد وذهبنا إلى الميناء. هناك حمل موظّفو الوكالة الشنط الى الباخرة. بعد تأخير قصير بدأنا السفر. دخلت الباخرة مواني مختلفةً ونزل بعض الركّاب هناك لجولة قصيرة. بعد الرحلة رجعنا بالطائرة إلى بيروت.

1 ... في البلد و .... 2 دخلت الباخرة ....
3 قد حجزنا عند .... 4 هناك حمل موظّفو الوكالة ....
5 بعد الرحلة .... 6 ... عملنا رحلةً بحريةً من ....

Now underline all the direct objects in the passage. Which ones are indefinite?

13 Questioning

- Questions

1. Questions requiring the answer 'yes' or 'no'

Questions asking for an answer 'yes' or 'no' are introduced by an interrogative word. For affirmative questions this word is هل *hal* or (less commonly) أ *'a-*, neither of which we translate into English. Compare simple statements and questions:

هو جندي. *huwa jundī.* He is a soldier.
هل هو جندي؟ *hal huwa jundī?* Is he a soldier?
نجحت المظاهرة. *najaḥat al-muẓāhara.* The demonstration succeeded.
هل نجحت\أنجحت المظاهرة؟ *hal najaḥat/'a-najaḥat al-muẓāhara?* Did the demonstration succeed?
هل توجد مشاكل كثيرة؟ *hal tūjad mashākil kathīra?* Are there many problems?

Adding هل\أ does not change the type of sentence (e.g. equation or verbal sentence).

The answer is نعم *na'am* 'yes' or لا *lā* 'no'. Either answer may of course be expanded to a full sentence:

نعم، هو جندي. *na'am, huwa jundī.* Yes, he is a soldier.
لا، هو مأمور. *lā, huwa ma'mūr.* No, he is an official.
نعم، نجحت. *na'am, najaḥat.* Yes, it did.
لا، فشلت. *lā, fashilat.* No, it failed.

In Chapter 23 we study how to make negative questions and answers.

2. Questions requiring other answers

Questions requiring answers other than 'yes' or 'no' also begin with or centre on an appropriate interrogative word, as they do in English.

Common examples are:

مَن *man* who	ماذا *mādha* what
أيّ\أيّة *'ayy, 'ayya* which/what	كم *kam* how much/many
ما (هو\هي) *mā (huwa/hiya)* what is/are	متى *mata* when
لماذا *li-mādha* why	أين *'ayna* where
كيف *kayfa* how	أيّ نوع من *'ayy naw' min* what kind of

All these words can be governed by a preposition where necessary (لماذا already has one). Note further:

- من *man*, m. sing., does not change for gender and number. It may be subject of a verb or equation, or direct or prepositional object of a verb:

  من القائد ؟ *man al-qā'id?* Who is the leader?

  من سألت مثل هذا السؤال؟ *man sa'alt mithl hādha s-su'āl?*
  (To) Whom did you ask such a question?

  من *min* and عن *'an* + من *man* become ممّن\عمّن *mimman, 'amman*:

  ممّن طلبوها ؟ *mimman ṭalabūha?* Whom did they ask for it?

  من *man* as the attribute of a construct gives 'whose':

  هذه شكوة من؟ *hādhihi shakwat man?*
  Whose complaint is this?

  'whose' as a pronoun (i.e. in place of a noun) is لمن *li-man*:

  لمن هذه الورقة؟ *li-man hādhihi l-warqa?*
  Whose is this paper?

- ماذا *mādha* is used mainly in equations, ما (هو\هي) *mā (huwa/hiya)* mainly in questions with verbs. They are the inanimate counterparts of من *man*, and function like it, except that the forms ما هو and ما هي have gender:

  ماذا طلب المتظاهرون؟ *mādha ṭalab al-mutaẓāhirūn?*
  What did the demonstrators demand?

  ما (هو) الغرض من الاحتجاج؟ *mā (huwa) l-gharaḍ min*

al-iḥtijāj? What is the purpose of the protest?

وما (هي) حقوق المتظاهرين؟ ... *... wa-mā (hiya) ḥuqūq al-mutaẓāhirīn?* ... and what are the protesters' rights?

Note ممّا *mimmā* (من *min* + ما) and عمّا *'ammā* (عن + ما):

عمّا سمعتم اليوم؟ *'ammā sami'tum al-yawm?*
What did you hear about today?

- أيّ\أيّة *'ayy, 'ayya* as an interrogative expresses 'which/what'. It functions exactly as in the meaning 'any' studied in Chapter 9:

لأيّ غرض ...؟ *li-'ayy gharaḍ ...?* To what end ...?

أيّة أسئلة سألوكم؟\سألوكم أيّة أسئلة؟
'ayya 'as'ila sa'alūkum?/sa'alūkum 'ayya 'as'ila?
What questions did they ask you?

مع أي (من) أعضاء المعارضة؟ *ma' 'ayy (min) 'a'ḍā' al-mu'āraḍa?* with which opposition members?

- كم *kam* is used either as a pronoun:

كم أخذوا؟ *kam 'akhadhū?* How much/many did they take?

كم من الكت أخذوا؟ *kam min al-kutub 'akhadhū?*
How many of the books did they take?

or with adjectival force, with its noun in the indefinite *accusative singular* (irrespective of the noun's function in the sentence):

كم كتابًا أخذوا؟ *kam kitāban 'akhadhū?*
How many books did they take?

- The four adverbial interrogatives متى *mata,* لماذا *li-mādha,* أين *'ayna* and كيف *kayfa* present no special problem:

متى\لماذا ذهبوا إلى لبرلمان؟ *mata/li-mādha dhahabū 'ila l-barlamān?* When/Why did they go to Parliament?

أين\كيف دخلوا؟ *'ayna/kayfa dakhalū?*
Where/How did they get in?

- أيّ نوع من *'ayy naw' min* is followed by a definite noun or a definite construct:

أيّ نوع من الأسلحة؟ *'ayy naw' min al-'asliḥa?*
What kind of weapons?

3. or

'or' in a question is expressed with أم *'am* (not أو):

هل نجحت أم فشلت؟ *hal najaḥat 'am fashilat?*
Did it succeed or fail?

4. Direct and indirect questions

The questions studied here are *direct* questions. *Indirect* questions, e.g. 'We asked *whether he would support us.*' are studied in Chapter 31.

5. Vocabulary: النزاع *an-nizā'* Conflict

إرهاب *'irhāb* terrorism
إنسان *'insān* (no pl.) human being
ثورة *thawra* revolution
جريمة جرائم *jarīma jarā'im* crime
جندي جنود *jundī junūd* soldier
جيش جيوش *jaysh juyūsh* army
حرب حروب *ḥarb ḥurūb* (f.) war
حق حقوق *ḥaqq ḥuqūq* right (noun), truth
رهينة رهائن *rahīna rahā'in* hostage
سلاح أسلحة *silāḥ 'asliḥa* weapon
شكوة شكوات *shakwa shakawāt* complaint
قائد قوّاد *qā'id quwwād* leader
قوة *quwa* force, strength
مجرم *mujrim* criminal
مسلح *musallaḥ* armed
مكافحة *mukāfaḥa* (a/the) fight against

Exercise 1. Make a question:

e.g.: ذهب المتظاهرون إلى السفارة.

← هل ذهب المتظاهرون إلى السفارة ؟

hal dhahab al-mutaẓāhirūn 'ila s-sifāra?

1 الوضع اخطر منذ الحرب. 2 إجراءات اليوم أشدّ.

3 توجد مظاهرة في الشارع. 4 أخذوا الرهائن معهم.

5 رفضوا هذه النقطة. 6 شرحت الحكومة الإجراءات الجديدة.

7 المجرمون مسلّحون. 8 يوجد خلاف داخل الحزب.

Exercise 2. Make a question based on the underlined expression:

e.g.: *mata waṣalū?* وصلوا أمس . ← متى وصلوا ؟

1 كتب الشكوة باليد.
2 نشرنا نحن الشكوة على الجيش.
3 نشروا شكوةً شديدةً بخصوص الشرطة.
4 نشروها لمساعدة الزملاء.
5 حضر الطلاّب هذه المظاهرة.
6 ركب الإرهابيون السفينة بالقوة.
7 رفضت السلطات احتجاج المتظاهرين.
8 حضر كثير من الشرطيين.
9 حمل الجنود أسلحةً خفيفة.
10 بدأت ثورة الفلاّحين في السنة الماضية.
11 هذه جريمة على حقوق العمّال.
12 هذه هي تذاكر هذا السيد.

Exercise 3. Answer the question with the help of the expression given in parentheses:

e.g.: *shakwat al-fallāḥīn* شكوة من؟ (الفلاّحون) ← شكوة الفلاّحين

1 كم شخصاً سألوا ؟ (شخصان)
2 حضر كم شخصاً ؟ (شخصان)
3 كيف ركبوا القطار ؟ (القوة المسلحة)
4 من أجل حقوق من؟ (الإنسان)

5 أيّ نوع من الثورة؟ (السلم)
6 متى بدأت هذه الحرب؟ (شهران)
7 مظاهرة لأيّ غرض؟ (حقوق العمّال)
8 أين سكنتم في مصر؟ (القاهرة)
9 ماذا نشروا؟ (احتجاج على الإجراءات الجديدة)
10 هل ركبتم القطار؟ (ركبنا القطار)

Now give your own alternative answer to each question.

Exercise 4. Give an expression with the same meaning:

e.g.: *'ayy shakhṣ?* من؟ ← أيّ شخص؟

1 لماذا؟ 2 ماذا؟ 3 متى؟
4 أين؟ 5 كيف؟ 6 ممّن؟

Exercise 5. Collect in groups words having the same root:

e.g.: *hāmm, 'ahammīya* هامّ، أهمّيّة

سلاح، عملية، مسؤوليات، مسلّحون، متظاهر، حقيقة، دولية، كثير، عمّال، أسلحة، أكثرية، عملت، الأحرار، حقّ، دولة، حرّية، أموال، أسئلة، مظاهرة، مالي

Exercise 6. Read the passage and answer the questions:

في هذه الأيّام إحدى أهمّ مشاكل العالمية هي مكافحة الجريمة الدولية مثل الإرهاب. واليوم الإرهابيون والمجرمون الآخرون مسلّحون بالأسلحة الأحدث على مستوى الجيوش. عملت الدول المختلفة مع بعض على هذه المشكلة وحتّى اليوم نجحت عدد من هذه العمليات. النتيجة الإيجابية لجميع هذه العمليات الدولية ضرورية من أجل امن و حرّية وسلام كل إنسان في العالم.

1 كيف مسلّحون الإرهابيون؟
2 هل عملت الدول مع بعض من أجل حلّ المشكلة؟
3 هل نجحت هذه العمليات؟
4 ما هي أهمّية مكافحة الجريمة الدولية من أجل الإنسان؟

14 Recounting – 2

- Past tense, Form I: doubled, hollow, final-weak and doubly weak verbs
- Direct object suffixes attached to vocalic root letters

1. Past tense of doubled verbs

Doubled verbs are sound verbs (see Chapter 11) whose last two root letters are identical. An example in Form I is دلّ على *dalla 'ala* 'to show'. Verbs of the doubled class follow the sound pattern in Form I except that in the 3rd persons singular and plural the identical root letters fall together.

دلّ *dalla* 'to show', past tense:

دللت *dalaltu*, دللت *dalalta*, دللت *dalalti*, دلّ *dalla*, دلّت *dallat*;
دللنا *dalalna*, دللتم *dalaltum*, دلّوا *dallū* I showed/have shown (etc.)

2. Past tense of hollow verbs

Hollow verbs have a vowel و or ي as the middle root letter. The personal endings are identical to those of the sound verbs, but the middle root vowel is *unstable*, i.e. it changes in the different parts of the verb. For the past tense of Form I:

- in the 1st and 2nd persons middle و *-ū-* becomes *-u-* and middle ي *-ī-* becomes *-i*,
- in the 3rd persons this vowel becomes ا *-ā-*.

ساق *sāqa* 'to drive' (middle و), past tense:

سقت *suqtu*, سقت *suqta*, سقت *suqti*, ساق *sāqa*, ساقت *sāqat*;
سقنا *suqna*, سقتم *suqtum*, ساقوا *sāqū* I drove/have driven (etc.)

طار *ṭāra* 'to fly' (middle ي), past tense:

طرت *ṭirtu*, طرت *ṭirta*, طرت *ṭirti*, طار *ṭāra*, طارت *ṭārat*;
طرنا *ṭirna*, طرتم *ṭirtum*, طاروا *ṭārū* I flew/have flown (etc.)

A few middle و verbs have the middle ي pattern in the past tense:

نام *nāma* 'to sleep', middle و , past tense:

نمت *nimtu,* نمت *nimta,* نمت *nimti,* نام *nāma,* نامت *nāmat;*

نمنا *nimna,* نمتم *nimtum,* ناموا *nāmū* I (have) slept (etc.)

so also: خاف (من) *khāfa (min)* 'to fear': خفت *khiftu* ... خاف *khāfa*

3. Past tense of final-weak verbs

Final-weak verbs have a vowel as third or final root letter, mostly ي but also, less commonly, و . Up to and including the second root letter, the verb follows the sound pattern, but the final vowel is unstable.

For Form I past tense we can divide these verbs into *aw*, *ay* and *ī* verbs, depending on what follows the second (sound) root letter:

	aw verbs	*ay* verbs	*ī* verbs
final root letter	...و	...ي	...ي
1st princ. part	...ا *-a*	...ى *-a*	...ي *-iya*
1st/2nd persons	...و... *-aw-*	...يـ... *-ay-*	...يـ... *-ī-*
3rd person m. s.	...ا *-a*	...ى *-a*	...ي *-iya*
f. s.	...ت *-at*	...ت *-at*	...يت *-iyat*
pl.	...وا *-aw*	...وا *-aw*	...وا *-ū*

In the 1st and 2nd persons the usual personal ending follows the final root vowel shown. The 3rd-person endings are a combination of final root vowel and personal ending.

Typical *aw* verb; رجا *raja* to request, hope for, expect, past tense:

رجوت *rajawtu,* رجوت *rajawta,* رجوت *rajawti,* رجا *raja,*

رجت *rajat;* رجونا *rajawna,* رجوتم *rajawtum,* رجوا *rajaw*

so also: دعا *da'a* to summon عفا عن *'afa 'an* to forgive

Typical *ay* verb; رمى *rama* to throw, past tense:

رميت *ramaytu,* رميت *ramayta,* رميت *ramayti,* رمى *rama,*

رمت *ramat;* رمينا *ramayna,* رميتم *ramaytum,* رموا *ramaw*

so also: مشى *masha* to walk بكى *baka* to weep

جرى *jara* to flow, proceed (discussion etc.)

Typical *ī* **verb**; نسي *násiya* to forget, past tense:

نسيت *nasītu,* نسيت *nasīta,* نسيت *nasīti,* نسي *násiya,*

نسيت *násiyat;* نسينا *nasīna,* نسيتم *nasītum,* نسوا *nasū*

so also: بقي *báqiya* to remain لقي *láqiya* to meet (people or things)

4. Past tense of doubly weak verbs

Doubly weak verbs have two vocalic root letters, or one vocalic root letter and ء *hamza*. Verbs of this class are best learned in Form I verb by verb. In many of them, one of the weak root letters is stable in the past tense, making the verb behave like e.g. an initial-*wāw* verb, or a hollow verb, or a final-weak verb.

Commoner doubly weak verbs in the past tense are:

رأى *ra'a* 'to see': the *hamza* is stable; for the rest it is like a final-weak *ay* verb:

رأيت *ra'aytu* ..... رأى *ra'a,* رأت *ra'at;* ..... رأوا *ra'aw*

ولي *wáliya* 'to administer': the initial و is stable (as in e.g. وصل *waṣala,* Chapter 11); for the rest this is like a final-weak verb of the *ī* type:

وليت *walītu* … ولي *wáliya,* وليت *wáliyat;* … ولوا *walū*

جاء *jā'a* 'to come': the final *hamza* is stable; the middle is hollow (root vowel ي). The only difficulty is in writing the *hamza*:

جئت *ji'tu* ..... جاء *jā'a,* جاءت *jā'at;* ..... جاؤوا *jā'ū*

Note also جاء ب *jā'a bi-* 'to bring'.

نوى *nawa* 'to intend': in roots with …وي or …يي, the middle و or ي stabilises as *w* or *y* respectively, making the verb final-weak. The final ى of the principal part of نوى makes it an *ay* verb:

نويت *nawaytu* … نوى *nawa,* نوت *nawat;* … نووا *nawaw*

حيّ *ḥayya* 'to live (= be alive)': middle ي is stable (see above), final ي shows it to be an *ī* verb:

حييت *ḥayītu* ... حيّ *ḥayya*, حيّت *ḥayyat*; ... حيّوا *ḥayyū*

سوي *sáwiya* 'to equal': stable middle و , final ي makes it an *ī* verb:

سويت *sawītu* ... سوي *sáwiya*, سويت *sáwiyat*; ... سووا *sawū*

5. Direct object suffixes attached to vocalic root letters

See Chapter 12. Pronoun direct objects are suffixed as usual to verb forms which end in a vowel:

نسيهم *násiyahum* he forgot them

except that final ى... *-a* becomes ا... *-ā́-* when the suffix is added (since *'alif maqṣūra* can occur only at the end of a word):

نواه *nawā́hu* he intended it

6. Vocabulary: doubled and hollow verbs, Form I

(Vocalic root letters are shown in square brackets after the verb.)

باع [ي] *bā'a* to sell
تمّ *tamma* to come to an end
حلّ *ḥalla* to solve
زاد [ي] (عن) *zāda* to increase, *('an)* to exceed
زار [و] *zāra* to visit
شكّ في *shakka fī* to doubt
صار [ي] *ṣāra* to become
ضمّ (إلى) *ḍamma ('ila)* to join (to)
ظنّ *ẓanna* to suppose
عاش [ي] *'āsha* to live
غاب [ي](عن) *ghāba ('an)* to be absent (from)
قاد [و] *qāda* to lead
قال [و] *qāla* to say
قام [و] *qāma* to rise, get up

مات [و] *māta* to die
مدّ *madda* to extend
مرّ (ب\على) *marra (bi-/ʿala)* to pass (by, through)
همّ *hamma* to concern, to be important (to)

Exercise 1. Put the verb into the correct form of the past tense:

e.g.: *qult* قلت ← (قال، أنا)

1 (رأى، نحن)	2 (صار، هي)	3 (زار، أنا)
4 (دلّ، نحن)	5 (نوى، هم)	6 (نسي، هم)
7 (نام، أنتم)	8 (مشى، نحن)	9 (دعا، هو)
10 (خاف، نحن)	11 (رمى، هم)	12 (بقي، هي)

Exercise 2. Make plural everything possible:

e.g.: *qādū wufūdan* .قادوا وفوداً ← .قاد وفداً

1 قاد المدير الوفد. 2 ماذا قال لك؟
3 قد تمّ المشروع الحكومي. 4 ساق السائح سيّارةً جديدةً.
5 مشيت (أنا) في المدينة القديمة. 6 شكّ في هذا التفصيل.
7 كيف جرى البحث بين الوفدين؟ 8 دعاني إلى المؤتمر المالي.
9 لقد حل الخبير المشكلة الفنّية. 10 هل باع السيارتين القديمتين؟

Exercise 3. Put the verb into the correct form of the past tense:

e.g.: *ṭirt ʾila miṣr.* .طرت إلى مصر ← (طار، أنا) إلى مصر

1 قد (تمّ) مشاريع الحكومة.
2 (دلّ، نحن) على طريق المطار.
3 (زاد) المشاكل الاقتصادية بعد الحرب.
4 من (دعا، هم) إلى الاجتماع؟
5 (رأى، نحن) الفرق بين الفكرتين.
6 (نسي، هم) أهمّ نقطة في البحث.
7 (قال، هم) لي تاريخ وموضوع المؤتمر الوزاري.
8 (بقي) الخبراء في المختبر و(حل) المشكلة.

9 لقد (باع، نحن) الشركة بسبب هذه النقطة الهامّة.
10 (طار) الخبراء إلى دمشق و (زار) الزملاء هناك.

Exercise 4. Select the only correct verb form for the subject:

e.g.: (شكّوا\شككنا\ظننّا، نحن) في الأرقام.
← شككنا في الأرقام. *shakakna fi l-'arqām.*

1 (نسيت\بقينا\نسوا\نسينا، نحن) العنوان.
2 (قاموا\قام\قامت) الطلاّب بعد درس الأستاذ.
3 (جروا\جرت\جرى) البحوث حول السياسة التجارية.
4 قد (بدأ\تمّ\تمّت) السنة الدراسية أمس.
5 قد (مررت\مددت\مرّ\مدّ) الزوّار بشوارع قديمة.

Exercise 5. Give the (a) أنا, (b) هي and (c) هم form in the past:

e.g.: *qult, qālat, qālū* قال ← قلت، قالت، قالوا

1 باع	2 مشى	3 مدّ
4 نام	5 عاش	6 جاء
7 دعا	8 زاد	9 صار
10 خاف	11 نوى	12 حي

Exercise 6. Replace the noun direct object with a pronoun:

e.g.: رمى النقود على الطاولة. ← رماها على الطاولة.
ramāha 'ala ṭ-ṭāwla.

1 رأوا الأصدقاء في الأوتيل.
2 نسوا التفاصيل.
3 دعوا الطلاّب إلى الصفّ.
4 نوى نفس الشيء.
5 قالوا لي الثمن.
6 قالوا لي الأثمان.
7 قاد الوزير الوفد.
8 باع لي الكتب.
9 ساق السيّارة من بيروت إلى دمشق.
10 زرت (أنا) ممثّل الشركة.

Exercise 7. Complete the sentence with a verb from this chapter:

e.g.: ... المدير نفس النقطة. ← نسي المدير نفس النقطة.

nasi l-mudīr nafs an-nuqṭa.

1 ... السيّاح عدد من المدن القديمة في العراق.
2 بعد هذا ... (نحن) على الجمرك.
3 كيف ... الخبير المشاكل الرئيسية الفنّية؟
4 ... (انا) في الأوتيل يومين.
5 ... صادرات البلاد خلال السنوات الماضية.
6 ... عدّة مشاريع هامّة هذه السنة.
7 ... البحوث بين الحكومتين وقتًا طويلاً.
8 ... (هم) النوّاب إلى المؤتمر.
9 ... الموظّفون في أهمّية هذا التفصيل.
10 ... (نحن) البضائع في الخارج.

Exercise 8. Rewrite each expression with the right preposition where necessary:

e.g.: مررت، جمرك ← مررت على الجمرك\بالجمرك.

marart 'ala l-jumruk/bi-l-jumruk.

زرنا ، المدينة ← زرنا المدينة. *zurna l-madina.*

1 خرجوا ، المطار، سيارة
2 قاد ، وفداً رسمياً
3 شككنا ، أهمية الأرقام
4 هل قال، نفس الشيء؟
5 بعنا ، ماكينات زراعية، خارج
6 جاء الأستاذ ، الكتب الجديدة
7 أخذ الأستاذ ، الكتب الجديدة
8 عاشوا ، سنوات كثيرة
9 لماذا خاف الولد الصغير، القطار؟
10 نام الأطفال، وقتًا طويلاً

Exercise 9. Replace the verb with one taken from this chapter:

e.g.: وصلوا إلى دمشق أمس. ← جاؤوا إلى دمشق أمس.

jā'ū 'ila dimashq 'ams.

1 حضرنا الاجتماع.
2 شرح المشكلة.

3 ذكروا نقطة هامّة. 4 حمل شيءاً ثقيلاً.
5 سمعنا الحقيقة حول الموضوع. 6 ماذا طلبوا؟
7 ذهبت إلى المكتب. 8 فهمناه.

Exercise 10. Read this passage aloud, then answer the questions:

قبل وقت قصير حضر ممثلو الشركة مؤتمراً حول مشكلة صادرات البلاد الزراعية. دعتنا إلى هذا المؤتمر وزارة التجارة. في المؤتمر لقينا ممثلي شركات أخرى. قاد الوفد الحكومي وزير التجارة. قد زادت أثمان البضائع، وفي نفس الوقت قد مرّ قطاع التجارة الخارجية بمشاكل كبيرة هذه السنة. خلال هذا البحوث شرح المندوبون أفكاراً مختلفةً بخصوص الخطوات الممكنة لحل هذه المشاكل.

1 متى حضروا المؤتمر؟
2 من دعاهم إليه؟ لماذا؟
3 أي أشخاص لقي فيه مندوبو الشركة؟
4 هل مرّ القطاع بسنة طيّبة؟
5 ماذا زادت خلال السنة؟
6 وماذا شرح المندوبون؟
7 جرت البحوث في أي موضوع؟

Underline each verb in the passage, and say to which class it belongs. If it is hollow, what is its middle root letter? If it has a weak final root letter, is it an ***aw***, ***ay*** or *ī* verb in the past tense?

15 Possessing

- Possessive adjectives

1. Possessive adjectives

The possessive adjectives ('my', 'your', 'her') (also called possessive pronouns, though they never occur without a noun) are expressed in Arabic with suffixes added to the noun possessed. The suffixes are identical to the pronoun suffixes attached to prepositions, for which see Chapter 6.

The term 'possessive' is used for convenience in this context; the relationship is not necessarily one of ownership.

The noun ending ة‎... -a becomes ت‎... -at before any suffix.

The suffix ي‎... -ī is added directly to singular, broken plural and sound f. pl. nouns:

راتبي‎ rātibī my salary

مع زملائي‎ ma' zumalā'ī my colleagues

علاقتي‎ 'alāqatī my relationship

مسؤولياتي‎ mas'ūlīyātī my responsibilities

The dual and sound m. pl. endings change before the suffix ي‎... :

dual ان‎... + ي‎... → اي‎... -āya, ين‎... + ي‎... → يَّ‎... -ayya

sound m. pl. ون‎\ين‎... both → يَّ‎... -īya:

صديقاي\مع صديقيَّ‎ ṣadīqāya/ma' ṣadīqayya

(with) my two friends

(مع) معلميَّ‎ (ma') mu'allimīya (with) my teachers

and note (weak noun, Chapter 10):

محاميَّ‎ muḥāmīya 'my lawyer' and 'my lawyers'.

Before any of the other suffixes, the ending of the noun is modified:

- the dual and sound m. pl. lose their final ن‎... :

زميلاكم‎ zamīlākum your two colleagues

لزميليكم *li-zamīlaykum* for your two colleagues
مهنديونا *muhandisūna* our engineers
لمهندسينا *li-muhandisīna* for our engineers

- for other nouns we have to restore the noun's definite case-ending which has been suppressed in short pronunciation. For singular and broken-plural nouns these endings are:

  -u for the *nominative* or subject case (الرفع *ar-raf'*)
  -a for the accusative (النصب *an-naṣb*, studied in Chapter 12)
  -i for the genitive (الجرّ *al-jarr*, Chapter 6):

  حسابه هنا. *ḥisābuhu huna* His account is here.
  قد زرنا منطقتهم. *qad zurna minṭaqatahum.* We have visited their region.
  من أجل استقلالنا *min 'ajl istiqlālina* for our independence

  and note the spelling for a noun ending in ...اء *-ā'* when a suffix is added:

  سفراؤنا ، سفراءنا ،سفرائنا *sufarā'**u**na, sufarā'**a**na, sufarā'**i**na*

  For sound f. pl. nouns (pl. ending *-āt*), the restored vowels are *-u* for the nominative and *-i* for both the accusative and genitive; [*-a*] does not occur:

  علاقاتنا مع الأمم المتّحدة *'alāqāt**u**na ma' al-'umam al-muttáḥida* our relations with the United Nations
  شرحت لهم علاقاتنا مع روسيا. *sharaḥt lahum 'alāqātina ma' rúsiya.* I explained to them our relations with Russia.
  أهمّية علاقاتنا *'ahammīyat 'alāqātina* the importance of our relations
  على رأس وفدنا *'ala ra's wafdina* at the head of our delegation

- When the noun, with its restored ending, for any reason ends in *-i*, *-ī*, or *-ay*, then any attached possessive ...ه or ...هم is pronounced *-hi*, *-him* respectively:

مع وكيليه *ma' wakīlayhi* with his two agents

هذا مسؤولية مهندسيهم. *hādha mas'ūlīyat muhandisīhim.* This is their engineers' responsibility.

أهمّية مفاوضاته مع الإسرائيليين *'ahammīyat mufāwaḍātihi ma' al-'isrā'īlīyīn* the importance of its negotiations with the Israelis

(See the same phenomenon in Chapter 6, with prepositions.)

2. Possessive expressions with a qualifying adjective, or in construct state

A noun with a possessive suffix is definite, so any qualifying adjective has the article:

لطرفي اتّفاقيتنا التجارية *li-ṭarafay ttifāqīyatina t-tijārīya* for both parties to ('of') our trade agreement

الاتّحاد الأروبّي وحدوده الشرقية *al-ittiḥād al-'urubbī wa-ḥudūduhu sh-sharqīya* the European Union and its eastern borders

Being explicitly definite, a possessive expression can be the attribute (but not the theme) of a definite construct (Chapter 7); see examples above.

3. Distributive expressions

See Chapter 9. All the *definite* constructs studied there can be replaced with possessive expressions. Examine:

دفع كلّه. *dafa' kullahu.* He paid all of it.

قالته نفسها. *qālat-hu nafsuha.* She said it herself.

and note: في العقود كلّها *fī l-'uqūd kulliha* in all the treaties ('in the treaties, all of them')

للأصدقاء بعضهم *li-l-'aṣdiqā' ba'ḍihim* for some of the friends ('for the friends, some of them')

This last structure is very common.

4. Vocabulary: العلاقات الدولية *al-ʿalāqāt ad-duwalīya*

International relations

الاتّحاد الأوربّي *al-ittiḥād al-'urubbī* European Union
اتّفاقية *ittifāqīya* (written) agreement
أزمة أزمات *'azma 'azamāt* crisis
استقلال *istiqlāl* independence
إسرائيل *'isrā'īl* Israel
الأمم المتّحدة *al-'umam al-muttáḥida* United Nations
أمن\أمان *'amn, 'amān* security
بحث *baḥatha* to discuss
البنك الدولي *al-bank ad-duwalī* World Bank
جماعة *jamāʿa* group (of people)
جنوب *janūb* south
حدّ حدود *ḥadd ḥudūd* border
حركة *ḥaraka* movement
حفظ *ḥifẓ* preservation
حيادي *ḥiyādī* neutral
دبلوماسي *diblumāsī* diplomat(ic)
دولة دول *dawla duwal* state (country)
دولة كبرى *dawla kubra* superpower
دولة نامية *dawla nấmiya* developing country
سفارة *sifāra* embassy
سفير سفراء *safīr sufarā'* ambassador
شرق *sharq* east
الشرق الأوسط *ash-sharq al-'awsaṭ* Middle East
شمال *shimāl* north
طرف أطراف *ṭaraf 'aṭrāf* party (to a contract etc.)
عقد عقود *ʿaqd ʿuqūd* (also:) treaty

العالم الثالث *al-'ālam ath-thālith* third world
غرب *gharb* west
فلسطين *falasṭīn* (f.) Palestine
قضية قضايا *qaḍīya qaḍāya* cause, case
مجموعة *majmū'a* group (of things)
مستقلّ *mustaqill* independent
مصلحة مصالح *maṣlaḥa maṣāliḥ* interest
مفاوضة *mufāwaḍa* negotiation

Exercise 1. Add the possessive to the noun (which is nominative unless clearly otherwise):

e.g.: *'amnuna* أمننا ← أمن (نا)

1 اتّفاقية (هم)
2 استقلال (هي)
3 من مكتب (هو)
4 سفراء (نحن)
5 بحثوا علاقات (هم) الدبلوماسية.
6 مع مشرفين (هم)
7 جميع زملاء (أنتم)
8 ضدّ مصالح (نحن)
9 ضدّ مصالح (أنا)
10 حجزنا تذاكر (أنتم).
11 لأمن حدود (هي)
12 بدأوا مفاوضات (هم) أمس.

Exercise 2. In your answers to Ex. 1, add or substitute an adjective of your choice:

e.g.: *'amnuna l-kāmil* أمننا الكاملي ← أمننا

Exercise 3. Make the underlined noun expression plural. Do not change its possessive suffix:

e.g.: يهمّ هذا السؤال سفيرنا الجديد.
← يهمّ هذا السؤال سفراءنا الجدد.
yahumm hādha s-su'āl sufarā'ana l-judud.

1 بحثوا اتّفاقيتهم المالية مع البنك الدولي.
2 في بحث مع ممثّلهم
3 بدأ مفاوضته أمس.

4 نتيجة إجرائهم الإداري 5 مع مساعدة معلّمي

6 ذكر جولته في الشرق الأوسط.

Exercise 4. Convert the construct into a possessive expression:

e.g.: *khilāl mufāwaḍatihi* خلال مفاوضته ← خلال مفاوضة العقد

1 استقلال دولة نامية 2 قوة الدولة الكبرى الوحيدة

3 لحرّية العالم الثالث 4 مسؤوليات سفارة

5 أهمّية وظيفة سفير 6 لحلّ مشاكلنا الدبلوماسية

7 بحث بين طرفي الاتّفاقية 8 حقوق الدول الصغرى

Exercise 5. Read the passage and answer the questions:

تحت عنوان(1) "علاقات دولية" نفهم أمور مختلفة مثل مفاوضة عقودنا وتطوّر تجارتنا مع بلدان أخرى وحفظ استقلالنا ومصالحنا العامّة. لأيّة دولة حديثة أحسن طريقة لتسوية خلافاتها الدولية هي الوسائل السلمية كالبحث والمفاوضة ولا(2) بواسطة أسلحتها أو قوتها الاقتصادية.

(1) عنوان *'unwān* (here:) heading (2) ولا *wa-lā* and not

1 ماذا نفهم تحت عنوان "علاقات دولية"؟

2 لماذا تهمنا التجارة الخارجية؟

3 ما هو أحسن أسلوب لحل مشاكلنا الدولية؟

4 ما هي مصالح أكثرية الدول في حقل علاقاتها مع الخارج؟

16 Revision – 1

- Nouns, pronouns and adjectives (NB: examples are in the nominative case unless otherwise indicated or necessitated.)

Exercise 1. Give the plural of the expression :

e.g.: *li-l-khubarā' al-'ajānib* للخبراء الأجانب ← للخبير الأجنبي

1	خلال تجربة فنية	2	مكتبهم الرئيسي	3	أهمّ موظّفه
4	سؤال واضح	5	فلاّح الريف	6	تأخير طويل
7	لأطول برنامج	8	لراكب هندي	9	أيّ معلّم؟
10	حلّ مشكلة معقّدة	11	مشرف نوبة	12	كتاب غال

Exercise 2. Give the dual of the expression:

e.g.: لشخصين مشهورين ← لشخص مشهور

li-shakhṣayn mashhūrayn

1	المدير المصري	2	المدراء الهنود
3	هذه المستشفيات	4	مشكلة فنّية
5	في بلد صغير	6	لمشروع هامّ
7	الأسئلة الصعبة	8	أهمّ شيء

Exercise 3. Give the singular of the expression:

e.g.: *khabīr fannī* خبير فنّي ← خبراء فنّيون

1	الأرقام الطويلة	2	تحت أوامر رسمية
3	أساتذة مشهورون	4	في وظائفهم
5	في التقارير كلّها	6	عند ناس لطفاء
7	فرص ممتازة	8	مع أستاذين

Exercise 4. Make the adjective agree:

e.g.: *al-baḍā'i' at-tijārīya* البضائع التجارية ← البضائع، تجاري

1	الأوتيل، غال	2	أوتيل، غال

3 ناس، طيّب	4 لناس، طيّب
5 دمشق، قديم	6 طلباتهم، رئيسي
7 مدن، جميل	8 طبيبة، هندي
9 المعلّمات، سوري	10 للمندوبين، إنجليزي
11 أصدقاؤه، عربي	12 الفكرة، أوّل

Exercise 5. Add (a) هذا and (b) ذلك in the right form:

e.g.: في رسالة رسمية ← في هذه\تلك الرسالة الرسمية

fī hādhihi/tilka r-risāla r-rasmīya

1 خطوات إدارية ضرورية	2 مع مهندس خبير
3 ذكر مبدئين أساسين	4 أفكار ممتازة
5 خطّ جوي	6 زملاء أجانب
7 زميلات أجنبيات	8 شحن كبير
9 مشرفون مسؤولون	10 بنتان صغيرتان

Exercise 6. Make an equation from the two elements:

e.g.: *an-nawba ṭawīla* النوبة، طويل ← النوبة طويلة

الإنتاج، أهمّ شيء ← الإنتاة هو أهمّ شيء.

al-'intāj huwa 'ahamm shay'.

1 الحقيقة، بسيط	2 هذا، التقرير المالي
3 هذا، تقريرنا المالي	4 في اقتصاد اليوم، مشكلتان
5 جواب على سؤالنا، أوّل خطوة	6 هذا، النيل الأزرق

7 جواب على سؤالنا، خطوة إيجابية

8 الطريقة الوحيدة، موافقة الطرفين

9 المكتبة، أقدم من البنايات الأخرى

10 المكتبة، أقدم بناية الجامعة كلّها

Exercise 7. Make the preposition govern the noun or pronoun:

e.g.: *ma' al-muhandisīn* مع (المهندسون) ← مع المهندسين

1 إلى (أصدقاؤه)	2 من أجل (زملاؤنا)

3 في (مكتبي الرئيسي)
4 خلال (سنتان طويلتان)
5 ل (مندوبو الشركة)
6 ضدّ (مصالح الموظّفين)
7 على (أنا)
8 ل (ها)
9 إلى (هم)
10 في (هو)
11 من أجل (نحن)
12 على (أنتم)
13 بخصوص (أنا)
14 من (أنا)

Exercise 8. Re-express the noun with the corresponding pronoun:

e.g.: *ma'ahum* معهم ← مع المهندسين

1 على هذا الأساس
2 لابني
3 بخصوص الأصدقاء
4 بسبب مشاكلنا
5 عل رغم تقريره
6 بالعقد التجاري

Exercise 9. Add an attribute of your choice to make a construct:

e.g.: *thaman al-baḍā'i'* ثمن البضائع ← الثمن

1 المدينة
2 للمندوبين
3 محام
4 هذه المشكلة
5 مسؤوليات
6 وظائف ... و...
7 الوزارة
8 حقوق
9 قبل الوصول
10 تحت قانون
11 راتب
12 في الجداول

Exercise 10. Make the adjective qualify the noun which is underlined:

e.g.: تذكرة المسافر (رخيص) ← تذكرة المسافر الرخيصة

tadhkarat al-musāfir ar-rakhīṣa

تذكرة المسافر (هذا) ← تذكرة هذا المسافر

tadhkarat hādha l-musāfir

1 حلّ مشاكل (دولي)
2 برنامجا الحزبين (هذا)
3 مأمورو المحكمة (محلّي)
4 مدير مدرسة (هذا)
5 دفع حساب (متأخّر)
6 دفع حساب (متأخّر)

Exercise 11. Add to the noun the possessive suffix appropriate to (a) أنا , (b) هو , (c) هي , (d) أنتم and (e) هم :

e.g.: وظيفة ← وظيفتي، وظيفته، وظيفتْها ، وظيفتكم، وظيفتهم

waẓīfatī, waẓīfatuhu, waẓīfatuha, waẓīfatukum waẓīfatuhum

1 جدول
2 معلّمون
3 أصدقاء
4 مساعدة
5 جميع المعلّمين
6 أخذ الكتب
7 دفع الحسابات
8 محامون
9 الحسابات هنا
10 تلميذ جديد
11 الزملاء
12 للزميلة

Exercise 12. Replace the attribute with a possessive suffix:

e.g.: *rawātibuhum* رواتب الموظّفين ← رواتبهم

1 حول رواتب الموظّفين
2 في كلّ الجداول
3 حقوق الإنسان أساسية.
4 حمل البوّاب شنطة الضيف
5 ذكر أسماء زملائه.
6 على طلب المشرف
7 أخذوا سيّارات الوفد.
8 أخذوا سيّارات الوزارة.
9 وصل بعض الضيوف.
10 مع جميع الأعضاء
11 رفضت الحكومة تقرير اللجنة الوزارية.
12 ضدّ سياسة حزبنا

Exercise 13. Replace the possessive suffix with an appropriate attribute:

e.g.: *mushrif an-nawba* مشرفها ← مشرف النوبة

1 سياسته الاقتصادية
2 لمكافحته
3 شرحنا برنامجه
4 مسؤولياتها
5 بعضهم
6 بعضها
7 أهمّها
8 وظائفهم
9 وصل أكثريتهم
10 في أقصرها
11 شرح مبدأه
12 فكرته الأساسية

Exercise 14. Make a meaningful expression with the preposition لـ:

e.g.: رئيس، لجنة وطنية، تنمية، الريف

← رئيس (الـ)لجنة (الـ)وطنية لتنمية الريف

ra'īs (al-)lajna (l-)waṭanīya li-tánmiyat ar-rīf

1 مشكلة صعبة، مكافحة، إرهاب دولي

2 تعويض، تكليف، رحلة جويّة

3 تفاصيل، برنامج سنوي، تنمية، التجارة

4 عضو جديد، لجنة، تنظيم، حزب

5 أهمّية كبيرة، حلّ، مشاكل حالية

6 إدارة، مصالح عامّة، طلاّب

Exercise 15. Add an appropriate colour to the noun:

e.g.: *warāq 'abyaḍ* ورق أبيض → ورق

1 النيل
2 زهرة
3 نهر
4 الحصان
5 بيوت
6 ماكينة
7 ناس
8 التفّاح
9 الأشجار
10 بيضتان

Exercise 16. Give the opposite of the underlined expression:

e.g.: *'ibāra 'aqṣar* عبارة أقصر → عبارة أطول

1 هذا البيت أكبر من ذلك.
2 المكتب وراء الأوتيل
3 أطول نهر البلاد
4 دخلوا المصرف.
5 قبل سنتين
6 كتب رسالةً.
7 خرج أقلّية* الناس.
8 فوق الأرض
9 سكنوا خارج القرية.
10 عملوا في مصلحة الشركة كلّها.

* *'aqallīya*: you can work this word out from Chapter 8, paragraph 2.

Exercise 17. Make a question based on the underlined expression:

e.g.: *hal 'araft hādha?* هل عرفت هذا ؟ → عرفت هذا .

1 طلبوه أنفسهم.
2 وصلوا اليوم.
3 كتبوا له رسالةً.
4 دفع هذا الثمن.
5 عمله في مصلحتهم.
6 درس في دمشق.

Exercise 18. Replace the noun direct object with the appropriate pronoun:

e.g.: *qara'nāha.* قرأناها. ← قرأنا الرسالة.

1 أخذوا القطار إلى القاهرة.
2 تركنا الأوتيل اليوم.
3 وجد الكتب العربية في المكتبة نفسها.
4 هل فهمت (أنت) أسئلة الولد؟
5 سألت البنت أمّها.
6 ركبنا التاكسي وذهبنا إلى دمشق.
7 ذكر السفير مشكلة تنمية الاقتصاد.
8 قد بدأوا الاجتماع بدون المدير.
9 لماذا حضرت أنت اجتماع لجنة الخبراء؟
10 شكرت (أنا) السفراء الحاضرين.

Exercise 19. Make definite with the article:

e.g.: *al-waqt al-fāḍī* الوقت الفاضي ← وقت فاض

1 قاض ومحام
2 أراض زراعية
3 شهر ماض
4 أسلوب جار
5 مستوىً واطئ
6 في قرىً بعيدة

Exercise 20. Make the expression (a) comparative, (b) superlative without the article:

e.g.: وقت أطول، أطول وقت ← وقت طويل

waqt 'aṭwal, 'aṭwal waqt

1 مبدأ هامّ
2 عضو غني
3 كتب غالية
4 فكرة طيّبة
5 آبار عميقة
6 قوة قليلة

17 Recounting – 3

- Present tense, verb Form I

1. Present tense of verbs, Form I – general

The Arabic present tense (المضارع *al-muḍāri'*) is used for current or imminent actions and situations: 'I go, I am going' (now or very soon).

The present tense is derived from the *second principal part*, which in the dictionary is shown either in full or by its characteristic vowel *a, u* or *i*, thus: كتب *kataba yaktubu* or كتب *kataba u*. This book uses the fuller notation كتب يكتب *kataba yaktubu*.

The second principal part itself is the 3rd person m. sing. of the present. For the other persons, drop the *ya-* prefix and the *-u* ending before adding the personal prefix and ending shown in the table. Thus, for كتب يكتب *kataba yaktubu* 'to write', we have:

Person	Singular	Plural
1 m./f.	أكتب *'aktubu* I write	نكتب *naktubu* we write
2 m. 2 f.	تكتب *taktubu* you (m.) write تكتبين *taktubīna* you (f.) write	تكتبون *taktubūna* you write
3 m. 3 f.	يكتب *yaktubu* he writes تكتب *taktubu* she writes	يكتبون *yaktubūna* they write

(or: I am writing etc.)

Note:

- For the use of the three persons see Chapters 5 and 11, and for the other persons (dual, f. pl.) see the Appendix.
- The final vowel *-u* shown in small type is normally silent when the verb has no object suffix (Chapter 12). You will note that this happens to the final *-u* of the هو form itself.

2. Sound and hamzated verbs

The pattern shown above is valid for sound verbs (= three unchanging consonants) and hamzated verbs. Some examples, present tense:

Sound: عمل يعمل *'amila ya'malu* to do, to work, to make:
أعمل *'amalu,* تعمل *ta'malu,* تعملين *ta'malīna,* يعمل *ya'malu,*
تعمل *ta'malu;* نعمل *na'malu,* تعملون *ta'malūna,* يعملون *ya'malūna*
عرف يعرف *'arafa ya'rifu* to know, to recognise:
أعرف *'arifu,* تعرف *ta'rifu,* تعرفين *ta'rifīna,* يعرف *ya'rifu,*
تعرف *ta'rifu;* نعرف *na'rifu,* تعرفون *ta'rifūna,* يعرفون *ya'rifūna*

Initial *hamza*: أمر يأمر (بـ) *'amara ya'muru (bi-)* to order:
*آمر *'āmuru,* تأمر *ta'muru,* تأمرين *ta'murīna,* يأمر *ya'muru,*
تأمر *ta'muru;* نأمر *na'muru,* تأمرون *ta'murūna,* يأمرون *ya'murūna*
* [أ + أ *'a + 'a*] becomes آ *'ā.*

Middle *hamza*: سأل يسأل *sa'ala yas'alu* to ask, to enquire:
أسأل *'as'alu,* تسأل *tas'alu,* تسألين *tas'alīna,* يسأل *yas'alu,*
تسأل *tas'alu;* نسأل *nas'alu,* تسألون *tas'alūna,* يسألون *yas'alūna*

Final *hamza*: قرأ يقرأ *qara'a yaqra'u* to read:
أقرأ *'aqra'u,* تقرأ *taqra'u,* تقرإين *taqra'īna,* يقرأ *yaqra'u,*
تقرأ *taqra'u;* نقرأ *naqra'u,* تقرأون *taqra'ūna,* يقرأون *yaqra'ūna*

(These are the easiest spellings; you will also encounter تقرئين *taqra'īna,* تقرؤون *taqra'ūna* and يقرؤون *yaqra'ūna.*)

Principal parts of the other sound and hamzated verbs met so far:

Present-tense vowel *a*:		بدأ يبدأ	*bada'a yabda'u*
بحث يبحث	*baḥatha yabḥathu*	بعث يبعث	*ba'atha yab'athu*
دفع يدفع	*dafa'a yadfa'u*	ذهب يذهب	*dhahaba yadhhabu*
ركب يركب	*rakiba yarkabu*	سمع يسمع	*sami'a yasma'u*
شرب يشرب	*shariba yashrabu*	شرح يشرح	*sharaḥa yashraḥu*
فتح يفتح	*fataḥa yaftaḥu*	فشل يفشل	*fashila yafshalu*
فهم يفهم	*fahima yafhamu*	نجح ينجح	*najaḥa yanjaḥu*

Present-tense vowel *u*:

أكل يأكل	*'akala ya'kulu*	ترك يترك	*taraka yatruku*
حجز يحجز	*ḥajaza yaḥjuzu*	حضر يحضر	*ḥaḍara yaḥḍuru*
خرج يخرج	*kharaja yakhruju*	دخل يدخل	*dakhala yadkhulu*
درس يدرس	*darasa yadrusu*	ذكر يذكر	*dhakara yadhkuru*
سكن يسكن	*sakana yaskunu*	شكر يشكر	*shakara yashkuru*
ضرب يضرب	*ḍaraba yaḍrubu*	طلب يطلب	*ṭalaba yaṭlubu*
نشر ينشر	*nashara yanshuru*		

Present-tense vowel *i*:

		جلس يجلس	*jalasa yajlisu*
حمل يحمل	*ḥamala yaḥmilu*	رجع يرجع	*raja'a yarji'u*
رفض يرفض	*rafaḍa yarfiḍu*	نزل ينزل	*nazala yanzilu*

3. Initial-*wāw* verbs

Initial-*wāw* verbs lose their first root letter و in the present tense.

وقف يقف *waqafa yaqifu* to (come to a) stop:

أقف *'aqifu*, تقف *taqifu*, تقفين *taqifīna*, يقف *yaqifu*, تقف *taqifu*;
نقف *naqifu*, تقفون *taqifūna*, يقفون *yaqifūna*

Principal parts of the other initial-*wāw* verbs studied so far:

Present-tense vowel *a*: وضع يضع *waḍa'a yaḍa'u*

Present-tense vowel *i*:

وجد يجد *wajada yajidu* وصل يصل *waṣala yaṣilu*

4. Doubled verbs

In doubled verbs it is the identical middle and final root letters which fall together in the present.

دلّ يدلّ *dalla yadullu* to show:

أدلّ *'adullu*, تدلّ *tadullu*, تدلّين *tadullīna*, يدلّ *yadullu*, تدلّ *tadullu*;
ندلّ *nadullu*, تدلّون *tadullūna*, يدلّون *yadullūna*

Principal parts of the other doubled verbs studied so far:

Present-tense vowel *u*: حلّ يحلّ *ḥalla yaḥullu*

شكّ يشكّ	*shakka yashukku*	ضمّ يضمّ	*ḍamma yaḍummu*
ظنّ يظنّ	*ẓanna yaẓunnu*	مدّ يمدّ	*madda yamuddu*
مرّ يمرّ	*marra yamurru*	همّ يهمّ	*hamma yahummu*
Present-tense vowel *i*:		تمّ يتمّ	*tamma yatimmu*

5. Hollow verbs

The middle root letter و or ي assumes its own form in the present;
middle و ; قام يقوم ب *qāma yaqūmu bi-* to undertake:
أقوم *'aqūmu,* تقوم *taqūmu,* تقومين *taqūmīna,* يقوم *yaqūmu,*
تقوم *taqūmu;* نقوم *naqūmu,* تقومون *taqūmūna,* يقومون *yaqūmūna*
middle ي ; صار يصير *ṣāra yaṣīru* to become:
أصير *'aṣīru,* تصير *taṣīru,* تصيرين *taṣīrīna,* يصير *yaṣīru,*
تصير *taṣīru;* نصير *naṣīru,* تصيرون *taṣīrūna,* يصيرون *yaṣīrūna*
– except that verbs of the small نام *nāma* group (see Chapter 14), have ...ا... *-ā-* in the present:
نام ينام *nāma yanāmu* to sleep:
أنام *'anāmu,* تنام *tanāmu,* تنامين *tanāmīna,* ينام *yanāmu,*
تنام *tanāmu;* ننام *nanāmu,* تنامون *tanāmūna,* ينامون *yanāmūna*
so also: خاف يخاف (من) *khāfa yakhāfu (min)* to fear

6. Final-weak verbs

See Chapter 14. The ***aw***, ***ay*** and ***ī*** groups go as follows in the present.
***aw* past → *ū* (*īna/ūna*) pres.**; عفا يعفو عن *'afa ya'fū 'an* to forgive:
أعفو *'a'fū,* تعفو *ta'fū,* تعفين *ta'fīna,* يعفو *ya'fū,* تعفو *ta'fū;*
نعفو *na'fū,* تعفون *ta'fūna,* يعفون *ya'fūna*
so also: دعا يدعو *da'a yad'ū* رجا يرجو *raja yarjū*
***ay* past → *ī* (*īna/ūna*) present**; نفى ينفي *nafa yanfī* to deny:
أنفي *'anfī* تنفي *tanfī,* تنفين *tanfīna,* ينفي *yanfī,* تنفي *tanfī;*
ننفي *nanfī,* تنفون *tanfūna,* ينفون *yanfūna*
so also: رمى يرمي *rama yarmī* مشى يمشي *masha yamshī*

بكى يبكي *baka yabkī* جرى يجري *jara yajrī*

ī past → a (ayna/awna) present; لقي يلقى *láqiya yalqa* to meet:

ألقى *'alqa* تلقى *talqa,* تلقين *talqayna,* يلقى *yalqa,* تلقى *talqa;*

نلقى *nalqa,* تلقون *talqawna,* يلقون *yalqawna*

so also: بقي يبقى *báqiya yabqa* نسي ينسى *násiya yansa*

7. Doubly weak verbs

The comment made in Chapter 14, paragraph 4 applies also here, if we allow that initial *w* is dropped in the present (see ولي *waliya* below):

جاء يجيء *jā'a yajī'u* to come:

أجيء *'ajī'u,* تجيء *tajī'u,* تجيئين *tajī'īna,* يجيء *yajī'u,* تجيء *tajī'u;*

نجيء *najī'u,* تجيؤون\تجيئون *tajī'ūna,* يجيؤون\يجيئون *yajī'ūna*

نوى ينوي *nawa yanwī* to intend:

أنوي *'anwī,* تنوي *tanwī,* تنوين *tanwīna,* ينوي *yanwī,* تنوي *tanwī;*

ننوي *nanwī,* تنوون *tanwūna,* ينوون *yanwūna*

*حيّ يحيا *ḥayya yaḥya* to live:

أحيا *'aḥya,* تحيا *taḥya,* تحيين *taḥyayna,* يحيا *yaḥya,* تحيا *taḥya;*

نحيا *naḥya,* تحيون *taḥyawna,* يحيون *yaḥyawna*

(* ى must be rewritten as ا after ي .)

سوي يسوى *sáwiya yaswa* to equal:

أسوى *'aswa,* تسوى *taswa,* تسوين *taswayna,* يسوى *yaswa,*

تسوى *taswa;* نسوى *naswa,* تسوون *taswawna,* يسوون *yaswawna*

Two important doubly weak verbs which are irregular in the present:

رأى يرى *ra'a yara* to see; the middle *hamza* is dropped in the present:

أرى *'ara,* ترى *tara,* ترين *tarayna,* يرى *yara,* ترى *tara;*

نرى *nara,* ترون *tarawna,* يرون *yarawna*

ولي يلي *wáliya yalī* to administer; *ī* pattern in both past *and* present:

ألي *'alī,* تلي *talī,* تلين *talīna,* يلي *yalī,* تلي *talī;*

نلي *nalī,* تلون *talūna,* يلون *yalūna*

8. Present tense with a direct object pronoun suffix

With a verb having a consonant as final root letter, the vowel of the personal ending, normally dropped in short pronunciation, is restored also in the present tense, when a direct-object pronoun suffix is added:

يعرفه. *ya'rifuhu*. He knows it.

Since ى *'alif maqṣūra* can occur only finally, it is replaced by ا *'alif* when a suffix is added. The *'alif* is pronounced long, *ā*:

رماه. *ramāhu*. He threw it.

Remember (Chapter 6) that after an ending *-ī* the suffixes ه... and هم... are pronounced *-hi, -him*:

ينفيه. *yanfīhi*. He denies it.

9. Present beginning in the past

The Arabic present tense is used also for actions or situations beginning in the past and lasting into the present. Compare Arabic and English:

يغيب منذ سنة. *yaghīb mundh sana*. He has been absent a year.

10. Vocabulary: Form I verbs

أخذ يأخذ *'akhadha ya'khudhu* to take
بلغ يبلغ *balagha yablaghu* to amount to
حدث يحدث *ḥadatha yaḥduthu* to happen
عقد يعقد *'aqada ya'qidu* to tie, to hold (e.g. a meeting)
كفى يكفي *kafa yakfī* to deny
منع يمنع (من\عن) *mana'a yamna'u (min/'an)* to prohibit
نظر ينظر (إلى) *naẓara yanẓuru ('ila)* to look (at)

Exercise 1. Give the second principal part:

e.g.: *yaḥḍur* حضر ← يحضر

1 حلّ	2 أكل	3 بقي
4 نزل	5 دخل	6 وجد

9 خاف	8 طار	7 نوى
12 ولِي	11 رأى	10 نجح
15 تمّ	14 فشِل	13 جاءَ
18 عرف	17 حيَّ	16 ضمّ

Exercise 2. Give the first principal part:

e.g.: qara'a قرأ ← يقرأ

3 ينشر	2 يجري	1 يقود
6 يدفع	5 يمرّ	4 يلقى
9 يرى	8 يغيب	7 يضع
12 يحجز	11 يبيع	10 يمشي

Exercise 3. Put into the present tense:

e.g.: دفعنا حساب الغرفة. ← ندفع حساب الغرفة.
nadfa' ḥisāb al-ghurfa.

1 غاب أكثرية الطلّاب.   2 ماذا أخذوا معهم؟
3 وصلنا إلى القاهرة اليوم.   4 نفى كلّ شيء.
5 جئت (أنا) بالوثائق الضرورية. 6 نزل السياح من الطائرة.
7 هل شككتم في الإمكانية؟   8 لا، قرأنا تقرير المحاسب.
9 نظروا إلى أرقام الميزانية.   10 هل فهمتها (أنت)؟
11 عقدت الوزارة مؤتمراً دولياً.   12 ماذا نوت اللجنة في الأمر؟

Exercise 4. Put present-tense verbs into the past and vice versa:

e.g. yarawna l-farq. رأوا الفرق. ← يرون الفرق.
ḥalalna l-mushkila. نحلّ المشكلة. ← حللنا المشكلة.

1 هل يجد أية إمكانية؟   2 مررنا على بنايات قديمة.
3 قمنا بتنظيم مؤتمر اقتصادي. 4 يسوق سيّارةً أمريكيةً.
5 تمّت البحوث التجارية اليوم. 6 كيف شرحوا الفرق؟
7 ماذا يعملون لتسوية الخلاف؟ 8 طلبوا مساعدتنا الفنّية.
9 فتحَت حسابين جديدين.   10 يجيئون ببعض الوثائق.

Exercise 5. Complete the sentence with a verb in the present tense:

e.g.: ... المندوبون مؤتمراً. ← يحضر المندوبون مؤتمراً.

yaḥḍur al-mandūbūn mu'tamaran.

1 متى ... اللجنة تقريرها ؟
2 ... الناس إلى الكنيسة.
3 ... شخصان عن مؤتمر الحزب.
4 من ... وفدنا ؟
5 ... (نحن) مساعدتكم المالية.
6 ... (هم) حقيقة الأمر.
7 ... زميله في نفس الحقل.
8 ... البحث وقتًا طويلاً.
9 ... (هم) تاكسيًا و... الأوتيل.
10 ... هذه التجربة السياسية.

Exercise 6. Re-express the object with a pronoun:

e.g.: *narāhum.* نراهم. ← نرى الزملاء.

1 تدعو المحكمة المجرمين.
2 يركبون الطائرة في باريس.
3 يشرح ميزانية الاستثمارات.
4 ندرس اللغة العربية.
5 زاروا مدن الصحراء القديمة.
6 ينسى أصدقاءه.
7 هل يقرأون رسالتنا ؟
8 كيف أكتب هذا الجواب؟
9 لماذا رفضتم كل طلباتهم؟
10 ينفي سبب الخلاف.

Exercise 7. Read the following passage. For each verb, give its principal parts and identify its class (sound, hamzated, initial-*wāw* etc.):

e.g.: sound *darasa yadrusu* درس يدرس ← ندرس اللغة العربية.

في هذا الصفّ ندرس اللغة العربية. يبدأ الدرس ونحن نقرأ وثيقةً (مثل تقريراً أو رسالةً) بالعربي ونشرحها. يسمع معلّمنا و يسألنا أسئلة حول تفاصيل الوثيقة. في كثير من الأوقات يجيء المعلّم نفسه بورقةٍ خاصّةٍ لهذا الغرض. ومن وقت لآخر* يجد أحدنا مشاكل في اللغة (أو قد نسي شيءاً من الدرس السابق) ويطلب مساعدة المعلّم أو التلاميذ الآخرين. خلال الدرس نحلّ كلّ مشكلة بواسطة السؤال والجواب وبدراسة كل تفصيل. يجري ويتمّ الدرس كله بهذه طريقة.

* من وقت لآخر *min waqt li-'ākhar* from time to time

18 Recounting – 4

- Predicated verbs
- Verbs followed by the present tense

1. Predicated verbs

In the equations, studied in Chapters 5 and 13, the statement or question must be affirmative and present in meaning (= the unstated verb is deemed to express 'am', 'is' or 'are' in English).

A statement or question with 'to be' in the past or future needs a verb. This verb is كان يكون *kāna yakūnu* (hollow, middle و) 'to be'. Its predicate, when a noun and/or adjective, stands in the *accusative* case:

كان هذا الحقل منتجاً. *kān hādha l-ḥaql muntijan.*

(not: [منتج]) This field was productive.

كان مصدراً هامّاً للاقتصاد. *kān maṣdaran hāmman li-l-iqtiṣād.*

It was an important source for the economy.

The present tense of this verb, used by itself (i.e. with no other verb) expresses the future, 'will be':

هل تكون الطاقة غاليةً؟ *hal takūn aṭ-ṭāqa ghāliya?*

Will energy be expensive?

يكونون مهندسي البترول. *yakūnūna muhandisi l-bitrōl.*

They will be petroleum engineers.

Remember (Chapter 12) that the indefinite ending ...اً\...ةً *-an/-atan* cannot be attached to the theme of a construct:

كان\يكون مصدر الطاقة هامّاً. *kān/yakūn maṣdar aṭ-ṭāqa hāmman.* It was/will be an important energy source.

A predicate other than a noun or adjective stands of course unchanged:

كانت\تكون هنا بئر عميقة. *kānat/takūn huna bi'r ʿamīqa.*

(بئر is *subject*, هنا is predicate) There was/will be a deep well here.

Other predicated verbs, some known to us and all expressing an aspect of 'being' or 'becoming', include:

ليس	*laysa*	not to be
صار يصير	*ṣāra yaṣīru*	to become
ظلّ يظلّ	*ẓalla yaẓallu*	to remain
بقي يبقى	*báqiya yabqa*	to remain
دام يدوم	*dāma yadūmu*	to last
عاد يعود	*'āda ya'ūdu*	to be(come) again
زال يزال	*zāla yazālu*	to cease to be

Note:

- ليس *laysa* is a hollow verb (middle ي); past tense:
  لست *lastu,* لست *lasta,* لست *lasti,* ليس *laysa,* ليست *laysat;*
  لسنا *lasna,* لستم *lastum,* ليسوا *laysū*
  It has only the past tense, which has (NB) *present* meaning; 'I am not, you are not (etc.)', giving us the negative of an equation:
  الخبراء حاضرون. *al-khubarā' ḥāḍirūn.* The experts are present.
  ليسوا حاضرين. *laysū ḥāḍirīn.* They are not present.
  The endings of this verb are always pronounced in full.
- صار يصير *ṣāra yaṣīru* and ظلّ يظلّ *ẓalla yaẓallu* are easy:
  هل يصير مهندساً ؟ *hal yaṣīr muhandisan?* Will he become an engineer?
  ظللنا مشغولين. *ẓalalna mashghūlīn.* We kept busy.
- دام *dāma* and عاد *'āda* are more commonly used in the negative of the past tense ما دام *mā dām* 'as long as' and ما عاد *mā 'ād* 'to be no longer'. Both forms can have either present or past meaning:
  ما دام الحقل منتجاً نحفر. *mā dām al-ḥaql muntijan naḥfur.* As long as the field is productive, we shall drill.
  ما عادت البئر منتجةً. *mā 'ādat al-bi'r muntija.* The well is/was no longer productive.

(We study the negative more fully in Chapter 23.)

- زال يزال *zāla yazālu* 'to cease to be' belongs to the نام *nāma* group (Chapters 11, 17). It also is commoner in its negative form ما زال، لا يزال *mā zal* (past), *lā yazāl* (present) 'still to be':
  ما زال الاستكشاف خطراً *mā zāl al-istikshāf khaṭiran,*
  Exploration was still dangerous,
  ولا يزال التكرير غالياً. *wa-lā yazāl at-takrīr ghāliyan.*
  and refining is still expensive.

Remember (Chapter 12) that certain indefinite nouns and adjectives do not take the ending *-an*:

صاروا أغنياء. *ṣārū 'aghniyā'*. They became rich.

The predicated verbs are called in Arabic أخوات كان *'akhawāt kāna* 'the sisters of *kāna*'.

2. Predicated verbs with the present tense

All the predicated verbs except ليس *laysa* can also be followed by a second verb in the present tense. In verbal sentence structure (Chapter 11), when the subject is stated with a pronoun, it stands between the two verbs; when the subject is a noun, it also stands between the two verbs and the rules for the agreement of verbs apply.

كان يكون + **present tense** makes the *continuous past* tense, used for continuous or repeated past actions or situations 'I was doing/used to do':

كنّا نحفر بئراً اختباريةً. *kunna naḥfur bi'ran ikhtibārīya.*
We were drilling an experimental well.

كانوا يعملون في بغداد. *kānū ya'malūna fī baghdād.*
They used to work/were working in Baghdad.

We study the continuous past tense further in Chapter 19.

صار يصير with the present tense has the meaning 'to begin (to do)':

بعد قليل صارت الطلمبة تعمل. *ba'd qalīl ṣārat aṭ-ṭulumba ta'mal.*

After a little the pump began to work.

The other predicated verbs keep their meaning in this use:

ظللنا\بقينا نحفر كلّ السنة. *ẓalalna/baqīna naḥfur kull as-sana.* We kept on drilling all year.

ما دام هو يغيب نحن حاضرون. *mā dām huwa yaghīb naḥnu ḥāḍirūn.* As long as he is away we are here.

عدنا ندرس المشاكل. *'udna nadrus al-mashākil.* We re-examined ('studied again') the problems.

ما عادت الشركة تقوم بالحفر. *mā 'ādat ash-sharika taqūm bi-l-ḥafr.* The company is no longer engaged in ('undertaking') drilling.

لا يزالون يسكنون في مصر. *lā yazālūna yaskunūna fī miṣr.* They still live in Egypt.

3. Other verbs with the present tense

Certain other verbs can be used in the same way, sometimes in a special meaning, with the present tense of a second verb:

بدأ يبدأ	*bada'a yabda'u*	to begin
أخذ يأخذ	*'akhadha ya'khudhu*	(here:) to begin
ترك يترك	*taraka yatruku*	(here:) to let
كاد يكاد	*kāda yakādu*	almost (to do) – نام *nāma* group

بدأ العمّال يطلبون أكثر. *bada' al-'ummāl yaṭlubūna 'akthar.* The workmen began to demand more.

تدور الطلمبة. نتركها تدور. *tadūr aṭ-ṭulumba. natrukuha tadūr.* The pump is turning. We are letting it turn.

كدنا ننسى أهمّ نقطة. *kidna nansa 'ahamm nuqṭa.* We almost forgot the most important point.

4. Vocabulary: البترول *al-bitrōl* Petroleum

اكتشاف	*iktishāf* discovery	بئر آبار	*bi'r 'ābār* (f.) well
بنزين	*binzīn* petrol, gasolene	تكرير	*takrīr* refining

حفر	*ḥafr* drilling	حفر يحفر	*ḥafara yaḥfuru* to drill
خام	*khām* crude (oil etc.)	دار يدور	*dāra yadūru* to turn
زيت زيوت	*zayt zuyūt* oil	طاقة	*ṭāqa* energy
طلمبة	*ṭulumba* pump	غاز	*ghāz* gas
مصدر مصادر	*maṣdar maṣādir* source	ناقلة	*nāqila* tanker, transporter
نفط	*nafṭ* petroleum		

Exercise 1. Complete the expression by adding the predicate:

e.g.: *kānū muhandisīn.* كانوا (مهندسون) ← كانوا مهندسين.

1 صار (غني)
2 كان (أغنى)
3 ما دام الإنتاج (رخيص)
4 ليست الطلمبة (مفيد)
5 كنّا كلّنا (غائب)
6 ظلّ زملاؤهم (مأمورو البلد)
7 لا يزالون (تلاميذ)
8 يكون الولد (طبيب مشهور)
9 لا يزالون (طلاّب)
10 ما عاد الاستكشاف (ممكن)
11 ما زال (مشغول) كلّ الصيف
12 ليست الناقلة (أجنبي)

Exercise 2. Make the sentence negative:

e.g.: *laysa z-zayt ghāliyan.* الزيت غال. ← ليس الزيت غاليًا.

1 نحن موظّفون جدد.
2 هذه أوّل بئرنا في المنطقة.
3 هم فاضون كلّ اليوم.
4 الطلمبة قوية.
5 النفط ضروري من أجل اقتصادنا.
6 هذا الشخص هو مديرنا.
7 إنتاجهم ممتاز هذه السنة.
8 أكثرية الطلاّب مجتهدون.
9 المشرف مسؤول عن هذا.
10 التجارب الآخرة إيجابية.

Now put the original sentence into the affirmative future:

e.g.: *yakūn az-zayt ghāliyan.* الزيت غال. ← يكون الزيت غاليًا.

Exercise 3. Make the sentence affirmative :

e.g.: *'ana/'anta ma'mūr.* لست مأمورًا. ← أنا\أنت مأمور.

1 ليسوا حاضرين في الصفّ.
2 ليست السيّدات حاضرات.
3 لسنا مشغولين.
4 لست مسؤولاً أنت.

5 ليس الأطفال في البستان. 6 ليس هذا أقدم حقلنا.
7 ليس هذا الأستاذ مشهوراً. 8 ليست النتائج إيجابيةً.
9 لستم ممثلي الشركة. 10 ليسوا عمّالاً بسطاء.

Exercise 4. Begin the sentence with the verb shown in parentheses:

e.g.: حفروا البئر. (بدأوا) ← بدأوا يحفرون البئر.

bada'ū yaḥfurūna l-bi'r.

1 تركنا كلّ الأوراق في المكتب. (كدنا)
2 نام الأطفال وقتًا طويلاً. (تركوا)
3 سأل أسئلةً حول مشاكل قسمه السابق. (لا يزال)
4 سأل أسئلةً حول مشاكل قسمه السابق. (ما زال)
5 عمل في المكتب السابق. (عاد)
6 حفرنا في الحقل القديم. (ما عدنا)
7 وجدت عدد من المشاكل في الترجمة. (صرت)
8 باعت الشركة منتجاتها على الأسواق الدولية. (بدأت)

Exercise 5. Put the verb into the continuous past tense:

e.g.: *kunna naḥfur bi'ran.* حفرنا بئراً. ← كنّا نحفر بئراً.

1 سكنت (أنا) في بغداد. 2 بعنا أكثر على سوق طوكيو.
3 فتحت الشركة حقلين جديدين. 4 فهموا رأي وزارة البترول.
5 وجدت اللجنة مشاكل جديدة. 6 نجحت عمليات الحفر.
7 شرحنا مبادئ الاستكشاف للزوّار. 8 ماذا سألتم؟

Exercise 6. Arrange these oil operations in chronological order:

1 عمليات ناقلات 2 اكتشاف مصدر
3 إنتاج النفط الخام 4 تكرير النفط الخام
5 أستكشاف المنطقة 6 النقل حتى السوق
7 حفر بئر اختبارية 8 إنتاج البنزين
9 دراسة نتائج التجارب 10 حفر آبار منتجة

19 Recounting – 5

- Compound tenses

1. Future tense

In Chapter 17 we learned that the present tense is commonly used for imminent actions and situations in the immediate future. A 'proper' future tense ('I shall/will do') also exists; it is used mainly to express planned or non-imminent future events. It is somewhat more formal.

The future tense is formed by putting the prefix س *sa-* or (less frequently) the particle سوف *sawfa* before the present tense:

سيلقون\سوف يلقون الوزير. *sa-yalqawna/sawfa yalqawna l-wazīr.*
They will meet the minister.

هل سيرفض طلبهم؟ *hal sa-yarfiḍ ṭalabahum?*
Will he reject their demand?

Remember that for كان يكون *kāna yakūnu* 'to be' the future is already expressed by the present form أكون, تكون *'akūn, takūn* (etc.); س\سوف *sa-/sawfa* can be used but is not essential:

(سـ)أكون أنا هناك لمساعدتكم. *(sa-)'akūn 'ana hunāka li-musā'adatikum.* I shall be there to help you ('for your help').

2. Use of the continuous past tense

The continuous past tense ('I was doing') was introduced in Chapter 18 with simple (= one-action) sentences. It is also used in compound sentences such as:

كانت تسكن في القدس عندما وصلت. *kānat taskun fi l-quds 'indamā waṣalt.* She was living in Jerusalem when I arrived.

in which the continuous action or situation كانت تسكن is punctuated by the single action وصلت. Similarly:

كان الأطفال ينامون عندما دخلنا. *kān al-'aṭfāl yanāmūna 'indamā dakhalna*. The children were sleeping when we went in.

The two actions in these sentences are connected by the conjunction عندما *'indamā* 'when'. متى *mata* (Chapter 13) can also be used here, but is mainly used as an interrogative.

The 'when' clause (see below) can come first, as in English:

عندما خرجت كان هو يكتب الجواب. *'indamā kharajt kān huwa yaktub al-jawāb*. When I left he was writing the answer.

A *clause* is a group of words centred on a verb, i.e. relating one action or situation, and making at least limited sense by itself. We study clauses in detail in later chapters.

The continuous past tense of كان itself is not used.

3. Pluperfect tense

The *pluperfect* tense ('I had done') is used for one past action or situation preceding another. It is formed with the past tense of كان *kāna* plus the past tense of the verb indicating the action. Like the continuous past, the pluperfect can be used in a simple sentence:

كانوا حفروا بئرين في سنة. *kānū ḥafarū bi'rayn fī sana*.
They had drilled two wells in a year.

but is also common in a compound sentence:

كان ترك الأوتيل عندما وصلت الشرطة. *kān tarak al-'utayl 'indamā waṣalat ash-shurṭa*. He had left the hotel when the police arrived.

For emphasis the particle قد *qad* (Chapter 11) may be put before the second verb:

كنّا قد رجعنا قبل يومين. *kunna qad raja'na qabl yawmayn*.
We had (already) returned two days earlier.

عندما دفعنا حسابه كان هو قد ذهب إلى الخارج.
'indamā dafa'na ḥisābahu kān huwa qad dhahab 'ila l-khārij.
When we paid his bill he had already gone abroad.

In verbal sentence structure (Chapter 11), when the subject is stated with a pronoun, it stands after the form of كان; when the subject is a noun, that also comes after the form of كان, and the rules for the agreement of verbs apply:

كان الزوّار (قد) تركوا الطائرة. *kān az-zuwwār (qad) taraku ṭ-ṭā'ira.* The visitors had left the aeroplane.

كنّا نحن تركناها أيضًا. *kunna naḥnu taraknāha 'ayḍan.* We had also left it.

The pluperfect is not consistently used; the past tense, with or without قد, is often used to express the same time-sequence, especially in simple sentences:

قد تمّت العملية منذ شهر. *qad tammat al-'amalīya mundh shahr.* The operation had ended a month earlier ('since a month').

The pluperfect of كان itself is not used.

4. Past beginning in the remote past

Look back to Chapter 17, paragraph 8. Just as the present tense is used for an action or situation beginning in the past and lasting into the present, so the past tense expresses an action or situation beginning in the remote past and lasting into the more recent past. English expresses this with the pluperfect; not so Arabic:

سكنّا هناك شهرين عندما وصل. *sakanna hunāka shahrayn 'indamā waṣal.* We had lived ('We lived') there two months when he arrived.

Exercise 1. Make the verb future with س:

e.g.: متى يبدأ المؤتمر؟ ← متى سيبدأ المؤتمر؟

mata sa-yabda' al-mu'tamar?

1 يشكّون فيه.
2 عاش سنوات كثيرة.
3 قد سألوا عدّة أسئلة صعبة.
4 كانت خرجت من الجامعة.
5 هل يعرفوه؟
6 جاء المندوب بطلب وفده.
7 تقوم الشركة بالحفر.
8 يبقون يومًا ولا أكثر.

9 نشرت اللجنة تقريره بعد شهر. 10 طلب أكثر.

Exercise 2. Make the verb pluperfect:

e.g.: بدأوا الحفر. ← كانوا (قد) بدأوا الحفر.

kānū (qad) bada'u l-ḥafr.

1 متى تمّت العملية؟. 2 رفضت السلطات طلباتنا.
3 سيقومون باستكشاف المنطقة. 4 وصل قبل شهرين.
5 تجري البحوث وقتًا طويلاً. 6 سألنا نفس السؤال قبل سنة.
7 نجد مشاكل أشدّ. 8 وجدنا مشاكل أشدّ.
9 صرنا نجد مشاكل أشدّ. 10 نلقى مشاكل أشدّ.

Exercise 3. Make a compound sentence with a clause from each column, joining them with عندما:

e.g.: كنت أدرس فى القاهرة | سمعت عنه

← كنت أدرس فى القاهرة عندما سمعت عنه.

kunt 'adrus fī l-qāhira 'indamā sami't 'anhu.

1 كانوا دعوا الخبراء | 6 كتب أوّل كتابه
2 كانت اللجنة قد بحثت الأمر | 7 نشروا نتائج الانتخاب
3 كان يعمل جولة على النيل | 8 بدأ المؤتمر
4 كان خرج قبل سنة من الجامعة | 9 صار مديراً عامًا
5 عمل وقتًا قصيراً في شركة | 10 ذكرنا المشكلة

Now substitute a 'when' clause of your own for each answer.

Exercise 4. Repeat Exercise 3, putting the 'when' clause first:

e.g.: كنت أدرس فى القاهرة | سمعت عنه

← عندما سمعت عنه كنت أدرس فى القاهرة .

'indamā sami't 'anhu kunt 'adrus fī l-qāhira.

Now substitute a *main* clause (i.e. other than the 'when' clause) of your own choice for each of your answers to this exercise.

20 Recounting – 6

- Increased forms of verbs
- Verbs of Forms II, III and IV

1. Increased forms of verbs

All the verbs studied so far are in the so-called Form I or basic form. Verbs also occur, with the same roots, in *increased forms* (in Arabic, المزيدات *al-mazīdāt*). In this book we study Forms II to VIII and X. Tenses of increased forms are made and used essentially in the same way as with Form I. No verb root occurs in all forms. Use only those you know or find in the dictionary.

The Arabic term for 'verb form' is وزن أوزان *wazn 'awzān* 'weight'.

2. Verb Form II

In Form II the middle root letter doubles. Model verbs for Form II are:

sound:	علّم يعلّم	*'allama yu'allimu*	to teach
hamzated:	أكّد يؤكّد	*'akkada yu'akkidu*	to confirm, assure
initial-*w*:	وظّف يوظّف	*waẓẓafa yuwaẓẓifu*	to recruit
doubled:	قرّر يقرّر	*qarrara yuqarriru*	to decide, report
hollow:	موّل يموّل	*mawwala yumawwilu*	to finance
	غيّر يغيّر	*ghayyara yughayyiru*	to change
final-weak:	ربّى يربّي	*rabba yurabbī*	to bring up, educate

Note:

- initial or middle (not final) root letters و and ي stabilise, i.e. become a consonant *w* or *y* respectively,
- the vowelling is regular, as in all increased forms:
  - past tense: *a-a*; present tense: *u* in the prefix, *a-i* in the root
  - in Form II all final-weak verbs follow the *ay* pattern in the past and the *ī* pattern in the present.

Middle-*hamza* and final-*hamza* verbs do exist in Form II, but are too rare to concern us. They follow the Form II sound pattern.

The only Form II doubly weak verbs of possible interest all have a (stable, i.e. consonantal) و *w* in them, and therefore follow one of the other patterns. An example is ولَّى يولِّي *walla yuwallī* 'to appoint'.

Past and present tenses of the classes shown above:

All classes except final-weak; past *a-a*, present *a-i*:

علَّمت *'allamtu*, ... علَّم *'allama*; علَّمنا *'allamna*, ... علَّموا *'allamū*

أعلِّم *'u'allimu*, ... يعلِّم *yu'allimu*; ... يعلِّمون *yu'allimūna*

Final-weak; past *a + ay* pattern, present *u-a + ī* pattern:

ربَّيت *rabbaytu*, ... ربَّى *rabba*; ربَّينا *rabbayna*, ... ربَّوا *rabbaw*

أربِّي *'urabbī*, ... يربِّي *yurabbī*; ... نربِّي *nurabbī*, ... يربُّون *yurabbūna*

ربَّوا\يربُّون الأطفال حسب مبادئ جديدة.

rabbaw/yurabbūna l-'aṭfāl ḥasab mabādi' jadīda.

They brought/are bringing up the children according to new principles.

Form II verbs take a direct object (Chapter 12). Many are causative, i.e. they cause the object to do the action:

علِم يعلَم *'alima ya'lamu* Form I to know

علَّم يعلِّم *'allama yu'allimu* II 'to cause to know' = to teach

علَّمتهم\أعلِّمهم العربية. *'allamtuhum/'u'allimuhum al-'arabīya.*

I taught/am teaching them Arabic.

(علَّم *'allama* II takes both person and thing as direct objects)

3. Verb Form III

Form III verbs follow the Form II tense pattern fully except that:

- they have long ...ا... -*ā*- after the first root letter instead of a doubled middle root letter, giving us the vowelling *ā-a* for the past and *ā-i* for the present, with the appropriate variants for the final-weak class.

- there are no common hamzated or doubled verbs in Form III.

Model verbs for Form III:

sound:	ناسب يناسب	*nāsaba yunāsibu*	to suit
initial-*w*:	وافق يوافق	*wāfaqa yuwāfiqu*	to agree on/to
hollow:	جاوب يجاوب	*jāwaba yujāwibu*	to answer
final-weak:	نادى ينادي	*nāda yunādī*	to call to, summon

Past and present tenses:

All classes except final-weak; past *ā-a*, present *u-ā-i*:

جاوبت *jāwabtu*, ... جاوب *jāwaba*; ... جاوبنا *jāwabna*, ... جاوبوا *jāwabū*

أجاوب *'ujāwibu*, ... يجاوب *yujāwibu*; ... يجاوبون *yujāwibūna*

Final-weak; past *ā + ay* pattern, present *u-ā + ī* pattern:

ناديت *nādaytu*, ... نادى *nāda*; ... نادينا *nādayna*, ... نادوا *nādaw*

أنادي *'unādī*, ... ينادي *yunādī*; ... ننادي *nunādī*, ... ينادون *yunādūna*

Form III verbs take a direct object, often expressing the person affected. Compare:

كتب يكتب (إلى) *kataba yaktubu* I (*'ila*) to write (to)

كاتب يكاتب *kātaba yukātibu* III to write to, correspond with

قد جاوبونا على طلبنا. *qad jāwabūna 'ala ṭalabina.*

They have given us an answer ('answered us') to our request.

4. Verb Form IV

Model verbs for Form IV:

sound:	أرسل يرسل	*'arsala yursilu*	to send
final-*hamza*:	أنشأ ينشئ	*'ansha'a yunshi'u*	to construct, create
initial-*w*:	أوقف يوقف	*'awqafa yūqifu*	to (bring to a) stop
doubled:	أهمّ يهمّ	*'ahamma yuhimmu*	to concern, be important to
hollow:	أضاف يضيف	*'aḍāfa yuḍīfu*	to add
final-weak:	أعطى يعطي	*'aṭa yu'ṭī*	to give to

Note:

- the first principal part/past tense is prefixed with *'alif hamza*,

- the vowelling for all classes is *a-a* (past) and *u-i* (present), with variants (see below) for hollow and final-weak,
- initial root letter و takes the form *w* in the past, *ū* in the present,
- in the doubled verbs the identical root letters come together or separate in the same way and in the same persons as in Form I,
- in all hollow verbs (middle و and ي), the vowelling is *a-ā, u-ī* before a single consonant and *a-a, u-i* before two consonants,
- all final-weak verbs have the *ay* pattern in the past and the *ī* pattern in the present, with vowelling *a-a* and *u-ī*.

Initial- and middle-*hamza* verbs exist, but are rare.

For doubly weak verbs, the comment made for Form II also applies to Form IV. One exception is the irregular Form IV of the root رأي :

أرى يري *'ara yurī* to show to

in which the middle root letter *hamza* is dropped throughout.

Past and present tenses:

Sound and final-*hamza*; past *'a-a*, present *u-i*:

أنشأت *'ansha'tu*, ... أنشأ *'ansha'a*; ... أنشأوا *'ansha'ū*

أنشئ *'unshi'u*, ... ينشئ *yunshi'u*; ... ينشئون *yunshi'ūna*

Initial-*w*; past *'aw-a*, present *yū-i*:

أوقفت *'awqaftu*, ... أوقف *'awqafa*; ... أوقبوا *'awqafū*

أوقف *'ūqifu*, ... يوقف *yūqifu*; ... نوقف *nūqifu*, ... يوقفون *yūqifūna*

Doubled; root letters follow Form I pattern; past *'a-a*, present *u-i*:

أهممت *'aḥmamtu*, ... أهمّ *'aḥamma*; ... أهمّوا *'ahammū*

أهمّ *'uhimmu*, ... يهمّ *yuhimmu*; ... يهمّون *yuhimmūna*

Hollow; past *'a-ā/'a-a*, present *u-ī*:

أضفت *'aḍaftu*, ... أضاف *'aḍāfa*; ... أضفنا *'aḍafna*, ... أضافوا *'aḍāfū*

أضيف *'uḍīfu*, ... يضيف *yuḍīfu*;... نضيف *nuḍīfu*, ... يضيفون *yuḍīfūna*

Final-weak; past *'a + ay* pattern, present *u + ī* pattern:

أعطيت *'a'ṭaytu*, ... أعطى *'a'ṭa*; ... أعطينا *'a'ṭayna*, ... أعطوا *'a'ṭaw*

أعطي *'u'ṭī*, ... يعطي *yu'ṭī*; ... نعطي *nu'ṭī*, ... يعطون *yu'ṭūna*

Form IV verbs take a direct object, and are often causative. Compare:

وقف يقف *waqafa yaqifu* I to (come to a) stop

أوقف يوقف *'awqafa yūqifu* IV to (bring to a) stop

Some, like أعطى يعطي *'a'ṭa yu'ṭī* IV 'to give to' and أرى يري *'ara yurī* IV 'to show to' (irregular, see above) have both person and thing direct objects:

قد أعطونا\أرونا رسالةً رسميةً. *qad 'a'ṭawna/'arawna risāla rasmīya.* They have given us/shown us an official letter.

5. Notation of verbs

In the text and vocabulary, we shall list new verbs as follows:

Form I: كتب يكتب *kataba yaktubu* I to write

Forms II-X: علّم *'allama* II to teach

6. Vocabulary: Verb Forms II, III and IV

أخبر (ب) *'akhbara* IV *(bi-)* to inform (of)

أذاع *'adhā'a* IV to broadcast

أشار إلى *'ashāra* IV *'ila* to point to

أصدر *'aṣdara* IV to issue, export

أضرب *'aḍraba* IV to strike (from work)

أفاد *'afāda* IV to benefit, to report, to inform

ألقى *'alqa* IV to throw, to deliver (speech, lecture)

أمّن *'ammana* II to insure

أنتج *'antaja* IV to produce

أنجز *'anjaza* IV to implement, accomplish

أوجب *'awjaba* IV to impose, obligate

أيّد *'ayyada* II to support

جدّد *jaddada* II to renew, renovate

جرّب *jarraba* II to try out, attempt

حاول *ḥāwala* III to try

حضّر *ḥaḍḍara* II to prepare
رقّى *raqqa* II to promote
ركّب *rakkaba* II to fix, install
ساعد *sā'ada* III to help
سافر *sāfara* III to travel
سلّم *sallama* II to deliver
صدّق *ṣaddaqa* II to believe
صلّى *ṣalla* II to pray
طبّق (على) *ṭabbaqa* II *('ala)* to apply (a measure etc.) (to)
غادر *ghādara* III to leave
فاوض *fāwaḍa* III to negotiate
فتّش (عن، على) *fattasha* II to inspect, *('an)* to look for, *('ala)* to supervise
فضّل *faḍḍala* II to prefer
فكّر (في) *fakkara* II *(fī)* to think (about)
قدّم *qaddama* II to offer, serve, present, submit
كلّف *kallafa* II to cost
لاقى *lāqa* III to encounter
ميّز *mayyaza* II to distinguish, differentiate
وصّل *waṣṣala* II to convey
وقّع *waqqa'a* II to sign

Exercise 1. Put the verb into the correct past and present form:

e.g.: *fāwaḍtum, tufāwiḍūna* فاوضتم، تفاوضون ← (فاوض، انتم)

1 (أشار، أنتم)	2 (وقّع، أنا)	3 (أهمّ، هي)
4 (نادى، أنتَ)	5 (أعطى، هم)	6 (أفاد، أنا)
7 (ساعد، نحن)	8 (أكّد، هي)	9 (موّل، هم)
10 (لاقى، نحن)	11 (أذاع، أنا)	12 (أنشأ، هم)

Exercise 2. Make past expressions present and vice versa:

e.g.: *tunādi l-'aṭfāl.* نادت الأطفال. ← تنادي الأطفال.

1 يفيد الاستثمار الشركة. 2 أكّدوا ثمن البضائع.
3 لا يزالون يذيعون البرنامج. 4 سافرنا إلى بغداد.
5 يشير هنا إلى أهمّ نقطة. 6 لاقينا نفس الوضع الخطر.
7 كانوا ينتجون أحسن بضائع. 8 نخبر الرئيس بالأرقام.
9 من قد موّل العملية؟ 10 هل يساعد البنك في الأمر؟

Now put all except no. 3 into the future tense:

e.g.: *sa-tunādi l-'aṭfāl.* نادت الأطفال. ← ستنادي الأطفال.

Exercise 3. Replace each noun object (direct or prepositional) in Exercise 2 with the right pronoun :

e.g.: *nādat-hum.* نادت الأطفال. ← نادتهم.

Exercise 4. Add the pronoun direct object:

e.g.: *sā'adūnī* ساعدوا (أنا) ← ساعدوني

1 أخبرتم (نحن) 2 أري (أنتم) 3 نادى (أنتم)
4 أيّدت أنا (أنتِ) 5 سأعطي (هم) 6 صدّقوا (نحن)
7 غادر (هو) 8 لماذا تؤيّدون (هم)؟ 9 أوقّع (هي)
10 كلّف (أنا) كثيراً 11 ينادي (هو) 12 يفيد (أنا)

Exercise 5. Make plural verb expressions singular and vice versa:

e.g.: *sā'adūnī* ساعدني ← ساعدوني

1 سأذيع النتائج. 2 لا نزال ننادي الأصدقاء.
3 كانوا يميّزون بين المرشّحين. 4 سنقدّم منتجات جديدة.
5 هل تفاوض مع المعارضة؟ 6 بدأنا نجرّب أسلوبًا آخر.

Exercise 6. For each word, give at least one other with the same root:

e.g.: *tajriba* جرّب ← تجربة

1 حضّر 2 أنتج 3 أوقف 4 جواب

5 مساعدة	6 راكب	7 رسالة	8 هامّ
9 سافر	10 دورة	11 علّم	12 حق

Exercise 7. Complete the sentence with a verb of Form II, III or IV:

e.g.: ...نا المحاسب بتفاصيل الميزانية.

← أخبرنا المحاسب بتفاصيل الميزانية.

'akhbarana l-muḥāsib bi-tafāṣīl al-mīzānīya.

1 صار الوضع خطراً و... قسم الحفر عملياتها.
2 ... المصنع ماكينات مختلفة للزراعة.
3 قرأ الوزير العقد و ...ه. بعد ذلك ...ه السكرتيرة للطرف الآخر.
4 ... عملية الاستكشاف نقوداً كثيراً. من سـ...ـها ؟
5 أيّ يوم ...كم لاجتماع المدراء؟
6 قد فشلت أول تجربة و... أسلوبًا آخر.
7 قد ... الأطراف تفاصيل العقد وبعد يوم ... عليها.
8 ... أعضاء اللجنة الدولية المطار و... إلى القدس.
9 ... الرئيس نفس الخطاب قبل شهر عندما ... إلى بغداد.
10 اليوم الأوتيل ممتاز، قد ...ه قبل شهرين.

Exercise 8. Read this passage and answer the questions on it:

عندما كنّا نفاوض تفاصيل عقدنا أمس لاقينا مشكلةً أساسيةً. قدّم ممثلو مصرف الاستثمارات فكرةً جديدةً. يفضّل المصرف مبدأ المدفوعات السنوية. وسيطبّق هذا الإجراء على جميع قروضه الصناعية بسبب تكاليفه الإدارية. ستؤثّر هذه الخطوة على وضعنا المالي وسيغيّر برنامج استثمارنا، وأخبرنا وفد المصرف بهذا المشكلة.

1 كيف غيّر مصرف الاستثمارات سياسته بخصوص قروضه؟
2 لماذا قرّر المصرف هذه السياسة؟
3 كيف تؤثّر هذه السياسة على الشركة؟
4 على أيّ نوع من القروض سيطبّق المصرف الإجراء الجديد؟
5 هل أخبرت الشركة الطرف الآخر بالمشكلة؟

21 Recounting – 7

- Verbs of Forms V and VI

1. Verb Form V

Form V follows the pattern of Form II (Chapter 20) except that:

- it has the prefix ...تَ *ta-* immediately before the first root letter,
- the vowel of the present-tense prefix is *-a-*,
- the vowel pattern for the root *in both tenses* is *a-a*; final-weak and doubly weak verbs have the *ay* pattern likewise in both tenses.

Model verbs for Form V are:

sound:	تعلّم يتعلّم	*ta'allama yata'allamu*	to learn
hamzated:	تأكّد يتأكّد	*ta'akkada yata'akkadu*	to be sure
	تنبّأ يتنبّأ	*tanabba'a yatanabba'u*	to forecast
initial-*w*:	توسّع يتوسّع	*tawassa'a yatawassa'u*	to expand
doubled:	تردّد يتردّد	*taraddada yataraddadu*	to hesitate
hollow:	تطوّر يتطوّر	*taṭawwara yataṭawwaru*	to develop
	تغيّر يتغيّر	*taghayyara yataghayyaru*	to be changed
final-weak:	تلقّى يتلقّى	*talaqqa yatalaqqa*	to receive

(Middle-*hamza* verbs exist in Form V, but are too rare to concern us; they follow the Form V sound pattern.)

Past and present tenses:

All classes except final-weak; past and present *a-a*:

تعلّمت *ta'allamtu*, ... تعلّم *ta'allama*; ... تعلّموا *ta'allamū*

أتعلّم *'ata'allamu*, ... يتعلّم *yata'allamu*; ... يتعلّمون *yata'allamūna*

Final-weak; past and present *a + ay* pattern:

تلقّيت *talaqqaytu*, ... تلقّى *talaqqa*; ... تلقّوا *talaqqaw*

أتلقّى *'atalaqqa*, ... يتلقّى *yatalaqqa*; ... يتلقّون *yatalaqqawna*

تغيّرت سياستنا بعد الحرب. *taghayyarat siyāsatuna ba'd al-ḥarb.*

Our policy (was) changed after the war.

Form V is associated with Form II, of which it often expresses the reverse or complementary action:

علم يعلم *ʿallama yuʿallimu* II to teach
تعلّم يتعلّم *taʿallama yataʿallamu* V to learn
(كنّا) نتعلّم المزيدات. *(kunna) nataʿallam al-mazīdāt.*
We were/are learning the increased forms.

2. Verb Form VI

Form VI is related to Form III. It follows or differs from the pattern of Form III exactly as does Form V in relation to Form II. Model verbs:

sound: تداخل يتداخل *tadākhala yatadākhalu* to interfere
hamzated: تآمر يتآمر *taʾāmara yataʾāmaru* to confer
تفاءل يتفاءل *tafāʾala yatafāʾalu* to be optimistic
initial-*w*: تواجه يتواجه *tawājaha yatawājahu* to face each other
hollow: تعاون يتعاون *taʿāwana yataʿāwanu* to cooperate

Final-*hamza*, doubled and middle-*y* verbs of Form VI all exist, but are too rare to concern us. The same is true of final- and doubly weak verbs, all of which have *a* in the root and the *ay* pattern in the ending, for both tenses.

Past and present tenses:

All classes shown above; past and present *a-a*:

تعاونت *taʿāwantu*, ... تعاون *taʿāwana*; ... تعاونوا *taʿāwanū*
أتعاون *ʾataʿāwanu*, ... يتعاون *yataʿāwanu*;... يتعاونون *yataʿāwanūna*
كان المأمورون يتداخلون في عمله. *kān al-maʾmūrūn yatadākhalūna fī ʿamalina.* The officials were interfering with our work.

Form VI sometimes denotes reciprocal or joint action. Compare:

كاتب يكاتب *kātaba yukātibu* III to correspond with
تكاتب يتكاتب *takātaba yatakātabu* VI to correspond with each other

3. Vocabulary: Verb Forms V and VI

تأخَّر   ta'akhkhara V to be delayed/late

تأسَّف (على\لـ)   ta'assafa V ('ala, li-) to be sorry (about)

تبادل   tabādala VI to exchange with each other

تحسَّن   taḥassana V to improve, get better

تخصَّص   takhaṣṣaṣa V to specialise

تدخَّل   tadakhkhala V to intervene

تذكَّر   tadhakkara V to remember

تسلَّم   tasallama V to get, receive

تظاهر   taẓāhara VI to demonstrate (politically)

تعرَّف بـ   ta'arrafa V bi- to get acquainted with

تعلَّق بـ   ta'allaqa V bi- to depend on, pertain to

تقدَّم   taqaddama V to advance, progress

تكلَّم   takallama V to speak, talk

تمكَّن من   tamakkana V min to be capable of, to possess

تناوب   tanāwaba VI to rotate, take turns at

توقَّف على   tawaqqafa V 'ala to depend on

Exercise 1. Put the verb into the correct past and present form:

e.g.: ta'assafū, yata'assafūna   (تأسَّف، هم) ← تأسَّفوا، يتأسَّفون

1 (تبادل، أنتم)   2 (تعاون، نحن)   3 (تكلَّم، أنا)

4 (تلقَّى، هي)   5 (تآمر، هم)   6 (تسلَّم، هو)

7 (تخصَّص، أنتَ)   8 (تأكَّد، نحن)   9 (تنبَّأ، هم)

10 (تأخَّر، أنتم)   11 (تناوب، هم)   12 (تذكَّر، أنا)

Exercise 2. Make past expressions present and vice versa:

e.g.: توقَّف على الثمن. ← يتوقَّف على الثمن.

yatawaqqaf 'ala th-thaman.

1 يتبادلون آراءهم.   2 قد تقدَّمنا في جميع الحقول.

3 هل يتكلَّمون العربية؟   4 نتردَّد وقتًا طويلاً.

5 هل تذكّرت أسماء زملائه؟ 6 كيف تطوّر وضعهم المالي؟
7 تتعلّق التنمية بمستوى الاستثمارات الحكومية.
8 تلقّينا أوامر واضحةً. 9 كانوا تناوبوا عمل القسم.
10 تدخّلت المحكمة في خلاف الطرفين.

Exercise 3. Make plural verb expressions singular and vice versa:

e.g.: *yataraddadūna* يتردّد ← يتردّدون

1 تعرّفنا به أمس. 2 تمكّنوا من قوة كبيرة.
3 ما دام يتعاون معنا. 4 قد تلقّاها.
5 ما زالوا يتقدّمون. 6 كانوا يتكلّمون عن الانتخاب.

Exercise 4. Collect in groups words having the same root:

e.g.: *dākhil, tadakhkhal* داخل، تدخّل

مغادرة، نوبة، تحسّن، تعلّمنا، منتج، تذكر، يتقدّمون، يوقفون، نتيجة، ألاقي، علوم، ذكر، قدّم، تعليم، فضّل، توقّف، أمّن، قديم، تأمين، يتناوب، تلقّيت، أفضل، غادر، إنتاج، أحسن، يلقى

Exercise 5. Complete the sentence with a verb of Form V or VI:

e.g.: ...نا مع الزملاء على العمل.
← تعاونّا مع الزملاء على العمل.
taʿāwanna maʿ az-zumalāʾ ʿala l-ʿamal.

1 ... الجيش حتّى النهر. 2 أين ...تم اللغة العربية؟
3 هل ... الشركة من حقوق الاستكشاف؟.
4 ... الشركة وصارت أكبر شركة في البلاد.
5 ...ها (أنا) من أيامنا في الجامعة.
6 سـ... معهم حول الموضوع عندما نراهم.
7 قد ... وضع صادراتنا هذه السنة وصار ممتازاً.
8 أرسلت لك رسالةً. هل ...ـها؟
9 في حلّ هذه المشكلة ... كلّ شيء على الأسلوب.
10 كان المحامون ... آراءهم في المحكمة.

22 Recounting – 8

- Verb Forms VII, VIII and X

1. Verb Form VII

Form VII has ن *n* before the first root letter. Model principal parts:

Sound: انسحب ينسحب *insáḥaba yansáḥibu* to withdraw

Final-*hamza**: انكفأ ينكفئ *inkáfa'a yankáfi'u*
to be turned away/over

Doubled: انحلّ ينحلّ *inḥalla yanḥallu* to be solved

Hollow*: انحاز ينحاز *inḥāza yanḥāzu* to isolate oneself

Final-weak*: انقضى ينقضي *inqáḍa yanqáḍī* to be finished

(* Rare. Also, no initial- or middle-*hamza* and no initial-*wāw* verbs.)

The only useful Form VII doubly weak verbs have a stable و *w* in them; an example is انزوى ينزوي *inzáwa yanzáwī* 'to keep to oneself'.

Many Form VII verbs have passive meaning (= suffering the action of the verb); none has a direct object.

The first syllable of Form VII verbs is never stressed; further, the initial *i-* of the first principal part/past tense is weak:

هو انسحب\ينسحب. *huwa nsáḥab/yansáḥib.*
He withdrew/withdraws.

Past and present tenses: in all classes the past has prefix انـ.. *in-* and the present prefix has *-an*. Further:

Sound and final-*hamza*; past root vowelling *a-a*, present *a-i*:

انسحبت *insaḥabtu*, ... انسحب *insáḥaba;* ... انسحبوا *insáḥabū*

أنسحب *'ansáḥibu*, ... ينسحب *yansáḥibu;* ... ينسحبون *yansaḥibūna*

انكفأت *inkafa'tu*, ... انكفأ *inkáfa'a;* ... انكفأوا *inkáfa'ū*

أنكفئ *'ankáfi'u*, ... ينكفئ *yankáfi'u;* ... ينكفئون *yankafi'ūna*

Doubled; past root vowelling as in Form I *a(-a)*, present *a*:

انحللت *inḥalaltu*, ... انحلّ *inḥalla;* ... انحلّوا *inḥallū*

أنحلّ *'anḥallu,...* ينحلّ *yanḥallu; ...* ينحلّون *yanḥallūna*

Hollow; middle root vowel is *-a-/-ā-* in the past, *ā* in the present:

انحزت *inḥaztu, ...* انحاز *inḥāza;* انحزنا *inḥazna, ...* انحازوا *inḥāzū*

أنحاز *'anḥāzu, ...* ينحاز *yanḥāzu; ...* ينحازون *yanḥāzūna*

Final-weak; past *a + ay* pattern, present *a + ī* pattern:

انقضيت *inqaḍaytu, ...* انقضى *inqáḍa; ...* انقضوا *inqaḍaw*

أنقضي *'anqáḍī, ...* ينقضي *yanqáḍī; ...* ينقضون *yanqaḍūna*

2. Verb Form VIII

Form VIII follows Form VII in structure, but with ت *-t* after the first root letter instead of ن *n* before it. Model principal parts:

Sound: اقترح يقترح *iqtáraḥa yaqtáriḥu* to propose

Initial-*hamza**: ائتمر يأتمر *i'támara ya'támiru* to deliberate

Middle-*hamza* (rare): التأم يلتئم *iltá'ama yaltá'imu* to come together

Final-*hamza:* ابتدأ يبتدئ *ibtáda'a yabtádi'u* to begin

Doubled: احتلّ يحتلّ *iḥtalla yaḥtallu* to occupy

Hollow: امتاز يمتاز *imtāza yamtāzu* to excel

Final-weak: اشترى يشتري *ishtára yashtárī* to buy

* In the initial-*hamza* root أخذ and in all initial-*wāw* verbs, the ء or و itself becomes ت *-t-*, giving..اتّـ..\يتّـ *itta-/yatta-* in the principal parts:

Root أخذ: اتّخذ يتّخذ *ittákhadha yattákhidhu* to take

Initial-*wāw:* اتّصل يتّصل ب *ittáṣala yattáṣilu bi-* to contact (this example: root وصل)

Some Form VIII verbs can have a direct object.

Some Form VIII verbs add a figurative meaning to the root. Compare:

أخذ نقوداً *'akhadha nuqūdan* I to take money

and: اتّخذ إجراءات\خطوات *ittákhadha* VIII *'ijrā'āt/khuṭwāt* to take measures/steps

فتح *fataḥa* I to open

and: افتتح *iftataḥa* VIII to inaugurate

but many have no identifiable special meaning.

The initial *i-* of Form VIII is weak, and the first syllable is unstressed:

متى ابتدأ\يبتدئ؟ *mata btáda' /yabtádi'?*
When did/does it begin?

Tenses follow the Form VII patterns wherever possible, except for having ت after the first root letter instead of ن before it.

Sound:

اقترحت *iqtaraḥtu,* ... اقترح *iqtáraḥa;* ... اقترحوا *iqtáraḥū*
أقترح *'aqtáriḥu,* ... يقترح *yaqtáriḥu;* ... يقترحون *yaqtariḥūna*

Hamzated; all follow the vowelling of Form VII final-*hamza*:

ائتمرت *i'tamartu,* ... ائتمر *i'támara;* ... ائتمروا *i'támarū*
آتمر *'ātámiru,* ... يأتمر *ya'támiru;* ... يأتمرون *ya'tamirūna*
(one irregular:) اتّخذت *ittakhadhtu;* ... اتّخذوا *ittákhadhū*
أتّخذ *'attákhidhu,* ... يتّخذ *yattákhidhu;* ... يتّخذون *yattakhidhūna*
التأمت *ilta'amtu,* ... التأم *iltá'ama;* ... التأموا *iltá'amū*
ألتئم *'altá'imu,* ... يلتئم *yaltá'imu;* ... يلتئمون *yalta'imūna*
ابتدأت *ibtada'tu,* ... ابتدأ *ibtáda'a;* ... ابتدأوا *ibtáda'ū*
أبتدئ *'abtádi'u,* ... يبتدئ *yabtádi'u;* ... يبتدئون *yabtadi'ūna*

Initial-*wāw*; the و becomes تّ *-tt-*; past *itta-a*, present *atta-i*:

اتّصلت *ittaṣaltu,* ... اتّصل *ittáṣala;* ... اتّصلوا *ittáṣalū*
أتّصل *'attáṣilu,* ...يتّصل *yattáṣilu;*... يتّصلون *yattaṣilūna*

Doubled:

احتللت *iḥtalaltu,* ... احتلّ *iḥtalla;* احتللنا *iḥtalalna,* ... احتلّوا *iḥtallū*
أحتلّ *'aḥtallu,* ... يحتلّ *yaḥtallu;* نحتلّ *naḥtallu,* ... يحتلّون *yaḥtallūna*

Hollow:

امتزت *imtaztu,* ... امتاز *imtāza;* امتزنا *imtazna,* ... امتازوا *imtāzū*
أمتاز *'amtāzu,* ... يمتاز *yamtāzu;* نمتاز *namtāzu,* ... يمتازون *yamtāzūna*

Final-weak:

اشتريت *ishtaraytu,* ... اشترى *ishtára;* ...اشتروا *ishtáraw*

أشتري *'ashtárī*, ... يشتري *yashtárī*; ... يشترون *yashtarūna*

The ت *t* of Form VIII is modified after some initial root letters:

- after initial ص\ض\ط\ظ *ṣ, ḍ, ṭ* or *ẓ* it becomes ط *ṭ*:

  اصطنع *iṣṭána'a* VIII to manufacture

  اضطرب *iḍṭáraba* VIII to clash

- after initial د\ذ\ز *d, dh* or *z* it becomes د *d*:

  ادّعى *iddá'a* VIII to allege

  ازداد *izdāda yazdādu* VIII to be increased

3. Verb Form X

Form X is most easily formed by deriving from Form IV (Chapter 20):

- All classes except initial-*wāw*:

  IV أ...\يـ... *'a-, yu-* → X استـ...\يستـ... *ista-, yasta-* respectively, with weak initial *i-*

- Initial-*wāw*:

  IV أو...\يو... *'aw-, yū-* → X استو...\يستو... *istaw-, yastaw-* respectively, with weak initial *i-*

Otherwise, Form X tenses follow the pattern of Form IV. Model principal parts:

Sound: استعمل يستعمل *ista'mala yasta'milu* to use

Initial-*hamza*: استأنف يستأنف *ista'nafa yasta'nifu* to resume

Initial-*wāw*: استورد يستورد *istawrada yastawridu* to import

Doubled: استحقّ يستحقّ *istaḥaqqa yastaḥiqqu* to deserve

Hollow: استشار يستشير *istashāra yastashīru* to consult

استجوب يستجوب **istajwaba yastajwibu* to interrogate

Final-weak: استثنى يستثني *istathna yastathnī* to except

* استجوب *istajwaba* (root جوب) has, exceptionally, stable middle *w*.

Form X middle- or final-*hamza* verbs and doubly weak verbs also occur but are rare.

Form X often implies 'seeking to ...' or 'considering ... to be ...'; but for some verbs it is difficult to ascribe any additional meaning.

Most Form X verbs take an object (direct or prepositional).

The initial *i-* of the first principal part is weak:

ماذا استعملوا؟ *mādha sta'malu?* What did they use?

Past and present tenses:

استعملت *ista'maltu,* استعمل *ista'mala;* ... استعملوا *ista'malū*
أستعمل *'asta'milu,* يستعمل *yasta'milu;* ... يستعملون *yasta'milūna*
استأنفت *ista'naftu,* استأنف *ista'nafa;* ... استأنفوا *ista'nafū*
أستأنف *'asta'nifu,* يستأنف *yasta'nifu;* ... يستأنفون *yasta'nifūna*
استوردت *istawradtu,* ... استورد *istawrada;* ... استوردوا *istawradū*
أستورد *'astawridu,* يستورد *yastawridu;* ... يستوردون *yastawridūna*
استحققت *istaḥqaqtu,* ... استحقّ *istaḥaqqa;* ... استحقّوا *istaḥaqqū*
أستحقّ *'astaḥiqqu,* يستحقّ *yastaḥiqqu;* ... يستحقّون *yastaḥiqqūna*
استشرت *istashartu,* استشار *istashāra;* ... استشاروا *istashārū*
أستشير *'astashīru;* ... يستشيرون *yastashīrūna*
استثنيت *istathnaytu,* ... استثنى *istathna;* ... استثنوا *istathnaw*
أستثني *'astathnī,* ... يستثني *yastathnī;* ... يستثنون *yastathnūna*

4. to continue

The doubled verb استمرّ (في) *istamarra* X *(fī)* ' to continue', used with or without a prepositional object:

استمرّت الزيارة يومين. *istamarrat az-ziyāra yawmayn.*
The visit went on for two days.

نستمرّ في بحوثنا. *nistamirr fī buḥūthina.*
We are continuing ('in') our discussions.

can alternatively be followed by a present tense, in the manner of e.g. بدأ *bada'a* I (see Chapter 18):

استمررنا نحتجّ. *istamrarna naḥtajj.*
We continued to protest.

5. Vocabulary: Verb Forms VII, VIII and X

اتّفق على	*ittáfaqa* VIII *'ala* to agree on/to
اجتمع	*ijtáma'a* VIII to meet, congregate
احتاج إلى	*iḥtāja* VIII *'ila* to need
احتجّ (على)	*iḥtajja* VIII *('ala)* to protest (against)
ارتفع	*irtáfa'a* VIII to rise, go up
استأجر	*ista'jara* X to rent (as tenant)
استبدل	*istabdala* X to replace
استثمر	*istathmara* X to invest
استراح	*istarāḥa* X to rest
استغرب (من)	*istaghraba* X *(min)* to be surprised (at)
استغنى عن	*istaghna* X *'an* to do without
استفاد من	*istafāda* X *min* to benefit from
استقبل	*istaqbala* X to receive (guests)
استلم	*istálama* VIII to receive (things)
اشترك (في)	*ishtáraka* VIII *(fī)* to participate (in)
اعتبر	*i'tábara* VIII to consider
اعتقد	*i'táqada* VIII to believe
اكتشف	*iktáshafa* VIII to discover
امتدّ	*imtadda* VIII to be extended
انتخب	*intákhaba* VIII to (s)elect
انتظر	*intáẓara* VIII to wait (for), expect
انتهى	*intáha* VIII to (come to an) end
انخفض	*inkháfaḍa* VII to be lowered/reduced
انفجر	*infájara* VII to explode
اهتمّ ب	*ihtamma* VIII *bi* to take care about

Exercise 1. Put the verb into the correct past and present form:

e.g.: *iktashafna, naktáshif* اكتشفنا ، نكتشف ← (اكتشف، نحن)

1 (استغرب، هي) 2 (اهتمّ، أنا) 3 (ابتدأ، هم)

4 (امتدّ، هو)	5 (انخفض، هو)	6 (اشترى، هم)
7 (امتاز، أنتم)	8 (ازداد، هي)	9 (استراح، أنا)
10 (ادّعى، نحن)	11 (اتّصل، هي)	12 (اتّفق، هم)

Exercise 2. Make past expressions present and vice versa:

e.g.: افتتحوا المستشفى. ← يفتتحون المستشفى.
yaftatiḥūna l-mustashfa.

1 اتّخذنا الإجراءات الضرورية.
2 أتّصل بهم من أجل حلّ مشكلتنا.
3 انحلّت المشكلة خلال الاجتماع.
4 استوردت الشركة بضائع مختلفة هذه السنة.
5 نشتري كمبيوتراً جديداً. هو مفيد من أجل تقاريرنا.
6 قد استفاد اقتصاد البلاد من التجارة الخارجية.
7 يجتمع مندوبو الوزارات في غرفة المؤتمرات.
8 قد استأنفنا البحوث بعد دراسة التقرير الأخير.
9 أستشير الخبراء حول هذا الموضوع المعقّد.
10 كان جميع الزملاء يشتركون في بحث ارقام الميزانية.

Exercise 3. Where possible, make singular expressions plural and plural singular:

e.g.: نشتري سيّارات جديدةً. ← أشتري سيّارةً جديدةً.
'ashtárī sayyāra jadīda.

1 استغنى عن مساعدة الخبراء.
2 سنستقبل الضيوف بعد وصولهم هنا.
3 يستأجرون بيوتًا خارج البلد من أجل موظّفيهم.
4 بدأ المندوب المؤتمر ببحث التقرير المالي الأخير.
5 كانوا يحتاجون إلى أرقام تقاريرنا الاقتصادية.

Exercise 4. Supply a suitable Form VII, VIII or X verb in the correct (a) past, (b) present and (c) continuous past form:

e.g.: (X) فرنسا منتجات مختلفةً من بلادنا.
← استوردت\تستورد فرنسا منتجات مختلفةً من بلادنا.
istawradat/tastawrid faransa mantajāt mukhtálifa min bilādina.
kānat faransa tastawrid .... كانت فرنسا تستورد ...

1 (X) نحن) من السياسة التجارية الجديدة.
2 (VIII) الوزير الزوّار الأجانب في مكتبه.
3 (VII) الجيش من الأقاليم الساحلية.
4 (X) أنا) عن مساعدته.
5 (VIII) الجيش المدن الرئيسية للبلاد.
6 (VIII) الاقتصاد إلى رأس مال جديد.

Exercise 5. Recast the sentence with the verb expression shown:
e.g.: *mā zilna nastaghrib.* (ما زال) استغربنا. ← ما زلنا نستغرب.

1 (يبدأ) استفاد من مساعدة البنك.
2 لماذا (استمررتم) استثمرتم في مثل هذا المشروع؟
3 (ما عادت) اكتشفت الشركة حقلاً منتجًا كلّ السنة.
4 (لا يزالون) استعمل العمّال ماكينات قديمةً.

Exercise 6. Read this passage aloud, then answer the questions on it:

قد اكتشفنا حقل نفط في هذه المنطقة قبل سنتين وابتدأت عمليات الحفر بعد ذلك تحت اتّفاقيتنا مع الحكومة. كان إنتاجنا خلال السنة الأولى ضعيفًا وزاد الى المستوى الحالي في أوائل هذه السنة. صار العمل في هذا المنطقة صعب وبسبب ذلك تبقى العمليات غاليةً. سنجرّب أساليب هندسيةً جديدةً بعد وقت قصير من أجل حلّ مشاكل الإنتاج هذه.

1 ماذا أكتشفوا؟ 2 أين اكتشفوه؟
3 تحت أية اتّفاقية ابتدأ الحفر؟
4 لأي غرض يجرّبون أساليب جديدةً؟
5 هل العمل صعب في هذه المنطقة؟
6 كيف كان الإنتاج خلال السنة الأولى؟

23 Negating and excepting

- Negative of verbs, adjectives and pronouns
- Exception

1. Negative of verbs – present tense

We negate the present tense by putting the invariable particle لا *lā* before it:

لا يحضرون المؤتمر. *lā yaḥḍurūna l-mu'tamar.*
They are not attending the conference.

لا يحضرونه. *lā yaḥḍurūnahu.* They are not attending it.

لا يشتري البضائع. *lā yashtári l-baḍā'i'.*
He does not buy/is not buying the goods.

لا يشتريها. *lā yashtárīha.*
He does not buy/is not buying/will not buy them.

لا يستأنفون الحفر. *lā yasta'nifūna l-ḥafr.*
They are not resuming (the) drilling.

Remember (Chapter 18) that the negative of a construct is expressed with the predicated verb ليس *laysa*:

ليسوا حاضرين. *laysū ḥāḍirīn.* They are not present.

The structure لا يكون *lā yakūn* (etc., from كان *kāna*), while present in form, is *future* in meaning in a main clause:

لا يكون ممكناً. *lā yakūn mumkinan.*
It will not be possible.

2. Negative of verbs – future tense

The negative future can be made with سوف لا *sawfa lā* + present tense:

سوف لا نرجع. *sawfa lā narji'.* We shall not return.

سوف لا يعرفه. *sawfa lā ya'rifuhu.* He will not know it.

But a commoner formula, which is more emphatic in meaning, is

لن *lan* + subjunctive tense

in which the particle لن is invariable. The subjunctive tense (in full, the imperfect subjunctive tense, المضارع المنصوب *al-muḍāri' al-manṣūb*) is formed from the present tense as follows:

All verbs except final- and doubly weak:

- change the full-pronunciation ending *-u* to *-a* (unwritten, and dropped in short pronunciation when no suffix follows),
- change personal endings ...ين *-īna* to ...ي *-ī* and ...ون *-ūna* to ...وا *ū* (the *'alif* being dropped when a suffix is added).

Typical subjunctive tense (كتب يكتب *kataba yaktubu* I, sound):

أكتب *'aktuba*, تكتب *taktuba*, تكتبي *taktubī*, يكتب *yaktuba*,
تكتب *taktuba*; نكتب *naktuba*, تكتبوا *taktubū*, يكتبوا *yaktubū*

Final- and doubly weak:

- the spelling ...و\...ي remains, but is pronounced *-uwa/-iya* before a pronoun suffix, otherwise *-ū/-ī* in short pronunciation,
- with final ى *-a*, make no change,
- change personal endings ...ين *-īna/-ayna* to ...ي *-ī/-ay* and ...ون *-ūna/-awna* to ...وا *ū/-aw* (the *'alif* is dropped before a suffix):

(و , I): أعفو *'afū/-uwa*; نعفو *na'fū/-iya*, ... يعفوا *ya'fū*
(ي , I): أرمي *'armī/-iya*; نرمي *narmī/-iya*, ... يرموا *yarmū*
أنوي *'anwī/-iya*; ننوي *nanwī/-iya*, ... ينووا *yanwū*

لن يحضروا المؤتمر. *lan yaḥḍuru l-mu'tamar.*
They will not attend the conference.

لن يحضروه. *lan yaḥḍurūhu.* They will not attend it.

لن يشتري البضائع. *lan yashtári l-baḍā'i'.*
He will not buy the goods.

لن يشتريها. *lan yashtáriyaha.* He will not buy them.

لن يستأنفوا الحفر. *lan yasta'nifu l-ḥafr.*
They will not resume (the) drilling.

For the negative future of كان *kāna* I, see the previous paragraph.

3. Negative of verbs – past tense

The simplest way to make the negative of the past tense is to put the invariable particle ما *mā* before it:

ما صدّقني. *mā ṣaddaqanī.* He did not believe me.

See the end of this paragraph for common uses of ما *mā* + past tense. However, for most verbs (including the one shown above) it is commoner, and preferred style, to use a different formula:

لم *lam* + jussive tense

The jussive tense (in full, the imperfect jussive tense, المضارع المجزوم *al-muḍāriʿ al-majzūm*) is formed from the subjunctive tense as follows:

Sound, hamzated, initial-*w* verbs (Forms I-X); Forms II and V of doubled and hollow verbs:

Drop the personal ending *-a*; change nothing else:

أكتب *'aktub,* تكتب *taktub,* تكتبي *taktubī,* يكتب *yaktub,*
تكتب *taktub;* نكتب *naktub,* تكتبوا *taktubū,* يكتبوا *yaktubū*

Doubled verbs, Forms other than II and V:

The jussive is the same as the subjunctive:

(أهمّ *'ahamma* IV): أهمّ *'uhimma,* ... تهمّي *tuhimmī,* يهمّ *yuhimma;*
نهمّ *nuhimma,* ... يهمّوا *yuhimmū*

Hollow verbs, Forms other than II and V:

Shorten the middle root letter و\ي *ū, ī* respectively to *u, i* (unwritten) when it is the last letter but one of the verb (discounting any pronoun suffix); otherwise no change:

(و , I): أقل *'aqul,* ... تقولي *taqūlī,* يقل *yaqul;* ... يقولوا *yaqūlū*
(ي , I): أبع *'abiʿ,* ... تبيعي *tabīʿī,* يبع *yabiʿ;* ... يبيعوا *yabīʿū*

Final- and doubly weak verbs:

Shorten the final root letter و\ى\ي *ū, a, ī* respectively to *u, a, i* (unwritten) when it is the last letter of the verb (discounting any pronoun suffix); otherwise no change:

(و , I): أعف *'afu,* ... تعفي *taʿfī;* نعف *naʿfu,* ... يعفوا *yaʿfū*

(ى , I): أبق *'abqa*, ...تبق *tabqa*; نبق *nabqa*; ... يبقوا *yabqaw*
أر *'ara*, تري *taray*, ير *yara*; ... نر *nara*; ... يروا *yaraw*
(ي , I): أرم *'armi*, ... ترم *tarmi*; ... نرم *narmi*, ... يرموا *yarmū*
أنو *'anwi*, ... تنو *tanwi*, ... ننو *nanwi*, ... ينووا *yanwū*

The jussive sounds the same in both full and short pronunciation.

لم يحضروا المؤتمر. *lam yaḥḍuru l-mu'tamar.*
They did not attend the conference.

لم يحضروه. *lam yaḥḍurūhu.* They did not attend it.

لم نعرف كيف. *lam na'rif kayfa.* We did not know how.

لماذا لم تساعدها؟ *li-mādha lam tusā'id-ha?*
Why did you not help her?

لم يشتر البضائع. *lam yashtári l-baḍā'i'.*
He did not buy the goods.

لم يشترها. *lam yashtáriha.* He did not buy them.

لم يستأنفوا الحفر. *lam yasta'nifu l-ḥafr.*
They did not resume/have not resumed (the) drilling.

'not ... yet' in the past is expressed with لم ... بعد *lam ... ba'du*:

لم يرجعوا بعد. *lam yarji'ū ba'd.*
They have not returned yet.

ما *mā* + **perfect**, shown at the beginning of this paragraph, is the commoner negative formula with كان *kān*, دام *dām*, زال *zāl* and عاد *'ād*, for which see Chapter 18:

ما كنّا ننتظرهم. *mā kunna nantaẓiruhum.*
We were not waiting for them.

ما زلنا نسكن في القدس. *mā zilna naskun fi l-quds.*
We were still living in Jerusalem.

4. Negative questions

See Chapter 13. The equivalent of هل *hal* in negative questions is أ *'a-*:

ألم تصدّقهم؟ *'a-lam tuṣaddiqhum?*

Did you not believe them?

Negative questions other than 'yes/no' questions are introduced as shown in Chapter 13; an example is given in paragraph 3 above.

5. Negative pronouns

'Nobody' and 'nothing' are expressed with أحد *'aḥad* '(some)one' and شيء *shay'* '(some)thing' respectively, with a negative verb:

لم يحضر أحد. *lam yaḥḍur 'aḥad.* Nobody attended.

لم نلاقِ أحداً. *lam nulāqi 'aḥadan.* We met no one.

لا يهمّنا شيء أكثر من هذا. *lā yuhimmuna shay' 'akthar min hādha.* Nothing concerns us more than this.

In this usage, شيء *shay'* can be intensified by adding أيّ *'ayy* 'any':

لن يهتمّوا بـ(أيّ)شيء. *lan yahtammū bi-('ayy)shay'.* They will concern themselves with nothing. ('They will not concern themselves with anything.')

6. There is no

'There is no ...' is expressed with لا *lā* followed by the appropriate noun, which has the unwritten accusative ending *-a* (see Chapter 15). In this structure the noun case-ending is usually pronounced, even in short pronunciation:

لا أمر أهمّ من هذا الخلاف. *lā 'amra 'ahamm min hādha l-khilāf.* There is no matter more important than this dispute.

We can also express 'there is/are no ...' with لا يوجد\لا توجد *lā yūjad/lā tūjad*, with the subject in the nominative case:

لا يوجد أمر أهمّ من ... *lā yūjad 'amr 'ahamm min ...*

7. Negative adjectives

Adjectives are negated with the word غير *ghayr* 'other (than)' in construct (Chapter 7):

رسمي *rasmī* official غير رسمي *ghayr rasmī* unofficial

واضح *wāḍiḥ* clear غير واضح *ghayr wāḍiḥ* unclear

هذه الإجراءات غير قانونية. *hādhihi l-'ijrā'āt ghayr qānūnīya.*
These measures are illegal.

زوّار غير مصريين *zuwwār ghayr miṣrīyīn*
non-Egyptian visitors

These constructs are indefinite; make them definite by adding the article to the original adjective (= the attribute), not to غير which is the theme:

بحثنا إجراءاتهم غير القانونية. *baḥathna 'ijrā'ātihim ghayr al-qānūnīya.* We discussed their illegal measures.

You will however sometimes meet the article wrongly attached to غير .

8. Exception

The preposition إلاّ *'illa* 'except (for)' is exceptional not only in meaning. Unlike all other prepositions, it does not always take the genitive case (Chapter 6).

Its commonest use is with a negative expression, with its noun in the case dictated by its own function in the sentence. In this structure it often expresses English 'only':

لا أعرف إلاّ نائبه. *lā 'a'rif 'illa nā'ibahu.*
I know only his deputy. ('I do not know except his deputy.')

لم يجئ إلاّ المندوبون الصغار. *lam yaji' 'illa l-mandūb**ūn** aṣ-ṣighār.* Only the junior ('small') delegates came.

In an affirmative statement (less common), the governed noun stands in the *accusative* case, irrespective of its grammatical function:

احتجّ الجميع إلاّ المحافظين. *iḥtajj al-jamī' 'illa l-muḥāfiẓ**īn**.*
Everybody protested except the conservatives.

إلاّ cannot take a pronoun suffix. Any pronoun governed by it is expressed with a subject pronoun, irrespective of grammatical function:

لا أعرف إلاّ هو. *lā 'a'rif 'illa huwa.*
I know only him.

Exercise 1. Make the verb negative in two ways:

e.g.: *mā dhahabū, lam yadhhabū* ذهبوا ← ما ذهبوا ، لم يذهبوا

1 رفضتُ (أنا)	2 استغربنا	3 نفى
4 احتللنا	5 قالت	6 اتّخذتم
7 سألتَ (أنتَ)	8 تذكّروا	9 اهتممنا
10 نسيتم	11 خفت (أنا)	12 جاوبنا

Exercise 2. Make affirmative:

e.g.: *'arafna* لم نعرف ← عرفنا

1 لم أقل	2 لم تنس	3 لم نشكّ
4 لم نفاوض	5 لم نصل	6 لم تنتظروا
7 لم نستشر	8 لم يسوقوا	9 لم نتعاون
10 ألم تتذكري؟	11 لم أناد	12 لم تفد

Exercise 3. Make negative (without using ما or لا سوف):

e.g.: *lan yadhhabū* سيذهبون ← لن يذهبوا

1 رئينا	2 سنقدّم	3 سنتقدّم
4 علّمتم	5 سكن	6 هو غائب
7 يشيرون	8 أساعد	9 هل تسافرين؟
10 سآخذ	11 أيّدوا	12 وافقنا

Exercise 4. Make affirmative:

e.g.: *sa'aqūl* لن أقول ← سأقول

1 لم نفهم	2 لا أوقف	3 لن تهمّني
4 لا تعطين	5 لن تعطي	6 لم تعط
7 لم يصلوا	8 ما بدأ يتكلّم	9 لا يرسلون
10 لن يجدّدوه	11 لا ينفيه	12 لا ينسحبون

Exercise 5. Make the expression (a) present, (b) future:

e.g.: *lā 'aqūl, lan 'aqūl* لم أقل ← لا أقول، لن أقول

1 لم يرجعوا
2 ما كان حاضراً
3 ألم تحتجّ؟
4 لم تعطي
5 لم يحتج إلى شيء
6 لم نر
7 لم نوافق
8 لم أتردّد
9 لم يضربوا
10 لم تدرسوا
11 لم تؤيّدوهم
12 لم ينفه

Exercise 6. Make the verb plural:

e.g.: *lam naqul* لم أقل ← لم نقل

1 لم تذهبْ (أنتَ)
2 لن ينسى
3 لن ينسحب
4 لم أتردّد
5 لم ينس
6 لن ينادي
7 لم يخف
8 سيلقي
9 لم يستفد

Exercise 7. Give the expression opposite meaning by negating (a) the adjective, (b) the verb or the equation:

e.g.: كان مفيداً ← كان غير مفيد، ما كان مفيداً

kān ghayr mufīd, mā kān mufīdan

1 تكون الدورة فنّيةً
2 الرسالة رسمية
3 حملت السيّارة نمرةً دبلوماسيةً
4 كان السبب واضحًا
5 شرح لنا التفاصيل الأساسية
6 هل المصنع منتج؟

Exercise 8. Add the idea 'only' using إلاّ + a negative:

e.g.: فهمت (أنا) أوّل درس. ← لم أفهم إلاّ أوّل درس.

lam 'afham 'illa 'awwal dars.

المعلّمون حاضرون. ← ليس حاضرين إلاّ المعلّمون.

laysa ḥādirīn 'illa l-mu'allimūn.

1 كان الدرس الأوّل مفيداً.
2 هي ساعدتني.
3 يعلّم الأستاذ أسس الهندسة.
4 يهمّنا المبدأ الأساسي.
5 سندفع على أساس العقد.
6 سألونا هذا الشيء البسيط.
7 نتّصل برئيس نفسه.
8 كانوا يحتاجون إلى قليل.

24 Attributing

- to have
- ذو *dhū* etc.

1. to have

The concept 'to have' is usually expressed in Arabic not with a verb but with a preposition + pronoun suffix or noun.

The preposition most commonly used in this context is عند *'inda* 'at, with'. Examine:

عندي جريدة. *'indī jarīda.* I have a newspaper. ('With me [is] a newspaper')

كان عند الجريدة محرّران. *kān 'ind al-jarīda muḥarrirān.* The newspaper had two editors.

عند المجلّة مصادر مختلفة. *'ind al-majalla maṣādir mukhtálifa.* The magazine has various sources.

(سوف) لا يكون عندهم وقت. *(sawfa) lā yakūn 'indahum waqt.* They will not have time.

عندنا مشكلة بخصوص هذه المقالة. *'indana mushkila bi-khuṣūṣ hādhihi l-maqāla.* We have a problem concerning this article.

In English, the thing possessed is the direct object of the verb 'to have'; in Arabic it is the *subject* of the verb كان *kāna* or of the (inverted) equation (Chapter 5). The term 'possessed' is used here for convenience; as the examples show, the association can be other than that of ownership.

عند is general in meaning; alternatively we can use ل *li-*, مع *ma'* or لدى *lada* 'with'. ل *li-* tends to accompany attributes seen as permanent and typical; مع *ma'* indicates having easily to hand, and لدى *lada* is used more in official language:

لهذة الجريدة سياسة اشتراكية. *li-hādhihi l-jarīda siyāsa shtirākīya.*

This paper has a socialist policy.

ليست لها بيانات مالية. *laysat laha bayānāt mālīya.*
It does not have financial notices.

هل معنا جريدة اليوم؟ *hal ma'ana jarīdat al-yawm?*
Do we have today's paper (= here) ?

لدى الحكومة صحيفة رسمية شهرية. *lada l-ḥukūma ṣaḥīfa rasmīya shahrīya.* The government has a monthly official journal.

لدى becomes ...لديـ *laday-* with a pronoun suffix; see إلى, Chapter 6.

2. ذو *dhū* etc.

ذو *dhū* is a word used to show attribution. It is always used in (indefinite or definite) construct:

حزب ذو قوة كبيرة *ḥizb dhū quwa kabīra*
(indefinite) a party with/having/of great power

المقرّر ذو المعلومات *al-muqarrir dhu l-ma'lūmāt*
(definite) the reporter with the information

Since the expression is a construct, it is only the attribute which gets the article when the expression is definite; ذو *dhū* itself cannot carry an article as it is always the theme.

ذو *dhū* has masculine and feminine, singular, dual and plural forms, to agree with the noun which it follows:

	Singular	Dual	Plural
m. nom.	ذو *dhū*	ذوا *dhawa*	ذوو *dhawū*
acc.	ذا *dha*	} ذوي *dhaway*	ذوي *dhawī*
gen.	ذي *dhī*		
f. nom.	} ذات *dhāt*	ذواتا *dhawāta*	} ذوات *dhawāt*
acc./gen.		ذواتي *dhawātay*	

(ذات *dhāt* and ذوات *dhawāt* have case-endings in full pronunciation; see Tables 1 and 3 in the Appendix.)

في شركة ذات مال كثير *fī sharika dhāt māl kathīr*
in a company with much property
لصحفي ذي علاقات ممتازة *li-ṣuḥufī dhī 'alāqāt mumtāza*
for/of a journalist with excellent relations
قد أذاعوا نشرة أخبار ذات أهمّية كبيرة.
qad 'adhā'ū nashrat 'akhbār dhāt 'ahammīya kabīra.
They have broadcast a news bulletin of great importance.

3. Vocabulary: المعلومات *al-ma'lūmāt* Information

اتّصال *ittiṣāl* contact, telephone call
إعلان *'i'lān* announcement, advertisement
أعلن *'a'lana* IV to announce, to advertise
إيميل *'īmayl* e-mail
بريد *barīd* post, mail
بريد إلكتروني *barīd 'iliktrōnī* e-mail
تحرير *taḥrīr* drafting, editing
تلفزيون *tilviziyōn* television
جاء يجيء *jā'a yajī'u* I (also:) to appear (in the press)
جاء يجيء ب *jā'a yajī'u bi-* I (also:) to carry (an article)
جريدة جرائد *jarīda jarā'id* newspaper
حكاية *ḥikāya* story, account, narrative
خبر أخبار *khabar 'akhbār* news
راديو *rādiyō* radio
صحافة *ṣiḥāfa* press
صحيفة صحف *ṣaḥīfa ṣuḥuf* newspaper
صوّر *ṣawwara* II to photograph, to film
صورة صور *ṣūra ṣuwar* picture, photograph
طبع يطبع *ṭaba'a yaṭba'u* I to print
فاكس *faks* telefax
فلم أفلام *film 'aflām* film

مركز مراكز *markaz marākiz* centre
معلومات (inan. pl.) *ma'lūmāt* information
مواصلات (inan. pl.) *muwāṣalāt* communications
موجز *mūjaz* extract, excerpt
مؤلّف *mu'allif* author, composer
نبأ أنباء *naba' 'anbā'* news
نسخة نسخ *nuskha nusakh* copy
نشرة *nashra* bulletin, edition
نصّ نصوص *naṣṣ nuṣūṣ* text

Exercise 1. Make a sentence with عند:

e.g.: أنا ، نصّ الإعلان ← عندي نصّ الإعلان. *'indī naṣṣ al-'i'lān.*
كان، أنا ، نصّ الإعلان ← كان عندي نصّ الإعلان.
kān 'indī naṣṣ al-'i'lān.

1 الصحفي، أهمّ معلومات
2 كان، نحن، حكاية هامّة
3 هو، مصدر داخل الحزب
4 الحزب، مصادر غير رسمية
5 المدينة، مطار دولي
6 هذة الجريدة، مراكز مختلفة
7 كلّ مركز، خبراء ماليون
8 يكون، أنتم، نسخة الإيميل
9 كلّ محرّر، مسؤولية كبيرة
10 كان، هي، نسختي الخطاب

Exercise 2. Make your answers to Exercise I negative:

e.g.: عندي نصّ الإعلان. ← ليس عندي نصّ الإعلان.
laysa 'indī naṣṣ al-'i'lān.
كان عندي نصّ الإعلان. ← ما كان عندي نصّ الإعلان.
mā kān 'indī naṣṣ al-'i'lān.

Exercise 3. In which of your answers to Exercise 1 might you replace عند with ل ? Do so, in those answers:

e.g.: عند الحزب قوة كبيرة . ← للحزب قوة كبيرة.
li-l-ḥizb quwa kabīra.

Exercise 4. Make an expression with the right form of ذو :

e.g.: مقرّر، مصدر هامّ. ← مقرّر ذو مصدر هامّ

muqarrir dhū maṣdar hāmm.

1 شخص، مال كبير
2 نشرة، بيانات حكومية
3 أخبار، أهمّية محلّية
4 صحيفة، محرّر ممتاز
5 النشرة، أرقام الميزانية
6 مع ناس، تعليم جامعي
7 الصحفيون، المعلومات المكتومة
8 لأعضاء، علاقات مفيدة لنا

Exercise 5. Make a pair of sentences on the model shown:

e.g.: مقرّر، معلومات هامّة

← هو مقرّر ذو معلومات هامّة. عند المقرّر معلومات هامّة.

huwa muqarrir dhū maʿlūmāt hāmma.

ʿind al-muqarrir maʿlūmāt hāmma.

1 سيّدة، ثقافة واسعة
2 الصحيفة، محرّر أجنبي
3 النشرة، أخبار اقتصادية
4 ولد، صحّة ضعيفة
5 الحزب، أكثرية في المجلس
6 صحف، آراء مختلفة
7 مجلّة، حكايات للأطفال
8 موظّفون، مسؤولية كبيرة

Exercise 6. Put the words from the list into the blanks in the passage:

جاءت ... الوطنية اليوم بـ... هامّ. حسب ... الرئيسية لجريدتنا قد ... مفاوضات ... التجارة العالمية. ألقى رئيس البنك الدولي ... عندما ... البحوث و... الصحيفة ... خطابه في إحدى مقالاتها. في نفس ... جاء ... حكومي. ... وزارة التجارة إجراءات جديدة لمساعدة قطاع ....

استأنفوا، إعلان، التجارة، خبر، موجز، المقالة، نشرت، اتّفاقية، النشرة، افتتحوا، خطابًا، الصحافة، تتخذ

25 Requesting and Commanding

- Imperative (الأمر *al-'amr*)

1. Imperative - general

The imperative or command form ('do!') of the verb exists only in the 2nd persons ('you').

Its main uses in written Arabic are in certain common formulæ found in correspondence, signs, advertising, form-filling and in written instructions for machinery, commercial products etc.:

- in correspondence:

  تفضّل\تفضّلي\تفضّلوا V *tafaḍḍal* (m. s.), *tafaḍḍalī* (f. s.), *tafaḍḍalū* (pl.) 'be so kind'. In writing it is often followed by a prepositional phrase with ب *bi-* + a noun denoting an action:

  تفضّلوا بالحضور. *tafaḍḍalū bi-l-ḥuḍūr*. Please do come. ('Be so kind with the presence.')

  تفضّلوا بقبول ... *tafaḍḍalū bi-qabūl* ... Please accept ... ('Be so kind with the acceptance of ...')

  In formal correspondence it is considered polite to use the plural.

- exhortations or instructions:

  اشرب\اشربي\اشربوا I *ishrab (-ī, -ū)* (m.s./f.s./pl.) drink
  اذكر\اذكري\اذكروا I *udhkur (-ī, -ū)* (on a form) mention
  افتح\افتحي\افتحوا I *iftaḥ (-ī, -ū)* open
  خذ\خذي\خذوا I *khudh (-ī, -ū)* take
  انظر\انظري\انظروا I *unẓur (-ī, -ū)* (in text reference) see
  قف I *qif* m. s. (from وقف يقف *waqafa yaqifu* I) STOP
  تمهّل V *tamahhal* m. s. (تمهّل *tamahhala* V) SLOW DOWN
  انتظر\انتظري\انتظروا VIII *intáẓir (-ī, -ū)* wait
  استعمل\استعملي\استعملوا X *ista'mil (-ī, -ū)* use

  All three forms are shown here; in the singular the m. is used for an unknown readership. قف and تمهّل are seen on traffic signs. An imperative may be accompanied by a formula of politeness such as

من فضلك\فضلكم *min faḍlika/faḍliki/faḍlikum*
('from your kindness') Please

لو سمحت\سمحتم *law samaḥt/samaḥti/samaḥtum*
('if you would permit') if you please

2. Forming the imperative

Paragraph 1 above gives the essentials of the use of the imperative in writing. It is, however, necessary to know how the imperative is formed. The following can be regarded provisionally as reference material.

The imperative is derived from the appropriate 'you' form (2nd. person m. s., f. s., pl.) of the *jussive*, see Chapter 23. This person has the prefix ...تو *tū-* or ...تـ *ta-*, *tu-*.

Prefix ...تو *tū-*. If the jussive form has this prefix, replace this with ...أو *'aw-* to make the imperative:

توقف *tūqif* (etc.) IV, أوقف\أوقفي\أوقفوا *'awqif (-ī, -ū)* stop

Prefix ...تـ *ta-, tu-*. If the jussive has one of these prefixes, remove the prefix. If the resultant form then begins with:

- *one consonant + a vowel*, go no further. This is the imperative:

تقل *taqul* (etc.) I, قل\قولي\قولوا *qul, qūlī, qūlū* say
تقف *taqif* (etc.) I, قف\قفي\قفوا *qif (-ī, -ū)* (come to a) stop
تدلّ *tadulla* (etc.) I, دلّ\دلّي\دلّوا *dulla, dullī, dullū* show
تعلّم *tu'allim* (etc.) II, علّم\علّمي\علّموا *'allim (-ī, -ū)* teach
تؤكّد *tu'akkid* (etc.) II, أكّد\أكّدي\أكّدوا *'akkid (-ī, -ū)* confirm
تتذكّر *tatadhakkar* (etc.) V, تذكّر\تذكّري\تذكّروا *tadhakkar (-ī, -ū)* remember

- *two consonants*, then an imperative prefix is needed; see below.

For Form IV, the imperative prefix to be added is ...أ *'a-*:

ترسل *tursil* (etc.) IV, أرسل\أرسلي\أرسلوا *'arsil (-ī, -ū)* send

For other than Form IV, look at the last vowel of the m. s. jussive form. If that vowel is *u*, add the imperative prefix ...ا *u-* (weak):

تكتب *taktub* (etc.) I, اكتب\اكتبي\اكتبوا *uktub (-ī, -ū)* write

تعف *ta'fu* (etc.) I, اعف\اعفي\اعفوا *u'fu, u'fī, u'fu* forgive

If that vowel is anything else, add the imperative prefix ...ا *i-* (weak):

تفتح *taftaḥ* (etc.) I, افتح\افتحي\افتحوا *iftaḥ (-ī, -ū)* open

ترم *tarmi* (etc.) I, ارم\ارمي\ارموا *irmi, irmī, irmū* throw

تنس *tansa* (etc.) I, انس\انسي\انسوا *insa, insay, insaw* forget

تنسحب *tansáḥib* (etc.) VII, انسحب\انسحبي\انسحبوا *insáḥib (-ī, -ū)* withdraw

تحتجّ *taḥtajja* (etc.) VIII, احتجّ\احتجّي\احتجّوا *iḥtajja, iḥtajjī, iḥtajjū* protest

تتّخذ *tattákhidh* (etc.) VIII, اتّخذ\ي\وا *ittákhidh (-ī, -ū)* take

We can summarise the rules in a table (the examples are all m. s.):

2nd pers. jussive	Changes	Imperative, e.g.
prefix تو *tū-*	→ Replace with ...أو *'aw-* →	أوقف *'awqif*
prefix تـ *ta-, tu-*	→ Remove; if form now begins: • one consonant + vowel → • two consonants, add prefix: - Form IV: prefix أ *'a-* → - others: last vowel of m. s. is *u*, prefix ا *u-* → last vowel of m. s. is *a/i*, prefix ا *i-* →	 علّم *'allim* أرسل *'arsil* اكتب *uktub* افتح *iftaḥ*

Three important Form I initial-*hamza* verbs drop their initial root letter entirely in the imperative:

تأخذ *ta'khudh* (etc.) I., خذ\خذي\خذوا *khudh, khudhī, khudhū* take

تأكل *ta'kul* (etc.) I., كل\كلي\كلوا *kul, kulī, kulū* eat

تأمر *ta'mur* (etc.) I., مر\مري\مروا *mur, murī, murū* order

Some other initial-*hamza* verbs have imperatives which need care, but these imperatives are too rare to concern us.

For the rarer persons (dual, f. pl.) of the imperative, see the Appendix.

3. Negative imperative

The negative imperative ('do not ...') is expressed with لا *lā* + the jussive form itself:

لا تنس\تنسي\تنسوا *lā tansa/tansay/tansaw* do not forget

لا تدخل\تدخلي\تدخلوا *lā tadkhul/tadkhulī/tadkhulū* do not enter

4. Vocabulary: المبيعات *al-mabīʿāt* Sales

بائع باعة *bāʾiʿ bāʿa* salesman

بائعة *bāʾiʿa* saleswoman

بيع بيوع *bayʿ buyūʿ* sale, selling

تخفيض *takhfīḍ* reduction

ترويج *tarwīj* promotion (sales, product)

تسويق *taswīq* marketing

تعليمات *taʿlīmāt* instructions

خفّض *khaffaḍa* II to reduce

دعاية ، إعلان داعي *diʿāya, ʾiʿlān dāʿī* publicity

روج *rawwaja* II to promote (sales, product)

زبون زبائن *zabūn zabāʾin* customer, client

سمح يسمح ل ب *samaḥa yasmaḥu li-* (person) *bi-* (thing) I to permit

ضريبة ضرائب *ḍarība ḍarāʾib* tax

مشتر\المشتري *mushtárin (al-mushtárī)* (weak) purchaser

مشترىً\المشترى *mushtáran (al-mushtára)* (weak) purchase

منافس *munāfis* competitor

منافسة *munāfasa* competition

منخفض *munkháfiḍ* reduced

Exercise 1. Give the affirmative and negative imperative, masculine singular, of the verb (shown by its first principal part):

e.g.: *iftaḥ, lā taftaḥ* فتح ← افتح، لا تفتح

1 ذكر	2 تذكّر	3 صوّر	4 ذهب
5 استعمل	6 دلّ	7 نام	8 أضرب
9 نظر	10 نسي	11 نادى	12 احتلّ
13 بدأ	14 اشترى	15 أعلن	16 وافق
17 بقي	18 رفض	19 أخذ	20 اتّخذ
21 ضرب	22 أيّد	23 باع	24 نفى

Now give the feminine singular and the plural of your answers.

Exercise 2. Make the imperative negative:

e.g.: *lā taftaḥī* افتحي ← لا تفتحي

1 استفيدوا	2 تعاونوا	3 اركبي	4 اشكر
5 استعملي	6 استمرّ	7 تداخلوا	8 وقّع
9 استبدلوا	10 اسألي	11 تكلّم	12 اقرأ
13 كل	14 أوقفوا	15 اتّصلي	16 غادروا
17 أضف	18 اشترك	19 ابكي	20 استرح

Exercise 3. From what verb is the imperative derived?:

e.g.: افتح ← I *fataḥa yaftaḥu* فتح يفتح

لا تسترح ← X *istarāḥa* استراح

1 لا تغب	2 صلوا	3 انزلوا	4 لا تشكّ
5 احتلّوا	6 انس	7 مر	8 مرّ
9 اعفي	10 لا تخف	11 أعطوا	12 اعتقد

Exercise 4. Substitute the right pronoun for the noun direct object of the imperative:

e.g.: *sā'id-hu.* ساعد الزبون. ← ساعده.

1 اطبع هذا الإعلان.

2 لا تنشروا نصّهم.

3 أذيعوا أخبار منتجاتنا الأخيرة. 4 اذكر الأسعار المنخفضة.
5 لا تنس مصالح الزبائن! 6 خذي صور البضائع معك.
7 لا تستعمل مثل هذه الدعاية. 8 انتظروا مبيعات آخر السنة.
9 أخبر المشتري بالتفاصيل كلّها. 10 قل له اسم منافسنا الرئيسي.

Exercise 5. Read the passage and answer the questions:

تعليمات مدير المبيعات للبائع او للممثل الجديد

ادرس تفاصيل منتجك.
ابحث المنتجات مع زملائك.
انظر ألى منتجات المنافسين واقرأ المعلومات بخصوصها.
تذكّر مبادئ التسويق وترويج المبيعات من وقت تدريبك.
استفد من أساليب الدعاية الحديثة.
احضر كل اجتماع على الوقت ولا تتأخّر.
قل الحقيقة في حسابك ولا تضع فيه إلاّ تكاليفك المهنية.
استعمل وقتك الفاضي لتنمية النفس.

لا تنس أهمّية علاقاتك الإيجابية مع الزبون او المشتري:
- افهم إرادات و مصالح الزبون.
- لا تزر المشتري بدون وثائقك.
- قدّم أحسن ثمن الممكن من أجل الزبون.
- لا تبع منتجًا او تحاول بيع منتج غير مفيد لغرض الزبون.
- اشرح البضائع للمشتري وجاوب على أسئلته.

1 هل يهمّ الممثّل دراسة منتجه؟ ودراسة منتجات المنافس؟
2 هل تحضر انت الاجتماعات علي الوقت؟
3 اذكر عدّة نقط ذات أهمّية من أجل العلاقات مع الزبون.
4 أية من هذه النقط أهمّ من الكلّ؟ اشرح رائيك.
5 هل تستعمل انت وقتك الفاضي لتنمية النفس؟
6 هل عملت كممثّل تجاري؟
7 ماذا يقول المدير بخصوص حساب تكاليف الممثّل؟

26 Describing the subject

- Active participles

1. Participles – general

A participle is a verbal adjective; it is derived from a verb, but has the function of an adjective or noun. Typical English participles are found in expressions like 'a working man' or 'a written agreement'. Arabic has the *active* participle qualifying or identifying the subject of the verb, and the *passive* participle qualifying or identifying the object. You already know several participial nouns and adjectives. This chapter explains the active participle (اسم الفاعل *ism al-fā'il*).

2. Active participle, Form I

Form I model is كاتب *kātib* 'writing', hence 'a writer, a clerk', from كتب *kataba*. So also, from verbs mostly known to you:

Sound, hamzated, initial *wāw*:

عامل	*'āmil* working, a worker	حامل	*ḥāmil* carrying, bearing
آكل	*'ākil* eating	قارئ	*qāri'* reading, reader
واقف	*wāqif* stopping, still, stationary		

Doubled; the *i* is dropped and the identical root letters fall together:

شاكّ	*shākk* doubting	هامّ	*hāmm* mattering, important
تامّ	*tāmm* complete		

Hollow; the weak middle root letter becomes *hamza*:

نائم	*nā'im* sleeping, asleep	طائر	*ṭā'ir* flying
بائع	*bā'i'* selling, a salesman	زائد	*zā'id* increasing

Final- and doubly weak; this is where many of the weak nouns and adjectives described in Chapter 10 originate:

جارٍ\الجاري	*jārin/al-jārī* current, ongoing
باقٍ\الباقي	*bāqin/al-bāqī* remaining, remainder

These are the m. s. forms. All these words can be made feminine/ inanimate plural where appropriate:

عاملة *ʿāmila* working woman, female worker
السيّارات الواقفة *as-sayyārāt l-wāqifa* the stationary cars
في الرسالة الحاملة اسمه *fī r-risāla l-ḥāmila smahu*
in the letter bearing his name
خذ باقيتة معك. *khudh bāqīyatahu maʿaka.*
Take the rest of it with you.
طائرة *ṭāʾira* aeroplane

and dual and animate plural; in Form I the participles when used as adjectives or f. nouns mostly have sound plurals, while as m. nouns their plural is often broken:

قارئان *qāriʾān* two readers
أطفال نائمون *ʾaṭfāl nāʾimūn* sleeping children
كاتبة كاتبات *kātiba kātibāt* female clerk, authoress
كاتب كتّاب *kātib kuttāb* clerk, writer

3. Active participle, Forms II to X

To form the (m. s.) active participle of an increased form, take the second principal part:

- remove the full-pronunciation ending *-u*, if any,
- in Forms V and VI, change the last vowel from *a* to *i*,
- replace the prefix ...يـ *ya-*, *yu-* with ...مـ *mu-* and the prefix ...يو *yū-* with ...مو *mū-*.

All classes except final- and doubly weak:

معلّم *muʿallim* II teacher	مموّل *mumawwil* II financier
مساعد *musāʿid* III assistant	موافق *muwāfiq* III agreeing
مرسِل *mursil* IV sender	موجب *mūjib* IV necessitating
مهمّ *muhimm* IV important	متأخّر *mutaʾakhkhir* V late
محتلّ *muḥtall* VIII	متعلّق ب *mutaʿalliq bi-* VIII

occupying, occupier — pertaining to, relating to, concerning

مبتدئ *mubtádi'* VIII beginner — مستثمر *mustathmir* X investor

مستورد *mustawrid* X importer — مستمر *mustamirr* X continuous

Final- and doubly weak:

مشترٍ\المشتري *mushtárin/al-mushtárī* (weak) VIII buying, purchaser

Make feminine and dual forms as usual. Almost all plurals are sound:

القوانين المتعلّقة بالعقود *al-qawānīn al-muta'alliqa bi-l-'uqūd*
laws relating to contracts

القوات المحتلّة المنطقة *al-quwāt al-muḥtalla l-minṭaqa*
the forces occupying the region

Only a few such participles used as m. nouns have a broken plural. In principle the participle takes the same kind of object (Chapter 12), if any, as its source verb; but a few (e.g. مفيد ل *mufīd li-* 'useful for' from أفاد *'afāda* IV 'to benefit') may differ. Also, the participle can be used as a noun in construct:

اجتماع مموّلي المشروع *ijtimā' mumawwili l-mashrū'*
a meeting of (the) financiers of the project

4. Negative

Like all adjectives, participles are negated with غير *ghayr*:

أسلوب غير مناسب *uslūb ghayr munāsib*
an unsuitable/inappropriate method

5. Vocabulary: اسم الفاعل *ism al-fā'il* Active participle

NB: As participles are regular, we list here only a few with additional or unexpected meanings, or derived from verbs not studied earlier.

ماشٍ\الماشي *māshin/al-māshī* (weak) walking, going — متقدّم *mutaqaddim* advanced, progressive

محتاج *muḥtāj* needy — مرتفع *murtáfi'* rising, high

مستأجر *musta'jir* tenant — مستعدّ *musta'idd* ready

Exercise 1. Give the (m. s.) active participle of:

e.g.: *ʿārif* عارف ← عرف I   *muʿlin* معلن ← أعلن IV

1 قرّر	2 سكن	3 سافر	4 تعاون
5 أذاع	6 كتب	7 خاف	8 أعطى
9 أكّد	10 احتجّ	11 طلب	12 انخفض
13 فهم	14 انتهى	15 اشترك	16 ساق
17 قدم	18 جلس	19 ناسب	20 تكلّم
21 اقترح	22 استعمل	23 ادّعى	24 احتاج
25 دلّ	26 أفاد	27 أوقف	28 زار

Now give any broken masculine plurals.

Exercise 2. Read the active participle, and give its source verb:

e.g.: *nāʾima, nāma yanāmu* I نام ينام ← نائمة

1 مفيدة	2 حاضرون	3 عارف	4 مستريح
5 المستمرّة	6 طلاّب	7 مستجوب	8 للمذيعين
9 مبتدئة	10 نازل	11 مجدّدة	12 المحتاج

Exercise 3. Complete the sentence with the active participle:

e.g.: لا تستعمل برنامجًا غير (ناسب). ← ... برنامجًا غير مناسب.

lā tastaʿmil barnāmajan ghayr munāsib.

1 أيّ كتاب (أفاد) لدراسة اللغة العربية؟
2 هل تعرف (موّل)ي هذه المشاريع؟
3 لا يهمّنا كم يكلّف، يدفع الـ(أمّن)ون!
4 "الوضع خطر" قال الـ(تكلّم) في خطابه أمام اللجنة البرلمانية.
5 ليس الأعضاء الجدد (غاب)ين، كلّهم (حضر)ون.
6 الـ(طار) (تأخّر)ة اليوم.
7 لا تشتر أيّة بضائع (قدم) بأسعار (ارتفع).
8 أين التلاميذ الـ(اشترك)ون في الامتحان؟

27 Describing the object

- Passive participles

1. Passive participle – general

See Chapter 26. The passive participle (اسم المفعول *ism al-maf'ūl*) qualifies or identifies the (direct or prepositional) object of the verb, i.e. the person or thing suffering the action. Like the active participle, it is an adjective which can also be a noun where appropriate.

2. Passive participle, Form I

Form I model for classes other than hollow, final- and doubly weak is مكتوب *maktūb* 'written', from كتب *kataba*. So also:

Sound and hamzated:

مفتوح *maftūḥ* open(ed)	معروف *ma'rūf* (well)known
مطلوب *maṭlūb* requested	مسؤول *mas'ūl* ('asked') responsible

Initial ***wāw***; the initial root letter و stabilises:

موضوع *mawḍū'* placed, subject

موجود *mawjūd* ('found') present, available

Doubled; the identical root letters separate:

محلول *maḥlūl* solved	مظنون *maẓnūn* supposed

Hollow; models are مقول *maqūl* 'said' (middle و and نام group) and مبيع *mabī'* 'sold' (middle ي). So also:

مزور *mazūr* visited	مخوف *makhūf* feared
مزيد *mazīd* excess, increased verb form	

Final- and doubly weak; models are مرجوّ *marjūw* 'requested' (final و) and منسيّ *mansīy* 'forgotten' (final ي). So also:

مدعوّ *mad'ūw* summoned	مرميّ *marmīy* thrown (away)

Fem./inan. pl., dual, plural and negative are formed where appropriate. A few masc. participles used as nouns have a broken plural:

جميع البضائع الموجودة *jamīʿ al-baḍāʾiʿ al-mawjūda*
all the available goods
مكتوب مكاتيب *maktūb makātīb* letter, message
موضوع مواضيع *mawḍūʿ mawāḍīʿ* subject
للأصدقاء المزورين اليوم *li-l-ʾaṣdiqāʾ al-mazūrīn al-yawm*
for the friends visited today
مشاكل غير محلولة *mashākil ghayr maḥlūla*
unsolved problems

3. Passive participle, Forms II to X

We form the (m. s.) passive participle of an increased form as follows: **All classes except final- and doubly weak:** change the last *i* or *ī* of the active participle to *a* or *ā* respectively; if the active participle already has *a* as its last vowel (Form VIII doubled), leave it unchanged:

مؤكّد *muʾakkad* II confirmed ممول *mumawwal* II financed
مرسل *mursal* IV sent موجب *mūjab* IV necessary, affirmative
محتل *muḥtall* VIII occupied مذاع *mudhāʿ* VIII broadcast
مستورد *mustawrad* X imported مستعمل *mustaʿmal* X used

Final- and doubly weak: change the final *-in* or ي... *-ī* of the active participle to ىً... *-an* or ى... *-a* respectively. The participle is weak:

مشترىً\المشترى *mushtáran/al-mushtára* VIII purchase(d)

Make fem./inan. pl., dual and negative forms as usual (except that the adjectival fem. sing./inan. pl. ending of the weak participles is اة... *-ā́*). A few participles used as m. nouns have a broken plural; otherwise, plurals are sound:

في الأراضي المحتلّة *fī l-ʾarāḍi l-muḥtalla*
in the occupied territories
ضريبة على المستوردات *ḍarība ʿala l-mustawradāt*
a tax on imports ('imported things')
مشتريات يومية *mushtarayāt yawmīya* daily purchases

(ال)كتب (الـ)مشتراة على الحساب *(al-)kutub (al-)mushtarā́ 'ala l-ḥisāb* books bought on account

Many Form VII verbs (Chapter 22) already have passive meaning; so the active participle of such verbs has passive force:

انخفض *inkháfaḍa* VII to be reduced

→ active participle منخفض *munkháfiḍ* reduced; no passive participle.

4. Instrument and agent: use of the passive participle

The Arabic passive participle can be accompanied by the *instrument* of the action (i.e. 'with what'):

مشاريع مموّلة بقروض حكومية *mashārī' mumawwala bi-qurūḍ ḥukūmīya* projects financed with government loans

but it is incorrect to state the *agent* of the action, (i.e. 'by whom/ what'). An expression such as 'financed *by the government*' is best cast differently, e.g. 'under government financing' or 'which the government financed'; we study these structures in Chapters 28 and 35.

5. Agreement of passive participles

A passive participle qualifying or identifying a direct object agrees fully with it:

الدراسات المنشورة خلال السنة المالية *ad-dirāsāt al-manshūra khilāl as-sana l-mālīya* the studies published during the financial year

but a passive participle qualifying or identifying a *prepositional* object is always *masculine singular*; the gender and number of the object are shown by adding the appropriate pronoun suffix to the preposition:

الدراسات المقوم بها خلال السنة المالية *ad-dirāsāt al-**maqūm biha** khilāl as-sana l-mālīya* the studies undertaken during the financial year

(قام يقوم ب *qāma yaqūmu bi-* I to undertake, Chapter 17.)

بين الخبراء المتّصل بهم *bayn al-khubarā' al-muttáṣal bihim* among the experts contacted

6. Participles as predicates

Active participles (Chapter 26), and also passive participles of verbs with a direct (not *prepositional)* object, are often used as predicates:

active: الوزير مسافر اليوم. *al-wazīr musāfir al-yawm.*
(= يسافر الوزير اليوم.) The minister is travelling today

passive: العربية مقروءة ومفهومة من العراق حتّى المغرب.
al-'arabīya maqrū'a wa-mafhūma min al-'irāq ḥatta l-maghrib.
Arabic is read and understood from Iraq to Morocco.

7. Vocabulary: اسم المفعول *ism al-maf'ūl*

Passive participle

NB: The note accompanying the vocabulary of Chapter 26 applies here.

متبادل *mutabādal* mutual
متوقّع *mutawaqqa'* expected
مستراح *mustarāḥ* lavatory
مستقبل *mustaqbal* future
مشترك *mushtárak* joint, common
معطيات *mu'ṭayāt* data
مقبول *maqbūl* accepted, acceptable
مقدّمة *muqaddama* preface, introduction
منشور *manshūr* (also:) notice, publication
مؤمّن عليه *mu'amman 'alayhi* insured

Exercise 1. Give the (m. s.) passive participle of:

e.g.: *ma'rūf* معروف ← عرف
muḥtāj 'ilayhi محتاج إليه ← احتاج إلى

1 مدّ	2 وافق على	3 ميز	4 شرح
5 فضّل	6 طبع	7 أكل	8 أعطى
9 استحقّ	10 فهم	11 باع	12 بعث ب
13 أوجب	14 رجا	15 رفض	16 أيّد

17 زاد عن	18 قرّر	19 استغنى عن	20 احتجّ على
21 اقترح	22 رقّي	23 استبدل	24 نسي
25 ذكر	26 صور	27 أنشأ	28 قرأ

Exercise 2. Complete the expression with the passive participle:

e.g.: *'iddat nuqaṭ madhkūra* عدّة نقط مذكورة ← عدّة نقط (ذكر)

النقط (أشار إلى) ← النقط المشار إليها

an-nuqaṭ al-mushār 'ilayha

1 المستشفى (افتتح) أمس	2 المساعدة (احتاج إلى)
3 مواضيع (تكلّم عن)	4 مقالات (طبع)
5 بين الأرقام (شكّ في)	6 بين الأرقام (كتب) هنا
7 الميزانية (انتظر) منذ شهر	8 أخطبة (ألقى) على الراديو
9 زبائننا (أمّن) في الخارج	10 من أجل الأعضاء (ذكر)
11 ناس (طلب من) مساعدتهم	12 إجراءات (منع) تحت القانون

Exercise 3. Read the passive participle, and give its source verb:

e.g.: *mawjūd, wajada yajidu* I وجد يجد ← موجود

1 مؤيّدون	2 منجز	3 محتاج إليه	4 مكتشف
5 مضاف	6 معطى	7 مؤكّد	8 ملقى
9 منشأ	10 مشتركة	11 محضّر	12 مستثناة

Which of these participles could, without pointing, be read as active? How would they then sound?

Exercise 4. Complete the passive expression:

e.g.: *al-ḥafr al-maqūm bihi* الحفر المقوم به ← الحفر المقوم ...

1 مساعدة محتاج ...	2 لشركة مسموح ... بالحفر
3 الإجراء الموافق ...	4 للزملاء المتّصل ...
5 معطيات مشكوك ...	6 المجرمون المشار ...

Exercise 5. Complete the predicate with an active or passive participle:

e.g.: أصدقاؤنا (وصل) اليوم ← أصدقاؤنا واصلون اليوم.

'aṣdiqa'una wāṣilūn al-yawm

المبدأ (فهم) عند الكلّ ← المبدأ مفهوم عند الكلّ.

al-mabda' mafhūm 'ind al-kull

1 جميع الطلاّب (اشترك) في التجربة.
2 الأرقام (أرى) في مقدّمة التقرير.
3 كانت الأسعار (انخفض) بسبب الوضع الاقتصادي الضعيف.
4 المدير (وافق) عليه.
5 المشروع (امتدّ) حتّى المنطقة الجنوبية.
6 الزوّار (مشى) في المدينة القديمة و(رجع) بعد قليل.
7 اسم وعنوان الطلاّب المذكورين (كتب) على الملفّ.
8 المكتبة (فتح) كلّ يوم خلال السنة الدراسية.

28 Naming the action

- Verbal nouns

1. Verbal noun – general

The verbal noun (المصدر *al-maṣdar*) is very important in Arabic. It denotes the action of the verb from which it is derived. In English, 'action' could be considered the verbal noun of 'to act'.

Although in principle every Arabic verb has a verbal noun (and some have two), not all the nouns are in common use. Also, some have unexpected or additional meanings.

The verbal noun has all the characteristics and functions of any noun.

2. Verbal noun, Form I

The Form I verbal noun is irregular. Here are the most useful verbal nouns (some already known to you) for the Form I verbs studied so far; first, those whose source verb is immediately obvious:

أخذ	*'akhdh* taking	أكل	*'akl* eating
أمر أمور	*'amr 'umūr* affair	أمر أوامر	*'amr 'awāmir* order
بيع بيوع	*bay' buyū'* sale	مبيع	*mabī'* sale
بحث بحوث	*baḥth buḥūth* discussion	تمام	*tamām* perfection, perfect, complete
حجز	*ḥajz* reservation		
حضور	*ḥuḍūr* presence	حفر	*ḥafr* drilling
حلّ حلول	*ḥall ḥulūl* solution	خوف	*khawf* fear
خروج	*khurūj* going out, exit	دخول	*dukhūl* entry
دراسة	*dirāsa* study	دفع مدفوعات	*daf' madfū'āt* payment
ذكر	*dhikr* mention, recollection	رأي آراء	*ra'y 'ārā'* opinion
رجاء	*rajā'* request	رجوع	*rujū'* return
رفض	*rafḍ* rejection, refusal	زيادة	*ziyāda* increase
زيارة	*ziyāra* visit	سؤال أسئلة	*su'āl 'as'ila* question

شرح *sharḥ* explanation   شكّ شكوك *shakk shukūk* doubt

شكر *shukr* thanks   طلب *ṭalab* request

طيران *ṭayarān* flight   عفو *'afw* forgiveness

عقد *'aqd* tying, holding   علم *'ilm* knowledge

عمل أعمال *'amal 'a'māl* action, work   غيبة *ghayba* absence

فشل *fashal* failure   فهم *fahm* understanding

قراءة *qirā'a* reading   قول أقوال *qawl 'aqwāl* saying

قيادة *qiyāda* leadership   قيام ب *qiyām bi-* undertaking

كتابة *kitāba* writing   كفاية *kifāya* sufficiency

كون *kawn* existence   مرور *murūr* passage, traffic

منع *man'* prohibition   موت *mawt* death

نجاح *najāḥ* success   نزول *nuzūl* descent

نشر *nashr* publication   نفي *nafy* denial

نوم *nawm* sleep   نية *niya* intention

وجود *wujūd* existence   وصول *wuṣūl* arrival

وضع أوضاع *waḍ' 'awḍā'* situation   وقوف *wuqūf* stop

Then those whose source verb (in parentheses) is less obvious:

حياة (حيّ) *ḥayá* life

مسألة مسائل (سأل) *mas'ala masā'il* matter

مطلب مطالب (طلب) *maṭlab maṭālib* request

معرفة (عرف) *ma'rifa* knowledge, acquaintance

معيشة (عاش) *ma'īsha* life

مهمّة مهامّ (همّ) *mahamma mahāmm* assignment

3. Verbal noun, Form II

All the increased forms make their verbal nouns on regular patterns.

All classes except final- and doubly weak; pattern *ta-ī*; doubled root letters separate:

تعليم *ta'līm* tuition   تجريب *tajrīb* test

تحضير *taḥḍīr* preparation   تطبيق *taṭbīq* application

تركيب تراكيب *tarkīb tarākīb* installation

تقرير *taqrīr* decision — تقرير تقارير *taqrīr taqārīr* report

تقديم *taqdīm* offer, presentation — تأييد *ta'yīd* support

تأكيد *ta'kīd* confirmation — تمويل *tamwīl* financing

تغيير *taghyīr* change — تمييز *tamyīz* discrimination

توظيف *tawẓīf* recruitment — توقيع *tawqī'* signature

A few Form II verbs, e.g. جرّب *jarraba*, have an alternative verbal noun on the f. pattern *ta-i-a*: تجربة تجارب *tajriba tajārib* 'experiment'.

Final- and doubly weak; pattern *tá-iya* (ending ة...):

تربية *tárbiya* education — ترقية *tárqiya* promotion

4. Verbal noun, Form III

All except final- and doubly weak; pattern *mu-ā-a-a* (with ة...):

مساعدة *musā'ada* help — مغادرة *mughādara* departure

مناسبة *munāsaba* occasion — موافقة *muwāfaqa* agreement

محاولة *muḥāwala* attempt — مفاوضة *mufāwaḍa* negotiation

A few Form III verbs, e.g. وافق *wāfaqa*, have an alternative verbal noun on the pattern *i-ā*: وفاق *wifāq* 'agreement'.

Final- and doubly weak; pattern *mu-ā-ā́* (ending اة...):

ملاقاة *mulāqā́* encounter — مناداة *munādā́* call

A few Form III verbs, e.g. نادى *nāda*, have an alternative verbal noun on the pattern *i-ā'* (with final *hamza*): نداء *nidā'* 'call'.

5. Verbal noun, Forms IV, VII, VIII and X

Form IV keeps its initial *hamza*; Forms VII-X keep their initial weak *i*-.

Sound, hamzated, doubled; pattern *'i-ā* (IV) and *i-i-ā* (VII-X); doubled root letters separate:

إرسال *'irsāl* IV despatch — إضراب *'iḍrāb* IV strike (labour)

انفجار *infijār* VII explosion — افتتاح *iftitāḥ* VIII inauguration

اقتراح *iqtirāḥ* VIII proposal — اكتشاف *iktishāf* VIII discovery

اتّخاذ *ittikhādh* VIII taking ابتداء *ibtidā'* VIII beginning
احتلال *iḥtilāl* VIII occupation اهتمام *ihtimām* VIII concern
استعمال *isti'māl* X use استثمار *istithmār* X investment
استئجار *isti'jār* X renting استئناف *isti'nāf* X resumption
استمرار *istimrār* X continuation استحقاق *istiḥqāq* X merit

Initial-*w*; pattern *'ī-ā* (IV) and *i-ī-ā* (X); Form VIII as for sound verbs:

إيجاب *'ījāb* IV obligation استيراد *istīrād* X importation
اتّصال *ittiṣāl* VIII contact

Hollow; pattern *'i-ā-a* (IV), *i-iyā* (VII, VIII), *i-i-ā-a* (X); IV and X end in ة... :

إشارة *'ishāra* IV sign, reference إذاعة *'idhā'a* IV broadcast
إضافة *'iḍāfa* IV addition احتياج *iḥtiyāj* VIII need
امتياز *imtiyāz* VIII distinction ازدياد *izdiyād* VIII increase
استراحة *istirāḥa* X rest

Final- and doubly weak; pattern *'i-ā'* (IV), *i-i-ā'* (VII-X); all end اء... :

إعطاء *'i'ṭā'* IV donation ادّعاء *iddi'ā'* VIII allegation
اشتراء *ishtirā'* VIII purchase استثناء *istithnā'* X exception

6. Verbal noun, Forms V and VI

All classes except final- and doubly weak; take the first principal part; change the *-a-* before the last root letter to *-u-*; drop the full-pronunciation ending *-a*:

تقدّم *taqaddum* V progress تأسّف *ta'assuf* V regret
تخصّص *takhaṣṣuṣ* V specialisation تردّد *taraddud* V hesitation
تداخل *tadākhul* VI interference تعاون *ta'āwun* VI cooperation

Final- and doubly weak (rare); weak patterns V *ta-a-in (at-ta-a-ī)*, VI *ta-ā-in (at-ta-ā-ī)*:

تلقّ\التلقّي *talaqqin/at-talaqqī* V reception

7. Use of verbal nouns

A verbal noun has the same type of object (if any) as its source verb. When a *direct* object is added to the verbal noun, the two are put into construct or into a prepositional structure with ل *li-*, see Chapter 7:

تطبيق قانون جديد *taṭbīq qānūn jadīd*
تطبيقهم لقانون جديد *taṭbīquhum li-qānūn jadīd*
the application/their application of a new law

A *prepositional* object added to a verbal noun keeps its preposition:

إشارة إلى قانون جديد *'ishāra 'ila qānūn jadīd*
إشارته إلى قانون جديد *'ishāratuhu 'ila qānūn jadīd*
a reference/his reference to a new law

8. Negative of verbal nouns

A verbal noun can be negated by putting it in definite construct after the verbal noun عدم *'adam* 'lack (of)':

عدم التعاون *'adam at-ta'āwun* non-cooperation
لعدم اهتمامه *li-'adam ihtimāmihi* through his inattention

عدم can also be used with a non-verbal noun, by interposing the verbal noun وجود *wujūd* 'existence', making a string construct:

عدم وجود الأموال *'adam wujūd al-'amwāl*
lack/absence ('non-existence') of funds

The connotation 'mis-' or 'wrong' can be added to a verbal noun by putting it in definite construct after the noun سوء *sū'* 'evil':

سوء الاستعمال *sū' al-isti'māl* misuse, abuse
لسوء الإدارة *li-sū' al-'idāra* through mismanagement
سوء فهمهم للقضية *sū' fahmihim li-l-qaḍīya*
their misunderstanding/wrong understanding of the case

9. Derivation from verbal nouns

Many relative adjectives ending ...ي *-ī* (Chapter 2) and abstract nouns ending ...ية *-īya* (Chapter 10) can be derived from verbal nouns. Examples:

تقدّمي *taqaddumī* progressive
استثنائي *istithnā'ī* exceptional
توسّعي ، توسّعية *tawassu'ī(ya)* expansionist, -ism
دراسي *dirāsī* academic
تعاونية *ta'āwunīya* cooperativism
عملي ، عملية *'amalī(ya)* practical, operation
استثنائي *istithnā'ī* exceptional

10. Vocabulary: المصدر *al-maṣdar* Verbal noun

NB: The most useful verbal nouns of Form I verbs already studied are listed in paragraph 2. Since the verbal nouns of increased forms are regular, this list shows only a few with additional or unexpected meanings, or derived from verbs not studied earlier.

استعداد *isti'dād* readiness
إصدار *'iṣdār* export(ation), issue
أخذ بعين الاعتبار *'akhadha* I *bi-'ayn al-i'tibār* to take into consideration
اعتماد (على) *i'timād ('ala)* confidence (in)
انقلاب *inqilāb* overthrow, coup d'état
تبادل *tabādul* mutual exchange
تدبير تدابير *tadbīr tadābīr* arrangement
تدخين *tadkhīn* smoking
تفاهم *tafāhum* mutual understanding
مقارنة *muqārana* comparison

Exercise 1. Give the verbal noun (with broken plural if any) of:

e.g.: *iḥtiyāj* احتياج ← احتاج   *khawf* خوف ← خاف

1 ناسب   2 شرح   3 خرج   4 تقدّم

5	رِكّب	6	قال	7	فشل	8	نجح
9	أضرب	10	وجد	11	حاوِل	12	أيّد
13	رجّع	14	زاد	15	حيّ	16	تخصّص
17	طبّق	18	ألقى	19	أضاف	20	جدّد
21	عرّف	22	استحقّ	23	تعاون	24	وظّف
25	ربّى	26	حضرِ	27	وضع	28	أمّن
29	امتاز	30	احتجّ	31	اقترح	32	اضطرب

Exercise 2. Give the verb from which the verbal noun is derived:

e.g.: استحقاق ← *istaḥaqqa* X استحقّ

1	إنشاء	2	تمييز	3	استكشاف	4	حلّ حلول
5	استغناء	6	إضافة	7	إفادة	8	ابتداء
9	احتياج	10	استغراب	11	معرفة	12	زيادة

Exercise 3. Put the words into columns as shown:

e.g.: معروف، عارف، معرفة

	active participle	passive participle	verbal noun
→	*'ārif* عارف	*ma'rūf* معروف	*ma'rifa* معرفة

1	مستحقّ، استحقاق، مستحقّ	2	حاجز، حجز، محجوز
3	مقول، قول، قائل	4	احتلال، محتلّ، محتلّ
5	محتاج، محتاج إليه، احتياج	6	معروف، عارف، معرف
7	تقديم، مقدّم، مقدّم	8	ملق، ملقي، إلقاء
9	زيارة، مزور، زائر	10	تأييد، مؤيد، مؤيّد

Exercise 4. Add the object to the verbal noun:

e.g.: حفرهم، البئر الجديدة ← حفرهم للبئر الجديدة

ḥafruhum li-l-bi'r al-jadīda

1	الفهم الكامل، الموضوع	2	الفهم، الموضوع الكامل
3	بسبب سوء قيادته، الحركة	4	الافتتاح الرسمي، المستشفى
5	اتّخاذ السلطات، إخراءات شديدة	6	تأكيد، تفاصيل الميزانية

7	تأكيد جزئي، تفاصيل الميزانية	8	احتجاج، خطاب الرئيس
9	اتّخاذ، إخراءات شديدة	10	لعدم ذكر، أهمّ احتياجاتهم

Exercise 5. Give the verbal noun which has opposite meaning:

e.g.: *ishtirā'* اشتراء ← بيع

1	نفي	2	دخول	3	انتهاء	4	حضور
5	فشل	6	كتابة	7	انخفاض	8	موت
9	إرسال	10	تعليم	11	مغادرة	12	استغناء

Exercise 6. We have not studied these verbal nouns or their source verbs. Work out the source verb and its form (II-X):

e.g.: *sallama* II سلّم ← تسليم

1	انضمام	2	تصفية	3	استنكار	4	تمدّن
5	إقامة	6	توزيع	7	اختيار	8	مناقشة
9	حوار	10	مقاتلة	11	اطّلاع	12	اتّحاد

Verbal nouns 8, 9 and 10 each have an alternative form. What is it?

(For the record, the source verbs and their verbal nouns mean:

1 to join/annexation, 2 to purify/purification,

3 to disapprove of/disapproval, 4 to be(come) civilised/civilisation,

5 to reside/residence, 6 to distribute/distribution, 7 to choose/choice,

8 to argue/argument, 9 to converse/dialogue, 10 to fight/fight,

11 to be aware/information, 12 to be united/union.)

29 Distinguishing – 2

- Comparative and superlative of derived adjectives
- ذو *dhū* with the comparative and superlative
- ممّا *mimmā*

1. Comparative of derived adjectives

Chapter 8 shows the comparative and superlative of simple adjectives. This chapter deals with *derived* adjectives, of two types:

- relative adjectives (Chapter 2), e.g. ضروري *ḍarūrī* 'necessary'
- participles of increased verb forms (Chapters 26, 27), e.g. متقدّم *mutaqaddim* 'advanced'

The comparative of these two examples is

أكثر ضرورةً	*'akthar ḍarūratan* ('greater in necessity') more necessary
أكثر تقدّمًا	*'akthar taqadduman* ('greater in advancement') more advanced

أكثر is of course the simple comparative of كثير *kathīr* 'much'. It is followed by the indefinite accusative form (Chapter 12) of the appropriate abstract noun, most often (not always) the source noun of the relative adjective or the verbal noun corresponding to the participle. The ending ةً... always gets its full pronunciation *-atan* in this structure.

More relative-adjective comparatives:

هذا الكتاب أكثر نظريةً ،	*hādha l-kitāb 'akthar naẓarīyatan,*
(for نظري *naẓarī* theoretical)	This book is more theoretical,
وأكثر فنًّا أيضًا.	*wa-'akthar fannan 'ayḍan.*
(for فنّي *fannī* technical)	and more technical too.

and participial comparatives:

أيّة مقالة أكثر تفصيلاً؟	*'ayya maqāla 'akthar tafṣīlan?*
(مفصّل *mufaṣṣal* detailed)	Which article is more detailed?

أفضّل شيئًا أكثر إفادةً. *'ufaḍḍil shay'an 'akthar 'ifādatan.*
(مفيد *mufīd* useful) I prefer something more useful.

هي أكثر ثقافةً من ابنها. *hiya 'akthar thaqāfatan min ibniha.*
(مثقّف *muthaqqaf* cultured) She is more cultured than her son.

In the derived comparatives أشدّ *'ashadd* is also used, less commonly, instead of أكثر. Diminishing comparison can be expressed with أقلّ *'aqall* 'less' instead of أكثر:

أسلوبك أشدّ\أقلّ تعقيداً. *'uslūbuka 'ashadd/'aqall ta'qīdan.*
(معقّد *mu'aqqad* complicated) Your method is more/less complicated.

Remember that the comparative is indefinite in meaning and invariable in form.

2. Superlative of derived adjectives

The superlative of derived adjectives is formed by making the comparative definite. This cannot be done using a construct, as it can with the simple adjectives. The superlative has to follow its noun:

الطلاّب الأكثر اجتهاداً *aṭ-ṭullāb al-'akthar ijtihādan*
(مجتهد *mujtáhid* hardworking) the most hardworking students

بالآلات الأكثر تعقيداً *bi-l-'ālat al-'akthar ta'qīdan*
with the most complicated instruments

3. ذو *dhū* etc. with comparative and superlative

See Chapter 24. The attributive word ذو *dhū* (etc.) can also be used in conjunction with a comparative or superlative:

شخص ذو علم أكثر للموضوع *shakhṣ dhū 'ilm 'akthar li-l-mawḍū'*
a person more knowledgeable about ('with more knowledge of') the subject

الشخص ذو العلم الأوسع للموضوع *ash-shakhṣ dhu l-'ilm al-'awsa' li-l-mawḍū'* the most widely knowledgeable person on the subject

4. ممّا *mimmā* than

Chapter 8 shows من *min* 'than'. من is used in this meaning only as a preposition, i.e. before a noun or with a pronoun suffix:

هو أكبر من صديقه\منه. *huwa 'akbar min ṣadīqihi/minhu.*
He is older ('bigger') than his friend/than him.

If the second half of the comparison has a verb, then من becomes the conjunction ممّا *mimmā* 'than (that which)':

يبيعون أقلّ ممّا ينتجون. *yabī'ūna 'aqall mimmā yuntijūna.*
They sell less than they produce.

بالفعل قال الوزير أكثر ممّا قرّروا في الصحافة. *bi-l-fi'l qāl al-wazīr 'akthar mimmā qarrarū fi-ṣ-ṣiḥāfa.*
In fact the minister said more than they reported in the press.

When a noun is compared with itself, and the second half of the comparison has no verb, the noun is suffixed again as a pronoun to من:

الأكل أغلى هنا منه في القاهرة. *al-'akl 'aghla huna minhu fi l-qāhira.* Food is more expensive here than in Cairo.

But if the second half has a verb, then we need ممّا as usual:

الأكل أغلى هنا ممّا كان في القاهرة. *al-'akl 'aghla huna mimmā kān fi l-qāhira.* Food is more expensive here than it was in Cairo.

5. Vocabulary

اجتهاد *ijtihād* effort, diligence
أكل *'akl* (also:) food
آلة *'āla* instrument, device, tool, machine
تعقيد *ta'qīd* complication, complexity
ضرورة *ḍarūra* necessity
فعل أفعال *fi'l 'af'āl* fact, act, action, verb
فعلي *fi'lī* actual, factual
فنّ فنون *fann funūn* art, craft
مفصّل *mufaṣṣal* detailed

Exercise 1. Give the comparative and superlative adjectives:

e.g.: *'aṭwal, al-'aṭwal* طويل ← أطول، الأطول
مفصّل ← أكثر تفصيلاً، الأكثر تفصيلاً
'akthar tafṣīlan, al-'akthar tafṣīlan

1 غني 2 مميّز 3 قصير 4 إيجابي
5 مفيد 6 سلمي 7 واضح 8 مثقّف

Exercise 2. Complete the sentence with the comparative:

e.g.: هم (مجتهدون، زملاؤهم).
← هم أكثر اجتهاداً من زملائهم.
hum 'akthar ijtihādan min zumalā'ihim.

1 في الماضي كنّا نسكن في بلاد (سلمي، هذا).
2 دفعت أنا (قليل، أنتَ).
3 دفعت أنا (قليل، دفعت أنتَ).
4 في هذا البلاد أهل المدن (محتاج، أهل القرى).
5 لا أعرف طالبةً (مستحقّة، تأييدنا الكامل).
6 يعرفون (كثير، يقولون لنا).
7 بعد الدورة الابتدائية سنبدأ دورةً (متقدّمةً).
8 لا شيء (بسيط ومفيد، هذه الآلة الصغيرة).

Exercise 3. من or ممّا? Complete:

e.g.: *ṭalab 'akthar minnī.* طلب أكثر، أنا ← طلب أكثر منّي.
طلب أكثر، طلبت أنا ← طلب أكثر ممّا طلبت أنا.
ṭalab 'akthar mimmā ṭalabt 'ana.

1 أعطينا أقلّ، استلمنا
2 هذا أحسن، رجونا
3 النتيجة أفضل، الشهر الماضي
4 النتيجة أفضل، كانت في الشهر الماضي
5 الجرائد أثقل في القاهرة، في بغداد
6 تقريره الآخر أكثر فعلاً، تقاريره السابقة

30 Revision – 2

- Verbs

Exercise 1. Give (a) the principal parts, (b) the m. s. imperative, (c) the m.s. active participle, (d) the m. s. passive participle, if any - with preposition if any, (e) the verbal noun and (f) the form (I-X) of each verb:

e.g.: كتب ← كتب يكتب، اكتب، كاتب، مكتوب، كتابة
kataba yaktubu, uktub, kātib, maktūb, kitāba I

1	تعلّم	2	عمل	3	اشترى	4	اتّصل
5	قرأ	6	احتاج	7	حاول	8	أرسل
9	انخفض	10	اهتمّ	11	درس	12	جدّد
13	صوّر	14	نوى	15	اعتبر	16	استبدل
17	طبع	18	نشر	19	تناوب	20	ألقى
21	أكل	22	ذكر	23	تذكّر	24	قال
25	أشار	26	أكّد	27	حلّ	28	اتّخذ
29	شكّ	30	أوجب	31	وجد	32	باع

Now make your imperatives of nos. 3, 5, 8, 20, 24, 25 and 32 (g) feminine and plural affirmative, and (h) masculine, feminine and plural negative.

Exercise 2. Put the verb into the present tense:

e.g.: نسيت (أنا) ← أنسى *'ansa*   أرسلناه ← نرسله *nursiluhu*

1	دخلْتَ	2	لم أنس	3	احتلّوا	4	ناسبهم
5	لن ينفوا	6	سأخرج	7	صاروا	8	اتّصل
9	أعلنّاه	10	تناوبتم	11	ربّيتم	12	أشار
13	استغربوا	14	أنجزوا	15	تردّدت (أنا)	16	بكى
17	رجوتم	18	خافت	19	دعونا	20	لم نبع
21	سيفهم	22	لن تقرإي	23	نشرتموه	24	وصلنا

Exercise 3. Put the sentence into the future:

e.g.: نخبرهم بالحقيقة. ← سنخبرهم بالحقيقة.
sa-nukhbiruhum bi-l-ḥaqīqa.

1 الزوّار حاضرون للمغادرة.
2 وصلوا على الوقت.
3 أشار إلى مقدّمة كتابه.
4 لم يزر البنايات القديمة.
5 كان يبيع كتب في السوق.
6 من ساعده؟ لا أحد اهتمّ به.
7 أنا مسؤول عنه.
8 وصل بعد وقت قليل.

Exercise 4. Make the verb singular:

e.g.: *fataḥ* فتح ← فتحوا

1 نمنا
2 ننام
3 تنادون
4 نويتم
5 تنوون
6 جئنا
7 تجيؤون
8 يحتاجون
9 اشترينا
10 يشيرون
11 زاروا
12 طرتم

Exercise 5. Identify the word as an active participle, a passive participle or a verbal noun, and give its source verb:

e.g.: انفجار → vb. noun, انفجر *infájara* VII

1 مدير
2 آكل
3 مفهوم
4 كاف
5 وفاق
6 وقوف
7 توسّع
8 مناد
9 إضراب
10 مأمور
11 مفتتح
12 استجواب
13 اقتراح
14 قراءة
15 وجود
16 تقديم
17 متقدّم
18 ارتفاع

Exercise 6. Make the sentence negative:

e.g.: اشترينا شيئًا. ← لم نشتر شيئًا.
lam nashtari shay'an.

1 ستجدون كتبًا جديدةً هناك.
2 جاء أحد من المكتب.
3 هل فهمت شرحه؟
4 امتاز ابني في المدرسة.
5 يمتاز ابني في المدرسة.
6 سينفون الادّعاء.

7 رأى الخبراء الفرق. 8 لماذا تركتم الاجتماع؟
9 هل وجدت الشرطة الأسلحة؟ 10 يوجد مبدأ أهمّ من هذا.
11 احتججت (أنا) على الادّعا. 12 قد ادّعوا جريمةً شديدةً.

Exercise 7. Make the statement (a) negative, (b) past affirmative and negative, and (c) future affirmative and negative:

e.g.: هو مجتهد في المدرسة.
← ليس\كان\ما كان\يكون\لا يكون مجتهداً في المدرسة.
laysa/kān/mā kān/yakūn/lā yakūn mujtahidan fi-l-madrasa.

1 الوضع بسيط. 2 الادّعاء شديد.
3 طلاّبي مهندسون مشهورون. 4 في الحكومة خلاف كبير.
5 اليوم اجتماع هامّ. 6 المحاضرة مفيدة للطلاّب.
7 اشتراكهم ضروري للنجاح. 8 الاحتلال غير قانوني.
9 أحسن طريقة هي الإضراب. 10 في المكتبة كتب قديمة.

Exercise 8. Put the parenthesised verb into the continuous past tense:

e.g.: (ذهب) الأطفال إلى المدرسة.
← كان الأطفال يذهبون إلى المدرسة.
kān al-'aṭfāl yadhhabūna 'ila l-madrasa.

1 (اتّصل) السكرتيرة بالوزير.
2 كيف (قام) المهندسون بعملياتهم بدون التمويل الضروري؟
3 (بحث) اللجنة تنظيم المبيعات عندما اتّصل المدير نفسه.
4 (لم ننتظر) إلاّ توقيع العقد.
5 ماذا (نوى) المدراء بخصوص تنظيم اليوم الافتتاحي؟
6 (عمل) الفنّيون على رأس البئر عندما حدث الانفجار.

Exercise 9. Add the right form of ما زال or لا يزال as appropriate:

e.g.: يسكن أصدقاؤه في القدس.
← لا يزال أصدقاؤه يسكنون في القدس.
lā yazāl 'aṣdiqā'uhu yaskunūna fi l-quds.

1 عملنا على رأس البئر.
2 أدرس المصادر العربية.
3 أنا طالب في القاهرة.
4 يبحثون الوضع المالي.
5 بحثوا الوضع الدولي.
6 كنت مشغولاً كلّ اليوم.
7 هل كنتم مشغولين أم فاضين؟
8 (نحن) فاضون، تفضّل.
9 احتجّ الزملاء على انخفاض رواتبهم.
10 أجد مشاكل في دراسة المزيدات.

Exercise 10. Form the active participle and make it agree:

e.g.: في الوقت (ناسب) ← في الوقت المناسب

fi l-waqt al-munāsib

1 أطفال (نام)
2 خذ (بقي) معك.
3 هو (غاب)، إسأل (ساعد)ه
4 ضدّ القوات (احتلّ)
5 هل تعرف (أرسل) المكتوب؟
6 للسياح (سافر) اليوم

Exercise 11. Form the passive participle and make it agree:

e.g.: المساعدة (قدّم) ← المساعدة المقدّمة

al-musā'ada l-muqaddama

المساعدة (احتاج إلى) ← المساعدة المحتاج إليها

al-musā'ada l-muḥtāj 'ilayha

1 العملية (قام ب)
2 جزء من التمويل (طلب)
3 تفاصيل (أشار إلى) في النصّ
4 نتائج (توقّع)
5 الحسابات (دفع)
6 إجراءات (احتجّ على)

Exercise 12. Make a verbal-noun expression on the pattern shown:

e.g.: *rafḍuhum li-d-daf'* رفضوا الدفع. ← رفضهم للدفع

1 دفع الحساب.
2 استلمنا رسالتكم.
3 قاموا بمشروع غال.
4 أشرنا إلى معلومات هامّة.
5 قرأت (أنا) العقد.
6 اتّخذوا إجراء إيجابي.

31 Starting with the subject

- Nominal sentences
- أنّ *'anna* and its derivatives
- Indirect statement and question

1. Nominal sentences

So far all sentences with verbs in this book have been verbal sentences, with the verb occurring earlier than its subject.

Arabic also uses the so-called *noun sentence* or *nominal sentence* (جملة اسمي *jumla smī*), in which the verb follows its subject and agrees fully with it, as in English. Compare these two sentences:

حضر المندوبون المؤتمر. *ḥaḍar al-mandūbūn al-mu'tamar.*
(verbal sentence) The delegates attended the conference.

المندوبون حضروا المؤتمر. *al-mandūbūn ḥaḍaru l-mu'tamar.*
(nominal sentence) The delegates attended the conference.

This nominal sentence is correct as it stands, but it is more usual style to introduce it with the conjunction إنّ *'inna.*

إنّ *'inna* adds no meaning to the sentence; it merely announces that a nominal sentence (in the form of a statement) follows. After إنّ *'inna*, the subject of the clause goes into the *accusative case* (Chapter 12):

إنّ المندوبين حضروا المؤتمر. *'inna l-mandūb**īn** ḥaḍaru l-mu'tamar.*

Further examples:

إنّ زميلنا يلقي خطاباً. *'inna zamīl**a**na yalqī khiṭāban.*
Our colleague is making a speech.

إنّ المشروع ابتدأ قبل شهر. *'inna l-mashrū' ibtáda' qabl shahr.*
The project began a month ago.

إنّ الموظّفين قد وافقوا على الاقتراح. *'inna l-muwaẓẓaf**īn** qad wāfaqū 'ala l-iqtirāḥ.* The employees have agreed to the proposal.

Examine now some variants:

إنّ المهندسين لا يحضرون.	*'inna l-muhandisīn lā yaḥḍurūna.* The engineers are not attending.
إنّهم لا يحضرون.	*'innahum lā yaḥḍurūna.* They are not attending.
إنّ المهندسين غائبون.	*'inna l-muhandisīn ghā'ibūn.* The engineers are absent.
إنّهم غائبون.	*'innahum ghā'ibūn.* They are absent.
إنّ المهندسين كانوا غائبين.	*'inna l-muhandisīn kānū ghā'ibīn.* The engineers were absent.
إنّهم كانوا غائبين.	*'innahum kānū ghā'ibīn.* They were absent.
إنّ المهندسين ليسوا حاضرين.	*'inna l-muhandisīn laysū ḥāḍirīn.* The engineers are not present.
إنّهم ليسوا حاضرين.	*'innahum laysū ḥāḍirīn.* They are not present.

Note:

- if the subject is a pronoun, it is suffixed to إنّ (e.g. إنّهم *'innahum*),
- equations (which are in fact nominal sentences) can also be introduced by إنّ (but see below); if so, the subject stands in the *accusative*, and the predicate remains in the nominative,
- when an equation is made negative, past or future, i.e. acquires a predicated verb ليس or كان, (Chapter 18), then the predicate still goes into the accusative following the rule for predicated verbs.

With equations, adding إنّ is not so clearly a preferred option; it is added mostly for emphasis or weight. Equations without إنّ are, as we have seen, very frequent.

When the sentence begins with إنّ we cannot omit a subject pronoun as we often can otherwise; the pronoun must be present in the form of a suffix on إنّ itself. For the first-person pronouns we have two possibilities. Here is the complete range of persons:

إنّني\إنّي، إنّكَ، إنّكِ، إنّه، إنّها؛ إنّنا\إنّا، إنّكم، إنّهم

'innanī/'innī, 'innaka, 'innaki, 'innahu, 'innaha;

'innana/'inna, 'innakum, 'innahum

Do not attempt at this stage to make a nominal sentence with a *dual* subject; this would require a dual verb and/or dual pronoun, neither of which we have studied.

2. أنّ *'anna* and its derivatives

إنّ is one of a group of conjunctions derived from أنّ *'anna* 'that'. The most important members of the group are:

أنّ	*'anna* that	إنّ	*'inna* (para. 1 above); that
(و)لكنّ	*(wa)lākinna* but	لأنّ	*li-'anna* because
كأنّ	*ka-'anna* as if		

The whole group is known in Arabic as إخوات أنّ *'akhawāt 'anna* 'the sisters of *'anna*'. They all behave similarly; any clause introduced by one of them follows the nominal-sentence pattern.

ولكنّ *walākinna* (less commonly, لكنّ *lākinna*) 'but' and لأنّ *li-'anna* 'because' present no complication:

طلبوا إضافةً ولكنّهم لم ينجحوا. *ṭalabū 'iḍāfa walākinnahum lam yanjaḥū.* They asked for an increase but they did not succeed.

رفضنا طلبهم لأنّ المحاسبين قد قرّروا ارتفاع تكاليف الإنتاج. *rafaḍna ṭalabahum li-'anna l-muḥāsibīn qad qarraru rtifā' takālīf al-'intāj.* We rejected their demand because the accountants had reported a rise in ('of') production costs.

The other three conjunctions shown are studied below.

3. Indirect statement

In reporting another's words, we have the choice of using so-called *direct statement* or *indirect statement.*

Direct statement quotes the speaker verbatim: 'He says: "I am working".' Indirect statement (also called reported statement) is commoner. It paraphrases the speaker's words: 'He says (that) he is working.'

After the verb قال يقول *qāla yaqūlu* I 'to say', the conjunction for indirect statement is إنّ *'inna*, which we encountered in paragraph 1 above, but which in this use expresses 'that':

يقول إنّه يعمل. *yaqūl 'innahu ya'mal.*

He says (that) he is working.

('that' can be omitted in English; إنّ must be present in Arabic.)

In Arabic the reported verb always reflects the tense or the timing of the original speaker. Compare the Arabic and English tenses of e.g.:

قال إنّه يعمل. *qāl 'innahu ya'mal.*

He said he was working ('is working').

قلنا إنّا سنحضر بعد قليل. *qulna 'inna sa-naḥḍur ba'd qalīl.*

We said we would ('will') be present in a while.

Similarly, if the reported statement is an equation, it remains so, i.e. reflecting present time:

قال إنّه مشغول. *qāl 'innahu mashghūl.*

(not: [كان مشغولاً]) He said he was busy.

إنّ *'inna* is the correct indirect-statement conjunction only after the verb قال يقول. After any other verb of reporting etc., the conjunction is أنّ *'anna*:

أعلنوا أنّ الطايرة وصلت. *'a'lanū 'anna ṭ-ṭā'ira waṣalat.*

They announced that the aeroplane had ('has') arrived.

أكّدنا أنّها متأخّرة. *'akkadna 'annaha muta'akhkhira.*

We confirmed that it was/is delayed.

Any preposition accompanying the verb of reporting is retained:

أخبرونا بالأفعال. *'akhbarūna bi-l-'af'āl.*

(ب *bi-* + thing-object) They informed us of the facts.

so also: أخبرونا بأنّهم يبقون. *'akhbarūna bi-'annahum yabqawna.*

They told us that ('informed us of that') they were staying.

The indirect-statement structure applies not only to speech, but to verbs of perception such as knowing, believing, hearing etc.:

يعرفون أنّنا نحفر. *ya'rifūna 'annana naḥfur.*
They know that we are drilling.

أعتقد أنّه قد فشل. *'a'taqid 'annahu qad fashil.*
I believe it has failed.

The conjunction كأنّ *ka-'anna* 'as if', although having nothing to do with indirect statement, nevertheless follows all the rules of indirect statement and is also best studied here:

كان يتكلّم كأنّه يعرفكم. *kān yatakallam ka-'annahu ya'rifukum.*
He was talking as if he knew ('knows') you.

4. Indirect question

Direct questions are studied in Chapter 13. Indirect questions expecting the answer 'yes' or 'no' are introduced by one of the conjunctions

هل *hal* (ما) إذا *(mā) 'idha* whether

سألنا هل\ما إذا\إذا سيؤيّدنا . *sa'alna hal/mā 'idha/'idha sa-yu'ayyiduna.* We asked whether he would ('will') support us.

For other questions, the usual interrogatives are used. Note that the tenses follow the indirect-statement pattern, and the question may retain its original word-order:

لم نعرف من المسؤول. *lam na'rif man al-mas'ūl.*
We did not know who was responsible.

اسأل لماذا تأخّرت الطائرة\لماذا الطائرة تأخّرت. *is'al li-mādha ta'akhkharat aṭ-ṭā'ira/li-mādha ṭ-ṭā'ira ta'akhkharat.*
Ask why the aeroplane is late.

and it may depend on a direct question, as in English:

هل عرفت لماذا يحضرون؟ *hal 'araft li-mādha yaḥḍurūna?*
Did you know why they were attending?

5. It is certain (etc.) that

Clauses like 'It is known/certain/clear that ...' introducing a fact, usually begin with ...من الـ *min al-* (which we do not translate into English):

من المعروف\الأكيد\الواضح أنّهم (كانوا) ضدّ الاقتراح.

min al-ma'rūf/al-'akīd/al-wāḍiḥ 'annahum (kānū) ḍidd al-iqtirāḥ.

It is known/certain/clear that they are (were) against the proposal.

Exercise 1. Recast the sentence, beginning with إنّ *'inna*:

e.g.: غاب الممثّلون. ← إنّ الممثّلين غابوا.

'inna l-mumaththilīn ghābū.

نحن حاضرون. ← إنّا\إنّنا حاضرون. *'innā/'innana ḥāḍirūn.*

1 كتب الصحفيون مقالات لشرح نتائج الانتخابات الإقليمية.
2 نشروا أيضًا أفكارهم حول الوضع السياسي للبلاد كلّه.
3 اتّفق مندوبو المؤتمر على أهمّ النقط المذكورة.
4 الخلاف بين أحزاب الحكومة أشدّ ممّا أعتقدنا.
5 هو أكثر اجتهاداً من الطلاّب الآخرين.
6 ما عدنا طلاّبًا عندما بدأت الحرب.
7 استأجرت العائلة بيتًا خارج البلد.
8 تظاهر المأمورون أمام البرلمان ضدّ ارتفاع الأسعار الأساسية.
9 خلال المفاوضات احتجّ الموظّفون على اقتراح قسم المالية.
10 قد حفروا عدّة آبار غير منتجة خلال هاتين السنتين.

Exercise 2. Rewrite as a verbal sentence where possible:

e.g.: إنّ المتظاهرين وقفوا أمام الوزارة.

← وقف المتظاهرون أمام الوزارة.

waqaf al-mutaẓāhirūn 'amām al-wizāra.

1 إنّ موظّفينا ينوون مفاوضة جدول رواتب جديد.
2 إنّنا لن نبحث المسألة معهم إلاّ بعد نشر الميزانية.
3 إنّ جميع موظّفينا قد أضربوا عندما سمعوا جوابنا.
4 إنّ المجرمين لم يأخذوا كثيراً من البنك، حسب الصحيفة.

5 إنّ الشرطة استجوبت شخصاً أمس.
6 إنّهم قد أكّدوا أنّهم لا يعرفون شيءاً عن الموضوع.
7 إنّ وزيرنا افتتح المصنع نفسة.
8 إنّ صحفيي كل بلاد يسألون ماذا حدث في بلادنا.

Exercise 3. Put into indirect statement or question as appropriate:

e.g.: أعلنوا: المشكلة محلولة. ← أعلنوا أنّ المشكلة محلولة.

'a'lanū' anna l-mushkila maḥlūla.

سألونا "هل ستذهبون؟". ← سألونا ما إذا سنذهب.

sa'alūna mā 'idha sa-nadhhab.

1 من مسؤول عن مثل هذا الفشل؟ إنّنا لا نعرف.
2 أخبرنا من فضلك. ماذا حدث؟
3 قد أخبرتكم به. المشرفون مسؤولون.
4 أكّدونا: سننشر النتائج في المستقبل القريب.
5 نشكّ فيه. سينشرون التفاصيل الكاملة.
6 ما زالوا يقولون "الوضع غير خطر".
7 اسألوا المشرف "هل وصلت الآلات الجديدة؟".
8 لاَ أحد يعرف: كان كم شخصاً في المشغل عند الانفجار؟

Exercise 4. Make statements combining one expression from each column (beginning the sentence with nos. 1-5):

e.g.: أكّدونا | الوضع غير خطر

← أكّدونا أنّ الوضع غير خطر.

'akkadūna 'anna l-waḍ' ghayr khaṭir.

1 سمعت (أنا)	6 تأخّروا
2 لا شكّ	7 ارتفعت التكاليف
3 جاء في الجرائد	8 المعلّمون مسؤولون
4 أخبرنا المدراء	9 ستتعاون كلّ الأحزاب
5 تشير النشرة	10 وجد الخبراء الحقل

Exercise 5. Add your own predicate to make a sentence:

e.g.: من الواضح أنّ ... ← من الواضح أنّها ذكية.

min al-wāḍiḥ 'annaha dhakīya.

1 كان من المعروف أنّ ...
2 من الأكيد أن ...
3 من الواضح أنّ ...
4 من المفهوم عند الكلّ أنّ ...

Exercise 6. Make these nominal sentences begin with إنّ:

e.g.: المشرفون كانوا غائبين. ← إنّ المشرفين كانوا غائبين.

'inna l-mushrifīn kānū ghā'ibīn.

1 نحن ضدّ الاقتراح الجديد بخصوص الإضراب العامّ.
2 صحفيو "أخبار الوطن" يعارضون الحكومة.
3 هي عملت سنتين في مدرسة ابتدائية.
4 عدد كبير من زملائنا اشتراكيون.
5 كلهم كانوا يؤيّدون الفكرة إلاّ ممثلي الحزب.
6 الموظّفون الصغار رفضوا التعويض. لا يكفيهم.

Exercise 7. Join the two sentences into one with the conjunction shown:

e.g.: لا نعرف. لم نتكلّم بعد مع المشرف. (لأنّ)
← لا نعرف لأنّا لم نتكلّم بعد مع المشرف.

lā na'rif li-'anna lam natakallam ma' al-mushrif.

1 كان يتكلّم. ليس عنده مسؤولية في الأمر. (كأنّ)
2 لم يخبرني بشيء إلاّ بهذا. ليس مسؤولاً نفسه. (أنّ)
3 ليس عندي علم بالأمر. سأسأل زملائي. (ولكنّ)
4 قال للجميع. يفهم كلّ شيء عن القضية. (? أنّ or إنّ)
5 أكّد للجميع. يفهم كلّ شيء عن القضية. (? أنّ or إنّ)

32 Modifying

- Adverbs
- Comparative and superlative of adverbs
- Negative of adverbs

1. Simple adverbs

An adverb (ظرف ظروف *ẓarf ẓurūf*) is a word modifying (i.e. describing or limiting) a verb, adjective or another adverb. In the following English sentences the underlined adverb modfies respectively the verb, the adjective, and the other adverb, all shown here in italics:

She *works* well. Her work is very *good*. She works very *well*.

The simplest Arabic adverbs are formed by putting the source word (most often an appropriate adjective or noun) into the indefinite accusative. Examples, from words already studied:

كثيراً *kathīran* much, greatly — قليلاً *qalīlan* (a) little
سهلاً *sahilan* easily — جديداً *jadīdan* recently
أخيراً *'akhīran* recently — أوّلاً *'awwalan* firstly
تماماً *tamāman* completely — عادةً *'ādatan* usually

Many relative adjectives form adverbs in the same way:

شخصياً *shakhṣīyan* personally — رسمياً *rasmīyan* officially
يومياً *yawmīyan* daily — سنوياً *sanawīyan* annually
أساسيًا *'asāsīyan* basically

Important adverbs from nouns not so far studied:

تقريب *taqrīb* approximation — تقريباً *taqrīban* approximately
مثل أمثال *mathal 'amthāl* example — مثلاً *mathalan* for example
خاصّة خواصّ *khāṣṣa khawaṣṣ* peculiarity — خاصّةً *khāṣṣatan* especially

and two from prepositions:

قبلاً *qablan* before(hand) — معاً *ma'an* together

Note also: كذا\هكذا\كذالك *(hā)kadha, ka-dhālika* thus, so
جيّداً *jayyidan* *well جداً *jiddan* very
(* no adverb is formed from طيّب *ṭayyib*)
In adverbs, the ending ةً... is always given full pronunciation, *-atan*.

2. Compound adverbs

Some adverbs consist of a preposition-and-noun phrase (sometimes definite, sometimes indefinite):

سرعة *sur'a* speed بسرعة *bi-sur'a* quickly
ضبط *ḍabṭ* precision بالضبط *bi-ḍ-ḍabṭ* precisely

An easy way to compound adverbs is with ... بصورة *bi-ṣūra* ... 'in a ... manner' :

بصورة رسمية *bi-ṣūra rasmīya* officially
بصورة خاصّة *bi-ṣūra khāṣṣa* especially
بصورة عامّة *bi-ṣūra 'āmma* in general, generally

and many others. It is a common formula.

All expressions of time and place, however formulated, e.g. اليوم *al-yawm*, هناك *hunāka*, are also adverbs.

3. Comparison of adverbs

For simple accusative adverbs the comparative adverb has the same form as the comparative adjective:

يسافر أكثر\أبعد منّي. *yusāfir 'akthar/'ab'ad minnī.*
He travels more/farther than I.
ولكنّه يتكلّم أقلّ. *walākinnahu yatakallam 'aqall.*
But he talks less.

Remember that the comparative is a diptote (Chapter 12) and cannot take the ending *-an*.

For the prepositional-phrase adverbs, add the comparative adjective أكثر *'akthar* to the noun (which must be indefinite):

بضبط أكثر *bi-ḍabṭ 'akthar* more precisely ('with more precision')

and for the compounds made with بصورة *bi-ṣūra*, make the qualifying adjective comparative:

بصورة أخصّ *bi-ṣūra 'akhaṣṣ* more especially

The adverb of degree 'much, (by) far' with a comparative is بكثير *bi-kathīr*:

أحسن بكثير *'aḥsan bi-kathīr* much/far better

The superlative degree for adverbs is best expressed with the comparative followed by an expression with e.g. أيّ *'ayy* or كلّ *kull*:

يقرأ أحمد أسرع من أيّ تلميذ. *yaqra' 'aḥmad 'asra' min 'ayy tilmīdh.* Ahmad reads faster than any (other) pupil.

إنّ الوزير يعرف المسألة أحسن من الكل. *'inna l-wazīr ya'rif al-mas'ala 'aḥsan min al-kull.* The minister knows the matter best ('better than all').

4. Negative of adverbs

Adverbs are negated with غير *ghayr* (see Chapter 23). The easiest formula is ... بصورة غير *bi-ṣūra ghayr* + adjective:

يتكلّم واضحًا. *yatakallam wāḍiḥan.* He speaks clearly.

يتكلّم بصورة غير واضحة. *yatakallam bi-ṣūra ghayr wāḍiḥa.* He speaks unclearly.

5. Vocabulary الظروف *aẓ-ẓurūf* Adverbs

ابتداءً من\اعتبارًا من *ibtidā'an min, i'tibāran min* with effect from

أبدًا *'abadan* at all, ever, (+ negative) not at all, never

الآن *al-'ān* now — دائمًا *dā'iman* always

على كلّ حال *'ala kull ḥāl* in any case

فورًا *fawran* immediately — قريبًا *qarīban* soon

Exercise 1. Give the corresponding adverb:

e.g.: *tamāman* تماماً ← تام

1	إيجابي	2	رئيسي	3	أقلّ	4	مستمرّ
5	شديد	6	أشدّ بكثير	7	حالي	8	طيّب جدّاً
9	محلّي	10	أوضح	11	حقيقة	12	جزئي

Exercise 2. Give the adverb with opposite meaning (using a negative if necessary):

e.g.: *qalīlan* قليلاً ← كثيراً

1	واضحًا	2	استثنائيًا	3	بصورة خاصّة	4	رسميًا
5	تقريبًا	6	كاملاً	7	أخيراً	8	قويًا

Exercise 3. Complete the sentence with an appropriate adverb:

e.g.: *'innahu yaktub wāḍiḥan.* إنّه يكتب واضحًا. ← إنّه يكتب ....

1	لا تتكلّم ...!	2	ينشرون الميزانية ....
3	رجعوا ... عندما سمع الخبر.	4	المدينة جميلة ....
5	لا يهم ...، سنستلم الجواب	6	قد طبّقوا الإجراء ....
7	سيخبروننا بالنتائج	8	... غير ممكن!
9	لماذا لم يخبر أحداً، المدير ...؟	10	احتجّ العمّال ....

Exercise 4. Make the adverb comparative:

e.g.: *'akthar* أكثر ← كثيراً

1	سريعًا	2	بالضبط	3	خاصّةً	4	جيّداً

33 Anticipating

- Verbs followed by the subjunctive or verbal noun
- Indirect command or request

1. Verbs of will, possibility, necessity

Certain verbs or verb forms expressing will, possibility or necessity, the most important of which include:

(a) أراد *'arāda* IV to want (to)

استطاع *istaṭā'a* X can, to be able (to)

فضّل *faḍḍala* II to prefer

حاول *ḥāwala* III to try

نوى ينوي *nawa yanwī* I to intend

(b) يجب (على) *yajib ('ala)* I it is necessary

يجوز (ل) *yajūz (li-)* I it is likely/permitted

يمكن *yumkinu* IV it is possible

are followed by the conjunction أنْ *'an* ('that') and a subjunctive verb (see Chapter 23) to express e.g. 'I want to ...', 'we can ...' and the like:

أريد أنْ أساعدكم. *'urīd 'an 'usā'idakum.* I want to help you. ('I want that I should help you.')

لا نستطيع أنْ نشترك. *lā nastaṭī' 'an nashtarik.* We cannot ('that we') participate.

نفضّل أن تحضره أنت. *nufaḍḍil 'an taḥḍurahu 'anta.* We prefer you to/that you attend it.

كانوا يحاولون أن يتّصلوا بكم. *kānū yuḥāwilūna 'an yattáṣilū bikum.* They were trying to contact you.

يجب أن يرسلها فوراً. *yajib 'an yursilaha fawran.* He must ('It is necessary that he') send it immediately.

يجوز أن يقولوا الحقّ. *yajūz 'an yaqūlu l-ḥaqq.* They may be ('It is likely that they are') telling the truth.

لا يمكن أن ينجح المشروع. *lā yumkin 'an yanjaḥ al-mashrū'.*
The project cannot ('It is not possible that the project should') succeed.
Note:

- the verbs under (a) agree with the subject; for أراد *'arāda* IV however the continuous past (كان يريد *kān yurīd* etc.) is used instead of the simple past:
  كنت أريد أن أساعدكم. *kunt 'urīd 'an 'usā'idakum.*
  I wanted to help you.
- altering the main verb (e.g. in tense) does not affect the verb following أنْ *'an*, which remains subjunctive. Further, the two verbs need not have the same subject.
- the verbs under (b) are always in the 3rd person s. form; for these also the continuous past (كان يجب *kān yajib*, كان يجوز *kān yajūz*, كان يمكن *kān yumkin*) is preferred to the simple past. See also paragraph 4 below.
- أنْ *'an* is quite distinct from أنّ *'anna* and its derivatives (Chapter 31). أنْ *'an* does not entail the accusative or take a pronoun suffix, and the clause following it has the structure of a verbal sentence, beginning with the subjunctive verb.

2. Indirect request and command

Direct request or command is the imperative, Chapter 25. Indirect request or command is expressed with a verb such as

أمر يأمر ب *'amara ya'muru* I *bi-* to order
طلب يطلب *ṭalaba yaṭlubu* I to request
رجا يرجو *raja yarju* I to request, expect
اقترح *iqtáraḥa* VIII to suggest

followed by أنْ (negative ألاّ *'allā*) and the subjunctive:

أمرناهم بأن ينسحبوا. *'amarnāhum bi-'an yansáḥibū.*
We ordered them to withdraw ('that they withdraw').

أقترح\أرجو ألاّ تجاوبي. *'aqtáriḥ/'arjū 'allā tujāwibī.*
I suggest that you do not reply./I request you not to reply.

اطلب أن يستأنفوا العمل. *uṭlub 'an yasta'nifu l-'amal.*
Ask them to resume ('Ask that they resume') work.

This last example shows an indirect request following a direct one.

The indirect-request structure can apply also after verbs with similar meaning, e.g. سمح يسمح ل *samaḥa yasmaḥu* I *li-* 'to permit, allow':

سمحنا لهم أن يشتركوا. *samaḥna lahum 'an yashtarikū.*
We allowed them to participate.

3. Use of verbal noun

It is very common, and often considered better style, to replace the أن + *subjunctive clause* with the appropriate definite verbal noun. Examine:

كنّا نريد أن نستبدل الماكينة. *kunna nurīd 'an nastabdil al-mākīna.*
We wanted to replace the machine.

كنّا نريد استبدال الماكينة. *kunna nurīd istibdāl al-mākīna.*
We wanted to replace ('We wanted the replacement of') the machine.

نوينا أن نجدّد العقد. *nawayna 'an nujaddid al-'aqd.*
نوينا تجديد العقد. *nawayna tajdīd al-'aqd.*
We intended to renew the contract.

إنّنا نحاول البيع على مستوى عالمي. *'innana nuḥāwil al-bay' 'ala mustawa(n) 'ālami.* We are trying to sell ('sale') at a world level.

سمحنا لهم بالاشتراك. *samaḥna lahum bi-l-ishtirāk* (NB ب *bi-*, see Chapter 25) We allowed them to participate ('the participation').

The subject of the second action can be made clearer with a possessive suffix on the verbal noun:

يجب تطبيقهم للقانون. *yajib taṭbīquhum li-l-qānūn.*
They must apply the law. ('Their application of the law is necessary.')

اقترح رفضهم للطلب. *iqtáraḥ rafḍahum li-ṭ-ṭalab.*
He suggested they refuse the request.

4. The third-person verbs

يجب *yajib*, يجوز *yajūz* and يمكن *yumkin* can show more clearly to whom or what they apply if we use a pronoun-object suffix. Two of the verbs take prepositional objects, the third a direct object:

يجب على   يجوز ل   يمكن + direct object

يجب عليه أن يؤيّدنا. *yajib ʻalayhi ʼan yuʼayyidana.*
He has to support us.

هل يمكنهم أن يفهموا هذه النقطة؟ *hal yumkinuhum ʼan yafhamū hādhihi n-nuqṭa?* Will they be able to understand this point?

and with a verbal noun:

يجب عليه تأييدنا. *yajib ʻalayhi taʼyīduna.* He has to support us.

يجوز لهم الرجوع الفوري. *yajūz lahum ar-rujūʻ al-fawrī.*
They may return immediately.

5. but

(و)لكنّ *(wa-)lākinna* 'but', which introduces a nominal sentence (Chapter 31) becomes (و)لكنْ *(wa)lākin* when introducing a verbal sentence:

ولكنّ المدير لا يريد أنْ ... *walākinna l-mudīr lā yurīd ʼan ...*
ولكنْ لا يريد المدير أنْ ... *walākin lā yurīd al-mudīr ʼan ...*
but the director does not want ...

Exercise 1. Recast the sentence as shown, using أنْ. All the sentences are situated in present time:

e.g.: (استطاع) أفهم الموضوع. ← أستطيع أن أفهم الموضوع.
ʼastaṭīʻ ʻan ʼafham al-mawḍūʻ.

1 (يجوز) يقترح شيئًا آخر عندما يسمع خبركم.
2 (يمكن) نقدّم شكوتنا للقاضي ولكن (يجوز) سيرفضها.
3 (يمكن) هل تشرحون تفاصيل العقد؟
4 (يجب) يعمل الجميع من أجل القضية العامّة.

5 (أراد ، نحن) يساعدون التلاميذ الجدد .
6 ألا (فضّل، أنت) ننشر مقالتك كمقالة رئيسية؟
7 (حاول) إنّ ممثلينا يفاوضون مع الإسرائيليين.
8 (نوى) سنخبرهم بأنّ الوضع اخطر ممّا ظننّا في الماضي.
9 (أراد ، الحكومة) تبدأ الوزارة تطبّق الضريبة فوراً.
10 (حاول) لا تبيعوا بضائع غير مفيدة للزبون.

Exercise 2. Do Ex. 1 again, nos. 1 to 9, putting the sentence into past time:

e.g.: أستطيع أن أفهم الموضوع. ← استطعت أن أفهم الموضوع.
istaṭaʿt ʿan ʾafham al-mawḍūʿ.

Exercise 3. Do Ex. 1 again, nos. 1 to 4, adding a pronoun or noun object to يجب , يجوز and يمكن:

e.g.: يجوز أن يرفض الطلب. ← يجوز له أن يرفض الطلب.
yajūz lahu ʾan yarfiḍ aṭ-ṭalab.

Exercise 4. Do Ex. 1 again, nos. 2 to 7, with a verbal noun instead of أن:

e.g.: أستطيع أن أفهم الموضوع. ← أستطيع فهم الموضوع.
ʾastaṭīʿ fahm al-mawḍūʿ.

Exercise 5. Put before each verb (a) نريد, (b) يريدون, (c) أستطيع, (d) تستطيعون , as shown. The whole expression has the same subject:

e.g.: ذهب ← نريد أن نذهب، يريدون أن يذهبوا،
أستطيع إن أذهب، تستطيعون أن تذهبوا
nurīd ʾan nadhhab, yurīdūna ʾan yadhhabū,
ʾastaṭīʿ ʾan ʾadhab, tastaṭīʿūna ʾan tadhhabū

1	استقبل	2	ساعد	3	بقي	4	زار
5	اتّصل	6	وافق	7	أرسل	8	أعطى

Now put يجب before each verb; make the subject of the sentence (a) هي , (b) هو :

e.g.: ذهب ← يجب أن تذهب، يجب أن يذهب

yajib 'an tadhhab, yajib 'an yadhhab

Exercise 6. Make an indirect command, beginning with (a) طلبنا, (b) نرجو, (c) أمرنا :

e.g.: يذهبون ← طلبنا\نرجو أن يذهبوا، أمرنا بأن يذهبوا

ṭalabna/narjū 'an yadhhabū, 'amarna bi-'an yadhhabū

1	تدخّل	2	تقول (أنتَ)	3	تجلسين	4	يرجعون
5	تتّخذون	6	تساعدوننا	7	تقفون	8	يبقون

Now add the person-object to the first verb :

e.g. يذهبون ← طلبنا منهم\نرجوهم أن يذهبوا، أمرناهم بأن يذهبوا

ṭalabna minhum/narjūhum 'an/'amarnāhum bi-'an yadhhabū

Exercise 7. Re-express the verbal noun with a clause beginning أنْ :

e.g.: لا يستطيعون شرح الموضوع.

← لا يستطيعون أن يشرحوا الموضوع.

lā yastaṭī'ūna 'an yashraḥu l-mawḍū'.

1 يجب علينا الاتّصال الفوري بمسؤولي الوزارة.

2 إنّ قسم المالية لا يريد إلاّ التعاون مع السلطات المناسبة.

3 هل يمكنهم الاشتراك الكامل؟ إنّنا نشكّ فيه.

4 حاولت السفارة عقد اجتماع مع وزارة الخارجية.

5 لا يزال الرئيس ينوي زيارته الرسمية في الأراضي المحتلّة.

6 إنّ المجلس لن يسمح للوفد الكامل بالحضور.

7 كان يجب علينا تأييد الحزب كلّه في مثل هذه المشكلة.

8 هل يمكننا تقديم لهم أيّ شيء؟

9 لم يستطع المقرّر كتابة مقالة مناسبة حول القضية.

10 إنّنا نحاول دراسة لغة مؤقّدة.

34 Intending

- Clauses of intent or purpose
- It is possible (etc.) that

1. Clauses of intent or purpose

Clauses showing intent or purpose are introduced by one of the following conjunctions, all meaning 'so that, in order that':

ل *li-* لأنْ *li-'an* حتّى *ḥatta* (لـ)كي *(li-)kay*

or the negative لئلاّ *li-'allā́* (NB stress) so that ... not

followed by a verb in the subjunctive. The purpose clause has the structure of a verbal sentence, beginning with the verb. The subjects of the main verb and the purpose clause may be the same or different:

شرحت العقد لأنْ يفهموه. *sharaḥt al-'aqd li-'an yafhamūhu.*

I explained the contract so that they would understand it.

أوقفنا الماكينة لكي نفتّشها. *'awqafna l-mākīna li-kay nufattishaha.*

We stopped the machine in order to inspect ('that we inspect') it.

دفعوا الضريبة ليساعدوا زملاءهم. *dafa'u ḍ-ḍarība li-yusā'idū zumalā'ahum.* They paid the tax to help their colleagues.

حاولنا المفاوضة لئلاّ يضرب العمّال.

ḥāwalna l-mufāwaḍa li-'allā́ yuḍrib al-'ummāl.

We tried negotiation/negotiating so that the workers would not strike.

We already know ل and حتّى as prepositions. As a conjunction, حتّى also means 'until', and the unfulfilled action stands in the subjunctive:

سنستمرّ حتّى ننجح. *sa-nastamirr ḥatta nanjaḥ.*

We shall continue until we succeed.

Distinguish also between لأنْ *li-'an* 'so that' + subjunctive, and لأنّ *li-'anna* 'because' (Chapter 31) which is followed by an accusative subject and nominal-sentence structure with a non-subjunctive verb.

2. Use of verbal noun

It is common to replace the *conjunction + subjunctive verb* (i.e. the purpose clause) with a *preposition + definite verbal noun*. The preposition is one showing purpose, e.g. لِ *li-* (most commonly) or من أجل *min 'ajl*. This structure can be used when the whole sentence has only one subject, and when the purpose clause is affirmative:

أوقفنا الماكينة من أجل التفتيش. *'awqafna l-mākīna min 'ajl at-taftīsh.* We stopped the machine to inspect ('for inspection').

أوقفنا الماكينة لتفتيشها. *'awqafna l-mākīna li-taftīshiha.* We stopped the machine to inspect it ('for its inspection').

This second example is more explicit, adding the object to the verbal noun as a possessive suffix.

دفعوا الضريبة لمساعدة زملائهم. *dafa'u ḍ-ḍarība li-musā'adat zumalā'ihim.* They paid the tax to help their colleagues ('for their colleagues' assistance').

See Chapter 33 for a similar structure replacing أَنْ clauses.

3. It is possible (etc.) that

Clauses like 'It is possible/likely/expected/not sure that ...' introducing an uncertain idea, usually begin with من الـ.. *min al-* + adjective and continue with أَنْ + subjunctive verb:

من الممكن أن يتغيّر الوضع. *min al-mumkin 'an yataghayyar al-waḍ'.* It is possible that the situation may change.

كان كم المحتمل أن يرقضه. *kān min al-muḥtámal 'an yarfiḍahu.* It was likely that he would refuse it.

هل من المتوقّع أن يجيؤوا؟ *hal min al-mutawaqqa' 'an yajī'ū?* Is it expected that they will come?

ليس من الأكيد أن يرفضوا الاقتراح. *laysa min al-'akīd 'an yarfiḍu l-iqtirāḥ.* It is not certain that they will reject the proposal.

(Contrast this with the affirmative example in Chapter 31, paragraph 5.)

Exercise 1. Join the two sentences into one with a conjunction, showing purpose,:

e.g.: كتبت الرسالة. عرفوا الحقيقة.

← كتبت الرسالة لـ\لأنْ\لكي\حتّى يعرفوا الحقيقة.

katabt ar-risāla li-/li-'an/li-kay/ḥatta ya'rifu l-ḥaqīqa.

1 استبدلنا ماكينتين. استمررنا في الإنتاج.
2 دجلت الشرطة البناية. فتّشت الشرطة عن الأسلحة.
3 إنّنا نتعلّم اللغة العربية. ندرس ثقافة العرب.
4 يذيعون صور المجرمين. عرف الناس المجرمين.
5 أوقفت قوات الأمن المظاهرة. لم تمرّ المظاهرة على البرلمان.
6 من الضروري أن ننتظر. ينشرون نصّ البيان.
7 أفضّل أن أبقى في المكتب. أستقبل زوّارنا عند وصولهم.
8 ذهب رئيسنا إلى القاهرة. سيلقي خطابًا هامًّا هناك.
9 كان يجب أن يخرج فوراً. لن نتأخّر في بيروت.
10 أرجوك أن تتكلّم واضحًا. يسمعك المندوبون جيّداً.

In which of your answers might you replace the purpose clause with a verbal-noun structure? Do so where possible:

e.g.: استعملنا آلات جديدةً لكي نخفّض التكاليف.

← استعملنا آلات جديدةً لتخفيض التكاليف.

ista'malna 'ālāt jadīda li-takhfīdh at-takālīf.

Exercise 2. Put ل before each verb to make the beginning of a purpose clause, with subject (a) أنا, (b) هي, (c) أنتم:

e.g.: ذهب ← لأذهب، لتذهبي، لتذهبوا

li-'adhhab, li-tadhhabī, li-tadhhabū

1	غيّر	2	حاول	3	اقترح	4	استغنى
5	صار	6	نسي	7	رأى	8	أرسل

Exercise 3. Replace the verbal noun with a purpose clause:

e.g.: *ji'na li-'an nu'ayyidakum.* جئنا لتأييدكم. ← جئنا لأن نؤيّدكم.

1 لم ننتج هذا النفط للبيع على السوق المحلّي.
2 هل اتّخذ المجلس هذا الإجراء لتأييد مصالحنا أم لا ؟
3 اشترينا جريدةً لقراءة مقالتها الرئيسية.
4 طار الوفد إلى دمشق لمفاوضة اتّفاقيتنا التجارية.
5 زرنا المدينة القديمة من أجل تصوير البنايات الجميلة.

Exercise 4. Add your own predicate to make a sentence:

e.g.: من المحتمل أنْ ... ← من المحتمل أن يضرب السوّاقون.

min al-muḥtámal 'an yuḍrib as-sawwāqūn.

1 من الممكن أن ...
2 من الضروري أن ...
3 يكون من المحتمل أن ...
4 ليس من الأكيد أن ...
5 كان من المتوقّع أن ...

Exercise 5. لأنْ or لأنّ ? Join the two sentences into one with the right conjunction, making any other necessary changes:

e.g.: عمل جيّداً. يستحقّ الترقية.

← عمل جيّداً لأنْ يستحقّ الترقية.

'amil jayyidan li-'an yastaḥiqq at-tárqiya.

يستحقّ الترقية. عمل جيّداً.

← يستحقّ الترقية لأنّه عمل جيّداً.

yastaḥiqq at-tárqiya li-'annahu 'amil jayyidan.

1 استشرنا الخبراء. كنّا نريد أنْ نعرف الحقيقة.
2 استشرنا الخبراء. نعرف الحقيقة.
3 استعمل الكمبيوتر. تجد النتيجة أسرع.
4 لم ينجح الطالب. لم يحضر المحاضرات الضرورية.
5 سافرنا إلى بيروت. زرنا الأصدقاء في الجامعة.
6 إنّا ندرس اللغة العربية. نفهم ثقافة واقتصاد العرب.

35 Relating

- Relative clauses

1. Definite relative clauses

إنّ الشخص الّذي كتب هذا صار مشهوراً.

'inna sh-shakhṣ allådhī katab hādha ṣār mashhūran.

The person who wrote this became famous.

هذه هي المجلة الّتي جاءت بمقالتنا.

hādhihi hiya l-majalla llatī jā'at bi-maqālatina.

This is the periodical which carried ('brought') our article.

هل تعرف الخبراء الّذين أرسلوا التقرير؟

hal ta'rif al-khubarā' alladhīna 'arsalu t-taqrīr?

Do you know the experts who sent the report?

A clause (see Chapter 19) is a group of words centred on a verb and its subject, and making at least limited sense. The clause beginning الّذي\الّتي\الّذين 'who', 'which' in each of these sentences is a *relative* clause. A relative clause is an extended adjective; it qualifies a noun (the *antecedent*) situated in the clause on which it depends. The antecedents in these examples are الشخص 'the person', المجلة 'the periodical' and الخبراء 'the experts'.

The pronouns الّذي *allådhī* who, which (masc. sing.)

الّتي *allåtī* who, which (fem. sing./inan. pl.)

الّذين *alladhīna* who (masc./mixed animate pl.)

are known as *relative* pronouns. They correspond in identity to the subject pronouns هو, هي and هم (Chapter 5) exactly. The relative pronoun begins with a weak letter, which does not carry or affect the stress of the word. Other relative pronouns (dual, feminine plural, shown in the Appendix) also exist but are too rare to concern us here.

In these sentences, the relative pronoun is subject of its own verb:

الّذي كتب	*alládhī katab*	who wrote
الّتي جاءت ب	*allátī jā'at bi-*	which carried
الّذين أرسلوا	*alladhīna 'arsalū*	who sent

When the relative pronoun is *direct object* of its own verb, the object is reiterated with the appropriate pronoun suffix on the verb:

الشخص الّذي لاقيته أمس مؤلّف مشهور.

ash-shakhṣ alládhī lāqaytuhu 'ams mu'allif mashhūr.

The person whom I met ('him') yesterday is a famous author.

المقالة الّتى كتبتها أمس تخرج قريبًا.

al-maqāla llatī katabtuha 'ams takhruj qarīban.

The article which I wrote ('it') yesterday is coming out soon.

إنّ جميع الخبراء الّذين استشرناهم موافقون.

inna jamī' al-khubarā' alladhīna stasharnāhum muwāfiqūn.

All the experts whom we have consulted ('them') are agreed.

Similary, when the relative pronoun is *prepositional object* of its own verb, we have the preposition with its appropriate suffix:

لن تخرج المقاله الّتى ذكر فيها الميزانية. *lan takhruj al-maqāla llatī dhakar fīha l-mīzānīya.* The article in which ('which in it') he mentioned the budget is not coming out.

المهدسون الّذين تكلّمنا معهم ... *al-muhandisūn alladhīna takallamna ma'ahum* ... The engineers to/with whom we spoke ...

A possessive relative ('whose') is expressed with the possessive suffix (Chapter 15):

سأعطيكم اسم السياسي الّذي حكايته جاءت في الجريدة أمس.

sa'u'ṭīkum ism as-siyāsi lladhī ḥikāyatuhu jā'at fi l-jarīda 'ams. I will give you the name of the politician whose ('who his') story appeared in the newspaper yesterday.

2. Indefinite relative clauses

The sentences shown above all have definite antecedents. With an *indefinite* antecedent, the relative clause has the same structure, except that the relative pronoun is omitted:

إنّه مقرّر يفهم العرب تماماً. *'innahu muqarrir yafham al-ʿarab tamāman.* He is a reporter who understands the Arabs completely.

هذه هي مقالة نشرها في الصحافة الوطنية.
hādhihi hiya maqāla nasharaha fi ṣ-ṣiḥāfa l-waṭanīya.
This is an article which he published in the national press.

قد نشروا تفاصيل مختلفة نستطيع أن نستغني عنها.
qad nasharū tafāṣīl mukhtálifa nastaṭīʿ 'an nastaghnī ʿanha.
They have published various details that we can do without.

شخص نمرته لا نعرفها ... *shakhṣ numratahu lā naʿrifuha ...*
a person whose number we do not know ...

The English relative pronoun can often be omitted at will: 'The/A man (whom) I know '; the Arabic relative pronoun is omitted only under the rule shown here.

Remember the use of ذو (etc., Chapter 24) which can often express the meaning of a possessive relative more simply:

هو شخص ذو علم واسعة. *huwa shakhṣ dhū ʿilm wāsiʿ.*
He is a person who has/having/with wide knowledge.

3. Relative ما *mā*, من *man*

ما يهمّنا أكثر هو ... *mā yuhimmuna 'akthar, huwa ...*
What ('That which') concerns us more is ...

لا أفهم ما يقترح\يقترحه. *lā 'afham mā yaqtariḥ/yaqtariḥuhu.*
I do not understand what he is proposing.

These are also relative sentences; the pronoun ما 'what' in the sense of 'that which' is both antecedent and relative pronoun rolled into one.

In these sentences the reiterated direct-object pronoun suffix can be omitted, and mostly is. But where the object is *prepositional*, the appropriate suffix must be attached:

ما وافقتم عليه غير مقبول. *mā wāfaqtum ʿalayhi ghayr maqbūl.*
What you have agreed to is unacceptable.

ما itself may be suffixed to a preposition, where the context demands it:

استغربنا ممّا جاء في المقالة. *istaghrabna mimmā jā' fi l-maqāla.*
We were astonished at what the article said ('at what appeared in ...').

فيما\عمّا أكّدوا... *fīmā/ʿammā 'akkadū ...*
in what/from what they have confirmed ...

The animate (i.e. human) counterpart of ما in such sentences is من *man* 'the person who', whoever'. The same rules apply as for ما :

من كتب هذا لا يعرف القاهرة. *man katab hādha lā yaʿrif al-qāhira.*
The person who/Whoever wrote this does not know Cairo.

لمن يهمّ\يهمّه العمل *li-man yuhimm al-ʿamal/yuhimmuhu l-ʿamal* To Whom It May Concern

الّذي and الّذين can be used, less commonly, in place of من in this usage:

الّذي يعتقد\الّذين يعتقدون هذا ... *alladhī yaʿtaqid/alladhīna yaʿtaqidūna hādha ...* He who believes/Those who believe this ...

Note also the structure ما ... من *mā ... min* with a definite noun:

يبيعون ما عندهم من المال. *yabīʿūna mā ʿindahum min al-māl.* They are selling what property they have ('what they have of property').

These relative structures should not be confused with the use of ما\من in *indirect questions* (Chapter 31, "لم نعرف من المسؤول." etc.).

4. Clause antecedent

In some sentences the whole first clause is the antecedent. In this case we add a neutral antecedent الأمر *al-'amr* 'the matter':

غاب المحاسب الأمر الّذي لم نفهمه.

ghāb al-muḥāsib al-amr alládhī lam nafhamhu.

The accountant was absent, which (fact) we did not understand.

Exercise 1. Join the two sentences, in the same order, into one relative sentence:

e.g.: هل نظرتم الاقتراح؟ أرسلناه إليكم.

← هل نظرتم الاقتراح الّذي أرسلناه إليكم؟

hal naẓartum al-iqtirāḥ alládhī 'arsalnāhu 'ilaykum?

1 كتبت أنا الرسالة. جاءت الرسالة في الجريدة.
2 إنّنا نستورد البضائع الكهربية. ينتجونها.
3 ينتجون بضائع كثيرةً. إنّنا نستورد بضائع كثيرةً.
4 من هو؟ ساعدكم بكتابة التقرير.
5 حضر المؤتمر مندوبون كثار. إنّنا لا نعرف المندوبين.
6 لم يحضر الاجتماع ممثّلو الوزارة. استغربنا منّه.
7 صار انفجار كبير. مات شخص في الانفجار.
8 لم ننشر اسم الشركة. فشل مشروع الشركة.
9 فاوضنا مع العمّال. كانوا العمّال يضربون.
10 سنستفيد كثيراً من الاتفاقية. وقّعنا الاتفاقية أمس.

Exercise 2. Add the correct relative pronoun, if any:

e.g.: قرأنا التقرير ... أرسلتموه إلينا. ← الّذي

qara'na t-taqrīr alládhī 'arsaltumūhu 'ilayna.

1 تسلّمنا تقريراً اقتصاديًا ... قد أصدرته الوزارة.
2 قد ذكروا نفس الأرقام ... ذكرناها نحن أخيراً.
3 هل تعرفون أعضاء الوفد ... سيحضرون المؤتمر؟.
4 ما هي المبالغ ... كان الرئيس يتكلّم عنها؟
5 هو وزير ... عنده مسؤليات هامّة جداً.
6 من هو المسؤول ... أرسلنا المقالة إليه؟
7 تبيع الشركة بضائع ... تساعد كثيراً اقتصاد البلاد.
8 عندهم خبراء ماليون ... يعرفون كلّ التفاصيل.
9 سنطلب مساعدة المحاسب ... وقّع التقرير.
10 شخص ... يقول كذالك لا يفهم المشكلة.
11 إنّ هذه نقطة صغيرة ... لا تهمّنا أبداً.

12 قد نسوا أهمّ نقطة ... ذكرها المحرّر.

Exercise 3. Add the correct preposition and/or pronoun suffix where necessary:

e.g.: الموضوع الّذي تكلّمنا ... ← عنه

al-mawḍū' alládhī takallamna 'anhu

1 المسؤول الّذي أعطانا ... الوثيقة
2 التفاصيل الّتي سألتم ...
3 حكاية يجب أن نشكّ ...
4 بضائع نحتاج ... بسرعة
5 زميل سألتم ... هذه التفاصيل

Exercise 4. Put together one expression from each column to make ten meaningful sentences (fifteen are possible):

e.g.: وظّفوا العمّال | الّذين كانوا يحتاجون إليهم

← وظّفوا العمّال الّذين كانوا يحتاجون إليهم.

waẓẓafu l-'ummāl alladhīna kānū yaḥtājūna 'ilayhim.

1 قرأنا التقارير	11 يصطنع هذه المنتجات
2 قد سمعنا أوامر	12 الّذي يصطنع هذه المنتجات
3 يمدّون المصنع	13 الّتي قرّرتها الحكومة
4 هناك مصنع	14 الّتي ذكروها في التقرير
5 عندي كتاب	15 الّتي حضّرها قسم الهندسة
6 اتّخذوا الإجراءات	16 نحتاج إليه من أجل المؤتمر
7 تسلّمنا تقريراً	17 لم نفهمها
8 لم نفهم الأرقام	18 أصدرها مديرنا
9 كتبوا أرقاماً في التقرير	19 وضعوا فيه تفاصيل جديدةً
10 هذا هو شيء	20 أكتب فيه تمارين اللغة العربية

Exercise 5. Make the antecedent and its relative pronoun plural:

e.g.: العملية الصناعية الّتي ... ← العمليات الصناعية الّتي ...

al-'amalīyāt aṣ-ṣinā'īya llatī ...

1 الشخص الّذي ... 2 الرسالة الطويلة الّتي ...
3 المساعد الفنّي الّذي ... 4 البيت الكبير الّذي ...
5 الشيء الأوّل الّذي ... 6 الإجراء الإداري الّذي ...

Exercise 6. Complete the sentence with **ما** or **من**, adding any necessary preposition:

e.g.: **إنّني أشكّ ... يقول. ← إنّني أشكّ فيما يقول.**

'innanī 'ashukk fīmā yaqūl.

سنؤكّده ... يشكّ فيه ← سنؤكّده لمن يشكّ فيه

sa-nu'akkiduhu li-man yashukk fīhi.

1 خبرونا ... وجدوا من الأرقام.
2 اسألوا ... يعرف أكثر.
3 اطلبوه ... مسؤول عن هذا.
4 ... يفيدنا اكثر هو تجديد العقد.
5 لا نستطيع المفاوضة ... يعمل هكذا.
6 لا نعرف شيئًا ... يسألون.

Exercise 7. Add your own words to make a complete relative sentence:

e.g.: **هو زميل ... ← هو زميل يساعد دائمًا الغير.**

huwa zamīl yusā'id dā'iman al-ghayr.

1 كان يجب أن ننتظر، ... 2 رفض السلطات الاقتراح ...
3 ... يريد أن يعمل ... 4 في البلد جنينة عامّة ...

Exercise 8. Read this passage aloud, then answer the questions on it:

اليابان تمنع إعلانات التدخين في الأماكن العامّة

طوكيو - تفيد الصحافة اليابانية أن الحكومة اليابانية تنوي تطبيق إجراءً لمنع إعلانات التبغ* في الأماكن العامّة مثل القطر ومحطّات المترو. وأفاد مسؤولون في وزارة المالية أن الغرض هو منع الشباب من اتّخاذ عادة التدخين. ومن المتوقّع أن السطات

تطبّق هذا الإجراء بعد وقت قصير، في جميع الأماكن العامّة باستثناء دكاكين لبيع التبغ.

(adapted from القدس العربي *al-quds al-'arabī* newspaper, 3.2.04)

* تبغ تبوغ *tibgh tubūgh* tobacco

1 ماذا تنوي الحكومة اليابانية؟
2 ما هو غرض الحكومة؟
3 هل إعلانات التبغ ممنوعة في بلادك؟
4 متى تطبّق السلطات هذا الإجراء؟
5 ما هو رائيك عن مثل هذا الإجراء؟
6 ما هو المترو؟ هل يوجد مترو في بلدك؟

36 Situating

- Clauses of time

1. Clauses of time

Clauses of time show when an action happens or a situation applies. They are introduced by various conjunctions, the commonest being:

عندما	*'indamā* when	قبل أنْ	*qabl 'an* before
بعد أنْ	*ba'd 'an* after	منذ أنْ	*mundh 'an* since
حتّى	*ḥatta* until	بينما	*baynamā* while
طالما	*ṭālamā* as long as	ما دام	*mā dām* as long as

The time clause has verbal-sentence structure. In the sentence the main and time clauses can appear in either order.

عندما **'indamā** is already known to us (Chapter 19). Followed by the past tense, it means 'when'. With the continuous past or the present tense it can mean either 'when' or 'whenever':

عرفتها عندما سكنت\كنت أسكن في بغداد.

'araftuha 'indamā sakant/kunt 'askun fī baghdād.

I knew her when I lived/was living/used to live in Baghdad.

عندما يتلاقون يبحثون السياسة. *'indamā yatalāqawna yabḥathūna s-siyāsa.* When(ever) they meet they discuss politics.

قبل أنْ **qabl 'an** 'before' is always followed by the subjunctive, whatever the timing of the whole sentence:

لم يوقّع الأمر قبل أنْ يخرج. *lam yuwaqqi' al-'amr qabl 'an yakhruj.* He did not sign the order before he left.

(This is the rule; you will however also find the past tense used when the sentence is situated in the past: قبل أنْ خرج *qabl 'an kharaj.*)

بعد أنْ **ba'd 'an** 'after' and منذ أنْ *mundh 'an* 'since' are followed by the past tense, whatever the timing of the sentence:

سنطبّقه بعد أنْ وقّعه. *sa-nuṭabbiqahu ba'd 'an*

waqqa'ahu. We shall apply it after he signs/has signed it.

تسكن العائلة في الخارج منذ أنْ احتلّوا الضفّة الغربية. *taskun al-'ā'ila fī l-khārij mundh 'an iḥtallu ḍ-ḍiffa l-gharbīya*. The family has lived ('lives') abroad since they occupied the West Bank.

(This is the rule; you will however also find the subjunctive after بعد أنْ when the action is unfulfilled, i.e. the sentence has present or future timing: بعد أنْ يوقّعه *ba'd 'an yuwaqqi'ahu*.)

حتّى *ḥatta* 'until', referring to an unfulfilled action takes the subjunctive:

انتظروا حتّى يصلوا. *intaẓarū hatta yaṣilū*.
Wait until they arrive./Wait for them to arrive.

(Compare حتّى meaning 'so that', Chapter 34.)

But referring to a *fact*, حتّى 'until' takes the past tense:

انتظرنا حتّى وصلوا. *intaẓarna ḥatta waṣalū*.
We waited until they arrived

بينما ***baynamā*** 'while' and طالما *ṭālamā* 'as long as' can take either past or present tense (or an equation) as logic demands. بينما *baynamā* can also mean 'whereas':

بينما\طالما يعمل تأكل عائلته. *baynamā/ṭālamā ya'mil ta'kul 'ā'ilatuhu*. While/As long as he works, his family eats.

بينما انخفض الإنتاج ارتفعت تكاليفنا. *baynama nkháfaḍ al-'intāj irtáfa'at takālīfuna*. Whereas production fell, our costs rose.

ما دام ***mā dām*** 'as long as' is a quasi-conjunction, in fact a negative predicated verb; see Chapter 18.

2. Use of verbal noun

As with other clauses, it is common to express the meaning of a time clause with a corresponding *preposition + definite verbal noun* instead. Some typical equivalents:

clause (conjunction + verb)	preposition + verbal noun
عندما وصل *'indamā waṣal*	عند وصوله *'ind wuṣūlihi*

when he arrived	on his arrival
قبل أن ينفجر *qabl 'an yanfájir* before it exploded/explodes	قبل الانفجار *qabl al-infijār* before the explosion
بعد أن رجع المدير *baʿd ʿan rajaʿ al-mudīr* after the director returns	بعد رجوع المدير *baʿd rujūʿ al-mudīr* after the director's return
بينما يغيبون *baynamā yaghībūna* while they are away	خلال غيبتهم *khilāl ghaybatihim* during their absence

3. Vocabulary: العالم العربي *al-ʿālam al-ʿarabī*
The Arab World

أبوظبي *'abū ẓabī* Abu Dhabi	الأردنّ *al-'urdunn* Jordan
الإمارات *al-'imārāt* Emirates	البحرين *al-baḥrayn* (f.) Bahrain
تونس *tūnis* (f.) Tunis(ia)	الجزائر *al-jazā'ir* (f.) Algiers, Algeria
خليج خلوج *khalīj khulūj* gulf	دبيّ *dubayy* Dubai
الرياض *ar-riyāḍ* Riyadh	السودان *as-sūdān* Sudan
ضفّة ضفف *ḍiffa ḍifaf* bank, shore	عمان *ʿumān* (f.) Oman
عاصمة عواصم *ʿāṣima ʿawāṣim* capital city	عمّان *ʿammān* Amman
غزّة *ghazza* Gaza	قطر *qaṭar* (f.) Qatar
قناة السويس *qanāt as-suways* Suez Canal	لبنان *lubnān* Lebanon
ليبيا *lībiya* (f.) Libya	اليمن *al-yaman* Yemen

Exercise 1. Join the two sentences into one, using the conjunction shown and keeping the clauses in the same order:

e.g.: نرسل الرسالة. وقّع الوزير الرسالة. (بعد أن)
← نرسل الرسالة بعد أن وقّعها الوزير.
nursil ar-risāla baʿd 'an waqqaʿaha l-wazīr.

1 لا ترسل الرسالة. قرأت أنا الرسالة أيضًا. (قبل أن)
2 استمرّت الحرب. ابتدأ أشدّ شتاء بذكر الإنسان. (حتّى)
3 بيتي بيتك. تحتاج إلى مساعدتي. (طالما)
4 نتعلّم شيئًا عن ثقافة العرب. ندرس لغة العرب. (بينما)

5 استكشفنا الحقل سنتين. وجدنا النفط بكمّيات* اقتصادية.
(*kammīya, abstract noun of كم kam. Make a guess.) (عندما)
6 ادرسوا الملفّ جيّداً. تبدأون المفاوضة. (قبل أن)
7 لا تنسوا أهمّية المصدر. تكتبون نصّاً عربياً. (عندما)
8 يجب أن تقرأ المقدّمة. تدرس تفاصيل التقرير. (قبل أن)
9 سنستبدل الزيت. نفتّش الطلمبة. (بعد أن)
10 لا تنس مصالح الزبون. تزور الزبون. (عندما)

Repeat the exercise for nos. 3 to 10, reversing the order of the clauses:

e.g.: نرسل الرسالة بعد أن وقّعها الوزير.
← بعد أن وقّع الوزير الرسالة نرسلها.
ba'd 'an waqqa' al-wazīr ar-risāla nursiluha.

Exercise 2. Re-express the time clause with a preposition + verbal noun, and vice versa:

e.g.: بعد أن وصلت الطائرة ← بعد وصول الطائرة
ba'd wuṣūl aṭ-ṭā'ira

1 حتّى ينتهي الإضراب
2 قبل أن يتمّ الدرس
3 بينما ينامون
4 حتّى توقيع اتّفاقيتنا
5 بينما ناموا
6 منذ أن ابتدأت المفاوضات
7 خلال احتلالهم للمنطقة
8 قبل ابتداء البحوث
9 عندما فتّشوا السيّارة
10 بعد أن نشرنا البيان
11 عند استقبالهم للضيوف
12 قبل مغادرة البلد

Exercise 3. Complete the time clause with your own words:

e.g.: استغربت (أنا) عندما .... ← ... عندما نظرت كيف الوضع.
... 'indamā naẓart kayf al-waḍ'.

1 لا تنتظري حتّى ....
2 بقينا هناك حتّى ....
3 هل عندك مشكلة عندما ...؟
4 تردّد قبل أن ....
5 يجب أن تفكّر فيه قبل أن ....
6 ينام الأطفال بينما ....
7 بعد أن ... سنرجع الى البيت.
8 احتجّ الطلاّب عندما ....

37 Stipulating

- Conditional clauses
- Concessive clauses

1. Conditional clauses – general

Conditional clauses show subject to what condition the sentence is true. We distinguish between *real* conditions, which can be fulfilled ('If it rains ...), and *unreal* conditions which are impossible ('If I had known ...') or unlikely ('If I were rich ...'). We can call the conditional clause the *condition* (الشرط *ash-sharṭ*, pl. شروط *shurūṭ*) and the non-conditional clause the *response* (الجواب *al-jawāb*).

2. Real conditions

Real conditions are introduced by the conjunction إذا *'idha* 'if'. The conditon most commonly has the structure of a verbal sentence, and its verb stands in *a past tense*, irrespective of the timing; the verb in the response can be in any tense:

إذا رفضوا نسأل القاضي. *'idha rafaḍū nas'al al-qāḍī.*
If they refuse we will ask the judge.

Note:

- *a past tense* here means the past, the continuous past, or the pluperfect (Chapters 18, 19),
- traditional grammar requires a past tense in both clauses, but in modern usage the choice is free for the response.

If the response begins with anything other than a past- or present-tense verb (with no negative or other particle), the clause is introduced by the particle ف *fa-*, which can be translated (if at all) by 'then'. If the response is a nominal sentence or an equation, it begins فإن *fa-'inna*:

إذا فشلت فحاول طلمبةً أقوى. *'idha fashilat fa-ḥāwil ṭulumba 'aqwa.* If it fails, (then) try a stronger pump.

إذا سمعت خبراً فستتّصل بنا. *'idha sami'at khabaran fa-sa-tattáṣil bina.* If she has heard news she will telephone ('contact') us.

إذا فشلت محاولتنا فإنّ الوضع غير ممكن.

'idha fashilat muḥāwalatuna fa-'inna l-waḍ' ghayr mumkin.

If our attempt fails/has failed then the situation is impossible.

ليس *laysa* is technically a past-tense verb but nevertheless it has ف *fa-*:

إذا كان الوضع كذلك فليس هو المسؤول.

'idha kān al-waḍ' ka-dhālika fa-laysa huwa l-mas'ūl.

If the situation is like that then *he* is not responsible.

If the condition and response are reversed, ف *fa-* is dropped:

هل سيعارضوننا إذا حاولنا؟ *hal sa-yu'āriḍūnana 'idha ḥāwalna?*

Will they oppose us if we try?

For the negative, ما is not used; the condition has لم *lam* + jussive, the response لم *lam,* لا *lā,* لن *lan* or ليس *laysa:*

إذا لم يعمل فلا يأكل أبداً. *'idha lam ya'mal fa-lā ya'kul 'abadan.* If he does not work he does not eat at all.

إذا لم يضربوا ندفع التعويض. *'idha lam yuḍribū nadfa' at-ta'wīḍ.*

If they do not strike we will pay the compensation.

Chapter 31 shows the use of إذا as 'whether/if' in indirect questions, which must not be confused with conditional sentences.

A much less common conjunction for real conditions is إنْ *'in* (not to be confused with إنّ *'inna*). It is now mostly found in set expressions like إنْ شاء الله *'in shā' 'allāh* (common modern pronunciation *'inshallah*) ('if God wishes'), equivalent to 'I/we hope (so)':

طيّب إن شاء الله. *ṭayyib 'inshallah.* Well, I hope?

Note also إن وجد(ت) *'in wujid(at)* 'if any (is/are found)', used so:

اذكر نمرة التلفون إن وجدت. *udhkur numrat at-tilifōn 'in wujidat.*

Give ('Mention') the telephone number if any.

وجد *wujid* is the m.s., وجدت *wujidat* the f. s./inan. pl.

3. Unreal conditions

Unreal conditions are introduced with the conjunction لو *law* 'if'. The verb in both condition and response is in a past tense (i.e past, continuous past or pluperfect). The response, when it follows, is mostly introduced by the particle لـ *la-*:

لو عرفناه لأخبرناكم. *law 'arafnāhu la-'akhbarnākum.*
If we knew it we would inform you.

لو كنّا قد عرفناه لقد أخبرناكم. *law kunna qad 'arafnāhu la-qad 'akhbarnākum.* If we had known it we would have informed you.

لو كان الحقّ لكان ممتازاً. *law kān al-ḥaqq la-kān mumtāzan.*
If it were the truth it would be excellent.

If the order of clauses is reversed, لـ *la-* is dropped:

عارضته لو استطعته. *'āraḍtuhu law istaṭa'tuhu.*
I would oppose him if I could.

A negative condition has لم *lam* + jussive, a negative response ما *mā* + past tense:

لو لم يغيبوا لقد عرفوا. *law lam yaghībū la-qad 'arafū.*
If they had not been away they would have known.

لو فهموا لما احتجّوا. *law fahimū la-ma ḥtajjū.*
If they understood they would not protest.

See Chapter 31 for 'as if', which is not regarded as a condition.

4. Concessive clauses

Concessive clauses show *despite* or *irrespective of* what condition the sentence is true. They are classed as conditional clauses in Arabic. Concessive clauses are introduced, inter alia, by:

حتّى ولو *ḥatta wa-law* even if	مَن *man* whoever
مهما *mahmā* whatever	كيفما *kayfamā* however
متى ما *mata mā* whenever	أينما *'aynamā* wherever

حتّى ولو ***ḥatta wa-law*** clauses follow the rules of unreal conditions:

حتّى ولو عرفنا لما أخبرناهم. *ḥatta wa-law ʿarafna la-mā ʾakhbarnāhum.* Even if we we knew we would not inform them.

The other introductory words shown follow the rules of the type of condition (mostly real) in which they are used:

مهما كان غرضه فشل. *mahmā kān gharaḍuhu fashil.* (real) Whatever his purpose was, he/it has failed.

كيفما عملنا تكون صعبًا. *kayfamā ʿamilna takūn ṣaʿban.* (real) Whatever ('However') we do, it will be difficult.

كيفما كنّا عملنا لكان صعبًا. *kayfamā kunna ʿamilna la-kān ṣaʿban.* (unreal) Whatever we had done, it would have been difficult.

Distinguish between من *man* 'whoever' used concessively and used relatively (Chapter 35). Compare:

من حاول فإنّ المهمّة تكون صعبةً. *man ḥāwal fa-ʾinna l-mahamma takūn ṣaʿba.* (concessive) Whoever tries, the task will be difficult.

من يحاول لن ينجح. *man yuḥāwil lan yanjaḥ.* (relative) Whoever/He who tries will not succeed.

Real concessive clauses (i.e. those referring to a fact) can also begin with مع أنّ *maʿ ʾanna* 'although' + a nominal sentence (which can be an equation), avoiding entirely the rules of conditional sentences:

مع أنّ المهمّة صعبة سأحاول. *maʿ ʾanna l-mahamma ṣaʿba sa-ʾuhāwil.* Although the task is difficult I will try.

Exercise 1. Join the two sentences as one conditional sentence beginning with إذا or لو as shown:

e.g.: يغيب. سنخفّض راتبه. (إذا) ← إذا غاب فسنخفّض راتبه.

ʾidha ghāb fa-sa-nukhaffiḍ rātibahu.

الشركة مسؤولة. نستغرب. (لو)

← لو كانت الشركة مسؤولةً لاستغربنا.

law kānat ash-sharika masʾūla la-staghrabna.

1 كانوا وجدوا بيتًا مناسبًا. استأجروا البيت. (لو)

2 يوافقون على اشتراء كمّيات كبيرة. نخفّض السعر. (إذا)
3 يضربون. نرفض دفع الإضافة. (إذا)
4 الوضع سلمي. يمكن الحكومة أن تعلن انتخابًا. (لو)
5 نعرف الأرقام بالضبط. نستعمل الأرقام لكتابة تقريرنا. (لو)
6 الشركة أغنى. نشتري طائرةً للمدراء. (لو)
7 المهمّة صعبة. اطلب المساعدة. (إذا)
8 ما زال يحتجّ. لا أحد يسمع. (إذا)

Rewrite answers 1 to 5, making real conditions unreal and vice versa:

e.g.: إذا غاب فسنخفّض راتبه. ← لو غاب لخفّضنا راتبه.

law ghāb la-khaffaḍna rātibahu.

Exercise 2. Make a negative condition with إذا or لو as shown:

e.g.: الوضع صعب (إذا) ← إذا لم يكن الوضع صعبًا

'idha lam yakun al-waḍ' ṣa'ban

1 نعرف التفاصيل (لو)
2 نستطيع أن نؤيّدكم (إذا)
3 تصل الطائرة الآن (إذا)
4 يوافقون على الميزانية (إذا)
5 استكشفوا الحقل (لو)
6 يستكشفون الحقل (إذا)
7 درست (هي) سنةً إضافيةً (لو)
8 يزور السيّاح البرلمان (إذا)

Now make your answers affirmative:

e.g.: إذا لم يكن الوضع صعبًا ← إذا كان الوضع صعبًا

'idha kān al-waḍ' ṣa'ban

Exercise 3. Add your own response at … :

e.g.: لو عرفنا ... ← لو عرفنا لأخبرناكم.

'law 'arafna la-'akhbarnākum.

1 إذا قرأ التقرير ...
2 ... لو لم يساعدنا.
3 ... إذا حضر.
4 لو احتلّت الشرطة البناية ...
5 لو لم تحتلّ الشرطة البناية ...
6 إذا حللنا هذه المشكلة ...
7 ... لو سمحت
8 ... إذا كان عندنا الوقت.

Exercise 4. Reverse the order of the two clauses:

e.g.: إذا حضر فنتكلّم معه. ← نتكلّم معه إذا حضر.

natakallam ma'ahu 'idha ḥaḍar.

1 لا تتردّد أنْ تطلب المساعدة إذا احتجت إليها.
2 لو كانوا قد حضروا المؤتمر لكنت تكلّمت معهم.
3 قد أرسلنا لكم نسخةً لو كان عندي عنوانكم.
4 مهما كنتم تحتاجون إليه نؤيّدكم دائمًا.
5 سنزور المنطقة الساحلية إيضًا إذا كان عندنا وقت كاف.
6 يكلّفهم أكثر كيفما عملوا.

Exercise 5. Complete the concessive clause with your own words:

e.g.: حتّى ولو ... لما تغيّر شيء. ← حتّى ولو دفعت أكثر ...

ḥatta wa-law dafa't 'akthar la-mā taghayyar shay'

1 مع أنّ ... لأستمررت أدرس. 2 أينما ... نجد الجيش.
3 متى ما ... فإنّا حاضرون. 4 مهما ... فلا أصدّقه.

Exercise 6. Read the passage and answer the questions:

تبدأ المدارس السعودية، في السنة الدراسية المقبلة (1) تدريس اللغة الإنكليزية اعتبارًا من الصفّ السادس (2) الابتدائي كمادّة أساسية، تنفيذًا لقرار (3) مجلس الوزراء في هذا الأمر. ويفيد مصدر "الحياة" أنّ وزير التربية والتعليم محمّد الرشيد *(muḥammad ar-rashīd)* أصدر تعليماته إلى إدارات التربية والتعليم (للبنين (4) والبنات) لتطبيق القرار الوزاري اعتبارًا من السنة الدراسية المقبلة.

(adapted from الحياة *al-ḥayā* newspaper, 21.5.04)

(1) مقبل *muqbil* next (2) سادس *sādis* sixth (3) تنفيذًا لقرار *tanfīdhan li-qarār* in implementation of the resolution (4) للبنين *li-l-banīn* for boys

1 ما هو رأيك حول هذه الخبر؟ هل هذه خطوة إيجابية؟
2 ما هي أهمّية تدريس اللغات بصورة عامّة؟
3 كيف صارت اللغة الإنكليزية أهمّ لغة في العالم الحديث؟
4 متي سيبدأ إنجاز القرار الوزاري؟

38 Counting

- Numerals; cardinal and ordinal numbers

1. Numerals

The Arabic numerals are shown below:

١	٢	٣	٤	٥	٦	٧	٨	٩	٠
1	2	3	4	5	6	7	8	9	0

European numerals are used in Northwest Africa, and in some newspapers and other documents throughout the Arab world.

Numerals are written *left to right* → in compounds: ٢٠٤٦٨ 20468.

2. Cardinal numbers

Cardinal numbers ('1, 2, 3 ...') are those used in counting and quantifying. Their written forms as words are so complicated that even educated Arabs prefer to use a simplified version. Common simplified forms are given below; paragraphs 2 to 4 relate to these forms. You are advised to use this pronunciation when reading aloud (regardless of the varied spelling encountered), and to write numbers with numerals:

١	*wāḥid, wāḥida* m./f.	٢	*ithnayn, thintayn* m./f.	٣	*thalātha*
٤	*'arba'a*	٥	*khamsa*	٦	*sitta*
٧	*sab'a*	٨	*thamāniya*	٩	*tis'a*
١٠	*'ashara*	١١	*'iḥd'ashar*	١٢	*ithn'ashar*
١٣	*thalatt'ashar*	١٤	*'arba't'ashar*	١٥	*khamst'ashar*
١٦	*sitt'ashar*	١٧	*sab'at'ashar*	١٨	*thamant'ashar*
١٩	*tis'at'ashar*	٢٠	*'ishrīn*	٢١	*wāḥid(a) u-'ishrīn*
٢٣	*thalātha u-'ishrīn*	٣٠	*thalāthīn*	٤٠	*'arba'īn*
٥٠	*khamsīn*	٦٠	*sittīn*	٧٠	*sab'īn*
٨٠	*thamānīn*	٩٠	*tis'īn*	١٠٠	*mīya*
١٤٥	*mīya u-khamsa u-'arba'īn*			٢٠٠	*mitayn*

٣٠٠	*thalāth mīya*	٤٠٠	*'arbaʿ mīya*	٥٠٠	*khams mīya*
٦٠٠	*sitt mīya*	٧٠٠	*sabaʿ mīya*	٨٠٠	*thamān mīya*
٩٠٠	*tisaʿ mīya*	١٠٠٠	*'alf*	٢٠٠٠	*'alfayn*

٣٠٠٠ ... ١٠٠٠٠ } *thalāthat 'ālāf, 'arbaʿat 'ālāf, khamsat 'ālāf, sittat 'ālāf, sabʿat 'ālāf, thamāniyat 'ālāf, tisʿat 'ālāf, ʿasharat 'ālāf*

١٠٠٠٠٠ *mīt 'alf* ١٠٠٠٠٠٠ *milyūn*

٢٠٠٠٠٠٠ *milyūnayn* ٣٠٠٠٠٠٠ *thalātha malāyīn*

Note:

- In counting with no noun, the masc. forms of 1 and 2 are used *(wāḥid, ithnayn ...)*. For quantifying a noun, see below.
- Compound numbers are built as in English, except that units precede tens. Elements are connected with و 'and', pronounced *u*.
- *mīya, 'alf* and *milyūn* are nouns, pl. *mi'āt, 'ulūf, malāyīn* when used in indeterminate quantities:

  مئات\ألوف\ملايين من الناس\منهم *mi'āt, 'ulūf, malāyīn min an-nās, minhum* hundreds/thousands/millions of people/of them
- decimal values are written and read so:

  ٤،٨٥ *'arbaʿa nuqṭa/faṣla khamsa u-thamānīn* 4·85

3. Quantifying a noun: one and two

Since 'one' and 'two' are already shown by the singular or dual respectively, numbers 1 and 2 are used only for emphasis. These numbers then behave like a singular and dual adjective respectively:

معلمة واحدة ولا أكثر *muʿallima wāḥida wa-lā 'akthar*
one teacher and no more

للشخصين الاثنين فقط *li-sh-shakhṣayn al-ithnayn faqaṭ*
for the two people only

4. Quantifying a noun: more than two

Numbers higher than 2 do not change for gender.

Indefinite noun expressions. With a number higher than 2 quantifying an *indefinite* noun or noun expression, the number precedes, and the noun or noun expression takes the following form, whatever its grammatical function in the sentence:

- after 3 to 10, the *genitive plural*:

  غاب أربعة مهندسين مصريين. *ghāb 'arba'a muhandisīn miṣrīyīn.* Four Egyptian engineers stayed away.

  Before a plural beginning with *hamza* it is common to pronounce *-t* at the end of the number 3 to 10:

  ثلاثة أيام *thalāthat 'ayyām* three days

- after 11 to 99, the *accusative singular*:

  مع خمسة عشر طلاّبًا أجنبيًا *ma' khamst'ashar ṭullāban 'ajnabīyan* with fifteen foreign students

  but *'alf* and *milyūn* (both are nouns) do not change after 11 to 99.

- after a round number of hundreds, thousand or millions, the *genitive singular*; *mīya* before a noun becomes *mīt*, and its dual (*mitayn*) drops its *-n*, as in the theme of a construct:

  تظاهر مئة ألف شخص تقريبًا. *taẓahar mīt 'alf shakhṣ taqrīban.* About a hundred thousand people demonstrated.

  أكثر من مئة\مئتي دينار *'akthar min mīt/mitay dīnār* more than one/two hundred dinars

The noun takes the form dictated by the last number preceding it:

مئة جنيه مصري *mīt jinayh miṣrī* £100 Egyptian

مئة وعشرة جنيهات مصرية *mīya u-'ashara jinayhāt miṣrīya* £110 Egyptian

خمس مرّات *khamsa marrāt* five times

خمس وعشرين مرّةً *khamsa u-'ishrīn marra* 25 times

Definite noun expressions. A number quantifying a *definite* noun expression behaves like an adjective, and none of the above applies:

للكتب المئة وخمسين. *li-l-kutub al-mīya u-khamsīn*

for the 150 books
قرأوا تقاريري الثلاثة. *qara'ū taqārīri th-thalātha.*
They read my three reports.

5. Ordinal numbers

Ordinal numbers ('first, second ...') show a place in a sequence:

أوّل	*'awwal* 1st	ثانٍ\الثاني	*thānin, ath-thānī* (weak) 2nd		
ثالث	*thālith* 3rd	رابع	*rābi'* 4th	خامس	*khāmis* 5th
سادس	*sādis* 6th	سابع	*sābi'* 7th	ثامن	*thāmin* 8th
تاسع	*tāsi'* 9th	عاشر	*'āshir* 10th		

These are used like superlative adjectives, see Chapter 8. Only أوّل has a special definite feminine form (Chapter 8 also); الثاني has f. الثانية *ath-thāniya*. The other feminines are regular:

أوّل مرّة\المرّة الأولى *'awwal marra, al-marra l-'ūla*
the first time
ثاني وثيقة\الوثيقة الثانية *thānī wathīqa, al-wathīqa th-thāniya*
the third document
رابع سنة\السنة الرابعة *rābi' sana, as-sana r-rābi'a*
the fourth year
عاشر مرشّح\المرشّح العاشر *'āshir murashshaḥ, al-murashshaḥ al-'āshir* the tenth candidate

Higher ordinals are all used as definite adjectives:

الحادي عشر، الحادية عشرة m. *al-ḥādī 'ashar,*
(not [الأوّل ...]) f. *al-ḥādiya 'ashra* (NB) the 11th
الثاني عشر، الثانية عشرة m. *ath-thānī 'ashar,*
f. *ath-thāniya 'ashra* the 12th (etc.)

The tens '20th' to '90th' have the form of masculine sound plurals:

العشرون\ين ... التسعون\ين *al-'ishrūn/-īn ... at-tis'ūn/-īn*
الخامس\الخامسة والثلاثون *al-khāmis(a) wa-th-thalāthūn* 35th
and note: المئة، الألف *al-mīya, al-'alf* 100th/1000th (m./f.)

Ordinal numbers can be written with words only, not with numerals.

6. Vocabulary: القياسات والنقود *al-qiyāsāt wa-n-nuqūd*

Measurement and money

أي *'ay* i.e., that is to say	جنيه *jinayh* pound (£)
درجة *daraja* degree	دولار *dōlār* dollar
دينار دنانير *dīnār danānīr* dinar	ريال *riyāl* rial, riyal
سنتيمتر ، سم *santimitr* centimetre, cm	طنّ أطنان *ṭunn 'aṭnān* ton
غرام ، غم *gram* gram, gm	قياس *qiyās* measurement
كيلو(غرام) ، كغ *kīlō(gram)* kilo(gram), kg	
كيلومتر ، كم *kīlōmitr* kilometre, km	
لتر *litr* litre	ليرة *līra* lira
متر أمتار ، م *mitr 'amtār* metre, m	مرّة *marra* a time
بالمئة (٪) *bi-l-mīya* per cent (%)	يورو *yūrō* euro

Exercise 1. Count aloud (a) in ones from ١ to ٣٠, (b) in tens from ٤٠ to ١٠٠, (c) in hundreds from ٢٠٠ to ١٠٠٠, (d) in thousands from ٢٠٠٠ to ١٠٠٠٠.

Exercise 2. Put the noun (+ adjective if any) with the number:

e.g.: *mīya u-khamsat 'ashkhāṣ* ← ١٠٥ (شخص)

١ ٢٠٠ (متر)	٢ ٣٥ (دينار كويتي)
٣ ٤ (يوم)	٤ ١٠ (دولار)
٥ ١٤ (يوم فاض)	٦ ٢٥ (شخص فاض)
٧ ٣٠٤ (جنيه مصري)	٨ ١٢ (كيلومتر)
٩ ١٤٢ (ريال سعودي)	١٠ ٣٠٠٠ (ليرة لبنانية)

Exercise 3. Put (a) ٨, (b) ١٦, and (c) ١٠٠ before the expression:

e.g.: شخص ← ٨ أشخاص، ١٦ شخصًا، ١٠٠ شخص

thamāniyat 'ashkhāṣ, sitt'ashar shakhṣan, mīt shakhṣ

١ جنيه مصري	٢ دولار أمريكي
٣ مرّة	٤ كتاب عربي
٥ سؤال	٦ مرشّح أجنبي
٧ تقرير فنّي	٨ متر
٩ ريال قطري	١٠ تلميذ لبناني جديد

Exercise 4. Put the number into ordinal form and read the expression:

e.g.: مرّة (٣) ← ثالث مرّة\المرّة الثالثة

thālith marra, al-marra th-thālitha

١ شارع (٢)	٢ درس (٦)
٣ سنة (١)	٤ تمارين (٤ و٥)
٥ سيّارة (١٢)	٦ بئر (٢١)

Exercise 5. Read the passage and answer the questions:

بيكين – قال مسؤول كبير في معهد (1) حكومي لأبحاث (2) الطاقة أمس أن من المتوقّع أن تستهلك (3) الصين ٢٨٠ مليون طنّ من النفط هذه السنة أي ٥،٧٤ مليون برميل (4) يوميًا بزيادة سنوية تبلغ ٧٫٧ بالمئة. وقال نائب المدير العامّ لمعهد أبحاث الطاقة أن الصين، سادس أكبر اقتصاد في العالم، استهلكت ٢٦٠ مليون طنّ أي ٥،٣٤ مليون برميل يوميًا من النفط في سنة ٢٠٠٣. وهذه الأرقام هي أوّل أرقام نشرها مصدر صيني متّصل (5) بالحكومة.

(adapted from القدس العربي *al-quds al-'arabī*, 21.5.04)

(1) معهد معاهد *ma'had ma'āhid* institute; (2) بحث أبحاث *baḥth 'abḥāth* (re)search; (3) استهلك *istahlaka* X to consume; (4) برميل براميل *barmīl barāmīl* barrel; (5) متّصل *muttásil* connected

١ من أصدر هذه الأرقام؟ ٢ ما هي أهمّية هذه الأرقام؟

٣ ما هي زيادة الاستهلاك السنوية؟

٤ كم استهلكت الصين من النفط في سنة ٢٠٠٣؟

٥ ما هو وضع اقتصاد الصين بالمقارنة مع دول العالم الأخرى؟

٦ كم برميلاً يوجد في طنّ واحد؟

39 Timing

- Clock and calendar

1. Clock – hours

'One o'clock' is الساعة الواحدة *as-sā'a l-wāḥida*. The other eleven hours are expressed with الساعة *as-sā'a* ('hour, clock, watch') and a following *ordinal* number. 'At' is في *fī*:

الساعة الثانية\الثالثة *as-sā'a th-thāniya, th-thālitha*
two, three o'clock

في الساعة الحادية عشرة *fī s-sā'a l-ḥādiya 'ashra*
at eleven o'clock

On radio and television this 'official' form is sometimes dropped, with simplified cardinal numbers (see Chapter 38) used throughout:

as-sā'a thnayn, thalātha; fī s-sā'a 'iḥd'ashar

2. Clock – half and quarter hours, 20 minutes

Time on the half-hour is expressed with والنصف *wa-n-niṣf* 'and the half' after the hour:

في الساعة الرابعة والنصف *fī s-sā'a r-rābi'a wa-n-niṣf*
at half-past four

'a quarter past' is والربع *wa-r-rub'*, 'a quarter to' إلاّ الربع *'illa r-rub'* (ربع أرباع *rub' 'arbā'* 'quarter'):

قبل الساعة الخامسة والربع *qabl as-sā'a l-khāmisa wa-r-rub'*
before a quarter past five

بعد الساعة السادسة إلاّ الربع *ba'd as-sā'a s-sādisa 'illa r-rub'*
after a quarter to six

The fraction ثلث أثلاث *thulth 'athlāth* 'a third' is used for '20 to/past':

في الساعة السابعة و\إلاّ الثلث *fī s-sā'a s-sābi'a wa-/'illa th-thulth*
at twenty past/twenty to seven

3. Clock – odd minutes

Minutes other than the half-, quarter- or third-hour are expressed with the noun دقيقة دقائق *daqīqa daqā'iq* 'minute', often omitted with a multiple of five:

الساعة الثامنة إلاّ ستّ دقائق *as-sā'a th-thāmina 'illa sitta daqā'iq* six minutes to eight

الساعة التاسعة وعشر (دقائق) *as-sā'a t-tāsi'a wa-'ashara (daqā'iq)* ten (minutes) past nine

The half-, quarter- and third-hours are also quoted as reference points, like the hours. Note e.g.:

الساعة العاشرة والثلث إلاّ أربع دقائق

as-sā'a l-'āshira wa-th-thulth 'illa 'arba'a daqā'iq

16 minutes past 10 ('four minutes to 20 past 10')

In most countries the speaking clock on the telephone announces all minutes as numbers (i.e. without نصف\ربع\ثلث):

عند الإشارة تكون الساعة: ١٥، ١٥، ٤٠٠ ... *'ind al-'ishāra takūn as-sā'a: ar-rābi'a wa-khamst'ashar daqīqa wa-khamst'ashar thāniya.*

At the sign the time will be: four fifteen and fifteen seconds.

Note also: كم الساعة؟ *kam as-sā'a?* What is the time?

4. Days of the week

The days of the week are:

(يوم) الجمعة *(yawm) al-jum'a* Friday

السبت *as-sabt* Saturday — الأحد *al-'aḥad* Sunday

الاثنين *al-ithnayn* Monday — الثلاثاء *ath-thalātha** Tuesday

الأربعاء *al-'arba'a** Wednesday — الخميس *al-khamīs* Thursday

The word يوم may precede any of the names in construct, especially those which resemble the numbers. 'On' with a day is في *fi*.

(* Strictly speaking *ath-thalāthā'*, *al-'arba'ā'* – but hardly ever heard as such. Use the pronunciations shown in the list [compare the usual pronunciation of 'Wednesday' with its spelling, in English].)

5. Months

The international calendar has two sets of names, one used in Asian Arab countries, one in African:

	Asia		Africa	
Jan.	كانون الثاني	*kānūn ath-thānī*	يناير	*yanāyir*
Feb.	شباط	*shubāṭ*	فبراير	*fibrāyir*
Mar.	آذار	*'ādhār*	مارس	*māris*
Apr.	نيسان	*nīsān*	أبريل	*'abrīl*
May	أيّار	*'ayyār*	مايو	*māyū*
Jun.	حزيران	*ḥazīrān*	يونيو	*yūniyū*
Jul.	تمّوز	*tammūz*	يوليو	*yūliyū*
Aug.	آب	*'āb*	أغسطس	*'aghusṭus*
Sep.	أيلول	*'aylūl*	سبتمبر	*sibtambar*
Oct.	تشرين الأوّل	*tishrīn al-'awwal*	أكتوبر	*'uktóbar*
Nov.	تشرين الثاني	*tishrīn ath-thānī*	نوفمبر	*novambar*
Dec.	كانون الأوّل	*kānūn al-'awwal*	ديسمبر	*disambar*

The Muslim calendar of 354 or 355 days is official in some countries, and is used everywhere for Muslim religious dates. Its months are:

صفر	٢	*ṣafar*	محرّم	١	*muḥarram*
ربيع الثاني	٤	*rabī' ath-thānī*	ربيع الأوّل	٣	*rabī' al-'awwal*
جمدى الثانية	٦	*j. th-thániya*	جمادى الأولى	٥	*jumada l-'ūla*
شعبان	٨	*sha'bān*	رجب	٧	*rajab*
شوّال	١٠	*shawwāl*	رمضان	٩	*ramaḍān*
ذو احجّة	١٢	*dhu l-ḥijja*	ذو القعدة	١١	*dhu l-qa'da*

Typical dates:

في يوم الثلاثاء عشرين تمّوز سنة ألفين وأربع ميلادية (م)

fī yawm ath-thalātha 'ishrīn tammūz sanat 'alfayn u-'arba'a mīlādīya on Tuesday 20th July 2004 AD

السبت سابع عشر ربيع الثاني سنة ألف وأربع مئة وخمس وعشرين هجرية (هـ) *as-sabt sābi' 'ashara rabī' ath-thānī sanat 'alf u-'arba' mīya u-khamsa u-'ishrīn hijrīya* Saturday 17 Rabi'-al-thani 1425 AH

Note: (م) ميلادية *mīlādīya* is 'AD'; (هـ) هجرية *hijrīya* is 'AH', the 'year of the flight' (of Muhammad from Mecca to Medina in 622 AD).

With dates written in numerals, the blocks are read from right to left ←:

٢٠٠٤\١٠\٢٤ 24/10/2004

6. Vocabulary: الوقت *al-waqt* Time

إجازة *'ijāza* holiday, leave
أسبوع أسابيع *'usbū' 'asābī'* week
بعد الظهر *ba'd az-zuhr* afternoon
ثانية ثوان\الثواني *thāniya thawānin, ath-thawānī* (weak) a second
صباحًا *ṣabāḥan* in the morning, a.m.
صبح أصباح *ṣubḥ 'aṣbāḥ* morning
ظهر أظهار *ẓuhr 'aẓhār* midday
عيد أعياد *'īd 'a'yād* feast-day
غداً *ghadan* tomorrow
قادم *qādim* next
لحظة لحظات *laḥẓa laḥaẓāt* moment
ليلة ليال\الليالي *layla layālin, al-layālī* (weak) night
مدّة مدد *mudda mudad* period
مساء أمساء *masā' 'amsā'* evening
مساءً *masā'an* in the evening, p.m.
مقبل *muqbil* next, future

Exercise 1. Read the time:

e.g.: *as-sā'a l-'āshira u-'arba't'ashar daqīqa* ← ١٠،١٤

١	٤،١٥	٢	٣،٤٥	٣	١٢،٠٠	٤	٩،٣٥
٥	٦،٢٠	٦	١١،٣٠	٧	٨،٥٨	٨	٢،٣٩

٩ ٢،٢٧ ١٠ ٥،٥٥ ١١ ١٠،١٠ ١٢ ٧،٤٠

Read all the times again, after (a) قبل, (b) في, (c) بعد and (d) حتّى.

Exercise 2. Write the time in figures:

e.g.: *as-sā'a l-khāmisa 'illa r-rub'* → ٤،٤٥

1 *as-sā'a th-thālitha wa-n-niṣf* 2 ... *r-rābi'a wa-th-thulth*

3 ... *t-tāsi'a 'illa khamsa* 4 ... *s-sābi'a wa-'ashara*

5 ... *s-sādisa 'illa thamániya daqā'iq* 6 ... *l-ḥádiya 'āshira*

7 ... *th-thāmina 'illa th-thulth* 8 ... *l-wāḥida wa-n-niṣf*

9 ... *th-thániya wa-n-niṣf 'illa khamsa* 10 ... *r-rābi'a wa-daqīqatayn*

Exercise 3. Announce the time as on the speaking clock:

e.g.: عند الإشارة تكون الساعة: ٠٨،٢٠،٢٠.

'ind al-'ishāra takūn as-sā'a: ath-thāmina wa-'ishrīn daqīqa wa-'ishrīn thániya.

١ ... ١٠،٢٥،١٥ ٢ ... ٠٤،٠٥،٠٥

٣ ... ١٢٠٠ بالضبط ٤ ... ٠٦،٣٣،٣٠

٥ ... ١١،٤١،٢٥ ٦ ... ٠٧،٢٩ بالضبط

٧ ... ١١،٤١،١٠ ٨ ... ٠٣،١٠،٤٥

Exercise 4. Recite (a) the days of the week, beginning with Friday and (b) the months of the international calendar in both styles.

Then give the Asian-style name of each African-style month shown, and vice versa:

١ كانون الثاني ٢ شباط ٣ مايو ٤ مارس

٥ تشرين الأوّل ٦ يوليو ٧ سبتامبر ٨ نيسان

Exercise 5. Read the date:

e.g.: يوم الجمعة ١٩٩٩\١٢\٣١ م

yawm al-jum'a, ḥādī wa-th-thalāthīn kānūn al-'awwal/

disambar, sanat 'alf u-tisa' mīya u-tis'a u-tisīn mīlādīya

١ يوم الثلاثاء ٢٠\١١\٢٠٠٧ م
٢ الأربعاء ٢٢\١٢\١٣٢٤ هـ
٣ يوم الأحد ١٢\١٠\١٩٦٩ م
٤ الاثنين ٥\٧\١٩٨٢ م

Exercise 6. Read the passage and answer the questions:

افتتاح القمّة(1) العربية غداً في تونس

تفتتح غداً جامعة(2) الدول العربية أعمال القمّة العربية السادسة عشرة في قصر(3) المؤتمرات في تونس في حضور ثلاثة عشر رئيس دولة وأربعة رؤساء حكومات، بعد أن أرجئت(4) في ٢٨ آذار (مارس) الماضي. وأفادت مصادر تونسية أنّ الجلسة(5) الافتتاحية الّتي ستكون عامّةً ستقتصر(6) على خطاب رئيس الوزراء البحريني الّذي يسلّم الرئاسة لتونس وخطاب الرئيس زين العابدين بن علي (*zayn al-'ābidīn bin 'alī*) وتقرير الأمين(7) العامّ للجامعة العربية.

(adapted from الحياة *al-ḥayā*, 21.5.04)

(1) قمّة قمم *qimma qimam* summit (2) جامعة *jāmi'a* (here:) league
(3) قصر قصور *qaṣr quṣūr* palace
(4) أرجئت *'urji'at* it was postponed
(5) جلسة جلسات *jalsa jalasāt* session
(6) اقتصر على *iqtáṣara* VIII *'ala* to be restricted to
(7) أمين أمناء *'amīn 'umanā'* Secretary

١ أين ومتى عقدوا القمّة العربية؟
٢ أرجئت القمّة من أيّ تاريخ؟
٣ من كان الرئيس السابق للجامعة العربية؟
٤ كيف كانت الجلسة الافتتاحية؟ من ألقى خطاباً؟
٥ أيّة كانت المواضيع والمحلاّت التي كان يمكن الرئيس السابق أن يقرّر عنها في قمّة سنة ٢٠٠٤ م؟

40 Revision – 3

- Sentence structures

Exercise 1. Recast the sentence, beginning with إنّ :

e.g.: حضر الممثّلون الاجتماع. ← إنّ الممثّلين حضروا الاجتماع.

'inna l-mumaththilīn ḥaḍaru l-ijtimā'.

١ اشتركنا تمامًا في تنظيم المؤتمر.
٢ كان المهندسون يحاولون أن يشرحوا المشكلة.
٣ لن تنجح مشاريعنا بدون تعاونكم.
٤ يساعدنا في العمليات المساعدون الفنّيون للوكالة.
٥ جاء خبراء الشركة وساعدونا.
٦ ليس حاضراً. كان غائبًا امس ايضًا.
٧ فشلت عدد من مشاريعهم بعد الحرب.
٨ نجح طلأبنا في امتحانهم.
٩ سيترك زوّارنا الأوتيل بعد زيارة المدينة.
١٠ يريد الممثلون أن ينشروا التقرير قريبًا.

Exercise 2. Make the expression negative (a) present, (b) past (use ما with predicated verbs only), and (c) future (avoid using لا سوف):

e.g.: قرأوا الكتاب. ← لا يقرأون\لم يقرأوا\لن يقرأوا الكتاب.

lā yaqra'ūna/lam yaqra'u/lan yaqra'u l-kitāb.

١ تعاونّا في العملية
٢ إنّها نسيت عنواني
٣ يرسلون تقريراً فنّيًا
٤ ينجح تمامًا
٥ خاف من نتيجة الانتخابات
٦ يستشيروننا
٧ كان حاضراً
٨ إنّني أفهم لماذا
٩ يصدّقهم
١٠ تردّدت (هي)

Exercise 3. Make a question based on the underlined expression:

e.g.: *hal ta'rif hādha?* هل تعرف هذا؟ ← تعرف (أنت) هذا.

١ طلبوه أنفسهم.
٢ إنّهم لا يحضرون.
٣ أرسلوا لك رسالةً.
٤ عملوا هكذا لهذا الغرض.
٥ وقّع المدير التقرير.
٦ وصلوا أمس.

Exercise 4. Make a sentence beginning with the expression shown in parentheses:

e.g.: (حاول المهندسون) استبدلوا الماكينة.

← حاول المهندسون أن يستبدلوا الماكينة.

ḥāwal al-muhandisūn ’an yastabdilu l-mākīna.

Then recast your answer, using the verbal noun:

e.g.: حاول المهندسون أن يستبدلوا الماكينة.

← حاول المهندسون استبدال الماكينة.

ḥāwal al-muhandisūn istibdāl al-mākīna.

١ (يجب) الوفود وافقت على هذه النقطة الأساسية.
٢ (إنّ مدير الإدارة يريد) يبتدأ برناجنا فوراً.
٣ (رجت الشركة) العملية ناجحة تماماً.
٤ (بدأنا) درسنا اقتراح العمّال الّذين كانوا يضربون.
٥ (هل يستطيع الخبراء؟) يهتمّون بهذه التفاصيل.

Exercise 5. Join the two sentences, in the same order, in one relative sentence:

e.g.: نقدّم لكم التقرير. حضّر مستشارونا التقرير.

← نقدّم لكم التقرير الّذي حضّره مستشارونا.

nuqaddim lakum at-taqrīr allādhī ḥaḍḍarahu mustashārūna.

١ سنرسل لهم البضائع. يحتاجون إلى هذه البضائع.
٢ ذكروا شيئاً. إنّنا جميعنا استغربنا منه.
٣ هذا هو مشروع. يهمّنا هذا المشروع كثيراً.
٤ استقبل الرئيس الزوّار. قد سافروا إلى البلاد لزيارة رسمية.
٥ استفاد الناس كثيراً من المشاريع. قد قامت بها الحكومة.
٦ قد قامت الحكومة بمشاريع مختلفة. لن نستفيد من المشاريع.

٧ إنّنا نشكّ في نجاح البرنامج. يشرحه المقرّر في مقالته.
٨ هل هذه هي التفاصيل؟ خبرتم الرئيس بالتفاصيل.
٩ خبرناهم بمعلومات. أخذنا المعلومات من الصحافة.
١٠ لن نشترك في بحوث. لا تفيدنا أبداً.

Exercise 6. Put into the right form the verb shown in parentheses:

e.g.: سيسألون الخبراء قبل أن (قرّر، هم).
← سيسألون الخبراء قبل أن يقرّروا.
sa-yas'alūna l-khubarā' qabl 'an yuqarrirū.

١ عندما (وصل، هم) قد انتهى المؤتمر.
٢ سننتظر حتّى (وصل، هم).
٣ انتظرنا حتّى (وصل، هم).
٤ استمررنا (درس) المشكلة.
٥ كان يجب أن (استبدل، نحن) الماكينة لكي (استأنف) الإنتاج.
٦ ظلّوا (استعمل) أساليب قديمة مع أنّها (كلّف) أكثر.
٧ يجب أن (قرأ، نحن) الميزانية قبل أن (قرّر).
٨ لن (حضر) ممثّلونا المؤتمر لأنّهم (ليس) في البلاد.
٩ (رفض، هم) طلب المرشّح عندما (سمع) الحكاية.
١٠ إنّنا قد (تدخّل) لكي (ساعد)كم. ألا (صدّق، أنتم)نا؟
١١ لو (يمكن)هم أن (أيّد)ك لقد(اتّصل) بك فوراً.
١٢ لهذا الغرض لم يبدأوا (ركّب) الكمبيوتر أمس.
١٣ إذا (درس، هم) الهندسة (يمكن) أن (سافر) إلى الخارج.
١٤ يحاول أن (تعلّم) كيف يجب أن (كتب) اللغة العربية.
١٥ حتّي ولو (ساعد، نحن)ك لما (نجح، انت).
١٦ فضّلنا أن (ألقى) المساعد الخطاب لأنّه (عرف) الموضوع.
١٧ لو (عرف) المساعد الموضوع لقد (ألقى) الخطاب.
١٨ إنّهم تردّدوا أن (استشار)نا قبل انتهاء الدراسة الفنّية.
١٩ لا تتردّد أن (استشار)هم إذا (كان) مشكلة.
٢٠ اعتقدنا أنّك (سافر) قريباً.

Exercise 7. Re-express the second clause with a verbal noun:

e.g.: سيسألون الخبراء قبل أن يجتمعوا.

← سيسألون الخبراء قبل اجتماعهم.

sa-yas'alūna l-khubarā' qabl ijtimā'ihim.

١ يريدون المهندسون أن يستبدلوا الماكينات.
٢ جاء بعض الخبراء لكي يساعدوه.
٣ انتظر الحزب نتيجة الانتخاب قبل أن يدرس سياستنا.
٤ أهمّ شيء هو أن يركّبوا الكهربا فوراً.
٥ إنّنا نفهم تماماً ما تحتاجون إليه.

Exercise 8. Rewrite the sentence, beginning with the verb:

e.g. إن المرشّحين نجحوا. ← نجح المرشّحون. *najaḥ al-murashshaḥūn.*

١ إن سياسة الحكومة قد فشلت.
٢ إنّهم كانوا يحتاجون إلى مساعدة البنك الدولي.
٣ إنّ النوّاب بدأوا يتكلمون عن ارتفاع ثمن الطاقة.
٤ إنّ المسافرين دفعوا حسابهم و تركوا الأوتيل.
٥ إنّني أعتقد أنّ السياسيين لا يهتمّون كثيراً بهذا.

Exercise 9. Make the question or command indirect, as shown:

e.g.: هل توافقون على الاقتراح ؟(سألتهم)

← سألتهم إذا يوافقون على الاقتراح.

sa'altuhum 'idha yuwāfiqūna 'ala l-iqtirāḥ.

انتظروا (طلبنا منكم) ← طلبنا منكم أن تنتظروا.

ṭalabna minkum 'an tantáẓirū.

١ لماذا ترفض طلبنا ؟(لم نعرف)
٢ قف! (أمرناه)
٣ هل سيحضرون؟ (لم يؤكّدوا)
٤ كيف ينوي أن يقوم به؟ (شرح)
٥ لا تنسوا هذه النقطة. (رجونا منهم)
٦ قل لنا اسمك. (طلبوا منّي)

Exercise 10. Re-express the underlined words:

e.g.: الأعداد التي ذكرها هنا ← الأعداد المذكورة هنا

al-'a'dād al-madhkūra huna

١ مسألة لها أهمّية كبيرة ٢ يجب عليه الاتّصال بنا.

٣ الطلاّب الحاضرون في الصفّ ٤ عقد ليس توقيع عليه

٥ لا يمكن أن نستقبلهم. ٦ بعد أن رجعوا اتّصلوا بنا.

Exercise 11. Read this passage aloud, then answer the questions on it:

وضع الأطفال-الجنود

عدد الأطفال-الجنود يبلغ ٢٠٠ ألف في حوالى ٢٠ بلداً، على رغم الاتّفاقيات الدولية ضدّ استعمال الأطفال في النزاعات المسلّحة. وتحتلّ أفريقيا المكان الأوّل في تجنيد (1) الأطفال بالقوة. وفي أوغندا اختطف (2) "جيش الرب المعارض" (3) حوالى ٨ آلاف طفل في السنة الماضية وضمّهم إلى صفوفه (4). وفي جمهورية الكونغو الديموقراطية شهد (5) النزاع المسلّح جرائم لا مقارنة بها على حق الأطفال.

(adapted from الحياة *al-ḥayā́*, 3.2.04)

(1) تجنيد: (verbal noun, root is جند) (2) اختطف *ikhtáṭafa* VIII to abduct

(3) جيش الربّ امعارض *jaysh ar-rabb al-mu'āriḍ* the Lord's Resistance Army (4) صفوف *ṣufūf* (here:) ranks

(5) شهد يشهد *shahida yashhadu* I to witness

١ ماذا حدث في اوغندا؟

٢ كيف يجري تجنيد الأطفال؟

٣ اذكر عدد الأطفال-الجنود في العالم.

٤ كيف الوضع في الكونغو؟

٥ ماذا يكتب المقرر بخصوص افريقيا؟

٦ في رائيك، ما هي حقوق الطفل؟

٧ هل توجد اتّفاقيات متعلّقة بهذه المسألة؟ هل نجحت أم لا؟

Key to exercises

N.B.: After Chapter 3, answers are transcribed only selectively.

Chapter 1. Ex. 1 1 *'umm wa-'ab* 2 *bint 'aw walad* 3 *shāī wa-qahwa* 4 *bayt wa-bustān.* 5 *bayt 'aw shaqqa/shiqqa* 6 *ṭayyib* 7 *kursī wa-ṭāwula* 8 *ism wa-'unwān* 9 *'ams* 10 *bāb wa-shubbāk* 11 *'ā'ila* 12 *ghurfa*

Ex. 2 3 قهوة *qạhwa* (*a* next to *q*) 5 شقّة *shạqqạ* (*a*'s next to *q*) 6 طيّب *ṭạyyib* (*a* next to *ṭ*) 7 طاولة *ṭạ̄wula* (*ā* next to *ṭ*)

Ex. 3 1 أمّ وأب 2 شاي أو قهوة 3 بيت وجنينة 4 اسم أو عنوتن 5 اسم وعنوان 6 صالون 7 صديق 8 غرفة 9 طيّب 10 عائلة 11 أمس 12 كرسي

Ex. 4 1 عائلة 3 أو 5 سأل 6 شيء 8 سؤال

Ex. 5 1 *ghúrfa* 2 *'unwā́n* 3 *junáyna* 4 *ṭáyyib* 5 *ṣadī́q* 6 *wálad* 7 *kúrsī* 8 *bustā́n*

Ex. 6 اسم، أمّ، أمس، بنت، بيت، شاي، شبّاك، شيء، غرفة، قهوة، كرسي، ولد.

Ex. 7 1 UNESCO 2 metro 3 Berlin 4 Shell 5 IBM 6 Reuters 7 Stalin 8 e-mail

Chapter 2. Ex. 1 1 *mudīr* m. 2 *tilifōn* m. 3 *mushkila* f. 4 *zamīl* m. 5 *taqrīr* m. 6 *maktab* m. 7 *kātiba* f. 8 *ra'īs* m. 9 *qism* m. 10 *mashghal* m. 11 *zamīla* f. 12 *kātib* m. 13 *muhandis* m. 14 *nawba* f. 15 *waẓīfa* f. 16 *mākīna* f.

Ex. 2 1 المدير *al-mudīr* 2 التلفون *at-tilifōn* 3 المشكلة *al-mushkila* 4 الزميل *az-zamīl* 5 التقرير *at-taqrīr* 6 المكتب *al-maktab* 7 الكاتبة *al-kātiba* 8 الرئيس *ar-ra'īs* 9 القسم *al-qism* 10 المشغل *al-mashghal* 11 الزميلة *az-zamīla* 12 الكاتب *al-kātib* 13 المهندس *al-muhandis* m. 14 النوبة *an-nawba* 15 الوظيفة *al-waẓīfa*

16 الماكينة *al-mākīna*

Ex. 3 1 مصري *miṣrī* 2 بسيطة *basīṭa* 3 أجنبي *'ajnabī* 4 أجنبية *'ajnabīya* 5 صعبة *ṣa'ba* 6 واضح *wāḍiḥ* 7 منتج *muntij* 8 قصيرة *qaṣīra* 9 مصرية *miṣrīya* 10 دولية *duwalīya* 11 رئيسي *ra'īsī* 12 طويلة *ṭawīla*

Ex. 4 1 الزميل المصري *az-zamīl al-miṣrī* 2 المشكلة البسيطة *al-mushkila l-basīṭa* 3 المدير الأجنبي *al-mudīr al-'ajnabī* 4 الشركة الأجنبية *ash-sharika l-'ajnabīya* 5 الوظيفة الصعبة *al-waẓīfa ṣ-ṣa'ba* 6 العقد الواضح *al-'aqd al-wāḍiḥ* 7 القسم المنتج *al-qism al-muntij* 8 العملية القصيرة *al-'amalīya al-qaṣīra* 9 الكاتبة المصرية *al-kātiba l-miṣrīya* 10 الشركة الدولية *ash-sharika d-duwalīya* 11 المكتب الرئيسي *al-maktab ar-ra'īsī* 12 النوبة الطويلة *an-nawba ṭ-ṭawīla*

Ex. 5 1 سوري، سورية *sūrī(ya)* 2 رئيسي، رئيسية *ra'īsī(ya)* 3 صناعي، صناعية *ṣinā'ī(ya)* 4 عراقي، عراقية *'irāqī(ya)* 5 هندسي، هندسية *handasī(ya)* 6 كهربي، كهربية *kahrabī(ya)*

Ex. 6 1 بسيطة *basīṭa* 2 قديم *qadīm* 3 صعبة *ṣa'ba* 4 صغير *ṣaghīr* 5 خفيفة *khafīfa* 6 قصير *qaṣīr*

Ex. 7 1 المشكلة البسيطة *al-mushkila al-basīṭa* 2 المشغل القديم *al-mashghal al-qadīm* 3 العملية الصعبة *al-'amalīya aṣ-ṣa'ba* 4 المصنع الصغير *al-maṣna' aṣ-ṣaghīr* 5 الصناعة الخفيفة *aṣ-ṣinā'a l-khafīfa* 6 العقد القصير *al-'aqd al-qaṣīr*

Ex. 8 1 الإنتاج الصناعي *al-'intāj aṣ-ṣinā'ī* 3 الكهربا *al-kahraba* 4 مصر *miṣr* (definite without the article) 7 العراق *al-'irāq* 8 العمل *al-'amal*

Ex. 9 1 سوري *sūrī* 2 فنّية *fannīya* 3 الصناعي *aṣ-ṣinā'ī* 4 الهامّة *l-hāmma* 5 مصر القديمة *miṣr al-qadīma*

Ex. 10 1 عراقي *'irāqī* 2 الرئيسية *r-ra'īsīya* 3 هندسية *handasīya* 4 السنوي *as-sanawī* 5 الكهربي *al-kahrabī* 6 الصناعي *aṣ-ṣinā'ī*

Chapter 3. Ex. 1 1 وفدان، وفود *wafdān, wufūd* 2 مندوبان، مندوبون *mandūbān, mandūbūn* 3 الكمبيوتران، الكمبيوترات *al-kambyūtirān, al-kambyūtirāt* 4 زميلان، زملاء *zamīlān, zumalā'* 5 لجنتان، لجان *lajnatān, lijān* 6 ممثّلان، ممثّلون *mumaththilān, mumaththilūn* 7 مكتبان، مكاتب *maktabān, makātib* 8 منظّمتان، منظّمات *munaẓẓamatān, munaẓẓamāt* 9 الوثيقتان، الوثائق *al-wathīqatān, al-wathā'iq* 10 الملفّان، الملفّات *al-milaffān, al-milaffāt* 11 رئيسان، رؤساء *ra'īsān, ru'asā'* 12 الكاتبان، الكتّاب *al-kātibān, al-kuttāb* 13 مهندسان، مهندسون *muhandisān, muhandisūn* 14 النوبتان، النوب *an-nawbatān, an-nuwab* 15 وظيفتان، وظائف *waẓīfatān, waẓā'if* 16 جوابان، أجوبة *jawābān, 'ajwiba* 17 بحثان، بحوث *baḥthān, buḥūth* 18 الصديقان، الأصدقاء *aṣ-ṣadīqān, al-'aṣdiqā'* 19 مصريان، مصريون *miṣrīyān, miṣrīyūn* 20 مديران، مدراء *mudīrān, mudarā'* 21 رأسان، رؤوس *ra'sān, ru'ūs*

Ex. 2 1 أصدقاء جدد *'aṣdiqā' judud* 2 أيّام طويلة *'ayyām ṭawīla* 3 المدراء الفنّيون *al-mudarā' al-fannīyūn* 4 مدراء سوريون *mudarā' sūriyūn* 5 أوقات صعبة *'awqāt ṣa'ba* 6 زميلات أجنبيات *zamīlāt 'ajnabīyāt* 7 المشاكل المعقّدة *al-mashākil al-mu'aqqada* 8 الممثّلون الطيّبون *al-mumaththilūn aṭ-ṭayyibūn* 9 المخازن القديمة *al-makhāzin al-qadīma* 10 الزملاء الرئيسيون *az-zumalā' ar-ra'īsīyūn* 11 الرؤساء الجدد *ar-ru'asā' al-judud* 12 شركات دولية *sharikāt duwalīya* 13 اجتماعات قصيرة *ijtimā'āt qaṣīra* 14 سكرتيرات طيّبات *sikritayrāt ṭayyibāt* 15 مهندسون عراقيون *muhandisūn 'irāqīyūn* 16 أرقام واضحة *'arqām wāḍiḥa* 17 المشرفون المسؤولون *al-mushrifūn al-mas'ūlūn* 18 أطفال صغار *'aṭfāl ṣighār* 19 البساتين الصغيرة *al-basātīn aṣ-ṣaghīra* 20 وظائف هامّة *waẓā'if hāmma*

Ex. 3 1 مدير جديد *mudīr jadīd* 2 بيت كبير *bayt kabīr* 3 وثيقة معقّدة *wathīqa mu'aqqada* 4 مدير جديد *mudīr jadīd* 5 مصنع منتج

maṣna' muntij 6 تقرير هامّ *taqrīr hāmm* 7 التقرير الهامّ *at-taqrīr al-hāmm* 8 عقد قديم *'aqd qadīm* 9 أسلوب مفيد *'uslūb mufīd* 10 النوبة اليومية *an-nawba l-yawmīya* 11 اجتماع طويل *ijtimā' ṭawīl* 12 وفد كبير *wafd kabīr* 13 اللجنة الرئيسية *al-lajna r-ra'īsīya* 14 بنت صغيرة *bint ṣaghīra* 15 الموظّف المسؤول *al-muwaẓẓaf al-mas'ūl* 16 رقم بيسط *raqm basīṭ* 17 العامل المنتج *al-'āmil al-muntij* 18 موظّف سوري *muwaẓẓaf sūrī* 19 الوثيقة الخاصّة *al-wathīqa l-khāṣṣa* 20 جواب طويل *jawāb ṭawīl*

Ex. 4 1 البسيطة *l-basīṭa* 2 بسيطة *basīṭa* 3 كبيرة *kabīra* 4 السوريون *as-sūrīyūn* 5 مسؤولون *mas'ūlūn*

Chapter 4. Ex. 1 1 هذا\ذلك المحاسب السعودي 2 هذه\تلك الرسالة 3 هؤلاء\أولئك المحاسبون الطيّبون 4 هذه\تلك المهنة الهامّة 5 هؤلاء\أولئك الناس 6 هذه\تلك المنظّمة اليابانية 7 هذه\تلك الوفود الغائبة 8 هذا\ذلك الوقت 9 هذان\ذانك المأموران الصينيان 10 هذه\تلك المبالغ الكبيرة 11 هذا\ذلك المبلغ الكبير 12 هذه\تلك المشاكل الشخصية 13 هؤلاء\أولئك الشرطيون 14 هذا\ذلك الشخص 15 هذا\ذلك السائق المجتهد 16 هذه\تلك المحلاّت القديمة 17 هؤلاء\أولئك التجّار الفرنساويون 18 هذه\تلك البنت الصغيرة 19 هؤلاء\أولئك الأشخاص 20 هذا\ذلك الزميل السابق

Ex. 2 1 هؤلاء السيدات الألمانيات 2 أولئك السادة الإنجليز 3 تلك المشاكل العامّة 4 هذه الكمبيوترات اليابانية 5 هؤلاء الأصدقاء العرب 6 هؤلاء الصديقات العربيات 7 هؤلاء السكرتيرات الهنديات 8 أولئك الزملاء الغائبون 9 هؤلاء البنات الصغيرات 10 هؤلاء المهندسون الهنود

Ex. 3 1 هذه 2 ذلك 3 هؤلاء 4 هذا 5 أولئك 6 ذلك 7 هذه 8 تلك

Ex. 4 1 الإيطالي 2 كويتي 3 سعودي 4 هندي

5 الفرنسي\الفرنساوي 6 الألماني 7 صيني 8 روسي

Ex. 5 1 هذه المشكلة البسيطة 2 تلك الرسالات القصيرة
3 أولئك المأمورمن الحاضرون 4 تلك المشكلة الخاصّة
5 ذلك المكتب القديم

Chapter 5. Ex. 1 1 هو 2 هم 3 هي 4 هي 5 هي 6 هي 7 هو
8 هي 9 هو 10 هي 11 هو 12 هي

Ex. 2 1 الطالبة سورية. 2 الدروس طويلة.
3 التدريب عملي ونظري 4 هي مثقّفة. 5 المدرّس في الصفّ.
6 المختبر هناك. 7 المختبر مشهور. 8 الإنشاء سهل.
9 الأستاذ خبير في الكهربا. 10 التلاميذ في المكتبة.
11 أفريقيا كبيرة. 12 الوثيقة طويلة. 13 نحن مصريون.
14 الرسالات مكتومة. 15 السوّاق حاضر.
16 الأستاذ السابق مشهور.

Ex. 3

equation	not an equation
3, 4, 5, 6, 8, 9, 10, 13, 14, 16	1, 2, 7, 11, 12, 15

Ex. 4 1 هذا الزميل هو الخبير الطبّي. 2 هم المعلّمون الأجانب.
3 المدرّس هو الخبير في الكمبيوتر. 4 التربية هي مشكلة كبيرة.
5 الموادّ الرئيسية هي الدراسات الطبّية والعلوم العامّة.

Ex. 5 1 هؤلاء الطلاّب أذكياء. 2 الدراسة نظرية.
3 المشرف مسؤول. 4 هؤلاء الزملاء خبراء. 5 الأساتذة زملاء.
6 في الصفوف مرشّحون أجانب. 7 المشاكل الرئيسية هي التراجم.
8 المشرفون حاضرون. 9 الامتحان العملي صعب.
10 التلاميذ هناك في الصفوف. 11 هم أشخاص مثقّفون.
12 الطالب غائب.

Ex. 6 1 معقّدة 2 طويلة 3 إيطالية 4 الإيطالية 5 قديم

Ex. 7 (possible answers:) 1 هذا الزميل 2 هذا الشابّ هو
3 التلاميذ 4 المرشّحون الجدد 5 هذه المدرسة هي 6 الطبّ

Ex. 8 1 ... خبير مشهور في العلم الطبّي. 2 ... تلاميذ جدد هنا.
3 ... في الدراسات الطبّية. 4 هذا الأستاذ ...

5 ...تعليم نظري وعملي. 6 ...كبيرة...
7... الكتب في المكتبة الطبّية. 8 ممتازة ...

Chapter 6. Ex. 1 1 تحت التجربة 2 في اليابان 3 في المشغل
4 في هذا الوقت 5 بعد الاجتماعين 6 كتلميذ 7 داخل المكاتب
8 منذ سنتين 9 خلال الدورة 10 خلال الدورات 11 ضد الموظّفين
12 للرئيس

Ex. 2 1 عليّ 2 فيكم 3 فيها 4 فيهم 5 جنبي 6 عنك 7 داخلها
8 خارجه 9 جنبه 10 بخصوصي 11 عنّي 12 لهم

Ex. 3 1 خلاله 2 لها 3 إليهم 4 فيه 5 خلالها 6 فيها 7 من أخله
8 له 9 ضدّه 10 بخصوصهم 11 عليه 12 عندهم

Ex. 4 1 بعد 2 ضدّ 3 تحتها 4 أليه 5 بدونه 6 من 7 منذ
8 وراءهم 9 إليّ 10 بالرغم من

Ex. 5 (possible answers:) 1 بعد المحاضرة 2 ضدّ الزملاء
3 وراء البيت 4 في الدرس 5 بخصوص الدورة 6 خلال الاجتماع
7 خلال النوبة 8 للطالبة 9 على الطاولة 10 المدير ألى
11 عند الأصدقاء 12 بالكتب

Ex. 6 1 هؤلاء الوكلاء\مع هذين الوكيلين
2 في المدارس\المدرستين 3 المدراء\المديرين وبيني
4 المشاكل الحاضرة\المشكلتين الحاضرتين في
5 اجتماعات طويلة\بعد اجتماعين طويلين
6 التجّار العرب\التاجرين العربيين 7 للممثّلين السابقين
8 عند الشرطين 9 بحوث خاصّة\خلال بحثين خاصّين
10 النوب اليومية\بخصوص النوبتين اليوميتين

Ex. 7 1 في العقد\للعقد\بالعقد
2 في الشركات\للشركات\بالشركات
3 في التقرير\للتقرير\بالتقرير 4 في البيت\للبيت\بالبيت
5 في الوظيفة\للوظيفة\بالوظيفة
6 في المختبرات\للمختبرات\بالمختبرات
7 في الصناعة\للصناعة\بالصناعة 8 في المدير\للمدير\بالمدير

9 في الرسالة\للرسالة\بالرسالة 10 في الزملاء\للزملاء\بالزملاء

11 في المكتب\للمكتب\بالمكتب 12 في المدراء\للمدراء\بالمدراء

1 في شركات\الشركات\بشركات 2 في عقد\العقد\بعقد

3 في بيت\البيت\ببيت 4 في تقرير\التقرير\بتقرير

5 في مختبرات\المختبرات\بمختبرات 6 في وظيفة\الوظيفة\بوظيفة

7 في مدير\المدير\بمدير 8 في صناعة\الصناعة\بصناعة

9 في رسالة\الرسالة\برسالة 10 في زملاء\الزملاء\بزملاء

11 في مكتب\المكتب\بمكتب 12 في مدراء\المدراء\بمدراء

Chapter 7. Ex. 1 1 استقرار البلاد 2 أسماء الأعضاء

3 حكومة مصر 4 برنامج الحكومة 5 هم مندوبو البرلمان

6 على رأس الوفد 7 مع مندوبي البرلمان 8 تحت رياسة الوزير

9 لحزبي الحكومة 10 ممثّل العراق حزب او برامج سياسة

Ex. 2 1 سياسة الحزب الرئيسية 2 سياسة الحزب الرئيسي

3 مأمور هذه الوزارة 4 مأمور الوزارة هذا

5 مسؤوليات هذه الوزارة الهامّة 6 قانون العمل الجديد

Ex. 3 1 الرئيس السابق للجنة المالية 2 إجراءات لدفاع بلاد

3 الصناعة الخفيف لهذا البلاد 4 الرئيس السابق للحزب

5 سياسة الحزب لتدريب الشباب

6 انتخابات برلمانية جديدة لحكومة\انتخابات برلمانية لحكومة جديدة

Ex. 4 Definite: 1, 2, 3, 5, 6, 7, 8. Indefinite: 4

Ex. 5 1 ... سياسات 2 ... ممثّلي

3 قوانين العمل المعقّدة 4 ... بلدان 5 ... عن مهندسي

6 انتخابات النوّاب السنوية

7 ... رؤساء وممثّلو 8 ... هم مندوبو

Ex. 6 1 ... عن سكرتيرات 2 ... عن مندوبي 3 ... عن أعضاء

4 ... عن نائبي 5 ... عن الاشتراكيين والأحرار والمحافظين

No. 5 is not a construct.

Ex. 7 1 استقرار البلدان العربية\الولايات المتّحدة\الإقليم

2 وزارات البلدان العربية\الولايات المتّحدة\الإقليم

تحت رئاسة الوزير\الولايات المتّحدة 4 مكتبة الجامعة الرئيسية 3
حكومة الولايات المتّحدة 6 مجلس الوزراء 5

Ex. 8 (possible answers:) 1 الولد 3 الجمهورية 2 أعضاء
مدارس 9 سياسة 8 مشاكل 7 المصنع 6 المالية 5 مكتب 4
مأمورين 10

Ex. 9 (possible answers:) 1 قانون 3 انتخاب الأعضاء 2 اللجنة
لممثّلي الحزب 6 مشاكل الإدارة 5 الصحّة 4 التربية
تاريخ ومحلّ المؤتمر 9 الحكومة 8 أساليب التدريس 7
وزارة الخارجية أو الداخلية 10

Ex. 10 (possible answers:) 1 الصحّة\المالية\الداخلية\التربية\
التربية\التاريخ 3 المالية\الإنتاج\التدريب\الصنع 2 الصناعة
(القديمة، الحديثة)

Chapter 8. Ex. 1 1 أهمّ 5 أقصر 4 أوضح 3 أطول 2 أشدّ
أسهل 12 أخفّ 11 أجدّ 10 أذكى 9 أصعب 8 أقوى 7 أضعف 6

Ex. 2 1 فكرة أوضح، أوضح فكرة 2 شيء أهمّ، أعمّ شيء
طريقة أحسن، إحسن طريقة 5 4 = 2 وضع أخطر، أخطر وضع 3
خلاف أعمق. أعمق خلاف 7 ناس ألطف، ألطف ناس 6
خطوة أشدّ، أشدّ خطوة 8

Ex. 3 (possible answers:) 1 أصعب من 3 أكبر من 2 أقصر من
أوضح من 6 أحسن من 5 أطول من 4

Ex. 4 1 الآراء الأوضح 3 أخطر خلاف 2 العبارة الأجمل
أحسن نتائج 7 الخطوة الأهمّ 6 أقصر جواب 5 الوضع الأصعب 4
النقطة الأخرى\الآخرة 8

Ex. 5 1 بيت أجدّ\احدث 3 آخر فرصة 2 عبارة أقصر
الخلاف الأصغر 6 أبعد عن المكتب 5 أوائل السنة 4
احترام أقلّ 8 الصناعات الأخفّ 7

Ex. 6 1 الجواب أطول من السؤال. 2 هو أقوى منّي.
الحقيقة أهمّ من رأي الناس. 3
الفكرة الأساسية أبسط وأسهل من ذلك. 4

Ex. 7 (possible answers:) 1 ... هي دراسة كامل للوضع.
2 ... أحسن فكرة. 3 ... (هو) تقرير بالأرقام الكاملة.
4 ... هذا الأضو 5 ... حزبنا 6 ... عن الوزارة.
Ex. 8 1 طويل 2 قصير 3 كبيرة 4 ذكي 5 هامّ 6 قليل 7 كثير
8 قديم 9 شديد 10 ثقيل 11 غني 12 واطئ
Ex. 9 (possible answers:) 1 أوّل كتاب 2 المبدأ الأوّل
3 عبارات أخرى 4 المدرسة الأقرب 5 التلميذ الأفضل
6 الفرصة الأولى 7 البلدان الكبرى 8 ماكينة أقوة 9 شركة أغنى
10 خطوة أشدّ

Chapter 9. Ex. 1
1 عدّة مصارف محلّية\عدد من المصارف المحلّية.
2 عدّة رواتب\عدد من الرواتب 3 عدّة حسابات\عدد من الحسابات
4 عدة أساتذة\عدد من الأساتذة 5 عدّة وكالات\عدد من الوكالات
6 عدّة مشاريع دولية\عدد من المشاريع الدولية
7 عدّة آراء\عدد من الآراء
8 عدّة مكاتب حكومية\عدد من المكاتب الحكومية
9 عدّة تكاليف\عدد من التكاليف
10 عدّة صادرات\عدد من الصادرات
11 عدّة أعضاء\عدد من الأعضاء
12 عدّة بضائع\عدد من هذه البضائع
Ex. 2 1 صغيرة 2 خاصّة 3 محلّي 4 معقّدة
5 هي المشكلة الوحيدة 6 رخيصة 7 حاضرون 8 غائبون
Ex. 3 1 أيّ 2 كلّ 3 عدد من 4 نفس 5 أيّة 6 كثير من
Ex. 4 1 العملية 2 ميزانية 3 القروض 4 صادرات الشركة
5 حساب 6 هذه القطاعات
Ex. 5 أكثرية، كثير، أكثر. مال، أموال، مالية.
أهمّية، أهمّ، هامّ. خلاف، مختلف. عدّة، عدد. جميع، جامعة.
كلّية، كلّ.

Chapter 10. Ex. 1 1 أزرق 2 زرقاء 3 البيضاء 4 عمي
5 الخضراء 6 حمراء 7 الأسود 8 أجانب
Ex. 2 1 القاضي السابق 2 المحلاّت الفاضية
3 على المستوى العالي 4 إلي المستشفى العامّ 5 للمحامي الغالي
6 بنايات القرى
Ex. 3 1 قرى المنطقة 2 في أيادي السلطات المحلّية
3 محامي هذه الشركة 4 محامو هذه الشركة
5 أراضي منطقة النيل الأبيض 6 طريق دمشق
Ex. 4 1 القرى المختلفة للمنطقة
2 في الأيادي الخبيرة للسلطات المحلّية
3 المحامي الغالي لهذه الشركة 4 المحامون السابقون لهذه الشركة
5 الأراضي الزراعية لمنطقة النيل الأبيض
6 الطريق الطويل\الطويلة لدمشق
Ex. 5 القاهرة هي أكبر مدينه أفريقيا وإحدى أقدم مدن العالم. مصر محل هامّ من أجل ثقافة وسياسة العالم العربي الشرقي والغربي. كتب الكتّاب المصريين مشهورة عند جميع العرب المثقّفين. وفي نفس الوقت مصر هامّة في المنظّمات الدولية. القاهرة علي نهر النيل. هذا النهر هو أطول نهر العالم، وهو هامّ لزراعة كلّ الإقليم.

Chapter 11. Ex. 1 1 دخل 2 دخل 3 شرحوا 4 ذهبنا 5 رجعتم
6 فهمَت 7 وصلوا 8 خرج 9 نجحَت 10 شربَت
Ex. 2 1 سمعنا وفهمنا 2 أكلت وشربت 3 بدأ ونجح
4 أخذوا ... وتركوا 5 كتبتم ونشرتم 6 قرأت 7 وجدنا 8 سكنوا
9 فتح 10 طلبوا
Ex. 3 1 كتب 2 دخلت 3 خرجوا 4 نشرَت 5 رجعتم 6 كتبنا
7 شرب ... وتركوا 8 ذهب 9 تركَت 10 فهِم
Ex. 4 1 سألنا 2 ذهب ... ورجعوا 3 نشرَت 4 عرفت ... وكتبت
5 وصلَت
Ex. 5 1 المهندسون 2 الشركة 3 السكرتيرة 4 الممثّل 5 الوفود

Ex. 6 (possible answers:) 1 رفض المدراء 2 فشلَت المشاريع
ذهب الممثّلون ... ورجعوا 6 المهندس 5 الخبير 4 قد بدأ الخبراء 3
Ex. 7 (possible answers:) 1 ترك الاشتراكيون البرلمان.
شرحوا 6 فشلَت 5 فهم 4 بحثَت 3 دخل 2
Ex. 8 1 ... وراء البيت توجد ... 3 هناك يوجد ... 2 توجد في ...
يوجد في الكلّية ... 5 توجد في التقرير ... 4
Ex. 9
كتب الخبراء الاقتصاديون التقرير السنوي على طلب الوزراء. 1
رفضوا عدّة تفاصيل. 2
ذكرت اللجنة عدد من المشاكل المالية المعقدة وطلبت دراسة عدّة 3
سأل أعضاء اللجنة أسئلةً فنّيةً مختلفةً. 4 نقط.
ذكرت اللجنة عدد من المشاكل المالية المعقدة. 5
درس الوزراء الوثيقة خلال اجتماع اللجنة المالية. 6

Chapter 12. Ex. 1 . Ex. 1 1 قطاراً خاصّاً 2 غرفتين 3 الغرفتين
التاكسي 6 تذكرتين للقطار 5 قطراً خاصّةً 4
موظّفي وكالة 9 أوتوبيساً 8 من المأمور تذاكر أرخص 7
تاكسياً 12 جدولاً جديداً 11 جداول جديدةً 10
Ex. 2 1 طلب المأمورون من الركّاب أجرات أخرى.
عرف موظّفو الجمرك سيّاحًا أجانب فى الطائرات. 2
طلب الركّاب من الوكلاء تذاكر للرجوع. 3
نشرت شركات السياحة جداول جديدةً. 4
سمعنا باواخر في المواني. 6 حملنا شنطًا كبيرةً معنا. 5
شرح لنا الوكلاء تفاصيل الجداول. 8 شكرنا الموظّفين المصريين. 7
شكرنا موظّفي شركات السياحة. 9
فهم المأمورون مشاكل التذاكر. 10
Ex. 3 1 دفعها إليه. 4 قرأوه 3 قرأوها 2 شرحته لهم.
أخذه المسافر. 8 طلبناه منه. 7 ركبه. 6 دفعها إليهم. 5
تركناه. 10 دفعناه. 9
Ex. 4 (possible answers:) 1 شرحوا الجدول للسيّاح. 2 من المطار

3 أخذ التذاكر. 4 دفع الأجرة 5 بدأ الرحلة 6 ركبنا التاكسي.
7 ركبنا الطائرة. 8 سمعوا الزوّار. 9 حمل الشنط.
10 تركوا الأوتيل 11 فهموا الجدول. 12 شكرنا الوكلاء.
Ex. 5 1 قطاراً خاصّاً 2 تذاكر 3 تأمينًا رخيصًا 4 رسالتين
5 أوتيلاً أرخص 6 سفراً طويلاً 7 جدولاً 8 نقطًا هامّةً
9 أوتيلاً جديداً 10 كتابًا معقّداً 11 جدولاً جويًّا 12 رحلةً أرخص
Ex. 6 (possible answers:) 1 الثقيلة 2 الأرخص 3 كبيرةً 4 مصريةً
5 أجنبيًا 6 الغالية 7 الدولي 8 جويًّا 9 المصريين 10 أخرى
11 محلّيين 12 أجانب
Ex. 7 1 ركبنا اتوبيسًا خاصًا في البلد وذهبنا إلى الميناء.
2 دخلت الباخرة مواني مختلفةً.
3 قد حجزنا عند وكالة سفر تذاكر لباخرة سيّاحية كبيرة.
4 هناك حمل موظّفو الوكالة شنطنا الى الباخرة.
5 بعد الرحلة رجعنا بالطائرة إلى بيروت.
6 خلال الربيع عملنا رحلةً بحريةً من بيروت.
Indef. dir. obj: رحلةً بحريةً، تذاكر، اتوبيسًا خاصًا، مواني مختلفةً
Definite direct objects: الشنط، السفر

Chapter 13. Ex. 1 1-8 هل ... ؟
Ex. 2 1 كيف كتب الشكوة؟ 2 من نشر الشكوة ... ؟
3 أيّ نوع من الشكوة نشروا بخصوص ... ؟ 4 لماذا نشروها ؟
5 أيّة مظاهرة حضر الطلاّب؟ 6 كيف ركب الإرهابيون السفينة؟
7 رفضت السلطات احتجاج من؟ 8 حضر كم شرطيًا؟
9 أيّ نوع من الأسلحة حمل الجنود؟ 10 متى بدأت ثورة الفلّاحين؟
11 هذه جريمة على حقوق من؟ 12 هذه (هي) تذاكر من؟
Ex. 3 1 سألوا شخصين. 2 حضر شخصان.
3 ركبوا القطار بالقوة المسلّحة. 4 من أجل حقوق الإنسان
5 ثورة سلمية 6 بدأت هذه الحرب قبل شهرين.
7 مظاهرة من أجل حقوق العمّال 8 سكنّا في القاهرة.
9 نشروا احتجاجًا على الإجراءات الجديدة.

10 . نعم (ركبنا القطار)

Ex. 4 1 في أيّ وقت؟ 2 لأيّ غرض؟ 3 أيّ شيء؟

4 من أيّ شخص؟ 5 بأيّة طريقة؟ 6 في أيّ محلّ؟

Ex. 5 سلاح، مسلّحون، أسلحة. عملية، عمّال، عملت.

مسؤوليات، أسئلة. متظاهر، مظاهرة. حقيقة، حقّ. دولية، دولة.

كثير، أكثرية. الأحرار، حرّية. أموال، مالي.

Ex. 6 1 هم مسلّحون بالأسلحة الأحدث على مستوى الجيوش.

2 نعم نجحت عدد منها. 3 نعم عملت دول مختلفة مع بعض.

4 المكافحة ضرورية من أجل أمن وسلام وحرّية الإنسان.

Chapter 14. Ex. 1 1 رأينا *ra'ayna* 2 صارَت 3 زرت 4 دللنا

5 نووا *nawaw* 6 نسوا *nasū* 7 تمّتم 8 مشينا *mashayna* 9 دعا

10 خفنا 11 رموا *ramaw* 12 بقيت *báqiyat*

Ex. 2 1 ماذا قالوا لكم؟ 2 قاد المدراء الوفود.

3 ساق السياح سيّارات جديدةً. 4 قد تمّت المشاريع الحكومية.

5 شكّوا في هذه التفصايل. 6 مشينا في المدن القديمة.

7 دعونا إلى المؤتمرات المالية. 8 كيف جرَت البحوث بين الوفود؟

9 هل باعوا السيارات القديمة؟ 10 لقد حل الخبراء المشاكل الفنّية.

Ex. 3 1 تمّت 2 دللنا 3 زادت 4 دعوا 5 رأينا 6 نسوا 7 قالوا

8 طار، زاروا 9 بعنا 10 بقي، حلّوا

Ex. 4 1 نسينا 2 قام 3 جرت 4 تمّت 5 مرّ

Ex. 5 1 مشيت، مشَت، مشوا 2 بعت، باعت، باعوا

3 نمت، نامت، ناموا 4 مددت، مدّت، مدّوا

5 جئت، جاءت، جاؤوا 6 عشت، عاشت، عاشوا

7 زدت، زادت، زادوا 8 دعوت، دعت، دعوا

9 خفت، خافت، خافوا 10 صرت، صارت، صاروا

11 حييت، حيّت، حيّوا 12 نويت، نوت، نووا

Ex. 6 1 رأوهم 2 نسوها 3 دعوهم 4 نواه 5 قالوه 6 قالوها

7 زرته 8 باعها 9 ساقها 10 قاده

Ex. 7 1 زار 2 مررنا 3 حلّ 4 بقيت 5 زادت 6 تمّت 7 جرَت

8 دعوا 9 شكّ 10 بعنا

Ex. 8 1 قاد وفداً رسمياً. 2 خرجوا من المطار بالسيارة.
3 هل قال نفس الشيء؟ 4 شككنا في أهمية الأرقام.
5 جاء الأستاذ بالكتب الجديدة. 6 بعنا ماكينات زراعيةً في الخارج.
7 عاشوا سنوات كثيرة. 8 أخذ الأستاذ الكتب الجديدة.
9 لماذا خاف الولد الصغير (من) القطار؟
10 نام الأطفال وقتاً طويلاً.

Ex. 9 1 غاب عن 2 حلّ 3 نسوا 4 جاء بشيء ثقيل. 5 قلنا
6 رجوا 7 جئت\جاءت 8 ظننّاه

Ex. 10 1 حضروه قبل وقت قصير.
2 دعتهم إليه وزارة التجارة لبحث مشاكل التجارة.
3 لا، قد مرّ بسنة صعبة. 4 لقوا ممثّلي شركات أخرى.
5 زادَت أثمان البضائع.
6 شرحوا أفكاراً مختلفةً بخصوص الخطوات الممكنة.
7 جرت البحوث في الصادرات الزراعية.
حضر sound; دعتنا final-weak, *aw*; لقينا final-weak, *ī*; قاد hollow, و ; زادت *hollow*, ي ; مرّ doubled; شرح sound

Chapter 15. Ex. 1 1 اتّفاقيتهم 2 استقلالها 3 من مكتبه
4 سفراؤنا 5 علاقاتهم 6 مشرفيهم 7 زملائكم 8 مصالحنا
9 مصالحي 10 تذاكركم 11 حدودها 12 مفاوضاتهم

Ex. 2 (possible answers:) 1 التجارية 2 الاقتصادي 3 الرئيسي
4 السابقون 5 المعقّدة 6 الجدد 7 الأجانب 8 السياسية 9 المالية
10 السياحية 11 الدولية 12 الطويلة

Ex. 3 1 اتّفاقياتهم المالية 2 ممثّليهم 3 بدأت مفاوضاته
4 إجراءاتهم 5 معلّميّ 6 جولاته

Ex. 4 1 استقلالها 2 قوتها 3 لحريّته 4 مسؤولياتها 5 أهمّيتها
6 لحلّها 7 طرفيها 8 حقوقها

Ex. 5 1 نفهم أمور مثل عقودنا وتجارتنا وحفظ استقلالنا.
2 تهمنا من أخل تطوير اقتصادنا.

‫3. أحسن أسلوب هو البحث والمفاوضة.‬
‫4. مصالحها هي تطوير اقتصادها بواسطة التجارة.‬

‫Chapter 16. Ex. 1 1 خلال تجارب فنّية 2 مكاتبهم الرئيسية‬
‫3 أهمّ موظّفيهم 4 أسئلة واضحة 5 فلّاحو الأرياف‬
‫6 تأخيرات طويلة 7 لأطول برامج 8 لركّاب هنود 9 أيّ معلّمين؟‬
‫10 حلول مشاكل معقّدة 11 مشرفو نوب 12 كتب غالية‬
‫Ex. 2 1 المديران المصريان 2 المديران الهنديان‬
‫3 مشكلتان فنّيتان 4 هذان المستشفيان 5 في بلدين صغيرين‬
‫6 لمشروعين هامّين 7 السؤالان الصعبان 8 أهمّ شيئين‬
‫Ex. 3 1 الرقم الطويل 2 تحت أمر رسمي 3 أستاذ مشهور‬
‫4 في وظيفته 5 في التقرير كلّه 6 عند شخص لطيف‬
‫7 فرصة ممتازة 8 مع أستاذ‬
‫Ex. 4 1 الغالي 2 غال 3 طيّبون 4 طيّبين 5 القديمة 6 الرئيسية‬
‫7 جميلة 8 هندية 9 السوريات 10 الإنجليز 11 العرب 12 الأولى‬
‫Ex. 5 1 هذه\تلك الخطوات الإدارية الضرورية‬
‫2 مع هذا\ذلك المهندس الخبير‬
‫3 ذكر هذين\ذينك المبدئين الأساسيين‬
‫4 هذه\تلك الأفكار الممتازة 5 هذا\ذلك الخطّ الجوي‬
‫6 هؤلاء\أولئك الزملاء الأجانب‬
‫7 هذا\ذلك الشحن الكبير 8 هؤلاء\أولئك الزميلات الأجنبيات‬
‫9 هؤلاء\أولئك المشرفون المسؤولون‬
‫10 هاتان\تانك البنتان الصغيرتان‬
‫Ex. 6 1. هذا هو التقرير المالي 2 الحقيقة بسيطة.‬
‫3. في اقتصاد اليوم مشكلتان. 4 هذا تقريرنا المالي.‬
‫5. هذا هو النيل الأزرق. 6 الجواب على سؤالنا هو أوّل خطوة.‬
‫7. الجواب على سؤالنا خطوة إيجابية.‬
‫8. الطريقة الوحيدة هي موافقة الطرفين.‬
‫9. المكتبة أقدم من البنايات الأخرى.‬
‫10. المكتبة هي أقدم بناية الجامعة كلّها.‬

Ex. 7 1 أصدقائه 2 زملائنا 3 مكتبي الرئيسي 4 سنتين طويلتين
5 مندوبي الشركة 6 مصالح الموظّفين 7 عليّ 8 لها 9 إليهم 10 فيه
11 من أجلنا 12 عليكم 13 بخصوصي 14 منّي
Ex. 8 1 عليه 2 له 3 بخصوصهم 4 بسببها 5 على رغمه 6 به
Ex. 9 (possible answers:) 1 مدينة دمشق 2 لمندوبي الحكومة
3 محامي الشركة 4 مشكلة ميزانيتنا هذه 5 مسؤوليات المدير
6 وظائف المشرف وعمّاله 7 وزارة المالية 8 حقوق موظّفينا
9 قبل وصول الطائرة 10 تحت قانون التجارة 11 راتب المأمورين
12 في جداول الخطّ الجوّي
Ex. 10 1 حلّ مشاكل دولية 2 برنامج هذين الحزبين
3 مأمورو المحكمة المحلّيون 4 مدير مدرسة هذا
5 دفع حساب متأخّر\دفع متأخّر لحساب 6 دفع حساب متأخّر
Ex. 11 1 جدولي، جدوله، جدولها، جدولكم، جدولهم
2 معلّميّ، معلّموه، معلّموها، معلّموكم، معلّموهم
3 أصدقائي، أصدقاؤه، أصدقاؤها، أصدقاؤكم، أصدقاؤهم
4 بمساعدتي، بمساعدته، بمساعدتها، بمساعدتكم، بمساعدتهم
5 معلّميّ، معلّميه، معلّميها، معلّميكم، معلّمينهم
6 كتبي، كتبه، كتبها، كتبكم، كتبهم
7 حساباتي، حساباته، حساباتها، حساباتكم، حساباتهم
8 محاميّ، محاموه، محاموها، محاموكم، محاموهم
9 حساباتي، حساباته، حساباتها، حساباتكم، حساباتهم
10 تلميذي\تلميذه\تلميذها\تلميذكم\تلميذهم الجديد
11 زملائي، الزملاؤه، الزملاؤها، الزملاؤكم، الزملاؤهم
12 لزميلتي، لزميلته، لزميلتها، لزميلتكم، لزميلتهم
Ex. 12 1 رواتبهم 2 كلّها 3 حقوقه 4 شنطته 5 أسماءهم 6 طلبه
7 سيّاراته 8 سيّاراتها 9 بعضهم 10 جميعهم 11 تقريرها
12 سياسته
Ex. 13 (possible answers:) 1 سياسة الحزب 2 لمكافحة الإرهاب
3 برنامج الوفد 4 مسؤوليات الوزارة 5 بعض الضيوف
6 بعض الكتب 7 أهمّ القضايا 8 وظائف زملائي

9 أكثرية الأعضاء 10 أقصر الرسالات 11 مبدأ الأسلوب
12 فكرة الخبير
Ex. 14 1 المشكلة الصعبة لمكافحة الإرهاب الدولي
2 تعويض التكليف لرحلة جوّية
3 تفاصيل البرنامج السنوي لتنمية التجارة
4 عضو جديد للجنة تنظيم الحزب
5 الأهمّية الكبيرة لحلّ (الـ)مشاكل (الـ)حالية
6 إدارة المصالح العامّة للطلاّب
Ex. 15 (possible answers:) 1 الأبيض 2 حمراء 3 أزرق 4 الأسود
5 بيضاء 6 سوداء 7 بيض 8 الأحمر 9 الخضراء 10 بيضاوان
Ex. 16 1 اصغر 2 أمام 3 أقصر 4 خرجوا من 5 بعد 6 قرأ
7 أكثرية 8 تحت 9 داخل 10 ضدّ\على
Ex. 17 1 هل ... ؟ 2 متى وصلوا؟ 3 ماذا كتبوا له؟
4 أيّ ثمن دفع؟ 5 لماذا عمله؟ 6 اين درس؟
Ex. 18 1 أخذوه 2 تركناه 3 وجدها 4 فهمتها 5 سألتها 6 ركبناه
7 ذكرها 8 بدأوه 9 حضرته 10 شكرتهم
Ex. 19 1 القاضي والمحامي 2 الأراضي الزراعية 3 الشهر الماضي
4 الأسلوب الجاري 5 المستوى الواطئ 6 في القرى البعيدة
Ex. 20 1 مبدأ أهمّ، أهمّ مبدأ 2 عضو أغنى، أغنى عضو
3 كتب أغلى، أغلى كتب
4 فكرة أحسن\أفضل، أحسن\أفضل فكرة
5 آبار أعمق، أعمق آبار 6 قوة أقلّ، أقلّ قوة

Chapter 17. Ex. 1 1 يحلّ *yahullu* 2 يأكل *ya'kulu* 3 يبقى *yabqa*
4 ينزل *yanzilu* 5 يدخل *yadkhulu* 6 يجد *yajidu* 7 ينوي *yanwī*
8 يطير *yaṭīru* 9 يخاف *yakhāfu* 10 ينجح *yanjaḥu* 11 يرى *yara*
12 يلي *yalī* 13 يجيء *yajī'u* 14 يفشل *yafshalu* 15 يتمّ *yatimmu*
16 يضمّ *yaḍummu* 17 يحيا *yaḥya* 18 يعرف *ya'rifu*
Ex. 2 1 قاد 2 جرى 3 نشر 4 لقي 5 مرّ 6 دفع 7 وضع
8 غاب 9 رأى 10 مشى 11 باع 12 حجز

Ex. 3 1 يغيب 2 يأخذون 3 نصل 4 ينفي 5 أجيء 6 ينزل
7 تشكّون 8 نقرأ 9 ينظرون 10 تفهمها 11 تعقد 12 تنوي
Ex. 4 1 وجد 2 نمرّ 3 نقوم 4 ساق 5 تتمّ 6 يشرحون
7 عملوا 8 يطلبون 9 تفتح 10 جاؤوا
Ex. 5 (possible answers:) 1 تنشر 2 يذهب\يجيء 3 يغيب 4 يقود
5 نطلب 6 ينفون\يقولون 7 يعمل 8 يجري 9 يأخذون ... ويتركون
10 تنجح\تفشل
Ex. 6 1 تدعوهم 2 يركبونها 3 يشرحها 4 ندرسها 5 زاروها
6 ينساهم 7 يقرأونها 8 أكتبه 9 رفضتموها 10 ينفيه
Ex. 7 درس يدرس: ندرس sound. بدأ يبدأ: يبدأ hamzated.
قرأ يقرأ: نقرأ hamzated. شرح يشرح: نشرح sound.
سمع يسمع: يسمع sound. سأل يسأل: يسأل hamzated.
جاء يجيء: يجيء doubly weak. وجد يجد: يجد initial-*wāw*.
نسي ينسِي: نسي final-weak. طلب يطلب: يطلب sound.
حلّ يحلّ: نحلّ doubled. جرى يجري: يجري final-weak.
تمّ يتمّ: يتمّ doubled.

Chapter 18. Ex. 1 1 غنيًا 2 أغنى 3 رخيصًا 4 مفيدةً 5 غائبين
6 مأموري البلد 7 تلاميذ 8 طبيبًا مشهوراً 9 طلاّبًا 10 ممكنًا
11 مشغولاً 12 أجنبيةً
Ex. 2 1 لسنا موظّفين جداً. 2 ليست هذه أول بئرنا ...
3 ليسوا فاضين ... 4 ليست الطلمبة قويةً. 5 ليس النفط ضروريًا
6 ليس هذا الشخص مديرنا. 7 ليس إنتاجهم ممتازاً ...
8 ليس أكثرية الطلاّب مجتهدين. 9 ليس المشرف مسؤولاً ...
10 ليست التجارب الآخرة إيجابيةً.
1 نكون موظّفين جداً. 2 تكون هذه أول بئرنا ...
3 يكونون فاضين ... 4 تكون الطلمبة قويةً. 5 يكون النفط ضروريًا
6 يكون هذا الشخص مديرنا. 7 يكون إنتاجهم ممتازاً ...
8 يكون أكثرية الطلاّب مجتهدين. 9 يكون المشرف مسؤولاً ...
10 تكون التجارب الآخرة إيجابيةً.

Ex. 3 السيّدات حاضرات. 2 هم حاضرون ... 1
الأطفال في البستان. 5 أنت مسؤول. 4 نحن مشغولون 3
هذا الأستاذ مشهور. 7 هذا (هو) أقدم حقلنا. 6
هم عمّال بسطاء. 10 أنتم ممثلو الشركة. 9 النتائج إيجابية. 8
Ex. 4 تركوا الأطفال ينامون ... 2 كدنا نترك كلّ الأوراق ... 1
عاد يعمل ... 5 ما زال يسأل أسئلةً ... 4 لا يزال يسأل أسئلةً ... 3
بدأت الشركة تبيع ... 8 صرت أجد ... 7 ما عدنا نحفر ... 6
Ex. 5 كانت الشركة تفتح ... 3 كنّا نبيع 2 كنت أسكن 1
كانت اللجنة تجد ... 5 كانوا يفهمون 4
ماذا كنتم تسألون؟ 8 كنّا نشرح 7 كانت عمليات الحفر تنجح. 6
Ex. 6 5, 2, 7, 9, 10, 3, 4, 8, 1, 6.

Chapter 19. Ex. 1 ستخرج 4 سيسألون 3 سيعيش 2 سيشكّون 1
سيطلب 10 ستنشر 9 سيبقون 8 ستقوم 7 سيجيء 6 سيعرفونه 5
Ex. 2 كانت (قد) رفضت 2 متى كانت (قد) تمّت 1
كانت (قد) جرت 5 كان (قد) وصل 4 كانوا (قد) قاموا 3
كنّا (قد) لقينا 10 كنّا (قد) وجدنا 7, 8, 9 كنّا (قد) سألنا 6
Ex. 3 1 + 7, 8, 10; 2 + 7, 8, 10; 3 + 6, 7, 9; 4 + 6, 9; 5 + 9.

Chapter 20. Ex. 1 وقّعت، أوقّع 2 أشرتم، تشيرون 1
أفدت، أفيد 6 أعطوا، تعطون 5 ناديت، تنادي 4 أهمّت، تهمّ 3
موّلوا، يموّلون 9 أكّدَت، تؤكّد 8 ساعدنا، نساعد 7
أنشأوا، ينشئون 12 أذعت، أذيع 11 لاقينا، نلاقي 10
Ex. 2 نسافر 4 ما زالوا يذيعون 3 يؤكّدون 2 أفاد 1
ساعد 10 من يموّل 9 أخبرنا 8 ينتجون 7 نلاقي 6 أشار 5
سينتجون 7 سنلاقي 6 سيشير 5 سنسافر 4 سيؤكّدون 2 سيفيد 1
سيساعد 10 سيموّل 9 سنخبر 8
Ex. 3 إليها 5 إلية 4 لا يزالون يذيعونه. 3 أكّدوه 2 يفيدها 1
فيه 10 موّلها 9 نخبره بها. 8 كانوا ينتجونها. 7 لاقيناه 6
Ex. 4 سأعطيهم 5 أيّدتكِ 4 ناداكم 3 أريكم 2 أخبرتمونا 1

6 صدّقونا 7 غادره 8 تؤيّدونهم 9 أوقّعها 10 كلّفني 11 يناديه
12 يفيدني

Ex. 5 1 سنذيع 2 لا أزال أنادي 3 كان يميّز 4 سأقدّم
5 تفاوضون 6 بدأت أجرّب

Ex. 6 1 حاضر، محاضرة 2 منتج، إنتاج، نتيجة 3 وقف
4 جاوب 5 ساعد 6 ركب، ركّب 7 أرسل 8 همّ، أهمّ، أهميّة
9 سفر، مسافر، سفير، سفارة 10 دار 11 علم، معلّم، تعليم
12 حقيقة

Ex. 7 1 أوقف 2 ينتج 3 وقّعه ... أرسلته 4 كلّفت ... سيموّلها
5 يناسبكم 6 جرّبوا\حاولوا 7 فاوض ... وافقوا 8 غادر ... سافروا
9 ألقى ... سافر 10 جدّدوه

Ex. 8 1 يفضل مبدأ المدفوعات السنوية.
2 قرّروها بسبب التكاليف الإدارية.
3 ستؤثّر هذه الخطوة على الوضع المالي وسيغيّر برنامج الاستثمار.
4 سيطبّق المصرف هذا الإجراء على جميع قروضه الصناعية.
5 نعم، أخبرت وفد المصرف بوضع الشركة.

Chapter 21. Ex. 1 1 تبادلتم، تتبادلون 2 تعاونّا، نتعاون
3 تكلّمت، أتكلّم 4 تلقّت، تتلقّي 5 تآمروا، يتآمرون
6 تسلّم. يتسلّم 7 تخصّصت، تتخصّص 8 تأكّدنا، نتأكّد
9 تنبّأوا، يتنبّأون 10 تأخّرتم، تتأخّرون 11 تناوبوا، يتناوبون
12 تذكّرت، أتذكّر

Ex. 2 1 تبادلوا 2 نتقدّم 3 تكلّموا 4 تردّدنا 5 تتذكّر 6 يتطوّر
7 تعلّقَت 8 نتلقّى 9 يتناوبون 10 تتدخّل

Ex. 3 1 تعرّفت 2 يتمكّنون 3 ما داموا يتعاونون 4 تلقّوها
5 ما زال يتقدّم. 6 كان يتكلّم

Ex. 4 مغادرة، غادر. نوبة، يتناوب. تحسّن، أحسن.
تعلّمنا، علوم، تعليم. منتج، نتيجة، إنتاج. تذكر، ذكر.
يتقدّمون، قدّم، قديم. يوقفون، توقّف. ألاقي، تلقّيت، يلقى.
فضّل، أفضل. أمّن، تأمين.

Ex. 5 1 تقدّم 2 تعلّمتم 3 تتمكّن 4 توسّعت 5 أتذكّرها
6 سنتكلّم 7 تحسّن 8 تسلّمتها 9 يتوقّف 10 يتبادلون

Chapter 22. Ex. 1 1 استغربت، تستغرب 2 اهتممت، أهتمّ
3 ابتدأوا، يبتدئون 4 امتدّ، يمتدّ 5 انخفض، ينخفض
6 اشتروا، يشترون 7 امتزتم، تمتازون 8 ازدادت، تزداد
9 استرحت، أستريح 10 ادّعينا، ندّعي 11 اتّصلت، تتّصل
12 اتّفقوا، يتّفقون

Ex. 2 1 نتّخذ 2 اتّصلت 3 تنحلّ 4 تستورد
5 كان مفيداً 6 اشترينا. 7 يستفيد 8 اجتمع 9 نستأنف استشرت
10 يشترك

Ex. 3 1 نستغني عن مساعدة الخبير.
2 سأستقبل الضيف بعد وصوله هنا.
3 يستأجر بيتًا ... من أجل موظّفه.
4 بدأ المندوبون المؤتمرات ببحوث التقارير المالية الأخيرة.
5 كان يحتاج إلى رقم تقريري الاقتصادي.

Ex. 4 1 كنّا نستفيد، نستفيد، استفدنا 2 (كان) ينتظر، انتظر
3 (كان) ينسحب، انسحب 4 (كنت) أستغني، استغنيت
5 (كان) يحتلّ، احتلّ 6 (كان) يحتاج، احتاج

Ex. 5 1 ... يستفيد 2 ... يبدأ 3 ... تستثمرون استمررتم لماذا
3 ... تكتشف الشركة ... 4 ما عادت يستعملون العمّال يزال لا

Ex. 6 1 اكتشفوه في هذه المنطقة. 2 اكتشفوا حقل نفط.
3 ابتدأ الحفر تحت اتّفاقية بين الشركة والحكومة.
4 يجرّبونها من أجل حلّ مشكلة تكليف العمليات.
5 كان الإنتاج ضعيفًا خلال السنة الأولى. 6 نعم، هو صعب.

Chapter 23. Ex. 1 1 لم أرفض، ما رفضت، 2 ما استغربنا،
3 لم لنستغرب ما احتللنا، لم نحتل 4 ما نفى، لم ينف
5 ما قالت، لم تقل 6 ما اتّخذتم، لم تتّخذوا 7 ما سألت، لم تسأل
8 لم تتذكّروا، ما تذكّروا 9 ما اهتممنا، لم نهتمّ

10 ما نسيتم، لم تنسوا 11 ما خفت، لم أخف
12 ما جاوبنا، لم نجاوب

Ex. 2 1 قلت 2 نسيت 3 شككنا 4 فاوضنا 5 وصلنا 6 انتظرتم
7 استشرنا 8 ساقوا 9 تعاونّا 10 هل تذكّرتِ؟ 11 ناديت
12 أفدت\أفادت

Ex. 3 1 لم نر 2 لن نقدّم 3 لن نتقدّم 4 لم تعلّموا 5 لم يسكن
6 ليس غائبًا 7 لا يشيرون 8 لا أساعد 9 ألا تسافرين؟ 10 لن آخذ
11 لم يؤيّدوا 12 لم نوافق

Ex. 4 1 فهمنا 2 أوقف 3 ستهمّني 4 تعطين 5 ستعطين
6 أعطيت\أعطت 7 وصلوا 8 بدأ يتكلّم 9 يرسلون 10 سيجدونه
11 ينفيه 12 ينسحبون

Ex. 5 1 لا يرجعون، لن يرجعوا
2 ليس حاضراً، لا\لن يكون حاضراً 3 ألا تحتجّ، ألن تحتجّ؟
4 لا تعطين، لن تعطي 5 لا يحتاج إلى شيء، لن يحتاج إلى شيء
6 لا نرى، لن نرى 7 لا نوافق، لن نوافق 8 لا أتردد، لن أتردّد
9 لا يضربون، لن يضربوا 10 لا تدرسون، لن تدرسوا
11 لا تؤيّدونهم، لن تؤيّدوهم 12 لا ينفيه، لن ينفيه

Ex. 6 1 لم تذهبوا 2 لن ينسوا 3 لن ينسحبوا 4 لم نتردّد
5 لم ينسوا 6 لن ينادوا 7 لم يخافوا 8 سيلقون 9 لم يستفيدوا

Ex. 7 1 تكون الدورة غير فنّية.\لا تكون الدورة فنّيةً.
2 الرسالة غير رسمية.\ليست الرسالة رسميةً.
3 حملت السيّارة نمرةً غير دبلوماسية.\ لم تحمل السيّارة نمرةً دبلوماسيةً.
4 كان السبب غير واضح.\ما كان السبب واضحًا.
5 شرح لنا التفاصيل غير الأساسية.\ لم يشرح لنا التفاصيل الأساسية.
6 هل المصنع غير منتج؟\أليس المصنع منتجًا؟

Ex. 8 1 ما كان مفيداً إلاّ الدرس الأوّل.
2 لا يعلّم الأستاذ إلاّ أسس الهندسة. 3 لم تساعدني إلاّ هي.
4 لن ندفع إلاّ على أساس العقد. 5 لا يهمّنا إلاّ المبدأ الأساسي.

لم يسألونا إلاّ هذا الشيء البسيط. 6
ما كانوا يحتاجون إلاّ إلى قليل. 8 لا نتّصل إلاّ برئيس نفسه. 7

Chapter 24. Ex. 1 عند الصحفي أهمّ معلومات. 1
عنده مصدر داخل الحزب. 3 كان عندنا حكاية هامّة. 2
عند المدينة مطار دولي. 5 عند الحزب مصادر غير رسمية. 4
عند كلّ مركز خبراء ماليون. 7 عند هذه الجريدة مراكز مختلفة. 6
عند كلّ محرّر مسؤولية كبيرة. 9 تكون عندكم نسخة الإيميل. 8
كانت عندها نسختي الخطاب. 10
Ex. 2 ليس ... 5 ليست ... 4 ليس ... 3 ما كانت ... 2 ليست ... 1
ما كانت ... 10 ليست ... 9 لا تكون ... 8 ليس ... 7 ليست ... 6
Ex. 3 للمدينة مطار ... 5 للحزب مصادر ... 4 له مصدر ... 3
لكلّ محرّر ... 9 لكلّ مركز ... 7 لهذه الجريدة ... 6
Ex. 4 ذات محرّر 4 ذات أهمّية 3 ذات بيانات 2 ذو مال 1
ذوو علاقات 8 ذوو المعلومات 7 ذوي تعليم 6 ذات أرقام 5
Ex. 5 هي سيّدة ذات ثقافة واسعة.\عند السيّدة ثقافة واسعة. 1
هذه هي الصحيفة ذات المحرّر الأجنبي.\ 2
عند الصحيفة محرّر أجنبي.
هذه هي النشرة ذات الأخبار الاقتصادية.\ 3
عند النشرة أخبار اقتصادية.
هو ولد ذو صحّة ضعيفة.\عند الولد صحّة ضعيفة. 4
هذا هو الحزب ذو الأكثرية في المجلس.\ 5
عند الحزب أكثرية في المجلس.
هم صحف ذوو آراء مختلفة.\عند الصحف آراء مختلفة. 6
هذه هي مجلّة ذات حكايات للأطفال.\ 7
عند المجلّة حكايات للأطفال.
هم موظّفون ذوو مسؤولية كبيرة.\عند الموظّفين مسؤولية كبيرة. 8
Ex. 6 جاءت الصحافة الوطنية اليوم بخبر هامّ. حسب النشرة
الرئيسية لجريدتنا قد استأنفوا مفاوضات اتّفاقية التجارة العالمية.
ألقى رئيس البنك الدولي خطاباً عندما افتتحوا البحوث ونشرت

الصحيفة موجز خطابه في إحدى مقالاتها. في نفس المقالة جاء إعلان حكومي. تتخذ وزارة التجارة إجراءات جديدة لمساعدة قطاع التجارة.

Chapter 25. Ex. 1 1 اذكر *udhkur* 2 تذكّر *tadhakkar* 3 صوّر *ṣawwir* 4 اذهب *idhhab* 5 استعمل *ista'mil* 6 دلّ *dulla* 7 نم *nam*
8 أضرب *'aḍrib* 9 انظر *unẓur* 10 انس *insa* 11 ناد *nādi*
12 احتلّ *iḥtalla* 13 ابدأ *ibda'* 14 اشتر *ishtari* 15 أعلن *'a'lin*
16 وافق *wāfiq* 17 ابق *ibqa* 18 ارفض *irfiḍ* 19 خذ *khudh*
20 اتّخذ *ittákhidh* 21 اضرب *uḍrub* 22 أيّد *'ayyid* 23 بع *bi'*
24 انف *infi*
1 اذكروا، اذكري 2 تذكّروا، تذكّري 3 صوّروا، صوّري
4 اذهبوا، اذهبي 5 استعملوا، استعملي 6 دلّوا، دلّي
7 ناموا، نامي 8 أضربوا، أضوربي 9 انظروا، انظري
10 انسوا، انسي *insay, insaw* 11 نادوا، نادي 12 احتلّوا، احتلّي
13 ابدأوا، ابدإي 14 اشتروا، اشيري 15 أعلنوا، أعلني
16 وافقوا، وافقي 17 ابقوا، ابقي *ibqay, ibqaw*
18 ارفضوا، ارفضي 19 خذوا، خذي 20 اتّخذوا، اتّخذي
21 اضربوا، اضربي 22 أيّدوا، أيّدي 23 بيعوا، بيعي
24 انفوا، انفي
Ex. 2 1 لا تستفيدوا 2 لا تتعاونوا 3 لا تركبي 4 لا تشكر
5 لا تستعملي 6 لا تستمرّ 7 لا تتداخلوا 8 لا توقّع
9 لا تستبدلوا 10 لا تسألي 11 لا تتكلّم 12 لا تقرأ 13 لا تأكل
14 لا توقفوا 15 لا تتّصلي 16 لا تغادروا 17 لا تضف
18 لا تشترك 19 لا تبكي 20 لا تسترح
Ex. 3 1 غاب I 2 وصل I 3 نزل I 4 شكّ I 5 احتلّ VIII 6 نسي I
7 أمر I 8 مرّ I 9 عفا I 10 خاف I 11 أعطى IV 12 اعتقد VIII
Ex. 4 1 اطبعه 2 لا تنشروه 3 أذيعوها 4 اذكرها 5 لا تنسها
6 خذيها 7 لا تستعملها 8 انتظروها 9 أخبره 10 قله
Ex. 5 1 نعم، دراسة المنتجات ضرورية.

2 نعم، أحضر على الوقت.\لا، لا أحضر على الوقت.
3 (any of the indented lines) 5 نعم، أستعمل ...\لا، لا أستعمل ....
6 نعم، عندما ....\لا، أبداً.
7 لا تضع على حسابك التكاليف الشخصية.

Chapter 26. Ex. 1 1 مقرّر 2 ساكن 3 مسافر 4 متعاون 5 مذيع
6 كاتب 7 خائف 8 معط، المعطي 9 مؤكّد 10 محتجّ 11 طالب
12 منخفض 13 فاهم 14 منته، المنتهي 15 مشترك 16 سائق
17 مقدّم 18 جالس 19 مناسب 20 متكلّم 21 مقترح 22 مستعمل
23 مدّع، المدّعي 24 محتاج 25 دالّ 26 مفيد 27 موقف 28 زائر
broken m. pl.: 2 سكّان 6 كتّاب 11 طلاّب 28 زوّار
Ex. 2 1 *mufīda* أفاد IV 2 *ḥāḍirūn* حضر I 3 *'ārif* عرف I
4 *mustarīḥ* استراح X 5 *al-mustamirra* استمرّ X 6 *ṭullāb* طلب I
7 *mustajwib* استجوب X 8 *li-l-mudhī'īn* أذاع IV
9 *mubtadi'a* ابتدأ VIII 10 *nāzil* نزل I 11 *mujaddada* جدّد II
12 *al-muḥtāj* احتاج VIII
Ex. 3 1 مفيد 2 مموّلي 3 المؤمّنون 4 المتكلّم 5 غائبين، حاضرون
6 الطائرة متأخّرة 7 مقدّمة ... مرتفعة 8 المشتركون

Chapter 27. Ex. 1 1 ممدّد 2 موافق عليه 3 مميّز 4 مشروح
5 مفضّل 6 مطبوع 7 مأكول 8 معطًى، المعطى 9 مستحقّ
10 مفهوم 11 مبيع 12 مبعوث به 13 موجب 14 مرجوّ 15 مرفوض
16 مؤيّد 17 مزيد عنه 18 مقرّر 19 مستغنًى\المستغني عنه
20 محتجّ عليه 21 مقترح 22 مرقًّى، المرقّى 23 مستبدل 24 منسيّ
25 مذكور 26 مصوّر 27 منشأ 28 مقروء
Ex. 2 1 المفتتح 2 المحتاج إليها 3 متكلّم عنها 4 مطبوعة
5 المشكوك فيها 6 المكتوبة 7 المنتظرة 8 ملقاة 9 المؤمّن عليهم
10 المذكورين 11 مطلوب منهم 12 ممنوعة
Ex. 3 1 *mu'ayyadūn* أيّد II 2 *munjaz* أنجز IV 3 *muḥtāj 'ilayhi*
احتاج VIII 4 *muktashaf* اكتشف VIII 5 *muḍāf* أضاف IV

IV ألقى mulqan 8 II أكّد mu'akkad 7 IV أعطى mu'ṭan 6

VIII اشترك mushtaraka 10 IV أنشأ munsha' 9

X استثنى mustathnā 12 II حضّر muḥaḍḍar 11

1 mu'ayyidūn 2 munjiz 3 muḥtāj 4 muktashif 7 mu'akkid

10 mushtarika 11 muḥaddir

Ex. 4 1 إليها 2 لها 3 عليه 4 بهم 5 فيها 6 إليهم

Ex. 5 1 مشتركون 2. مرآة 3 منخفضة 4 موافق 5 ممتدّ

6 راجعون ... ماشون 7 مكتوبة 8 مفتوحة

Chapter 28. Ex. 1 1 مناسبة 2 شرح 3 خروج 4 تقدّم

5 تراكيب تركيب 6 أقوال قول 7 فشل 8 نجاح 9 إضراب

10 وجود 11 محاولة 12 تأييد 13 رجوع 14 زيادة 15 حياة

16 تخصّص 17 يطبق 18 إلقاء 19 إضافة 20 تجديد 21 معرفة

22 استحقاق 23 تعاون 24 توظيف 25 تربية 26 حضور

27 وضع أوضاع 28 تأمين 29 امتـياز 30 احتجاج 31 اقتراح

32 أضطراب

Ex. 2 1 أنشأ IV 2 ميّز II 3 استكشف X 4 حلّ I 5 استغنى X

6 أضاف IV 7 أفاد IV 8 ابتدأ VIII 9 احتاج VIII 10 استغرب X

11 عرف I 12 زاد I

Ex. 3 active participles: 1 مستحقّ 2 حاجز 3 قائل 4 محتلّ

5 محتاج 6 عارف 7 مقدّم 8 ملق 9 زائر 10 مؤيّد

passive participles: 1 مستحقّ 2 محجوز 3 مقول 4 محتلّ

5 محتاج إليه 6 معروف 7 مقدّم 8 ملقًى 9 مزور 10 مؤيّد

verbal nouns: 1 استحقاق 2 حجز 3 قول 4 احتلال 5 احتياج

6 معرفة 7 تقديم 8 إلقاء 9 زيارة 10 تأييد

Ex. 4 1 الفهم الكامل للموضوع 2 فهم الموضوع الكامل

3 سوء قيادته للحركة 4 بسبب الافتتاح الرسمي للمستشفى

5 اتّخاذ السلطات لإخراءات شديدة 6 تأكيد تفاصيل الميزانية

7 تأكيد جزئي لتفاصيل الميزانية 8 احتجاج على خطاب الرئيس

9 اتّخاذ إخراءات شديدة 10 لعدم ذكر أهمّ احتياجاتهم

Ex. 5 1 تأكيد 2 خروج 3 ابتداء 4 غيبة 5 نجاح 6 قراءة
7 ارتفاع 8 حياة 9 تسلّم 10 تعلّم 11 وصول 12 استعمال
Ex. 6 1 انضمّ VII 2 صفّى II 3 استنكر X 4 تمدّن V 5 أقام IV
6 وزّع II 7 اختار VIII 8 ناقش VI 9 حاور VI 10 قاتل VI
11 اطّلع VIII 12 اتّحد VIII
alternatives: 8 نقاش VI 9 حوار VI 10 قتال VI

Chapter 29. Ex. 1 1 أغنى، الأغنى
2 أقصر، الأقصر 3 أكثر امتيازاً، الأكثر امتيازاً
4 أكثر إفادةً، الأكثر إفادةً 5 أكثر إيجابًا، الأكثر إيجابًا
6 أوضح، الأوضح 7 أكثر سلمًا، الأكثر سلمًا
8 أكثر ثقافةً، الأكثر ثقافةً
Ex. 2 1 أقلّ ممّا دفعت أنت 2 أقلّ منك 3 أكثر سلمًا من هذا
4 أكثر استحقاقًا لتأييدنا الكامل 5 أشدّ احتياجًا من أهل القرى
6 أكثر تقدّمًا 7 أكثر ممّا يقولون لنا
8 أبسط و أكثر إفادةً من هذه الآلة الصغيرة
Ex. 3 1 ... أحسن ممّا رجونا. 2 ... أقلّ ممّا استلمنا.
3 ... أفضل ممّا كانت ... 4 ... أفضل من الشهر الماضي.
5 ... أكثر فعلاً من تقاريره ... 6 ... أثقل في القاهرة من في ...

Chapter 30. Ex. 1 1 علّم يعلّم، علّم، معلّم، معلّم، تعليم II
2 عمل يعمل، اعمل، عامل، معمول، عمل I
3 اشترى يشتري، اشتر، مشتر\المشتري، مشترًى\المشترى، اشتراء
VIII 4 اتّصل يتّصل، اتّصل، متّصل، متّصل به، اتّصال VIII
5 قرأ يقرأ، اقرأ، قارئ، مقروء، قراءة I
6 احتاج يحتاج، احتج، محتاج، محتاج إليه، احتياج VIII
7 حول يحاول، حاول، محاول، محاول، محاولة III
8 أرسل يرسل، أرسل، مرسل، مرسل، إرسال IV
9 انخفض ينخفض، انخفض، منخفض، -، انخفاض VII
10 اهتمّ يهتمّ، اهتمّ، مهتمّ، مهتمّ به، اهتمام VIII

11 ادرس يدرس، ادرس، دارس، مدروس، دراسة I

12 جدّد يجدّد، جدّد، مجدّد، مجدّد، تجديد II

13 صوّر يصوّر، صوّر، مصوّر، مصوّر، تصوير II

14 نوى ينوي، انو، ناو\الناوي، منويّ، نية I

15 اعتبر يعتبر، اعتبر، معتبر، معتبر، اعتبار VIII

16 استبدل يستبدل، استبدل، مستبدل، مستبدل، استبدال X

17 طبع يطبع، اطبع، طابع، مطبوع، طبع I

18 نشر ينشر، انشر، ناشر، منشور، نشر I

19 تناوب يتناوب، تناوب، متناوب، متناوب، تناوب VI

20 ألقى يلقي، ألق، ملقٍ\الملقي، ملقًى\الملقى، الِقاء IV

21 أكل يأكل، كل، آكل، مأكول، أكل II

22 ذكر يذكر، اذكر، ذاكر، مذكور، ذكر I

23 تذكّر يتذكّر، تذكّر، متذكّر، متذكّر، تذكّر V

24 قال يقول، قل، قائل، مقول، قول I

25 أشار يشير، أشر، مشير، مشار إليه، إشارة IV

26 أكّد يؤكّد، أكّد، مؤكّد، مؤكّد، تأكيد II

27 حلّ يحلّ، حلّ، حالّ، محلول، حلّ II

28 اتّخذ يتّخذ، اتّخذ، متّخذ، متّخذ، اتّخاذ VIII

29 شكّ يشكّ، شكّ، شاكّ، مشكوك فيه، شكّ I

30 أوجب يوجب، أوجب، موجب، موجب، إيجاب IV

31 وجد يجد، جد، واجد، موجود، وجود I

32 باع يبيع، بع، بائع، مبيع، بيع I

3 اشتري اشتروا، لا تشتر\تشتري\تشتروا

5 اقرإي اقرأوا، لا تقرأ\تقرإي\تقرأوا

8 أرسلي أرسلوا، لا ترسل\ترسلي\ترسلوا

20 ألقي ألقوا، لا تلق\تلقي\تلقوا

24 قولي قولوا، لا تقل\تقولي\تقولوا

25 أشيري أشيروا، لا تشر\تشيري\تشيروا

32 بيعي بيعوا، لا تبع\تبيعي\تبيعوا

Ex. 2 1 تدخل 2 لا أنسى 3 لا يحتلّون 4 يناسبهم 5 لا ينفون

6 أخرج 7 يصيرون 8 يتّصل 9 نعلنه 10 تتناوبون 11 تربّون
12 يشير 13 يستغربون 14 ينجزون 15 أتردّد 16 يبكي 17 ترجون
18 تخاف 19 يدعون 20 لا نبيع 21 يفهم 22 لا تقرإين 23 تنشرونه
24 نصل

Ex. 3 1 (سـ)يكون الزوّار حاضرين للمغادرة. 2 سيصلون ...
3 سيشير إليّ ... 4 لن يزور ... 5 سيبيع كتب...
6 أنا (سـ)أكون مسؤولاً عنه. 7 من سيساعده؟ لا أحد سيهتم به.
8 سيصل ...

Ex. 4 1 نمت 2 أنام 3 تنادي 4 نويت 5 تنوي 6 جئت 7 تجيء
8 يحتاج 9 اشتريت 10 يشير 11 زار 12 طرت

Ex. 5 1 act. part., أدار IV 2 act. part., أكل I 3 pass. part., فهم I
4 act. part., كفي I 5 vb. noun, وافق III 6 vb. noun, وقف I
7 vb. noun, توسع VI 8 act. part., نادى III 9 vb. noun, أضرب IV
10 pass. part., أمر I 11 act./pass. part., افتتح VIII
12 vb. noun, استجوب X 13 vb. noun اقترح VIII 14 vb. noun, قرأ I
15 vb. noun, وجد I 16 vb. noun, قدّم II 17 act. part., تقدّم V
18 vb. noun, ارتفع VIII

Ex. 6 1 لن تجدوا كتباً ... 2 لم يجئ أحد ... 3 ألم تفهم شرحه؟
4 لم يمتز ابني ... 5 لا يمتاز ابني ... 6 لن ينفوا الادّعاء.
7 لم ير الخبراء الفرق. 8 لماذا لم تتركوا الاجتماع؟
9 ألم تجد الشرطة ... 10 لا يوجد مبدأ ... 11 لم أحتجّ على الادّعا.
12 لم يدّعوا جريمةً شديدةً.

Ex. 7 1 ليس\كان\ما كان\يكون\لا يكون الوضع بسيطًا
2 ليس\كان\ما كان\يكون\لا يكون الادّعاء شديداً.
3 ليس\كان\ما كان\يكون\لا يكون طلابي مهندسين مشهورين.
4 ليس\كان\ما كان\يكون\لا يكون في الحكومة خلاف كبير.
5 ليس\كان\ما كان\يكون\لا يكون اليوم اجتماع هامّ.
6 ليست\كانت\ما كانت\تكون\لا تكون المحاضرة مفيدةً للطلاّب.
7 ليس\كان\ما كان\يكون\لا يكون اشتراكهم ضروريًا للنجاح.
8 ليس\كان\ما كان\يكون\لا يكون الاحتلال غير قانوني.

9 ليست\كانت\ما كانت\تكون\لا تكون أحسن طريقة الإضراب.
10 ليست\كانت\ما كانت\تكون\لا تكون في المكتبة كتب قديمة.
Also possible: 4 لا يوجد\كان\لم يوجد\سيوجد\لن يوجد في ...
10 لا توجد\كانت\لم توجد\ستوجد\لن توجد في ...

Ex. 8 1 كانت السكرتيرة تتّصل بالوزير.
2 كيف كان المهندسون يقومون ...؟ 3 كانت اللجنة تبحث ...
4 ما كنّا ننتظر ... 5 ماذا كان المدراء ينوون ...؟
6 كان الفنّيون يعملون ...

Ex. 9 1 ما زلنا نعمل ... 2 لا أزال أدرس ... 3 ما زلت طالبًا ...
4 لا يزالون يبحثون ... 5 ما زالوا يبحثون ...
6 ما زلت مشغولاً ... 7 أما زلتم مشغولين أم فاضين؟
8 لا نزال فاضين، تفضّل. 9 ما زالوا الزملاء يحتجّون على ...
10 لا أزال أجد ...

Ex. 10 1 نائمون 2 الباقية 3 غائب ... مساعده 4 المحتلّة
5 مرسل 6 المسافرين

Ex. 11 1 المقوم بها 2 المطلوب 3 مشار إليها 4 متوقّعة
5 المدفوعة 6 محتجّ عليها

Ex. 12 1 دفعه للحساب 2 استلامنا لرسالتكم
3 قيامهم بمشروع غال 4 إشارتنا إلي معلومات هامّة
5 قراءتي للعقد 6 اتّخاذهم لإجراء إيجابي

Chapter 31. Ex. 1 1 إنّ الصحفيين كتبوا مقالات ...
2 إنّهم نشروا أيضًا ... 3 إنّ مندوبي المؤتمر اتّفقوا علي ...
4 إنّ الخلاف بين ... 5 إنّه أكثر اجتهاداً من ...
6 إنّا\إنّنا ما عدنا طلاّبًا ... 7 إنّ العائلة استأجرت بيتًا ...
8 إنّ المأمورين تظاهروا ...
9 إنّ الموظّفين احتجّوا خلال المفاوضات على ...
10 إنّهم قد حفروا عدّة آبار ...

Ex. 2 1 ينوي موظّفونا ... 2 لن نبحث المسألة ...
3 قد أضرب جميع موظّفينا عندما سمعوا ...

4 ... استجوبت الشرطة ... 5 لم يأخذ المجرمون
6 ... افتتح وزيرنا ... 7 قد أكّدوا أنّهم لا يعرفون شيءاً
8 ... يسأل صحفيي كلّ بلاد
Ex. 3 1 ... إنّنا لا نعرف من مسؤول عن
2. أخبرنا من فضلك بماذا حدث.
3. قد أخبرتكم بأنّ المشرفين مسؤولون.
4 ... نشكّ فيما إذا سينشرون ... 5 أكّدوا أنّهم سينشرون النتائج
6. ما زالوا يقولون إنّ الوضع غير خطر.
7. اسألوا المشرف هل\إذا وصلت الآلات الجديدة.
8 ... لا أحد يعرف كم شخصاً كان
Ex. 4 1+6. سمعت أنّهم تأخّروا\يتأخّرون.
1+7. سمعت أنّ التكاليف ارتفعت\ترتفع.
1+8. سمعت أنّ المعلّمين مسؤولون.
1+9. سمعت أنّ كلّ الآحزاب ستتعاون.
1+10. سمعت أنّ الخبراء وجدوا الحقل.
2+6. لا شكّ في أنّهم تأخّروا\يتأخّرون.
2+7. لا شكّ في أنّ التكاليف ارتفعت\ترتفع.
2+8. لا شكّ في أنّ المعلّمين مسؤولون.
2+9. لا شكّ في أنّ كلّ الآحزاب ستتعاون.
2+10. لا شكّ في أنّ الخبراء وجدوا الحقل.
3+6. خاء في الجرائد أنّهم تأخّروا\يتأخّرون.
3+7. خاء في الجرائد أنّ التكاليف ارتفعت\ترتفع.
3+8. خاء في الجرائد أنّ المعلّمين مسؤولون.
3+9. خاء في الجرائد أنّ كلّ الآحزاب ستتعاون.
3+10. خاء في الجرائد أنّ الخبراء وجدوا الحقل.
4+6. أخبرنا المدراء بأنّهم تأخّروا\يتأخّرون.
4+7. أخبرنا المدراء بأنّ التكاليف ارتفعت\ترتفع.
4+8. أخبرنا المدراء بأنّ المعلّمين مسؤولون.
4+9. أخبرنا المدراء بأنّ كلّ الآحزاب ستتعاون.
4+10. أخبرنا المدراء بأنّ الخبراء وجدوا الحقل.

5+6 تشير النشرة إلى أنّهم تأخّروا.
5+7 تشير النشرة إلى أنّ التكاليف ارتفعت\ترتفع.
5+8 تشير النشرة إلى أنّ المعلّمين مسؤولون.
5+9 تشير النشرة إلى أنّ كلّ الآحزاب ستتعاون.
5+10 تشير النشرة إلى أنّ الخبراء وجدوا الحقل.
Ex. 5 (possible answers:) 1 ... أنّ الحكومة ضعيفة.
2 ... أنّه غير مسؤول. 3 ... أنّهم يحتاجون إلى مساعدتنا.
4 ... أنّ المشروع قد فشل.
Ex. 6 1 إنّا\إنّنا ضدّ ... 2 إنّ صحفيي "أخبار الوطن" ...
3 إنّها عملت سنتين ... 4 إنّ عدداً كبيراً من ... 5 إنّ كلهم كانوا ...
6 إنّ الموظّفين الصغار .... إنّه لا يكفيهم.
Ex. 7 1 كان يتكلّم كأنّ ليس عنده مسؤولية في الأمر.
2 لم يخبرني بشيء إلاّ بأنّه ليس مسؤولاً نفسه.
3 ليس عندي علم بالأمر ولكنّي سأسأل زملائي.
4 قال للجميع إنّه يفهم كلّ شيء عن القضية.
5 أكّد للجميع أنّه يفهم كلّ شيء عن القضية.

Chapter 32. Ex. 1 1 إجابيًا 2 رئيسيًا 3 أقلّ 4 مستمراً 5 شديداً
6 أشدّ بكثير 7 حاليًا 8 جيّداً جداً 9 محلّيًا 10 أوضح (بصورة)
11 حقيقةً\في الحقيقة 12 جزئيًا
Ex. 2 1 غير واضحًا 2 عامًّا\غير استثنائيًا 3 بصورة عامّة
4 شخصيًا\غير رسميًا 5 بالضبط 6 جزئيًا 7 قريبًا 8 ضعيفًا
Ex. 3 (possible answers:) 1 بسرعة 2 سنويًا 3 فوراً 4 جداً
5 كثيراً ... قريبًا 6 جزئيًا 7 بعد قليل 8 هكذا 9 مثلاً 10 شديداً
Ex. 4 1 (بصورة) أسرع 2 بضبط أكثر 3 بصورة أخصّ 4 أحسن

Chapter 33. Ex. 1 1 يجوز أن يقترح ...
2 يمكن أن نقدّم شكوتنا للقاضي ولكن يجوز أن يرفضها.
3 هل يمكن أن تشرحوا ... 4 يجب أن يعمل الجميع ...
5 نريد أن يساعدوا ... 6 ألا تفضّل أن ننشر ...

إنّ ممثّلينا يحاولون أن يفاوضوا مع ... 7
تريد الحكومة أن تبدأ الوزارة ... 9 ننوي أن نخبرهم بأنّ ... 8
حاولوا ألاّ تبيعوا بضائع ... 10

Ex. 2 1 كان يجوز أن يقترح شيئًا آخر عندما سمع خبركم.
كان يمكن أن نقدّم شكوتنا للقاضي ولكن كان يجوز أن يرفضها. 2
كان يجب أن يعمل الجميع ... 4 هل كان يمكن أن تشرحوا ... 3
ألم تفضّل أن ننشر ... 6 كنّا نريد أن يساعدوا ... 5
إنّ ممثّلينا حاولوا أن يفاوضوا مع ... 7
نوينا أن نخبرهم بأنّ ... 8
كانت تريد الحكومة أن تبدأ الوزارة ... 9

Ex. 3 1 يجوز له أن يقترح ...
يمكننا أن نقدّم شكوتنا للقاضي ولكن يجوز له أن يرفضها. 2
يجب على الجميع أن يعمل ... 4 هل يمكنكم أن تشرحوا ... 3

Ex. 4 3 هل يمكن شرحكم لتفاصيل العقد؟
نريد مساعدة ... 5 يجب عمل الجميع من أجل ... 4
إنّ ممثّلينا يحاولون المفاوضة مع ... 7 ألا تفضّل نشرنا لمقالتك ... 6

Ex. 5 1 نريد أن نستقبل، يريدون أن يستقبلوا،
أستطيع أن أستقبل، تستطيعون أن تستقبلوا
نريد أن نساعد، يريدون أن يساعدوا، 2
أستطيع أن أساعد، تستطيعون أن تساعدوا
نريد أن نبقى، يريدون أن يبقوا، 3
أستطيع أن أبقى، تستطيعون أن تبقوا
نريد أن نزيد، يريدون أن يزيدوا، 4
أستطيع أن أزيد، تستطيعون أن تزيدوا
نريد أن نتّصل، يريدون أن يتّصلوا، 5
أستطيع أن أتّصل، تستطيعون أن تتّصلوا
نريد أن نوافق، يريدون أن يوافقوا، 6
أستطيع أن أوافق، تستطيعون أن توافقوا
نريد أن نرسل، يريدون أن يرسلوا، 7
أستطيع أن أرسل، تستطيعون أن ترسلوا

8 نريد أن نعطي، يريدون أن يعطوا،
أستطيع أن أعطي، تستطيعون أن تعطوا
1 يجب أن تستقبل، يجب أن يستقبل
2 يجب أن تساعد، يجب أن يساعد
3 يجب أن تزيد، يجب أن يزيد 4 يجب أن تبقى، يجب أن يبقى
5 يجب أن تتّصل، يجب أن يتّصل
6 يجب أن توافق، يجب أن يوافق
7 يجب أن ترسل، يجب أن يرسل
8 يجب أن تعطي، يجب أن يعطي
Ex. 6 1 طلبنا\نرجو أن تدخّل، أمرنا بأن تدخّل
2 طلبنا\نرجو أن تقول، أمرنا بأن تقول
3 طلبنا\نرجو أن تجلسي، أمرنا بأن تجلسي
4 طلبنا\نرجو أن يرجعوا، أمرنا بأن يرجعوا
5 طلبنا\نرجو أن تتّخذوا، أمرنا بأن تتّخذوا
6 طلبنا\نرجو أن تساعدونا، أمرنا بأن تساعدونا
7 طلبنا\نرجو أن تقفوا، أمرنا بأن تقفوا
8 طلبنا\نرجو أن يبقوا، أمرنا بأن يبقوا
1 طلبنا منك\نرجوك أن تدخّل، أمرناك بأن تدخّل
2 طلبنا منك\نرجوك أن تقول، أمرناك بأن تقول
3 طلبنا منك\نرجوك أن تجلسي، أمرناك بأن تجلسي
4 طلبنا منهم\نرجوهم أن يرجعوا، أمرناهم بأن يرجعوا
5 طلبنا منكم\نرجوكم أن تتّخذوا، أمرناكم بأن تتّخذوا
6 طلبنا منكم\نرجومك أن تساعدونا، أمرناكم بأن تساعدونا
7 طلبنا منكم\نرجومك أن تقفوا، أمرناكم بأن تقفوا
8 طلبنا منهم\نرجوهم أن يبقوا، أمرناهم بأن يبقوا
Ex. 7 1 .يجب علينا أن نتّصل فوراً بمسؤولي الوزارة
2 .إنّ قسم المالية لا يريد إلاّ أن يتعاون مع السلطات المناسبة
3 .هل يمكنهم أن يشتركوا كاملاً؟ إنّنا نشكّ فيه
4 .حاولت السفارة أن تعقد اجتماعًا مع وزارة الخارجية
5 .لا يزال الرئيس ينوي أن يزور رسميًا الأراضي المحتلّة

6 .إنّ المجلس لن يسمح أن يحضر الوفد الكامل
7 .كان يجب أن نؤيّد الحزب كلّه في مثل هذه المشكلة
8 هل يمكننا أن نقدّم لهم أيّ شيء؟
9 .لم يستطع المقرّر أن يكتب مقالةً مناسبةً حول القضية
10 .إنّنا نحاول أن ندرس لغةً مؤقّتةً

Chapter 34. Ex. 1 1 .استبدلنا ماكينتين لأن نستمرّ في الإنتاج
2 .دجلت الشرطة البناية لأن تفتّش عن الأسلحة
3 .إنّنا نتعلّم اللغة العربية لكي ندرس ثقافة العرب
4 .يذيعون صور المجرمين لأن يعرفهم الناس
5 .أوقفت قوات الأمن المظاهرة لئلاّ تمرّ على البرلمان
6 .من الضروري أن ننتظر حتّى ينشروا نصّ البيان
7 .أفضّل أن أبقى في المكتب لأستقبل زوّارنا عند وصولهم
8 .ذهب رئيسنا إلى القاهرة حتّى يلقي خطابًا هامًّا هناك
9 .كان يجب أن يخرج فوراً لئلاّ نتأخّر في بيروت
10 .أرجوك أن تتكلّم واضحًا لكي يسمعك المندوبون جيّداً
1 .استبدلنا ماكينتين للاستمرار في الإنتاج
2 .دجلت الشرطة البناية من أجل التفتيش عن الأسلحة
3 .إنّنا نتعلّم اللغة العربية لدراسة ثقافة العرب
6 .من الضروري أن ننتظر نشرهم لنصّ البيان
7 .أفضّل أن أبقى في المكتب لاستقبال زوّارنا عند وصولهم
8 .ذهب رئيسنا إلى القاهرة لإلقاء خطاب هامّ هناك

Ex. 2 1 لأحاول، لتحتول، لتحاولوا 2 لأغيّر، لتغيّر، لتغيّروا
3 لأستغني، لتستغني، لتستغنوا 4 لأقترح، لتقترح، لتقترحوا
5 لأنسى، لتنسى، لتنسوا 6 لأصير، لتصير، لتصيروا
7 لأرسل، لترسل، لترسلوا 8 لأرى، لترى، لتروا

Ex. 3 1 .لم ننتج هذا النفط لأن نبيعه على السوق المحلّي
2 هل اتّخذ المجلس هذا الإجراء لكي يؤيّد مصالحنا أم لا؟
3 .اشترينا جريدةً لنقرأ مقالتها الرئيسية
4 .طار الوفد إلى دمشق حتّى يفاوض اتّفاقيتنا التجارية

5 زرنا المدينة القديمة لكي نصوّر البنايات الجميلة.

Ex. 4 (possible answers:) 1 ... يتأخّر الزوّار.
2 ... تستقبل الوفد في المطار. 3 ... يغيبوا كلّهم.
4 ... يستطيع أن يساعدنا. 5 تعارضنا اللجنة.

Ex. 5 1 لأنّا\لأنّنا 2 لأنْ 3 لأنْ 4 لأنّه 5 لأنْ نزور 6 لأنْ

Chapter 35. Ex. 1 1 كتبت أنا الرسالة الّتي جاءت في الجريدة.
2 إنّنا نستورد البضائع الكهربية الّتي ينتجونها.
3 ينتجون بضائع كثيرةً نستوردها.
4 من (هو) الّذي ساعدكم بكتابة التقرير؟
5 حضر المؤتمر مندوبون كثار لا نعرفهم.
6 لم يحضر الاجتماع ممثّلو الوزارة الأمر الّذي استغربنا منه.
7 صار انفجار كبير مات شخص فيه.
8 لم ننشر اسم الشركة الّتي فشل مشروعها.
9 فاوضنا مع العمّال الذين كانوا يضربون.
10 سنستفيد كثيراً من الاتفاقية الّتي وقّعناها أمس.

Ex. 2 1 – 2 الّتي 3 الّذين 4 الّتي 5 – 6 الّذي 7 – 8 – 9 الّذي
10 – 11 – 12 الّتي

Ex. 3 1 – 2 سألتموها\سألتم عنها 3 فيها 4 إليها 5 سألتموه

Ex. 4 1+15 2+17 or 18 3+12 4+11 5+20 6+13 or 14
7+16 or 19 8+14 or 15 9+17 or 18 10+16

Ex. 5 1 الأشخاص الّذين 2 الرسالات الطويلة الّتي
3 المساعدون الفنّيون الّذين 4 البيوت الكبيرة الّتي
5 الأشياء الأولى الّتي 6 الإجراءات الإدارية الّتي

Ex. 6 1 بما 2 من 3 ممّن 4 ما 5 مع من 6 عمّا

Ex. 7 (possible answers:) 1 الأمر الّذي لم يناسبنا أبداً.
2 الّذي قد قدّمه الفلاّحون. 3 عندنا مرشّح يريد أن يعمل الترجمة.
4 أنشأوها قبل سنتين.

Ex. 8 1 تنوي منع إعلانات التبغ في الأماكن العامّة.
2 الغرض هو منع الشباب من اتّخاذ عادة التدخين.

3 لا ، غير ممنوعة\نعم، ممنوعة في عدّة محلاّت.
4 ستطبّقه بعد وقت قصير.
5 أعتبر أنّه إجرا مفيد\غير مفيد لأنّ ...
6 المترو هو سكّة حديدية تحت الأرض. في بلدي (لا) يوجد مترو.

Chapter 36. Ex. 1 1 لا ترسل الرسالة قبل أن أقرأها أنا أيضًا.
2 استمرّت الحرب حتّى ابتدأ أشدّ شتاء بذكر الإنسان.
3 بيتي بيتك طالما تحتاج إلى مساعدتي.
4 نتعلّم شيئًا عن ثقافة العرب بينما ندرس لغة العرب.
5 استكشفنا الحقل سنتين عندما وجدنا النفط بكمّيات اقتصادية.
6 ادرسوا الملفّ جيّداً قبل أن تبدأوا المفاوضة.
7 لا تنسوا أهمّية المصدر عندما تكتبون نصًّا عربيًا.
8 يجب أن تقرأ المقدّمة قبل أن تدرس تفاصيل التقرير.
9 سنستبدل الزيت بعد أن فتّشنا الطلمبة.
10 لا تنس مصالح الزبون عندما تزوره.
3 طالما تحتاج إلى مساعدتي بيتي بيتك.
4 بينما ندرس لغة العرب نتعلّم شيئًا عن ثقافة العرب.
5 عندما وجدنا النفط بكمّيات اقتصادية (قد) استكشفنا الحقل سنتين.
6 قبل أن تبدأوا المفاوضة ادرسوا الملفّ جيّداً.
7 عندما تكتبون نصًّا عربيًا لا تنسوا أهمّية المصدر.
8 قبل أن تدرس تفاصيل التقرير يجب أن تقرأ المقدّمة.
9 بعد أن فتّشنا الطلمبة سنستبدل الزيت.
10 عندما تزور الزبون لا تنس مصالحه.

Ex. 2 1 قبل انتهاء الدرس 2 حتّى انتهاء الإضراب
3 خلال نومهم 4 خلال نومهم 5 حتّى يوقّع (أحد) اتّفاقيتنا
6 بينما احتلّوا المنطقة 7 منذ ابتداء المفاوضات
8 عند تفتيشهم للسيّارة 9 قبل أنْ تبتدئ البحوث
10 عندما استقبلوا\يستقبلون الضيوف 11 بعد نشرنا للبيان
12 قبل أنْ أغادر\تغادر(ي\وا)\يغادر(وا)\نغادر البلد

Ex. 3 (possible answers:) 1 يرجعوا. 2 رجعوا. 3 تكتب العربية؟
4 يوقّع الوثيقة. 5 تجاوب. 6 أعمل على التمارين.
7 بعد أنْ تمّت المحاضرة ... 8 رأوا الشرطة.

Chapter 37. Ex. 1

1 لو كانوا (قد) وجدوا بيتًا مناسبًا لاستأجروه.
2 إذا وافقوا على اشتراء كمّيات كبيرة نخفّض السعر.
3 إذا أضربوا نرفض دفع الإضافة.
4 لو كان الوضع سلميًا لكان يمكن الحكومة أن تعلن انتخابًا.
5 لو عرفنا الأرقام بالضبط لاستعملناها لكتابة تقريرنا.
6 لو كانت الشركة أغنى لاشترينا طائرةً للمدراء.
7 إذا كانت المهمّة صعبةً فاطلب المساعدة.
8 إذا لم يزل يحتجّ فلا يسمع أحد.
1 إذا وجدوا بيتًا مناسبًا يستأجرونه.
2 لو وافقوا على اشتراء كمّيات كبيرة لخفّضنا السعر.
3 لو أضربوا لرفضنا دفع الإضافة.
4 إذا كان الوضع سلميًا يمكن الحكومة أن تعلن انتخابًا.
5 إذا عرفنا الأرقام بالضبط نستعملها لكتابة تقريرنا.

Ex. 2 1 لو لم نعرف التفاصيل 2 إذا لم نستطع أن نؤيّدكم
3 إذا لم تصل الطائرة الآن 4 إذا لم يوافقوا على الميزانية
5 لو لم يستكشفوا الحقل 6 إذا لم يستكشفوا الحقل
7 لو لم تدرس سنةً إضافيةً 8 إذا لم يزر السيّاح البرلمان
1 لو عرفنا التفاصيل 2 إذا استطعنا أن نؤيّدكم
3 إذا وصلت الطائرة الآن 4 إذا وافقوا على الميزانية
5 لو استكشفوا الحقل 6 إذا استكشفوا الحقل
7 لو درسَت سنةً إضافيةً 8 إذا زار السيّاح البرلمان

Ex. 3 (possible answers:) 1 يفهم كلّ شيء.
2 فشلت كلّ محاولاتنا 3 يكون أحسن بكثير
4 لكان يمكنهم أن يجدوا الفلوس. 5 لما وجدوا شيئاً
6 فسيساعدنا كثيراً. 7 وقّع لي هذا

8 كان يمكننا أن نبحث القضية

Ex. 4 1. إذا احتجت إلى المساعدة فلا تتردّد أنْ تطلبها.
2. كنت تكلّمت معهم لو كانوا قد حضروا المؤتمر.
3. لو كان عندي عنوانكم لقد أرسلنا لكم نسخةً.
4. نؤيّدكم دائمًا مهما كنتم تحتاجون إليه.
5. إذا كان عندنا وقت كاف فسنزور المنطقة الساحلية أيضًا.
6. كيفما عملوا يكلّفهم أكثر.

Ex. 5 (possible answers:) 1 مع أنّ الدورة كانت صعبةً
2 مهما قال 3 إينما نظرنا 4 متى ما طلبتمونا

Ex. 6 1. هذا الخبر إيجابي لأنّ اللغة الإنجليزية مفيدة.
2. إنّ دراسة لغاة أخرى تمدّ ثقافة من يدرسها.
3 يوجد سببان: أولاً أهمّية العالمية السابقة لبريطانيا و بعد ذلك قوة الولايات المتّحدة في حقول مثل العلوم والسياسة والمواصلات.
4. سيبتدأ في أوّل السنة الدراسية المقبلة.

Chapter 38. Ex. 1 (a) *wāḥid, ithnayn, thalātha, 'arba'a, khamsa, sitta, sab'a, thamāniya, tis'a, 'ashara, 'iḥd'ashar, ithn'ashar, thalatt'ashar, 'arba't'ashar, khamst'ashar, sitt'ashar, saba't'ashar, thamant'ashar, tis'at'ashar, 'ishrīn, wāḥid u-'ishrīn, ithnayn u-'ishrīn, thalātha u-'ishrīn, 'arba'a u-'ishrīn, khamsa u-'ishrīn, sitta u-'ishrīn, sab'a u-'ishrīn, thamāniya u-'ishrīn, tis'a u-'ishrīn, thalāthīn.*

(b) *'arba'īn, khamsīn, sittīn, sab'īn, thamānīn, tis'īn, mīya.*

(c) *mitayn, thalāth mīya, 'arba' mīya, khams mīya, sitt mīya, saba' mīya, thamān mīya, tisa' mīya, 'alf.*

(d) *'alfayn, thalāthat 'ālāf, 'arba'at 'ālāf, khamsat 'ālāf, sittat 'ālāf, saba'at 'ālāf, thamāniyat 'ālāf, tis'at 'ālāf, 'asharat 'ālāf.*

Ex. 2 1 متر 2 ديناراً كويتياً 3 أيّام 4 دولارات
5 كيلومتراً 6 يومًا فاضيًا 7 شخصًا فاضيًا 8 جنيهات مصرية
9 ريالاً سعوديًا 10 ليرة لبنانية

Ex. 3 1 جنيهات مصرية، جنيهًا مصريًا، جنيه مصري
2 دولارات أمريكية، دولاراً أمريكيًا، دولار أمريكي
3 كتب عربية، كتابًا عربيًا، كتاب عربي 4 مرّات، مرّةً، مرّة
5 أسئلة، سؤالاً، سؤال
6 مرشّحين أجانب، مرشّحًا أجنبيًا، مرشّح أجنبي
7 أمتار، متراً، متر 8 تقارير فنّية، تقريراً فنّيًا، تقرير فنّي
9 ريالات قطرية، ريالاً قطريًا، ريال قطري
10 تلاميذ لبنانيين جدد، تلميذاً لبنانيًا جديداً، تلميذ لبناني جديد
Ex. 4 1 ثاني شارع، الشارع الثاني
2 إوّل سنة، السنة الأولى 3 سادس درس، الدرس السادس
4 رابع وخامس تمارين، التمارين الرابع والخامس
5 البئر الحادية عشرة 6 السيّارة الثانية عشرة
Ex. 5 1 أصدرها المعهد الحكومي لأبحاث الطاقة في الصين.
2 هذه هي أوّل أرقام الّتي نشرها مصدر رسمي في الصين.
3 الزيادة السنوية هي ٧،٧٪.
4 استهلكت ٢٦٠ مليون طنّ أي ٥،٣٤ مليوت برميل يوميًا.
5 عند الصين سادس اقتصاد في العالم.
6 توجد ٧،٥ براميل (٧ براميل والنصف) تقريبًا في طنّ واحد.

Chapter 39. Ex. 1 1 الساعة الرابعة والربع
2 الساعة الثانية عشرة\الظهر 3 الساعة الرابعة إلاّ الربع
4 الساعة السادسة والثلث 5 الساعة التاسعة والنصف وخمسة
6 الساعة التاسعة إلاّ دقيقتين 7 الساعة الحادية عشرة والنصف
8 الساعة الثانية والنصف وتسعة دقائق
9 الساعة الثانية والنصف إلاّ ثلاث دقائق
10 الساعة العاشرة وعشر 11 الساعة السادسة ألاّ خمس
12 الساعة الثامنة ألاّ الثلث
Ex. 2 1 ٣،٣٠ 2 ٤،٢٠ 3 ٨،٥٥ 4 ٧،١٠ 5 ٥،٥٢
6 ١١،٠٠ 7 ٧،٤٠ 8 ١،٣٠ 9 ٢،٢٥ 10 ٤،٠٢
Ex. 3 1 عند الإشارة تكون الساعة: العاشرة وخمس وعشرون

دقيقةً وخمس عشرة ثانيةً

2 الرابعة وخمس دقائق وخمس ثوان :...

3 الثانية عشرة\ظهر بالضبط :...

4 السادسة وثلاث وثلاثون دقيقةً وثلاثون ثانيةً :...

5 الحادية عشرة وواحدة وأربعون دقيقةً وخمس وعشرون ثانيةً :...

6 السابعة وتسع وعشرون دقيقةً بالضبط :...

7 الحادية عشرة وواحدة وأربعون دقيقةً وعشر ثوان :...

8 الثالثة وعشر دقائق و خمس وأربعون ثانيةً :...

Ex. 4 (a) *yawm al-jum'a, yawm as-sabt, yawm al-'aḥad, yawm al-ithnayn, yawm ath-thalātha, yawm al-'arbaʻa, yawm al-khamīs.* (b) *kānun ath-thānī, shubāṭ, 'ādhār, nīsān, 'ayyār, ḥazīrān, tammūz, 'āb, 'aylūl, tishrīn al-'awwal, tishrīn ath-thānī, kānūn al-'awwal. yanāyir, fibrāyir, māris, 'abrīl, māyu, yūniyū, yūliyū, 'aghusṭus, sibtambar, 'uktóbar, novambar, disambar.*

1 يناير 2 فبراير 3 أيّار 4 آذار 5 أكتوبر 6 تمّوز 7 أيلول
8 أبريل

Ex. 5 1 *yawm ath-thalātha, 'ishrīn tishrīn ath-thānī/novambar, sanat 'alfayn u-sabʻa mīlādīya* 2 *al-'arbaʻa, thānī u-'ishrīn dhi l-ḥijja, sanat 'alf u-thalāth mīya u-'arbaʻa u-'ishrīn hijrīya* 3 *yawm al-'aḥad, thānī 'ashar tishrīn al-'awwal/'uktóbar, sanat 'alf u-tisaʻ mīya u-tisʻa u-sittīn mīlādīya* 4 *al-ithnayn, khāmis tammūz/yūliyū, sanat 'alf u-tisaʻ mīya u-thnayn u-thamānīn mīlādīya*

Ex. 6 1 عقدوها في ثاني والعشرين أيّار\مايو سنة ألفين وأربعة، في تونس.

2 أرجئت من ثامن عشر آذار\مارس من نفس السنة.

3 كان رئيس وزراء البحرين الرئيس السابق.

4 كانت الجلسة عامةً. ألقى خطاباً الرئيسان السابق والجديد.

5 كان يمكنه ذكر قضايا مختلفة، بينها فلسطين وإسرائيل، والعراق، ومكافحة الإرهاب، والتطوّرات في العالم العربي مثلاً.

Chapter 40. Ex. 1 1 إنّا\إنّنا اشتركنا تمامًا في تنظيم المؤتمر.
2 إنّ المهندسين كانوا يحاولون أن يشرحوا المشكلة.
3 إنّ مشاريعنا لن تنجح بدون تعاونكم.
4 إنّ المساعدين الفنّيين للوكالة يساعدوننا في العمليات.
5 إنّ خبراء الشركة جاؤوا وساعدونا.
6 إنّه ليس حاضراً. إنّه كان غائبًا امس ايضًا.
7 إنّ عدد من مشاريعهم فشلت بعد الحرب.
8 إنّ طلاّبنا نجحوا في امتحانهم.
9 إنّ زوّارنا سيتركون الأوتيل بعد زيارة المدينة.
10 إنّ الممثّلين يريدون أن ينشروا التقرير قريبًا.
Ex. 2 1 لا\لم\لن نتعاون في العملية
2 إنّها لا تنسى\لم تنس\لن تنسى عنواني
3 لا يرسلون\لم يرسلوا\لن يرسلوا تقريراً فنّيًا
4 لا\لم\لن ينجح تمامًا
5 لا يخاف\لم يخف\لن يخاف من نتيجة الانتخابات
6 لا يستشيروننا\لم يستشيرونا\لن يستشيرونا
7 ليس\ما كان (لم يكن)\لا يكون حاضراً
8 لا\لم\لن يصدّقهم 9 إنّني لا\لم\لن أفهم لماذا
10 لا\لم\لن تتردّد
Ex. 3 1 ألا يحضرون؟ 2 هل طلبوه أنفسهم؟
3 لماذا\لأيّ غرض عملوا هكذا؟ 4 ماذا أرسلوا لك؟
5 متى وصلوا؟ 6 من وقّع التقرير؟
Ex. 4 1 كان يجب أن الوفود توافق على هذه النقطة الأساسية.
كان يجب وفاق الوفود على هذه النقطة الأساسية.
2 إنّ مدير الإدارة يريد أن يبتدأ برناجنا فوراً.
إنّ مدير الإدارة يريد ابتداء برناجنا الفوري.
3 رجت الشركة أن تكون العملية ناجحةً تمامًا.
رجت الشركة نجاح العملية التامّة.
4 بدأنا ندرس اقتراح العمّال الّذين كانوا يضربون.
بدأنا دراسة اقتراح العمّال الّذين كانوا يضربون.

5 هل يستطيع الخبراء أن يهتمّوا بهذه التفاصيل؟
هل يستطيع الخبراء اهتمام بهذه التفاصيل؟

Ex. 5 1 سنرسل لهم البضائع الّتي يحتاجون إليها.
2 ذكروا شيئًا جميعنا استغربنا منه.
3 هذا هو مشروع يهمّنا كثيراً.
4 استقبل الرئيس الزوّار الّذين قد سافروا إلى البلاد لزيارة رسمية.
5 استفاد الناس كثيراً من المشاريع الّتي قد قامت بها الحكومة.
6 قد قامت الحكومة بمشاريع مختلفة لن نستفيد منها.
7 إنّنا نشكّ في نجاح البرنامج الّذي يشرحه المقرّر في مقالته.
8 هل هذه هي التفاصيل الّتي خبرتم الرئيس بها؟
9 خبرناهم بمعلومات أخذناها من الصحافة.
10 لن نشترك في بحوث لا تفيدنا أبداً.

Ex. 6 1 عندما وصلوا قد انتهى المؤتمر.
2 انتظرنا حتّى وصلوا. 3 سننتظر حتّى يصلوا.
4 استمررنا ندرس المشكلة.
5 كان يجب أن نستبدل الماكينة لكي نستأنف الإنتاج.
6 ظلّوا يستعملون أساليب قديمة مع أنّها كلّفت أكثر.
7 يجب أن نقرأ الميزانية قبل أن نقرّر.
8 لن يحضر ممثّلونا المؤتمر لأنّهم ليسوا في البلاد.
9 رفضوا طلب المرشّح عندما سمعوا الحكاية.
10 إنّنا قد تدخّلنا لكي نساعدكم. ألا تصدّقوننا؟
11 لو كان يمكنهم أن يؤيّدوك لقد اتّصلوا بك فوراً.
12 لهذا الغرض لم يبدأوا يركّبون الكمبيوتر أمس.
13 إذا درسوا الهندسة يمكن أن يسافروا إلى الخارج.
14 يحاول أن يتعلّم كيف يجب أن يكتب اللغة العربية.
15 حتى ولو ساعدناك لما نجحت.
16 فضّلنا أن يلقي المساعد الخطاب لأنّه يعرف الموضوع.
17 لو كان قد عرف المساعد الموضوع لقد ألقى الخطاب.
18 إنّهم تردّدوا أن يستشيرنا قبل انتهاء الدراسة الفنّية.
19 لا تتردّد أن تستشيرهم إذا كانت مشكلة.

20 اعتقدنا أنّك تسافر قريبًا.

Ex. 7 1 يريدون المهندسون استبدال الماكينات.

2 جاء بعض الخبراء لمساعدته.

3 انتظر الحزب نتيجة الانتخاب قبل دراسة سياستنا.

4 أهمّ شيء هو تركيب الفوري للكهربا.

5 إنّنا نفهم تمامًا احتياجهم.

Ex. 8 1 قد فشلت سياسة الحكومة.

2 كانوا يحتاجون إلى مساعدة البنك الدولي.

3 بدأ النوّاب يتكلمون عن ارتفاع ثمن الطاقة.

4 دفع المسافرون حسابهم و تركوا الأوتيل.

5 أعتقد أنّ السياسيين لا يهتمّون كثيراً بهذا.

Ex. 9 1 لم نعرف لماذا ترفض طلبنا.

2 لم يؤكّدوا هل\إذا\ما إذا سيحضرون. 3 أمرناه بأن يقف.

4 شرح كيف ينوي أن يقوم به.

5 رجونا منهم ألا ينسوا هذه النقطة.

6 طلبوا منّي أن أقول لهم اسمي.

Ex. 10 1 الّذين يحضرون\حاضرون 2 أن يتّصل 3 ذات

4 بعد رجوعهم 5 لا نستطيع 6 غير موقّع

Ex. 11 1 اختطف "جيش الربّ المعارض" حوالى ٨ آلاف طفل.

2 يجري تجنيد الأطفال بالقوة.

3 عدد الأطفال-الجنود مئتي ألف تقريبًا.

4 في الكنغو حدثت جرائم لا مقارنة بها على حقوق الأطفال.

5 تحتلّ أفريقية أوّل مكان في تجنيد الأطفال-الجنود.

6 حقوق الطفل هي مثلاً: الأمن والأكل والصحّة والاهتمام والتربية.

7 توجد اتّفاقيات ولكنّها لم نجحت في كلّ بلاد العالم.

Vocabulary index

Numbers indicate the chapter (or the chapter/paragraph) containing the first or most useful appearance of the word. Words always preceded by the article ...ال *al-* (etc.) are listed with the article, but in their own alphabetical position. For noun and adjective entries, see Chapters 3/5 and 10/4; for verb entries see Chapters 17/1, 20/5 and 28/2. For brevity, the particle 'to' is omitted from the English infinitive. The sign → refers an entry to a related entry (e.g. broken pl. to sing., irregular fem. to masc.), wherever the two entries are not adjacent.

ا\آ\أ\إ

أ *'a-* see 13/1, 23/4

ائتمر *i'támara* VIII deliberate 22

آب *'āb* August 39

أب آباء *'ab 'ābā'* father 1

بئر ← آبار

ابتدأ *ibtáda'a* VIII begin 22

ابتداء *ibtidā'* beginning 28; ابتداءً من *ibtidā'an min* with effect from 32

ابتدائي *ibtidā'ī* primary, elementary 5

بحث ← أبحاث

بحر ← أبحر

أبداً *'abadan* at all, ever; (+ neg.) not at all, never 32

أبريل *'abrīl* April 39

إبل *'ibil* camels 10

ابن أبناء *ibn 'abnā'* son 1

أبوظبي *'abū ẓabī* Abu Dhabi 36

باب ← أبواب

أبيض بيضاء بيض *'abyaḍ bayḍā' bīḍ* white 10

الاتّحاد الأوربّي :اتّحاد *al-ittiḥād al-'urubbī* European Union 15

اتّخاذ *ittikhādh* taking 28

اتّخذ *ittákhadha* VIII take 22

اتّصال *ittiṣāl* contact, telephone call 24, 28

اتّصل ب *ittáṣala* VIII *bi* contact 22

اتّفاقية *ittifāqīya* (written) agreement 15

اتّفق على *ittáfaqa* VIII *'ala* agree on/to 22

ثمن ← أثمان

اثنا عشر *ithn'ashar* twelve 38

اثنين *ithnayn*, f. *thintayn* two 38

الاثنين *al-ithnayn* Monday 39

إجازة *'ijāza* holiday 39

أجنبي ← أجانب

اجتماع *ijtimā'* meeting 3

أربع مئة *'arba' mīya* four hundred 38

أربعة *'arba'a* four; أربعة عشر *'arba'at'ashar* fourteen 38

أربعين *'arba'īn* forty 38

ارتفع *irtáfa'a* VIII rise, go up 22

أرجئت *'urji'at* it was postponed 39

الأردنّ *al-'urdunn* Jordan 36

إرسال *'irsāl* despatch 28

أرسل *'arsala* IV send 20

أرض أراض\الأراضي *'arḍ 'arāḍin, al-'arāḍī* (f. weak) land 10

إرهاب *'irhāb* terrorism 13

أرى يري *'ara yurī* IV show to 20

ازداد *izdāda yazdādu* VIII be increased 22

ازدياد *izdiyād* increase 28

أزرق زرقاء زرق *'azraq zarqā' zurq* blue 10

أزمة أزمات *'azma 'azamāt* crisis 15

أسبوع → أسابيع

أستاذ → أساتذة

أساس أسس *'asās 'usus* basis 8

أساسي *'āsasī* basic 5; أساسيًا *'asāsīyan* basically 32

أسلوب → أساليب

سبب → أسباب

أسبوع أسابيع *'usbū' 'asābī'* week 39

استأجر *ista'jara* X rent (as tenant) 22

أستاذ أساتذة *'ustādh 'asātidha* professor 5

استأنف *ista'nafa* X resume 22

استبدال *istibdāl* replacement 33

استبدل *istabdala* X replace 22

استثمار *istithmār* investment 9, 28

استثمر *istathmara* X invest 22

استثناء *istithnā'* exception 28

استثنائي *istithnā'ī* exceptional 28

استثنى *istathna* X except 22

استجوب يستجوب *istajwaba yastajwibu* X interrogate 22

استحقّ *istaḥaqqa* X deserve 22

استحقاق *istiḥqāq* merit 28

استراح *istarāḥa* X rest 22, 28

استشار *istashāra* X consult 22

استطاع *istaṭā'a* X can, to be able 33

استعداد *isti'dād* readiness 28

استعمال *isti'māl* use 28

استعمل *ista'mala* X use 22

استغرب (من) *istaghraba* X *(min)* be surprised (at) 22

استغنى عن *istaghna* X *'an* do without 22

استفاد من *istafāda* X *min* benefit from 22

استقبل *istaqbala* X receive (guests) 22

استقرار *istiqrār* stability 7

استقلال *istiqlāl* independence 15

استكشاف *istikshāf* exploration 18

استلم *istálama* VIII receive (things) 22

استمرّ (في) *istamarra* X (*fī*) continue 22

استمرار *istimrār* continuation 28

استنكار *istinkār* disapproval 28

استهلك *istahlaka* X consume 38

استورد *istawrada* X import 22

استئجار *isti'jār* renting 28

استيراد *istīrād* importation 28

استئناف *isti'nāf* resumption 28

إسرائيل *'isrā'īl* Israel 15

أساس → أسس

سعر → أسعار

سلاح → أسلحة

أسلوب أساليب *'uslūb 'asālīb* method 3

اسم أسماء *ism 'asmā'* name 1

سمكة → أسماك

سوق → أسواق

أسود سوداء سود *'aswad sawdā' sūd* black 10

سؤال → أسئلة

أشار إلى *'ashāra* IV *'ila* point to 20

إشارة *'ishāra* sign, reference 28

اشتراء *ishtirā'* purchase 28

اشتراكي *ishtirākī* socialist 7

اشتراكية *ishtirākīya* socialism 10

اشترك (في) *ishtáraka* VIII (*fī*) participate (in) 22

اشترى *ishtára* VIII buy 22

شتاء → أشتية

شجرة → أشجار

شخص → أشخاص

شديد → أشدّاء

شهر → أشهر

شيء → أشياء

صبح → أصباح

إصدار *'iṣdār* export(ation), issue 28

أصدر *'aṣdara* IV issue, export 20

صديق → أصدقاء

اصطنع *iṣṭána'a* VIII manufacture 22

أصفر صفراء صفر *'aṣfar ṣafrā' ṣufr* yellow 10

صيف → أصياف

أضاف *'aḍāfa* IV add 20

إضافة *'iḍāfa* addition 28

إضراب *'iḍrāb* strike (labour) 28

أضرب *'aḍraba* IV strike (labour) 20

اضطرب *iḍṭáraba* VIII clash 22

طبيب → أطبّة

طرف → أطراف

أطرش طرشاء طرش *'aṭrash*

ṭarshā' ṭursh deaf 10
طفل ← أطفال
اطّلاع *iṭṭilā'* information 28
طنّ ← أطنان
أطيب *'aṭyab* kinder, pleasanter 8
ظهر ← أظهار
أخذ بعين الاعتبار :اعتبار
'akhadha I *bi-'ayn al-i'tibār*
take into consideration 28;
اعتباراً من *i'tibāran min*
with effect from 32
اعتبر *i'tábara* VIII consider 22
اعتقد *i'táqada* VIII believe 22
عدد ← أعداد
عضو ← أعضاء
إعطاء *'i'ṭā'* donation 28
أعطى *'a'ṭa* IV give to 20
إعلان *'i'lān* announcement, advertisement 24
أعلن *'a'lana* IV
announce, advertise 24
عمل ← أعمال
أعمى عمياء عمي *'a'ma 'amyā'*
'umy blind 10
عالم ← أعوالم
عيد ← أعياد
غرض ← أغراض
أغسطس *'aghusṭus* August 39
غني ← أغنياء
أفاد *'afāda* IV
benefit, report, inform 20
إفادة *'ifāda*
benefit, usefulness 29
افتتاح *iftitāḥ* inauguration 28
افتتح *iftátaḥa* VIII inaugurate 22
أفريقيا *'afrīqiya* Africa 4
أفضل *'afḍal* better 8
فعل ← أفعال
فكرة ← أفكار
فلم ← أفلام
أقارب *'aqārib* relatives 8
إقليم ← أقاليم
إقامة *'iqāma* residence 28
اقتراح *iqtirāḥ*
proposal, suggestion 28
اقترح *iqtáraḥa* VIII
propose, suggest 22
اقتصاد *iqtiṣād* economy 9
اقتصر على *iqtáṣara 'ala* VIII
be restricted to 39
قسم ← أقسام
قليل ← أقلاّء
إقليم أقاليم *'iqlīm 'aqālīm*
region 7
قوي ← أقوياء
أكابر *'akābir* adults,
older/prominent people 8
اكتشاف *iktishāf* discovery 18, 28
اكتشف *iktáshafa* VIII discover 22
اكتوبر *'uktóbar* October 39
أكثرية *'aktharīya* majority 9
أكّد *'akkada* II confirm, assure 20
آكل *'ākil* eating 26
أكل *'akl* eating 28; food 29

أكل يأكل *'akala ya'kulu* I
eat 11, 17
أكيد *'akīd* certain, sure (facts) 29
إلاّ *'illa* except (for),
(with neg. verb) only 23
ألف ← آلاف
التأم *ilta'ama* VIII
come together 22
الّتى *allátī* who, which 35
الّذي *alládhī* who, which 35
الّذين *alladhīna* who 35
ألف آلاف\ألوف *'alf 'ālāf, 'ulūf*
thousand;
الألف *al-'alf* thousandth 38
ألقى *'alqa* IV throw, deliver
(speech, lecture) 20
ألمانيا *'almániya* Germany 4
آلة *'āla* instrument, device, tool,
machine 29
ألف ← ألوف
إلى *'ila* to 6
أم *'am* or (in a question) 13
أمّ أمّهات *'umm 'ummahāt*
mother 1
الإمارات *al-'imārāt* Emirates 36
مكان ← أماكن
أمام *'amām* in front of 6
أمان *'amān* security 15
متر ← أمتار
امتاز *imtāza* VIII excel 22
امتحان *imtiḥān* examination 5
امتدّ *imtadda* VIII
be extended 22
امتياز *imtiyāz* distinction 28
مثل ← أمثال
أمر (ب) *'amara ya'muru* I *(bi-)*
order 17
أمر أمور *'amr 'umūr*
matter, affair 3
أمر أوامر *'amr 'awāmir*
command 3
أمريكا *'amrīka* America 2
أمريكي *'amrīkī* American 2
أمس *'ams* yesterday 1
مساء ← أمساء
إمكانية *'imkānīya* possibility 8
أمم: الأمم المتّحدة *al-'umam al-muttáḥida* United Nations 15
أمّن *'ammana* II insure 20
أمن *'amn* security 15
مال ← أموال
أمر ← أمور
أمين أمناء *'amīn 'umanā'*
secretary (-general etc.) 39
الآن *al-'ān* now 32
أنْ *'an* that see 33
إنْ: إن شاء الله *'in shā' 'allāh,*
'inshallāh one hopes,
hopefully 37;
إن وجد(ت) *'in wujid(at)*
if any, as the case may be 37
أنّ *'anna* that see 31
إنّ *'inna* that see 31
أنا *'ana* I (pronoun) 5

نبأ ← أنباء

أنت *'anta/'anti* you (m./f.) 5

إنتاج *'intāj* production 2

أنتج *'antaja* IV produce 20

انتخاب *intikhāb* (s)election 7

انتخب *intákhaba* VIII (s)elect 22

انتظر *intáẓara* VIII wait (for), expect 22

أنتم *'antum* you (pl.) 5

انتهى *intáha* VIII (come to an) end 22

أنجز *'anjaza* IV implement, accomplish 20

أنجلترا *'ingiltira* England, Gt. Britain 4

إنجليزي إنجليز *'ingilīzī 'ingilīz* English, British 4

انحاز *inḥāza* VII isolate oneself 22

انحلّ *inḥalla* VII be solved 22

انخفض *inkháfaḍa* VII be lowered/reduced 22

انزوى *inzáwa* VII keep to oneself 22

إنسان *'insān* human being 13

انسحاب *insiḥāb* withdrawal 28

انسحب *insáḥaba* VII withdraw 22

أنشأ *'ansha'a* IV construct, create 20

إنشاء *'inshā'* essay 5

انضمام *inḍimām* annexation 28

... انفجر *infájara* VII explode 22

نفس ← أنفس

انقضى *inqáḍa* VII be finished 22

انقلاب *inqilāb* overthrow, coup d'état 28

انكفأ *inkáfa'a* VII be turned away/over 22

إنكلترا *'ingiltira* England, Great Britain 4

إنكليزي إنكليز *'ingilīzī 'ingilīz* English, British 4

نهر ← أنهر

أهل ← أهال\الأهالي

اهتمّ ب *ihtamma* VIII *bi* be concerned by/about 22

اهتمام *ihtimām* concern 28

أهل أهال\الأهالي: أهل *'ahl 'ahālin, al-'ahālī* relative (weak); أهل القرى *'ahl al-qura* country people; أهل المدن *'ahl al-mudun* townspeople 10

أهمّ *'ahamma* IV concern, be important to 20

أهمّيّة *'ahammīya* importance 8

أو *'aw* or 1

آخر ← أواخر

أمر ← أوامر

أوّل ← أوائل

أوتوبيس *'otobīs* bus 12

أوتيل *'utayl* hotel 12

أوجب *'awjaba* IV impose, obligate 20

ورقة ← أوراق

وزن ← أوزان

وضع ← أوضاع

وطن ← أوطان

وقت ← أوقات

أوقف *'awqafa* IV (bring to a) stop 20

أوّل أوائل *'awwal 'awā'il* first 8, 38; أوّلاً *'awwalan* firstly 32

ولد ← أولاد

أولئك *'ūlā'ika* those 4

أي *'ay* i.e., that is to say 38

أيّ *'ayy* any 9; which, what 13; ← نوع

يد ← أياد\الأيادي

أيار *'ayyār* May 39

يوم ← أيّام

إيجاب *'ījāb* obligation 28

إيجابي *'ījābī* positive 8

أيّد *'ayyada* II support 20

أيضاً *'ayḍan* also 19

إيطاليا *'īṭāliya* Italy 4

أيلول *'aylūl* September 39

إيميل *'īmayl* e-mail 24

أين *'ayna* where 13

ب

ب *bi-* in, with, by means of 6

باب أبواب *bāb 'abwāb* door 1

باخرة بواخر *bākhira bawākhir* ship 12

باص *bāṣ* bus 12

باع يبيع *bā'a yabī'u* I sell 14

باق\الباقي *bāqin/al-bāqī* (weak) remaining, remainder 26

بائع باعة *bā'i' bā'a* salesman 25

بائعة *bā'i'a* saleswoman 25

بترول *bitrōl* petroleum 18

بحث يبحث *baḥatha yabḥathu* I discuss 15, 17

بحث بحوث *baḥth buḥūth* discussion 3; بحث أبحاث *baḥth 'abḥāth* (re)search 38

بحر أبحار *baḥr 'abḥār* sea 12

البحرين *al-baḥrayn* (f.) Bahrain 36

بحث ← بحوث

بدأ يبدأ *bada'a yabda'u* I begin 11, 17

برنامج ← برامج

برلمان *barlamān* parliament 7

برميل براميل *barmīl barāmīl* barrel 38

برنامج برامج *barnāmaj barāmij* programme 7

بريد *barīd* post, mail; بريد إلكتروني *barīd 'iliktrōnī* e-mail 24

بريطانيا *barīṭāniya* Britain 4

بستان بساتين *bustān basātīn* garden 1

بسيط بسطاء *basīṭ busaṭā'* simple 2

بضاعة بضائع *biḍā'a baḍā'i'* merchandise 9

بعث يبحث (ب) *ba'atha* *yab'athu* I *(bi-)* to send 12

بعد *ba'd* after 6; بعد أن *ba'd 'an* after 36; لم ... بعد *lam ... ba'd* not yet 23

بعض *baḍ'* each other; (in construct) some 9

بعيد (عن) *ba'īd ('an)* far (from) 8

بغداد *baghdād* Baghdad 18

بقر *baqar* cattle 10

بقرة *baqara* cow 10

بقي يبقى *báqiya yabqa* I remain 14, 17

بكى يبكي *baka yabkī* I weep 14, 17

بلاد بلدان *bilād buldān* country 4; → بلد

بلد بلاد *balad bilād* (m./f.) town 10

بلاد → بلدان

بلدية *baladīya* municipality 10

بلغ يبلغ *balagha yablaghu* I amount to 17

بنت → بنات

بناية *bināya* building 10

بنت بنات *bint banāt* girl, daughter 1

بنزين *binzīn* petrol, gasolene 18

بنك بنوك *bank bunūk* bank 9; البنك الدولي *al-bank ad-duwalī* World Bank 15

بنون *banūn* boys 37

بوّاب *bawwāb* doorman 4

باخرة → بواخر

بيان *bayān* notice 24

بيت بيوت *bayt buyūt* house 1

بئر آبار *bi'r 'ābār* (f.) well 18

بيروت *bayrūt* Beirut 10

بيض *bayḍ* eggs 10

أبيض → بيض\بيضاء

بيضة *bayḍa* egg 10

بيع بيوع *bay' buyū'* sale 25

بين *bayna* between, among 6

بينما *baynamā* while 36

بيت → بيوت

بيع → بيوع

ت

تاجر تجّار *tājir tujjār* merchant, trader 4

تأخّر *ta'akhkhara* V be late/delayed 21

تأخير *ta'khīr* delay 12

تاريخ تواريخ *tārīkh tawārīkh* date, history 3

تاسع *tāsi'* ninth 38

تأسّف *ta'assuf* regret 28

تأسّف (على\ل) *ta'assafa* V *('ala, li-)* be sorry (about) 21

تأكّد *ta'akkada* V be sure 21

تاكسي *taksī* taxi 12

تأكيد *ta'kīd* confirmation 28

تامّ *tāmm* complete 26

تآمر *ta'āmara* VI confer 21

تأمين *ta'mīn* insurance 12
تانك *tānika* those two 4
تأييداً *ta'yīd* support 28
تبادل *tabādala* VI exchange with each other 21; *tabādul* mutual exchange 28
تبغ تبوغ *tibgh tubūgh* tobacco 35
تاجر → تجّار
تجارة *tijāra* trade 9
تجديد *tajdīd* renewal 33
تجربة تجارب *tajriba tajārib* test, experiment 5
تجريب *tajrīb* test 28
تجنيد *tajnīd* conscription 40
تحت *taḥt* below, under 6
تحرير *taḥrīr* drafting, editing 24
تحسّن *taḥassana* V improve, get better 21
تحضير *taḥḍīr* preparation 28
تخصّص *takhaṣṣaṣa* V specialise 21; *takhaṣṣus* specialisation 28
تخفيض *takhfīḍ* reduction 25
تدبير → تدابير
تداخل *tadākhala* VI interfere 21; *tadākhul* interference 28
تدبير تدابير *tadbīr tadābīr* arrangement 28
تدخّل *tadakhkhala* V intervene 21
تدخين *tadkhīn* smoking 28
تدريب *tadrīb* training 5
تدريس *tadrīs* instruction 5
تذكرة → تذاكر
تذكّر *tadhakkara* V remember 21
تذكرة تذاكر *tadhkara tadhākir* ticket 12
ترجمة → تراجم
تركيب → تراكيب
تربية *tárbiya* education 5
ترجمة تراجم *tarjama tarājim* translation 5
تردّد *taraddada* V hesitate 21; *taraddud* hesitation 28
ترقية *tárqiya* promotion 28
ترك يترك *taraka yatruku* I leave 11, 17
تركيب تراكيب *tarkīb tarākīb* installation 28
ترويج *tarwīj* promotion (sales, product) 25
تسع مئة *tisa' mīya* nine hundred 38
تسعة *tis'a* nine; تسعة عشر *tis'at'ashar* nineteen 38
تسعين *tis'īn* ninety 38
تسلّم *tasallama* V get, receive 21
تسليم *taslīm* delivery 28
تسويق *taswīq* marketing 25
تسوية *táswiya* settlement (of dispute) 8
تشرين: تشرين الأوّل *tishrīn al-'awwal* October; تشرين الثاني *tishrīn ath-thānī* November 39
تصفية *táṣfiya* purification 28

تطبيق *taṭbīq* application 28
تطوّر *taṭawwara* V develop 21; *taṭawwur* development 9
تظاهر *taẓāhara* VI demonstrate (politically) 21
تعاون *ta'āwana* VI cooperate 21; *ta'āwun* cooperation 28
تعاونية *ta'āwunīya* cooperativism 28
تعرّف ب *ta'arrafa* V *bi-* get acquainted with 21
تعقيد *ta'qīd* complication, complexity 29
تعلّق ب *ta'allaqa* V *bi-* depend on, pertain to 21
تعلّم *ta'allama* V learn 21
تعليم *ta'līm* tuition, education 5; تعليمات (inan. pl.) *ta'līmāt* instructions 25
تعويض *ta'wīḍ* compensation 9
تغيّر *taghayyara* V be changed 21
تغيير *taghyīr* change 28
تفّاح *tuffāḥ* apples 10
تفاءل *tafā'ala* VI be optimistic 21
تفصيل تفاصيل *tafṣīl tafāṣīl* detail 8
تفاهم *tafāhum* mutual understanding 28
تفضّل *tafaḍḍala* V be so kind 25
تقرير → تقارير
تقدّم *taqaddama* V advance, progress 21; *taqaddum* progress 28
تقدّمي *taqaddumī* progressive 28
تقديم *taqdīm* offer, presentation 28
تقريب *taqrīb* approximation 32
تقريبًا *taqrīban* approximately 32
تقرير *taqrīr* decision 2
تقرير تقارير *taqrīr taqārīr* report 2
تكاتب *takātaba* VI correspond with each other 21
تكليف → تكاليف
تكرير *takrīr* refining 18
تكلّم *takallama* V speak, talk 21
تكليف تكاليف *taklīf takālīf* cost, expense 9
تلميذ → تلاميذ
تلفزيون *tilviziyōn* television 24
تلفون *tilifōn* telephone 2
تلقٍّ\التلقّي *talaqqin, at-talaqqī* (weak) reception 28
تلقّى *talaqqa* V receive 21
تلك *tilka* that 4
تلميذ تلامذ *tilmīdh talāmīdh* pupil 5
تليفون *tilifōn* telephone 2
تمّ يتمّ *tamma yatimmu* I (come to an) end 14, 17
تمرين → تمارين
تمام *tamām* perfect(ion), complete 28;

ج

جاء يجيء *jā'a yajī'u* I come 14, 17; appear (in the press) 24; جاء يجيء ب *jā'a yajī'u* I *bi-* bring 14; carry (in the press) 24

جار جيران *jār jīrān* neighbour 1

جار\الجاري *jārin, al-jārī* (weak) current 10, ongoing 26

جامعة *jāmi'a* university 5; league 39

جاوب *jāwaba* III answer 20

جبل جبال *jabal jibāl* mountain 10

جداً *jiddan* very 32

جدول ← جداول

جديد ← جدد

جدّد *jaddada* II renew, renovate 20

جدول جداول *jadwal jadāwil* schedule, timetable 12

جديد جدد *jadīd judud* new 2; جديداً *jadīdan* recently 32

جريدة ← جرائد

جريمة ← جرائم

جرّب *jarraba* II try out, attempt 20

جرى يجري *jara yajrī* I flow, proceed (talks etc.) 14, 17

جريدة جرائد *jarīda jarā'id* newspaper 24

جريمة جرائم *jarīma jarā'im* crime 13

الجزائر *al-jazā'ir* (f.) Algiers, Algeria 36

جزء أجزاء (من) *juz' 'ajzā' (min)* part (of) 7

جلس يجلس *jalasa yajlisu* I sit 11, 17

جلسة جلسات *jalsa jalasāt* session 39

جمادى الأولى *jumada l-'ūla,* جمدى الثانية *jumada th-thāniya* see 39/5

جمرك ← جمارك

جماعة *jamā'a* group (of people) 15

جمرك جمارك *jumruk jamārik* customs 12

الجمعة *al-jum'a* Friday 39

جمل أجمال *jamal 'ajmāl* camel 10

جمهورية *jumhūrīya* republic 7

جميع *jamī'* whole, all 9

جميل *jamīl* beautiful 8

جنينة ← جنائن

جنب *jamb* beside 6

جندي جنود *jundī junūd* soldier 13

جنوب *janūb* south 15

جندي ← جنود

جنينة جنائن *junayna junā'in* garden 1

جنيه *jinayh* pound (£) 38

جواب أجوبة *jawāb 'ajwiba* answer 3

حكومة *ḥukūma* government 7
حلّ يحلّ *ḥalla yaḥullu* I solve 14, 17
حلّ حلول *ḥall ḥulūl* solution 7
حمّال *ḥammāl* porter, carrier 4
أحمر ← حمر\حمراء
حمل يحمل *ḥamala yaḥmilu* I carry 11
حوار *ḥiwār* dialogue 28
حوالى\حول *ḥawāla, ḥawl* about 6
حيّ يحيا *ḥayya yaḥya* I live 14, 17
حيادي *ḥiyādī* neutral 15
حياة *ḥayā* life 28
حيوان *ḥayawān* animal 10

خ

خارج *khārij* outside 6; إلى\في الخارج *'ila/fi l-khārij* abroad 12
خارجية *khārijīya* Foreign Affairs 7
خاصّ *khāṣṣ* special, private 3; بصورة خاصّة *bi-ṣūra khāṣṣa* especially 32
خاصّة خواصّ *khāṣṣa khawāṣṣ* peculiarity 32
خاصّةً *khāṣṣatan* especially 32
خاف يخاف (من) *khāfa yakhāfu (min)* I fear 14, 17
خال\الخالي *khālin, al-khālī* (weak) empty 10
خام *khām* crude (oil etc.) 18
خامس *khāmis* fifth 38
خبر أخبار *khabar 'akhbār* news 24
خبير خبراء *khabīr khubarā'* expert 5
خرج يخرج (من) *kharaja yakhruju* I *(min)* go/come out (of) 11, 17
خروج *khurūj* going out, exit 28
خريف *kharīf* autumn 10
خصوص: بخصوص *bi-khuṣūṣ* concerning 6
أخضر ← خضر\خضراء
خطّ خطوط *khaṭṭ khuṭūṭ* line 12
خطاب أخطبة *khiṭāb 'akhṭiba* speech, address 7
خطر *khaṭir* dangerous 8
خطّ ← خطوط
خطوة *khuṭwa* step 8
خفّض *khaffaḍa* II reduce 25
خفيف *khafīf* light (weight) 2
خلاف *khilāf* dispute, disagreement 8
خلال *khilāl* during 6
خليج خلوج *khalīj khulūj* gulf 36
خمس مئة *khams mīya* five hundred 38
خمسة *khamsa* five; خمسة عشر *khamst'ashar* fifteen 38
خمسين *khamsīn* fifty 38
الخميس *al-khamīs* Thursday 39
خاصّة ← خواصّ

ذكي أذكياء *dhakī 'adhkiyā'* intellient 5

ذلك *dhālika* that 4

ذهب يذهب *dhahaba yadhhabu* I go 11, 17

ذو\ذوا\ذوات\ذواتا\ذواتي\ ذوو\ذوي\ذي *dhū, dhawā, dhawāt, dhawāta, dhawātay, dhawū, dhawī/dhaway, dhī* see 24/2

ر

رابع *rābi'* fourth 38

راتب رواتب *rātib rawātib* salary 9

راديو *rādiyō* radio 24

رأس رؤوس *ra's ru'ūs* head 3

رأسمال *ra'smāl* capital (fin.) 9

رأسمالية *ra'smālīya* capitalism 10

راكب ركّاب *rākib rukkāb* passenger, rider 12

رأى يرى *ra'a yara* I see 14, 17

رأي آراء *ra'y 'ārā'* opinion 8

ربّ أرباب *rabb 'arbāb* lord 40

ربّى *rabba* II educate, bring up 20

ربيع *rabī'* spring (season) 10; ربيع الأوّل *rabī' al-'awwal*, ربيع الثاني *rabī' ath-thānī* see 39/5

رجا يرجو *raja yarjū* I request, hope for, expect 14, 17

رجاء *rajā'* request 28

رجب *rajab* see 39/5

رجع يرجع *raja'a yarji'u* I go/come back 11, 17

رجوع *rujū'* return 12

رحلة *riḥla* trip, tour 12

رخيص *rakhīṣ* cheap 9

رسالة *risāla* letter 3

رسمي *rasmī* official 7; رسميًا *rasmīyan*, بصورة رسمية *bi-ṣūra rasmīya* officially 32

رفض يرفض *rafaḍa yarfiḍu* I reject, refuse 11, 17

رفض *rafḍ* rejection, refusal 28

رغم: بالرغم من\على رغم *bi-r-raghm min, 'ala raghm* despite 6

رقم أرقام *raqm 'arqām* figure 3

رقّى *raqqa* II promote 20

راكب ← ركّاب

ركب يركب *rakiba yarkabu* I get on/into 11, 17

ركّب *rakkaba* II fix, install 20

رمضان *ramaḍān* see 39/5

رمى يرمي *rama yarmī* I throw 14, 17

رهينة رهائن *rahīna rahā'in* hostage 13

راتب ← رواتب

روج *rawwaja* II promote (sales, product) 25

رئيس ← رؤساء

روسيا *rūsiya* Russia 4
رأس ← رؤوس
رئاسة\رياسة *ri'āsa, riyāsa* chairmanship, presidency 7
الرياض *ar-riyāḍ* Riyadh 36
ريال *riyāl* rial, riyal 38
رئيس رؤساء *ra'īs ru'asā'* chairman, president, chief 2; رئيس وزراء *ra'īs wuzarā'* Prime Minister 7
رئيسي *ra'īsī* principal 2
ريف أرياف *rīf 'aryāf* country(side) 10

ز

زاد يزيد (عن) *zāda yazīdu* I increase, *('an)* exceed 14
زار يزور *zāra yazūru* I visit 14
زال يزال *zāla yazālu* I cease to be 18; → ما زال
زائد *zā'id* increasing 26
زائر زوّار *zā'ir zuwwār* visitor 12
زبون زبائن *zabūn zabā'in* customer, client 25
زراعة *zirā'a* agriculture10
أزرق ← زرق\زرقاء
زميل زملاء *zamīl zumalā'* colleague 2
زهر *zahr* flowers 10
زهرة زهور *zahra zuhūr* flower 10
زائر ← زوّار
زيادة *ziyāda* increase 28
زيارة *ziyāra* visit 28
زيت زيوت *zayt zuyūt* oil 18

س

س *sa-* will, shall 19
سابع *sābi'* seventh
سابق *sābiq* former 4
ساحل سواحل *sāḥil sawāḥil* coast 10
سيّد ← سادة
سادس *sādis* sixth 37, 38
ساعد *sā'ada* III help 20
ساعة *sā'a* hour, clock, watch 39
سافر *sāfara* III travel 20
ساق يسوق *sāqa yasūqu* I drive 14
سأل يسأل *sa'ala yas'alu* I ask (enquire) 11, 17
سائح سيّاح *sā'iḥ suyyāḥ* tourist 12
سائق *sā'iq* driver 4
سبب أسباب *sabab 'asbāb* cause, reason 8; بسبب *bi-sabab* because of 6
سبتمبر *sibtambar* September 39
سبع مئة *saba' mīya* seven hundred 38
سبعة *sab'a* seven; سبعة عشر *saba't'ashar* seventeen 38
سبعين *sab'īn* seventy 38
ستّ مئة *sitt mīya* six hundred 38
ستّة *sitta* six; ستّة عشر *sitt'ashar* sixteen 38
ستّين *sittīn* sixty 38

سريع ← سراع
سرعة *sur'a* speed;
بسرعة *bi-sur'a* quickly 32
سريع سراع *sarī' sirā'* fast 8
سعر أسعار *si'r 'as'ār* price, rate 9
السعودية *as-sa'ūdīya* Saudi Arabia 4
سفارة *sifāra* embassy 15
سفر *safar* journey, travel 12
سفير ← سفراء
سفينة ← سفن
سفير سفراء *safīr sufarā'* ambassador 15
سفينة سفن *safīna sufun* ship 12
سكرتيرة *sikritayra* secretary 2
سكّة ← سكك
سكن يسكن *sakana yaskunu* I live 11, 17
سكّة (سكك) حديدية *sikka* (pl. *sikak*) *ḥadīdīya* railway 12
سلاح أسلحة *silāḥ 'asliḥa* weapon 13
سلام *salām* peace 7
سلطة *sulṭa* authority 7
سلّم *sallama* II deliver 20
سلم *silm* peace 7
سمح يسمح ل، ب *samaḥa yasmaḥu* I *li-* (person), *bi-* (thing) permit; لو سمحت\سمحتم *law samaḥt(i/um)* ('if you would permit') please 25
سمع يسمع *sami'a yasma'u* I hear 11, 17
سمك *samak* fish 10
سمكة أسماك *samaka 'asmāk* fish 10
سنتيمتر، سم *santimitr* centimetre, cm 38
سنة سنوات *sana sanawāt* year 2
سنوي *sanawī* annual 2; سنويًا *sanawīyan* annually 32
سهل *sahil* easy 2; سهلاً *sahilan* easily 32
ساحل ← سواحل
سوّاق *sawwāq* driver 4
سؤال أسئلة *su'āl 'as'ila* question 8
سوء *sū'* evil, mis-, wrong 28
أسود ← سود\سوداء
السودان *as-sūdān* Sudan 36
سوري *sūri* Syrian 2
سوريا *sūriya* (f.) Syria 2
سوف *sawfa* will, shall 19; سوف لا *sawfa lā* will/shall not 23
سوق أسواق *sūq 'aswāq* (f.) market 9
سوي يسوى *sáwiya yaswa* I equal 14, 17
سائح ← سيّاح
سياحة *siyāḥa* tourism 12
سيّارة *sayyāra* car 12
سياسة *siyāsa* policy, politics 7

سياسي *siyāsī* political, politician 7
سيّد سادة *sayyid sāda* gentleman, Mr 1
سيّدة *sayyida* lady, Mrs 1

ش

شابّ شباب *shābb shabāb* young man, young person 1
شارع شوارع *shāri' shawāri'* street 10
شاكّ *shākk fī* doubting 26
شاي *shāī* tea 1
شابّ ← شباب
شبّاك ← شبابيك
شباط *shubāṭ* February 39
شبّاك شبابيك *shubbāk shabābīk* window 1
شتاء أشتية *shitā' 'áshtiya* winter 10
شجر *shajar* trees 10
شجرة أشجار *shajara 'ashjār* tree 10
شحن *shaḥn* load 12
شخص أشخاص *shakhṣ 'ashkhāṣ* person 4
شخصيًا *shakhṣīyan* personally 32
شديد أشدّاء *shadīd 'ashiddā'* severe, vigorous 8
شرب يشرب *shariba yashrabu* I drink 11, 17
شرح يشرح *sharaḥa yashraḥu* I explain 11, 17
شرح *sharḥ* explanation 28
شرطة *shurṭa* police 4
شرطي *shurṭī* policeman 4
شرق *sharq* east; الشرق الأوسط *ash-sharq al-'awsaṭ* Middle East 15
شركة *sharika* company 2
شعبان *sha'bān* see 39/5
شقّة شقق *shiqqa/shaqqa shiqaq* apartment 1
شكّ شكوك *shakk shukūk* doubt 28
شكّ يشكّ في *shakka yashukku* I *fī* doubt 14, 17
شكر *shukr* thanks 28
شكر يشكر *shakara yashkuru* I thank 11, 17
شكّ ← شكوك
شكوة شكوات *shakwa shakawāt* complaint 13
شمال *shimāl* north 15
شنطة شنط *shanṭa shunaṭ* suitcase 12
شهادة *shahāda* certificate 5
شهد يشهد *shahida yashhadu* I witness 40
شهر أشهر *shahr 'ashhur* month 8
شارع ← شوارع
شوّال *shawwāl* see 39/5
شيء أشياء *shay' 'ashyā'* (some)thing 8

ص

صادرات *ṣādirāt* exports 9
صار يصير *ṣāra yaṣīru* I become 14, 17
صالون *ṣālūn* living-room 1
صباحًا *ṣabāḥan* in the morning, a.m. 39
صبح أصباح *ṣubḥ 'aṣbāḥ* morning 39
صحراء ← صحارى
صحافة *ṣiḥāfa* press 24
صحراء صحارى *ṣaḥrā' ṣaḥāra* (f.) desert 10
صحيفة ← صحف
صحفي *ṣuḥufī* journalist 24
صحّة *ṣiḥḥa* health 7
صحيفة صحف *ṣaḥīfa ṣuḥuf* newspaper 24
صدّق *ṣaddaqa* II believe 20
صديق أصدقاء *ṣadīq 'aṣdiqā'* friend 1
صعب صعاب *ṣa'ab ṣi'āb* difficult 2
صغير صغار *ṣaghīr ṣighār* small, junior 2
صفّ صفوف *ṣaff ṣufūf* class(room) 5; rank 40
صفر *ṣafar* see 39/5
أصفر ← صفر\صفراء
صفّ ← صفوف
صلّى *ṣalla* II pray 20
صناعة *ṣinā'a* industry 2
صناعي *ṣinā'ī* industrial 2
صنع *ṣan', ṣun'* manufacture 2
صوّر *ṣawwara* II photograph, film 24
صورة صور *ṣūra ṣuwar* picture, photograph 24; عامّ، رسمي، خاصّ ←
صيف أصياف *ṣayf 'aṣyāf* summer 10
الصين *aṣ-ṣīn* China 4

ض

ضبط *ḍabṭ* precision; بالضبط *bi-ḍ-ḍabṭ* precisely 32
ضدّ *ḍidd* against 6
ضريبة ← ضرائب
ضرب يضرب *ḍaraba yaḍrubu* I hit 11, 17
ضرورة *ḍarūra* necessity 29
ضروري *ḍarūrī* necessary 7
ضريبة ضرائب *ḍarība ḍarā'ib* tax 25
ضعيف ضعفاء *ḍa'īf ḍu'afā'* weak 3
ضفّة ضفف *ḍiffa ḍifaf* bank, shore 36
ضمّ يضمّ (إلى) *ḍamma yaḍummu* I *('ila)* join (to) 14, 17
ضيف ضيوف *ḍayf ḍuyūf* guest 12

ط

طار يطير *ṭāra yaṭīru* I fly 14

طالب طلاّب *ṭālib ṭullāb* student 5
طاقة *ṭāqa* energy 18
طاولة *ṭāwula* table 1
طائر *ṭā'ir* flying 26
طائرة *ṭā'ira* aeroplane 12
طبّ *ṭibb* medicine 5
طبع يطبع *ṭaba'a yaṭba'u* I print 24
طبّق (على) *ṭabbaqa* II *('ala)* apply (a measure etc.) (to) 20
طبيب أطبّة *ṭabīb' aṭibba* doctor 5
طريقة ← طرائق
أطرش ← طرش\طرشاء
طرف أطراف *ṭaraf 'aṭrāf* party (to contract etc.) 15
طريق طرق *ṭarīq ṭuruq* (m./f.) road 10
طريقة طرائق *ṭarīqa ṭarā'iq* way 8
طفل أطفال *ṭifl 'aṭfāl* child 1
طالب ← طلاّب
طلب يطلب *ṭalaba yaṭlubu* I ask for 11, 17
طلب *ṭalab* order, demand, request 2
طلمبة *ṭulumba* pump 18
طنّ أطنان *ṭunn 'aṭnān* ton 38
طويل ← طوال
طوب *ṭūb* bricks 10
طويل طوال *ṭawīl ṭiwāl* long 2
طيّب *ṭayyib* good 1
طير طيور *ṭayr ṭuyūr* bird 10
طيران *ṭayarān* flight 28
طير ← طيور

ظ

ظلّ يظلّ *ẓalla yaẓallu* I remain 18
ظنّ يظنّ *ẓanna yaẓunnu* suppose 14, 17
ظهر أظهار *ẓuhr 'aẓhār* midday; بعد الظهر *ba'd aẓ-ẓuhr* afternoon 39

ع

عاد يعود *'āda ya'ūdu* I be(come) again 18; ← ما عاد
عادة عوائد *'āda 'awā'id* habit 8; عادةً *'ādatan* usually 32
عارض *'āraḍa* III oppose 37
عاش يعيش *'āsha ya'īshu* I live 14
عاشر *'āshir* tenth 38
عاصمة عواصم *'āṣima 'awāṣim* capital city 36
عال\العالي *'ālin, al-'ālī* (weak) high 10
عالم أعوالم *'ālam 'a'wālim* world 9; العالم الثالث *al-'ālam ath-thālith* third world 15
عامّ *'āmm* general, public 4; بصورة عامّة *bi-ṣūra 'āmma* in general, generally 32
عامل عمّال *'āmil 'ummāl* worker, operative 2
عائلة *'ā'ila* family 1
عبارة *'ibāra* expression 8

عدد أعداد *'adad 'a'dād* number 9
عدّة *'idda* number 9
عدم *'adam* lack (of), in-, non- 28
العراق *al-'irāq* Iraq 2
عراقي *'irāqī* Iraqi 2
عربي عرب *'arabī 'arab* Arab(ian), Arabic 4
عرف يعرف *'arafa ya'rifu* I know, recognise 11, 17
عشرة *'ashara* ten 38
العشرون *al-'ishrūn* twentieth 38
عشرين *'ishrīn* twenty 38
عضو أعضاء *'uḍw 'a'ḍā'* member 7
عفا يعفو عن *'afa ya'fū* I *'an* forgive 14, 17
عفو *'afw* forgiveness 28
عقد *'aqd* tying, holding 28;
عقد عقود *'aqd 'uqūd* contract 2; treaty 15
عقد يعقد *'aqada ya'qidu* I tie, hold (e.g. a meeting) 17
عقد ← عقود
علاقة *'alāqa* relation(ship) 15
علّم *'allama* II teach 20
علم يعلم *'alima ya'lamu* I know 20
علم علوم *'ilm 'ulūm* science, knowledge 5, 28
على *'ala* on 6
عامل ← عمّال
عمان *'umān* (f.) Oman 36
عمّان *'ammān* Amman 36
عمل يعمل *'amila ya'malu* I do, work, make 11, 17
عمل أعمال *'amal 'a'māl* work 2
عملي *'amalī* practical 5
عملية *'amalīya* operation, process 2
أعمى ← عمي\عمياء
عميق *'amīq* deep 8
عن *'an* from, about 6
عنوان ← عناوين
عنب *'inab* grapes 10
عند *'ind* at, among, with 6, 24
عندما *'indamā* when 19, 36
عنوان عناوين *'unwān 'anāwīn* address 1
عاصمة ← عواصم
عادة ← عوائد
عيد أعياد *'īd 'a'yād* feast-day 39

غ

غاب يغيب (عن) *ghāba yaghību* I *('an)* be absent (from) 14
غادر *ghādara* III leave 20
غاز *ghāz* gas 18
غال\الغالي *ghālin, al-ghālī* (weak) expensive 10
غائب *ghā'ib* absent 4
غداً *ghadan* tomorrow 39
غرام ، غم *gram* gram, gm 38
غرب *gharb* west 15

غرض أغراض *gharaḍ 'aghrāḍ* purpose 8

غرفة غرف *ghurfa ghuraf* room 1; غرفة تجارة *ghurfat tijāra* Chamber of Commerce 9

غزّة *ghazza* Gaza 36

غني أغنياء *ghanī 'aghniyā'* rich 8

غيبة *ghayba* absence 28

غير *ghayr* other than, not 23

غيّر *ghayyara* II change 20

ف

ف *fa-* so, then 37

فاض\الفاضي *fāḍin, al-fāḍī* (weak) vacant, free 10

فاكس *faks* telefax 24

فاوض *fāwaḍa* III negotiate 20

فبراير *fibrāyir* February 39

فتح يفتح *fataha yaftaḥu* I open 11, 17

فتّش (عن، على) *fattasha* II inspect, (*'an*) look for, (*'ala*) supervise 20

فرصة فرص *furṣa furaṣ* opportunity 8

فرق فروق *farq furūq* difference 8

فرنسا *faransa* France 4

فرنساوي *faransāwī* French 4

فرنسة *faransa* France 4

فرنسي *faransī* French 4

فرق → فروق

فشل *fashal* failure 28

فشل يفشل *fashila yafshalu* I fail 11, 17

فصلة *faṣla* comma, decimal point 38

من فضلك\فضلكم :فضل *min faḍlika, faḍliki, faḍlikum* ('from your favour') please 25

فضّل *faḍḍala* II prefer 20

فعل أفعال *fi'l 'af'āl* fact, act, action, verb 29

فعلي *fi'lī* actual, factual 29

فقط *faqaṭ* only 38

فكّر (في) *fakkara* II (*fī*) think (about) 20

فكرة أفكار *fikra 'afkār* idea 8

فلاّح *fallāḥ* farmer, peasant 10

فلسطين *falasṭīn* (f.) Palestine 15

فلم أفلام *film 'aflām* film 24

فلوس (inan. pl.) *fulūs* money 9

فنّ فنون *fann funūn* art, craft 29

فنّي *fannī* technical, technician 2

فهم يفهم *fahima yafhamu* I understand 11, 17

فهم *fahm* understanding 28

فوراً *fawran* immediately 32

فوري *fawrī* immediate 33

فوق *fawq* above, over 6

في *fī* in 1

ق

قاد يقود *qāda yaqūdu* I lead 14

قادم *qādim* next 39

قاض\القاضي قضاة *qāḍin, al-qāḍī* (weak) *quḍā* judge 10

قارئ *qāri'* reading, reader 26
قال يقول *qāla yaqūlu* I say 14
قام يقوم *qāma yaqūmu* I rise, get up 14; قام يقوم ب *qāma yaqūmu* I *bi-* undertake 17
قانون قوانين *qānūn qawānīn* law 7
القاهرة *al-qāhira* Cairo 10
قائد قوّاد *qā'id quwwād* leader 13
قبل *qabl* before, ago 6; قبل أن *qabl 'an* before 36; قبلاً *qablan* before(hand) 32
قبول *qabūl* acceptance 25
قد *qad* see 11/6
القدس *al-quds* Jerusalem 19
قدّم *qaddama* II offer, serve, present, submit 20
قديم قدماء *qadīm qudamā'* old (things), ancient 2
قرأ يقرأ *qara'a yaqra'u* I read 11, 17
قراءة *qirā'a* reading 28
قرار *qarār* resolution 37
قرّر *qarrara* II decide, report 20
قرض قروض *qarḍ qurūḍ* loan 9
قرية ← (الـ)قرى
قريب (من) *qarīb (min)* near (to) 8; قريبًا *qarīban* soon 32
قرية (الـ)قرى *qáriya quran, al-qura* (weak) village 10
قسم أقسام *qism 'aqsām* department 2
قصير ← قصار
قصر قصور *qaṣr quṣūr* palace 39
قصير قصار *qaṣīr qiṣār* short 2
قاض ← قضاة
قضية قضايا *qaḍīya qaḍāya* cause, case 15
قطار قطر *qiṭār quṭur* train 12
قطاع *qiṭā'* sector 9
قطار ← قطر
قطر *qaṭar* (f.) Qatar 36
قعدة: ذو القعدة *dhu l-qa'da* see 39/5
قليل أقلاء *qalīl 'aqillā'* little, slight 3; قليلاً *qalīlan* (a) little 32
قمّة قمم *qimma qimam* summit 39
قناة السويس *qanāt as-suways* Suez Canal 36
قهوة *qahwa* coffee 1
قائد ← قوّاد
قانون ← قوانين
قول *qawl* saying 28
قوة *quwa* force, strength 13
قوي أقوياء *qawī 'aqwiyā'* strong 8
قيادة *qiyāda* leadership 28
قياس *qiyās* measurement 38
قيام ب *qiyām bi-* undertaking 28

ك

ك *ka-* as, like 6
كاتب *kātaba* III write to, correspond with 20

كاتب كتّاب *kātib kuttāb* clerk 2
كاد يكاد *kāda yakādu* I almost to do 18
كامل كملة *kāmil kamala* complete, perfect 8
كان يكون *kāna yakūnu* I be 18
كأنّ *ka-'anna* as if 31
كانون الأوّل: كانون *kānūn al-'awwal* December; كانون الثاني *kānūn ath-thānī* January 39
كبير كبار *kabīr kibār* big, senior 2
كتاب كتب *kitāb kutub* book 5
كاتب ← كتّاب
كتابة *kitāba* writing 28
كتاب ← كتب
كتب يكتب *kataba yaktubu* I write 11
كثير كثار *kathīr kithār* much, many 3; كثيراً *kathīran* greatly; بكثير *bi-kathīr* much, (by) far (with comparative) 32
كذا *kadha* thus, so 32
كذلك *ka-dhālika* thus, so 32
كرسي كراسي *kursī karāsī* chair 1
كفاية *kifāya* sufficiency 28
كفى يكفي *kafa yakfī* I suffice 17
كلّ *kull* each, every, whole, all 9
كلّف *kallafa* II cost 20
كلّية *kullīya* college, faculty 5
كم *kam* how much/many 13
كمبيوتر *kambyūtir* computer 3
كامل ← كملة
كمّية *kammīya* quantity 36
كنيسة كنائس *kanīsa kanā'is* church 10
كهربا *kahraba* electricity 2
كون *kawn* existence 28
الكويت *al-kuwayt* (f.) Kuwait 4
كي *kay* so that, in order that 34
كيف *kayf* how 13; كيفما *kayfamā* however 37
كيلو(غرام)، كغ *kīlō(gram)* kilo(gram), kg 38
كيلومتر، كم *kīlōmitr* kilometre, km 38

ل

ل *li-* for, of 6, so/in order that 34
لا *lā* no 13; do not, does not 23; ← سوف
لاقى *lāqa* III encounter 20
لأن *li-'an* so that, in order that 34
لأنّ *li-'anna* because 31
لبنان *lubnān* Lebanon 36
لتر *litr* litre 38
لجنة لجان *lajna lijān* committee 3
لحظة لحظات *laḥẓa laḥaẓāt* moment 39
لدى *lada* at, with 24
لطيف لطفاء *laṭīf luṭafā'* kind (adj.) 8
لعب يلعب *la'iba yal'abu* I play 11

لغة *lugha* language 8
لقد *laqad* see 11/6
لقي يلقى *láqiya yalqa* I meet 14, 17
لكنْ *lākin* but 33
لكنّ *lākinna* but 31
لكي *li-kay* so/in order that 34
لم *lam* did not 23; → بعد
لماذا *li-mādha* why 13
لمن *li-man* whose (is/are) 13
لن *lan* will not 23
لو *law* if 37; → حتّى, سمح
ليلة → ليال\الليالي
ليبيا *lībiya* (f.) Libya 36
ليرة *līra* lira 38
ليس *laysa* I not to be 18
ليلة ليال\الليالي *layla layālin, al-layālī* (weak) night 39

م

ما *mā* did not 23; what, that which 35
ما إذا *mā 'idha* whether 31
ما دام *mā dām* I as long as 18
ما زال لا يزال *mā zāl lā yazāl* I still to be/do 18
ما عاد *mā 'ād* I be/do no longer 18
ما هو\ما هي *mā huwa/mā hiya* what is/are 13
مات يموت *māta yamūtu* I die 14
مادّة موادّ *mādda mawādd* material, (school) subject 5
ماذا *mādha* what 13
مارس *māris* March 39
ماش\الماشي *māshin, al-māshī* (weak) walking, going 26
ماض\الماضي *māḍin, al-māḍī* (weak) past 10
ماكينة *mākīna* machine 2
مال أموال *māl 'amwāl* property 9
مالي *mālī* financial 7
مالية *mālīya* finance 7
مأمور *ma'mūr* official 4
مايو *māyū* May 39
مبدأ → مبادئ
مبلغ → مبالغ
مبتدئ *mubtádi'* beginner 26
مبدأ مبادئ *mabda' mabādi'* principle 8
مبلغ مبالغ *mablagh mabāligh* amount 3
مبيع *mabī'* sale, sold 25
متأخر *muta'akhkhir* delayed, late 12
متبادل *mutabādal* mutual 27
متخرّج *mutakharrij* graduate 5
متر أمتار، م *mitr 'amtār* metre, m 38
متّصل *muttáṣil* connected 38; متّصل به *muttáṣal bihi* contacted 27
متظاهر *mutaẓāhir* demonstrator 13

متعلّق ب *muta'alliq bi-* pertaining to, relating to, concerning 26
متقدّم *mutaqaddim* advanced 26
متوسّط *mutawassiṭ* middle (adj.) 5
متوقّع *mutawaqqa'* expected 27
متى *mata* when 13;
متى ما *mata mā* whenever 37
مثقّف *muthaqqaf* cultured, educated 5
مثل *mithl* like 6
مثل أمثال *mathal 'amthāl* example;
مثلاً *mathalan* for example 32
مجلس ← مجالس
مجتهد *mujtáhid* hardworking 4
مجرم *mujrim* criminal 13
مجلس مجالس *majlis majālis* assembly, مجلس وزراء *majlis wuzarā'* cabinet 7
مجلّة *majalla* magazine 24
مجموعة *majmū'a* group (of things) 15
محاسب *muḥāsib* accountant 4
محاضرة *muḥāḍara* lecture 5
محافظ *muḥāfiẓ* conservative 7
محكمة ← محاكم
محام\المحامي *muḥāmin, al-muḥāmī* (weak) lawyer 10
محاولة *muḥāwala* attempt 28
محتاج *muḥtāj* needy 26; محتاج إليه *muḥtāj 'ilayhi* needed 27
محتلّ *muḥtall* occupying 26; occupied 27
محتمل *muḥtámal* likely 34
محرّر *muḥarrir* editor 24
محرّم *muḥarram* see 39/5
محطّة *maḥaṭṭa* station 12
محكمة محاكم *maḥkama maḥākim* law-court 10
محلّ *maḥall* place 4
محلول *maḥlūl* solved 27
مخزن ← مخازن
مختبر *mukhtábar* laboratory 5
مختلف *mukhtálif* varied, various 5
مخزن مخازن *makhzan makhāzin* store 2
مخوف *makhūf* feared 27
مدّ يمدّ *madda yamuddu* I extend 14, 17
مدرسة ← مدارس
مدّة ← مدد
مدير ← مدراء
مدرّس *mudarris* instructor 5
مدرسة مدارس *madrasa madāris* school 5
مدعوّ *mad'ūw* summoned 27
مدفوع *madfū'* paid 27
دفع ← مدفوعات
مدينة ← مدن
مدّة مدد *mudda mudad* period 39
مدير مدراء *mudīr mudarā'*

director, manager 2
مدينة مدن *madīna mudun* city 10
مذاع *mudhā'* broadcast 27
مرّ يمرّ (ب\على) *marra yamurru* I *(bi-/'ala)* pass (by) 14, 17
مركز → مراكز
مرتفع *murtafi'* rising, high 26
مرجو *marjūw* requested 27
مرسل *mursil* sender 26; *mursal* sent 27
مرشّح *murashshah* candidate 5
مركز مراكز *markaz marākiz* centre 24
مرميّ *marmīy* thrown (away) 27
مرّة *marra* a time 38
مرور *murūr* passing, traffic 28
مزور *mazūr* visited 27
مزيد *mazīd* excess, increased verb form 27
مساء أمساء *masā' 'amsā'* evening; مساءً *masā'an* in the evening, p.m 39
مسجد → مساجد
مساعد *musā'id* assistant 26
مساعدة *musā'ada* aid, help 8
مسافر *musāfir* traveller 12
مسألة مسائل *mas'ala masā'il* matter 28
مستأجر *musta'jir* tenant 26
مستثمر *mustathmir* investor 26
مستراح *mustarāh* lavatory 27
مستشار *mustashār* consultant, adviser 27
(الـ)مستشفى *mustashfan, al-mustashfa* (weak) hospital 10
مستعدّ *musta'idd* ready 26
مستعمل *musta'mal* used 27
مستقبل *mustaqbal* future 27
مستقلّ *mustaqill* independent 15
مستمرّ *mustamirr* continuous 26
مستورد *mustawrid* importer 26; *mustawrad* imported 27
مستوردات *mustawradāt* imports 9
(الـ)مستوى *mustawan, al-mustawa* (weak, noun/adj.) level 10
مسجد مساجد *masjid masājid* mosque 10
مسلّح *musallah* armed 13
مسؤول *mas'ūl* responsible 2
مسؤولية *mas'ūlīya* responsibility 7
مشروع → مشاريع
مشغل → مشاغل
مشكلة → مشاكل
مشترك *mushtárak* joint, common 27
مشتر\المشتري *mushtárin, al-mushtárī* (weak) purchaser 25, buying 26
(الـ)مشترى *mushtáran, al-mushtára* (weak) purchase 25, purchased 27

مشرف *mushrif* supervisor 2
مشروع مشاريع *mashrū'* *mashārī'* project 9
مشغل مشاغل *mashghal* *mashāghil* workshop 2
مشغول *mashghūl* busy 18
مشكلة مشاكل *mushkila* *mashākil* problem 2
مشكوك فيه *mashkūk fihi* doubted 27
مشهور *mashhūr* famous 3
مشى يمشي *masha yamshī* I walk 14, 17
مصدر ← مصادر
مصرف ← مصارف
مصلحة ← مصالح
مصنع ← مصانع
مصدر مصادر *maṣdar maṣādir* source 18; verbal noun 28
مصر *miṣr* (f.) Egypt 2
مصرف مصارف *maṣrif maṣārif* bank 9
مصري *miṣrī* Egyptian 2
مصلحة مصالح *maṣlaḥa maṣāliḥ* interest 15
مصنع مصانع *maṣna' maṣāni'* factory 2
مطار *maṭār* airport 12
مطلب مطالب *maṭlab maṭālib* request 28
مطلوب *maṭlūb* requested 27
مظاهرة *muẓāhara* demonstration 13
مظنون *maẓnūn* supposed 27
مع *ma'a* with 6; معًا *ma'an* together 32
معارضة *mu'āraḍa* opposition 7
معهد ← معاهد
معرفة *ma'rifa* knowledge, acquaintance 28
معروف *ma'rūf* (well) known 27
معطيات *mu'ṭayāt* (inan. pl.) data 27
معقّد *mu'aqqad* complicated 2
معلّم *mu'allim* teacher 5
معلومات (inan. pl.) *ma'lūmāt* information 24
معهد معاهد *ma'had ma'āhid* institute 38
معيشة *ma'īsha* life 28
مغادرة *mughādara* departure 12
المغرب *al-maghrib* Morocco 27
مفتوح *maftuḥ* open 27
مفصّل *mufaṣṣal* detailed 29
مفهوم *mafhūm* understood 27
مفيد *mufīd* useful 2
مقاتلة *muqātala* fight 28
مقارنة *muqārana* comparison 28
مقالة *maqāla* (press) article 24
مقبل *muqbil* next, future 37, 39
مقبول *maqbūl* accepted, acceptable 27
مقدّمة *muqaddama* preface, introduction 27

مقرّر *muqarrir* reporter 24
مقروء *maqrū'* read 27
مقول *maqūl* said 27
مقوم به *maqūm bihi* undertaken 27
مكتبة , مكتب ← مكاتب
مكتوب ← مكاتيب
مكافحة *mukāfaḥa* fight against 13
مكان أماكن *makān 'amākin* place 10
مكتب مكاتب *maktab makātib* office 2
مكتبة مكاتب *maktaba makātib* library 5
مكتوب *maktūb* written; مكتوب مكاتيب *maktūb makātīb* letter, message 27
مكتوم *maktūm* confidential 3
ملاقاة *mulāqā* encounter 28
مليون ← ملايين
ملفّ *milaff* file (of papers) 3
مليون ملايين *milyūn malāyīn* million 38
ممّا *mimmā* than 29
ممتاز *mumtāz* excellent, distinguished 5
ممثّل *mumaththil* representative 3
ممكن *mumkin* possible 8
مموّل *mumawwil* financier 26; *mumawwal* financed 27
من *min* from 6; than 8, 29; *man* who(m); whose (in construct) 13; the person who, whoever 35
مناداة *munādā* call 28
مناسب *munāsib* suitable, appropriate 26
مناسبة *munāsaba* occasion 28
منطقة ← مناطق
منافس *munāfis* competitor 25
منافسة *munāfasa* competition 25
مناقشة *munāqasha* argument 28
منتج *muntij* productive, *muntaj* product 2
منتخب *muntákhab* elected 27
منخفض *munkháfiḍ* reduced 25
مندوب *mandūb* delegate 3
منذ *mundh* since 6
منسيّ *mansīy* forgotten 27
منشور *manshūr* published, notice 27
منطقة مناطق *minṭaqa manāṭiq* area, region 7
منظّمة *munaẓẓama* organisation 3
منع *man'* prohibition 28
منع يمنع (من\عن) *mana'a yamna'u* I *(min/'an)* prohibit 17
مهاجرة *muhājara* immigration 12
مهمّة ← مهامّ
مهمّ *muhimm* important 26
مهما *mahma* whatever 37
مهمّة مهامّ *mahamma mahāmm*

assignment, task 28
مهنة ← مهن
مهندس *muhandis* engineer 2
مهنة مهن *mihna mihan* profession 4
مادّة ← موادّ
مواصلات *muwāṣalāt* communications 24
موت *mawt* death 28
موضوع ← مواضيع
موافق على *muwāfiq 'ala* agreeing on/to 26
موافقة *muwāfaqa* agreement, consent 8
مؤتمر *mu'tamar* conference 7
موجب *mūjib* necessitating 26; *mūjab* necessary, affirmative 27
موجز *mūjaz* extract, excerpt 24
موجود *mawjūd* present, available 27
موضوع مواضيع *mawḍū' mawāḍī'* subject, theme 5
موظّف *muwaẓẓaf* employee 2
مؤكّد *mu'akkad* confirmed 27
موّل *mawwala* II finance 20
مؤلّف *mu'allif* author, composer 24
مؤمّن عليه *mu'amman 'alayhi* insured 27
مئتين *mitayn* two hundred 38
ميدان ميادين *maydān mayādīn* square 10
ميّز *mayyaza* II distinguish, differentiate 20
ميزانية *mīzānīya* budget 9
ميلادية *mīlādīya* A.D. 39
ميناء موان\الموانى *mīnā' mawānin, al-mawānī* (weak) port 12
مئة *mīya, mīt* hundred; المئة *al-mīya* hundredth; بالمئة (٪) *bi-l-mīya* per cent (%) 38

ن

نادى *nāda* III call to, summon 20
ناس (an. pl.) *nās* people 4
ناسب *nāsaba* III suit 20
ناقلة *nāqila* tanker, transporter 18
نام ينام *nāma yanāmu* I sleep 14, 17
نائب نوّاب *nā'ib nuwwāb* deputy, member of parliament 7
نائم *nā'im* sleeping, asleep 26
نبأ أنباء *naba' 'anbā'* news 24
نتيجة نتائج *natīja natā'ij* result 8
نجاح *najāḥ* success 28
نجح ينجح *najaḥa yanjaḥu* I succeed 11, 17
نحن *naḥnu* we 5
نداء *nidā'* call 28
نزاع *nizā'* conflict 13
نزل ينزل *nazala yanzilu* I go/come/get down 11, 17
نزول *nuzūl* descent 28

نسخة نسخ *nuskha nusakh* copy 24
نسي ينسى *násiya yansa* I forget 14, 17
نشر ينشر *nashara yanshuru* I publish 11, 17
نشر *nashr* publication 28
نشرة *nashra* bulletin, edition 24
نصّ نصوص *naṣṣ nuṣūṣ* text 24
نظر ينظر (إلى) *naẓara yanẓuru* I *('ila)* look (at) 17
نظري *naẓarī* theoretical 5
نظرية *naẓarīya* theory 10
نعم *na'am* yes 13
نفس *nafs* same see 9; نفس أنفس *nafs 'anfus* self, soul 9
نفْط *nafṭ* petroleum 18
نفى ينفي *nafa yanfī* I deny 17
نفي *nafy* denial 28
نقطة نقط *nuqṭa nuqaṭ* point 8; decimal point 38
نقل *naql* transport 12
نقود (inan. pl.) *nuqūd* money 9
نمرة نمر *numra numar* number (in a series) 3
نهر أنهر *nahr 'anhur* river 10
نوبة نوب *nawba nuwab* shift 2
أيّ نوع من :نوع *'ayy naw' min* what kind of 13
نوفمبر *nūfambr* November 39
نوم *nawm* sleep 28
نوى ينوي *nawa yanwī* I intend 14, 17
نيسان *nīsān* April 39
النيل *an-nīl* the Nile 10
نية *niya* intention 28

هـ

هاتان *hātān* these two 4
هامّ *hāmm* important 2
هجرية *hijrīya* A.H. 39
هذا *hādha* this 4
هذان *hādhān* these two 4
هذه *hādhihi* this, these 4
هكذا *hākadha* thus, so 32
هل *hal* see 13/1; whether 31
هم *hum* they 5
همّ يهم *hamma yahummu* I concern, be important (to) 14, 17
هنا *huna* here 4
هناك *hunaka* there 4
الهند *hind* India 4
هندسة *handasa* engineering 2
هندي هنود *hindī hunūd* Indian 4
هندي → هنود
هو *huwa* he, it 5
هواء *hawā'* air 12
هؤلاء *hā'ulā'i* these 4
هوية *huwīya* identity 10
هي *hiya* she, it, they (inan.) 5

و

و *wa-* and 1
واحد *wāḥid* one 38
بواسطة :واسطة *bi-wāsiṭat*

by means of 7
واسع *wāsiʿ* wide 8
واضح *wāḍiḥ* clear 2
واطئ *wāṭiʾ* low 8
وافق على *wāfaqa* III agree on/to 20
واقف *wāqif* stopping, still, stationary 26
وثيقة وثائق *wathīqa wathāʾiq* document 3
وجد: وجد يجد *wajada yajidu* I find 11, 17; إن وجد(ت) *ʾin wujid(at)* if any 37
وجود *wujūd* existence 28
الوحيد *al-waḥīd* the only 9
وراء *warāʾ* behind 6
ورق *waraq* foliage, paper 10
ورقة أوراق *waraqa ʾawrāq* leaf, sheet of paper 10
وزارة *wizāra* ministry 7
وزراء → رئيس , مجلس , وزير
وزن أوزان *wazn ʾawzān* weight, verb form 20
وزير وزراء *wazīr wuzarāʾ* minister 7
وسيلة وسائل *wasīla wasāʾil* means 8
وصل يصل *waṣala yaṣilu* I arrive 11, 17
وصّل *waṣṣala* II convey 20
وصول *wuṣūl* arrival 12
وضع يضع *waḍaʿa yaḍaʿu* I put, place 11, 17
وضع أوضاع *waḍʿ ʾawḍāʿ* situation 8
وطن أوطان *waṭan ʾawṭān* homeland 7
وطني *waṭanī* national 7
وظيفة → وظائف
وظّف *waẓẓafa* II recruit 20
وظيفة وظائف *waẓīfa waẓāʾif* job 2
وفاق *wifāq* agreement 28
وفد وفود *wafd wufūd* delegation 3
وقت أوقات *waqt ʾawqāt* time 3
وقّع *waqqaʿa* II sign 20
وقف يقف *waqafa yaqifu* I (come to a) stop 17
وقوف *wuqūf* stop 28
وكالة *wikāla* agency 9
وكيل وكلاء *wakīl wukalāʾ* agent 3
ولكنْ *walākin* but 33
ولكنّ *walākinna* but 31
ولّى *walla* II appoint 20
ولايات: الولايات المتّحدة *al-wilāyāt al-muttáḥida* United States 4
ولد أولاد *walad ʾawlād* boy, child 1
ولي يلي *wáliya yalī* I administer 14, 17

ي

اليابان *al-yābān* Japan 4

يجب (على) *yajib* I (*'ala*)
it is necessary see 33

يجوز (ل) *yajūz* I (*li-*)
it is likely see 33

يد أياد\الأيادي *yad 'ayādin, al-'ayādī* (f. weak) hand 10

يمكن *yumkin* IV
it is possible see 33

اليمن *al-yaman* Yemen 36

يناير *yanāyir* January 39

يوجد *yūjad* there is 11, 23

يورو *yūrō* euro

يوليو *yūliyu* July 39

يوم أيّام *yawm 'ayyām* day 3;
يوميًا *yawmīyan* daily 32;
اليوم *al-yawm* today 3

يونيو *yūniyū* June 39

Appendix

- Grammatical tables: nouns, adjectives, pronouns, verbs

1. Nouns and adjectives

Table 1 - Regular, indefinite (upper line) and definite (lower line), singular and broken plural

base word	nominative	accusative	genitive
final *consonant* (including cons. + *hamza* but not ...ا ء *-ā'*); sing. or broken plural	كتابٌ *kitābun* كتابُ *kitābu*	كتاباً *kitāban* كتابَ *kitāba*	كتابٍ *kitābin* كتابِ *kitābi*
	so also consonantal broken plural, e.g. كتب *kutub*		
	جزءٌ *juz'un* جزءُ *juz'u*	جزءاً *juz'an* جزءَ *juz'a*	جزءٍ *juz'in* جزءِ *juz'i*
final ...ي *-ī* (relative adj.)	فنّيٌّ *fannīyun* فنّيُّ *fannīyu*	فنّيّاً *fannīyan* فنّيَّ *fannīya*	فنّيٍّ *fannīyin* فنّيِّ *fannīyi*
final ...ة *-a* sing./broken pl.	دورةٌ *dawratun* دورةُ *dawratu*	دورةً *dawratan* دورةَ *dawrata*	دورةٍ *dawratin* دورةِ *dawrati*
	also ...ة broken pls., e.g. أسئلة *'as'ila*, قضاة *quḍā*		
final ...ا ء *-ā'* (where ا or ء is a *root letter*)	إنشاءٌ *'inshā'un* إنشاءُ *'inshā'u*	إنشاءً *'inshā'an* إنشاءَ *'inshā'a*	إنشاءٍ *'inshā'in* إنشاءِ *'inshā'i*
	so also a few ...ا ء broken pls., e.g. أجزاء *'ajzā'*		
ذات *dhāt* (def.)	ذاتُ *dhātu*	ذاتَ *dhāta*	ذاتِ *dhāti*
Also, all diptotes (Table 6) are regular when definite.			

Table 2 - Dual, indefinite or definite

base word	nominative	accusative and genitive
final *consonant*	كتابانِ *kitābāni*	كتابينِ *kitābayni*
or cons. + ء	جزآنِ *juz'āni*	جزئينِ *juz'ayni*
final ي... -*ī*	فنّيّانِ *fannīyāni*	فنّيّينِ *fannīyayni*
final ى... -*a*	مستويانِ *mustawayāni*	مستويينِ *mustawayayni*
final ة... -*a*	دورتانِ *dawratāni*	دورتينِ *dawratayni*
ا...ء -*ā'* m.s.	إنشاءانِ *inshā'āni*	إنشائينِ *inshā'ayni*
ا...ء -*ā'* f. s.	حمراوانِ *ḥamrāwāni*	حمراوينِ *ḥamrāwayni*

Table 3 - Feminine sound plural, indefinite (upper) and definite (lower)

base word	nominative	accusative and genitive
final *consonant* incl. ا...ء in	ملفّاتٌ *milaffātun* ملفّاتُ *milaffātu*	ملفّاتٍ *milaffātin* ملفّاتِ *milaffāti*
m. s. (ا or ء is a *root letter*)	إنشاءاتٌ *inshā'ātun* إنشاءاتُ *inshā'ātu*	إنشاءاتٍ *inshā'ātin* إنشاءاتِ *inshā'āti*
final ة... -*a*	دوراتٌ *dawrātun* دوراتُ *dawrātu*	دوراتٍ *dawrātin* دوراتِ *dawrāti*
final ى... -*a* in weak m. s.	مستوياتٌ *mustawayātun* مستوياتُ *mustawayātu*	مستوياتٍ *mustawayātin* مستوياتِ *mustawayāti*
final ا...ء -*a'* f. s. (rare)	صحراواتٌ *ṣaḥrāwātun* صحراواتُ *ṣaḥrāwātu*	صحراواتٍ *ṣaḥrāwātin* صحراواتِ *ṣaḥrāwāti*
ذوات *dhawāt*	ذواتُ *dhawātu*	ذواتِ *dhawāti*

Table 4 - Masculine sound plural, indefinite or definite

base word	nominative	accusative and genitive
final *consonant*	طَيِّبونَ *ṭayyibūna*	طَيِّبينَ *ṭayyibīna*
final ...ي *-ī*	فَنِّيّونَ *fannīyūna*	فَنِّيِّينَ *fannīyīna*

Table 5 - Weak, indefinite

base word	nominative and genitive	accusative
final ...ٍ indef.	محامٍ *muḥāmin (-ī)*	محامياً *muḥấmiyan*
m.s./broken pl.	أراضٍ *'arāḍin (-ī)*	→ diptote, Table 6
final ...ىً s./pl.	مستوىً\قوىً *mustawan/quran*	

Note the distribution of the cases.
The definite form of the m. s. weak active participles (e.g. المحامي *al-muḥāmī*) follows the relative-adjective pattern, Table 1. Feminines are regular, (الـ)محامية *(al-)muḥấmiya*, Table 1. But note that the stress remains on the root in these forms.
Masc. plurals are mostly sound, محامون *muḥāmūn* Table 4 (but قضاة *quḍā* Table 1).
Weak plurals like أراضٍ *'arāḍin* are *diptote* (Table 6) in the indefinite accusative form, أراضيَ *'arấḍiya*. Note the stress. The singular (e.g. أرض *'arḍ*) is regular, Table 1.
The indefinite ending ...ىً *-an* (typical of increased-form m. s. weak passive participles) becomes ...ى *-a* in the definite form. Both endings are invariable for case. Where the sing. has ...ىً\...ى *-an/-a*, the pl. is mostly sound feminine in ...يات *-ayāt*, Table 3.

Table 6 - Diptotes, indefinite

word pattern	nominative	accusative and genitive
e.g. *'akbar*	أكبرُ *'akbaru*	أكبرَ *'akbara*
broken plurals	تقاريرُ *taqārīru*	تقاريرَ *taqārīra*
a-ā-ī, -a-ā-i	تذاكرُ *tadhākiru*	تذاكرَ *tadhākira*
...اء (ا, ء are	حمراءُ *ḥamrā'u*	حمراءَ *ḥamrā'a*
not root letters)	زملاءُ *zumalā'u*	زملاءَ *zumalā'a*
All diptotes are regular (Table 1) when definite. The last group can also be categorised (and in Chapter 12 it is) as 'all feminine and almost all broken plurals ending ...اء -'ā (but e.g. the plural noun أجزاء *'ajzā'* 'parts', Table 1, is regular because the final *hamza* is a root letter).		

2. Pronouns

Table 7 - Dual and feminine plural subject pronouns and pronoun and possessive-adjective suffixes

Person	dual	feminine plural
2	أنتما *'antuma* you both ...كما *-kuma*	أنتنّ *'antunna* you ...كنّ *-kunna* you, your
3	هما *huma* they both ...هما *-huma** (of) them both	هنّ *hunna* they ...هنّ *-hunna** them, their
The dual and feminine plural are found only in the 2nd and 3rd persons. The dual pronouns and suffixes do not vary for gender. The feminine plural is used for a group exclusively of female persons; for mixed company, the masculine plural is used. (* *-hima, -hinna* after word ending *-i, -ī* or *-ay* in full pronunciation.)		

Table 8 - Dual and feminine plural relative pronoun

	dual		feminine plural
	nominative	accusative + genitive	all cases
m.	اللذان *alladhāni*	اللذين *alladhayni*	
f.	اللتان *allatāni*	اللتين *allatayni*	اللواتي *allawātī*

These are spelt, anomalously, with two letters *lām*. Of all the relative pronouns, only the dual has different endings for case. The feminine plural is used for a group exclusively of female persons; for mixed company, the masculine plural is used.

3. Dual and feminine plural verb forms – general

The dual and feminine plural are found only in the 2nd and 3rd persons. The dual does not vary for gender in the 2nd person. The feminine plural is used for a group exclusively of female persons.

The rules of verb agreement for verbal and nominal sentences apply also for these forms.

4. Dual and feminine plural verb forms, past and present

The endings shown apply to the type(s) of verb indicated, throughout Forms I to X. Only Form I is shown

Final-weak verbs are shown by the last letter of their first or second principal part, as appropriate to the tense shown. Doubly-weak verbs follow the pattern dictated by their final root letter.

For the f. pl. persons, in both tenses:

- in doubled verbs the identical root letters separate,
- in hollow verbs the middle root vowel is short, *u* or *i*.

Table 9 - Dual and feminine plural verbs, past tense

Pers.	verb class	dual		feminine plural	
2	sound	كتبتما	*katabtuma*	كتبتنّ	*katabtunna*
	hamzated	قرأتما	*qara'tuma*	قرأتنّ	*qara'tunna*
	initial-*wāw*	وصلتما	*waṣaltuma*	وصلتنّ	*waṣaltunna*
	doubled	دللتما	*dalaltuma*	دللتنّ	*dalaltunna*
	hollow	قلتما	*qultuma*	قلتنّ	*qultunna*
	fin.-wk. ...و	رجوتما	*rajawtuma*	رجوتنّ	*rajawtunna*
	fin.-wk. ...ى	رميتما	*ramaytuma*	رميتنّ	*ramaytunna*
	fin.-wk. ...ي	نسيتما	*nasītuma*	نسيتنّ	*nasītunna*
3 m.	sound	كتبا	*katabā*		
	hamzated	قرآ	*qara'ā*		
	initial-*wāw*	وصلا	*waṣalā*		
	doubled	دلاّ	*dallā*		
	hollow	قالا	*qālā*		
	fin.-wk. ...و	رجوا	*rajawā*		
	fin.-wk. ...ى	رميا	*ramayā*		
	fin.-wk. ...ي	نسيا	*násiyā*		
3 f.	sound	كتبتا	*katabatā*	كتبن	*katabna*
	hamzated	قرأتا	*qara'atā*	قرأن	*qara'na*
	initial-*wāw*	وصلتا	*waṣalatā*	وصلن	*waṣalna*
	doubled	دلّتا	*dallatā*	دللن	*dalalna*
	hollow	قالتا	*qālatā*	قلن	*qulna*
	fin.-wk. ...و	رجوتا	*rajawatā*	رجون	*rajawna*
	fin.-wk. ...ى	رميتا	*ramayatā*	رمين	*ramayna*
	fin.-wk. ...ي	نسيتا	*násiyatā*	نسين	*nasīna*

Table 10 - Dual and feminine plural verbs, present tense

Pers.	verb class	dual		feminine plural	
2	sound	تكتبان	*taktubāni*	تكتبن	*taktubna*
	hamzated	تقرآن	*taqra'āni*	تقرأن	*taqra'na*
	initial-*wāw*	تصلان	*taṣilāni*	تصلن	*taṣilna*
	doubled	تدلاّن	*tadullāni*	تدللن	*tadlulna*
	hollow	تقولان	*taqūlāni*	تقلن	*taqulna*
	fin.-wk. ...و	ترجوان	*tarjuwāni*	ترجون	*tarjūna*
	fin.-wk. ...ى	تنسيان	*tansayāni*	تنسين	*tansayna*
	fin.-wk. ...ي	ترميان	*tarmiyāni*	ترمين	*tarmīna*
3 m.	sound	يكتبان	*yaktubāni*		
	hamzated	يقرآن	*yaqra'āni*		
	initial-*wāw*	يصلان	*yaṣilāni*		
	doubled	يدلاّن	*yadullāni*		
	hollow	يقولان	*yaqūlāni*		
	fin.-wk. ...و	يرجوان	*yarjuwāni*		
	fin.-wk. ...ى	ينسيان	*yansayāni*		
	fin.-wk. ...ي	يرميان	*yarmiyāni*		
3 f.	sound	تكتبان	*taktubāni*	يكتبن	*yaktubna*
	hamzated	تقرآن	*taqra'āni*	يقرأن	*yaqra'na*
	initial-*wāw*	تصلان	*taṣilāni*	يصلن	*yaṣilna*
	doubled	تدلاّن	*tadullāni*	يدللن	*yadlulna*
	hollow	تقولان	*taqūlāni*	يقلن	*yaqulna*
	fin.-wk. ...و	ترجوان	*tarjuwāni*	يرجون	*yarjūna*
	fin.-wk. ...ى	تنسيان	*tansayāni*	ينسين	*yansayna*
	fin.-wk. ...ي	ترميان	*tarmiyāni*	يرمين	*yarmīna*

5. Dual and feminine plural verb forms – subjunctive, jussive and imperative

The subjunctive and jussive of these persons are the same. They are made from the appropriate person of the present tense (Table 12):

- *dual*: remove the final ...ن *-ni*:

  تكتبان *taktubāni* → تكتبا *taktubā*

  ينسيان *yansayāni* → ينسيا *yansayā*

- *feminine plural*: this is identical to the present-tense form.

The dual imperative is made from the jussive as shown for the other 2nd persons in Chapter 25.

Grammatical Index

Upright figures: Chapter no./paragraph no. *Italic* figures: paragraph no. or Table no. in the Appendix. → refers to another entry in the Index.

ARABIC-ENGLISH ENGLISH-ARABIC
PRACTICAL DICTIONARY

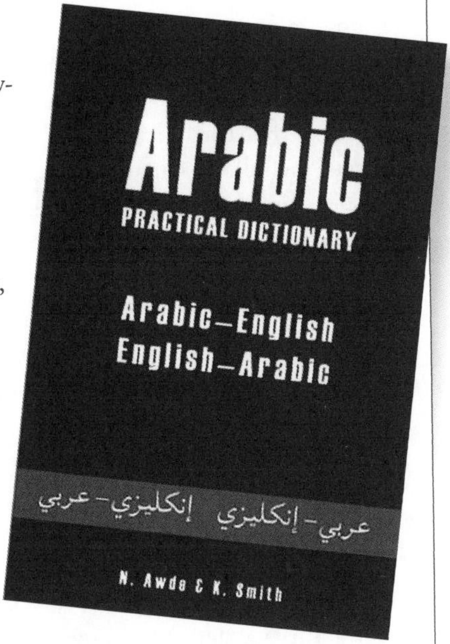

This dictionary is an essential resource for students of Arabic and English alike. It covers their needs with the most up-to-date entries in handy reference form, and will especially prove to be an aid in navigating the growing vocabulary of politics, telecommunications, technology, the Internet, tourism, business, and travel. Compact and concise, the dictionary includes more than 18,000 entires in clear, easy-to-read format the Arabic is provided with Romanized transliterations and the English with phonetic transliterations, while grammatical forms such as verb conjugations and plurals, are given for each word in both languages. The selection of current words and expressions and their practical arrangement make this a comprehensive and reliable dictionary that is not only a principal tool for the study of Modern Standard Arabic, bit also a perfect two-way portal for students of both Arabic and English.

400 pages • 4 3/8 x 7 • ISBN: 0-7818-1045-0
W • 18,000 entries • $22.50 PB

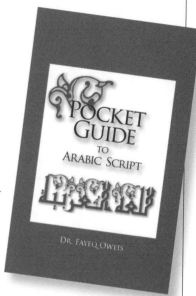